Echoes of the Intifada

Echoes of the Intifada

Regional Repercussions of the Palestinian-Israeli Conflict

EDITED BY

Rex Brynen

Routledge
Taylor & Francis Group
LONDON AND NEW YORK

First published 1991 by Westview Press

Published 2018 by Routledge
52 Vanderbilt Avenue, New York, NY 10017
2 Park Square, Milton Park, Abingdon, Oxon OX14 4RN

Routledge is an imprint of the Taylor & Francis Group, an informa business

Library of Congress Cataloging-in-Publication Data
Echoes of the Intifada : regional repercussions of the Palestinian
-Israeli conflict / edited by Rex Brynen.
p. cm. — (Westview special studies on the Middle East)
Includes bibliographical references and index.
ISBN 0-8133-8171-1
1. West Bank—History—Palestinian Uprising, 1987– —Influence.
2. Gaza Strip—History—Palestinian Uprising, 1987– —Influence.
3. Middle East—Politics and government—1979– . I. Brynen, Rex.
II. Series.
DS110.W47E24 1991
956.9405'4—dc20

90-22513
CIP

ISBN 13: 978-0-367-01660-9 (hbk)
ISBN 13: 978-0-367-16647-2 (pbk)

Contents

Preface vii

INTRODUCTION: The Palestinian Uprising
Rex Brynen and Neil Caplan 1

PART ONE: Israel and Palestine: Implications of the *Intifada* 5

1 The Palestinian Movement in Transition: Historical Reversals and the Uprising, *Salim Tamari* 13

2 Israel and the Palestinians: Human Rights in the Occupied Territories, *Raja Shehadeh* 29

3 The Impact of the *Intifada* on Israeli Political Thinking, *Mark Tessler* 43

4 Palestinians in Israel: Responses to the Uprising, *Nadim Rouhana* 97

PART TWO: Regional Repercussions of the Uprising 119

5 The PLO in Regional Politics, *Paul Noble* 131

6 Jordan, *Lamis Andoni* 165

7 Egypt, *Bahgat Korany* 195

8 Syria, *Fred Lawson* 215

PART THREE: The Superpowers 235

9 Soviet Union, *Tamar Weinstein (with Adam Jones)* 241

10 United States, *Fred Khouri* 265

About the Editor and Contributors 305
Index 307

Preface

Important historical turning points often seem to be unpredicted until they are upon us. For most observers (this writer included) the Palestinian uprising that erupted in December 1987 was unexpected—not because the depth of Palestinian national aspirations or the growing strength of Palestinian socio-political organization under occupation were unclear, but rather because it seemed unlikely that resistance to Israeli occupation could so quickly escalate and that once set in motion could be sustained in such an intense and continuing manner.

Yet the *intifada* has continued through a second and a third year. The West Bank and Gaza Strip have seen protest, violence and repression; Israeli politics has been beset by both turmoil and paralysis; the diplomatic arena has experienced bouts of rapid political change beset by periods of apparent blockage and inertia. The Palestine Liberation Organization has declared the formation of an independent Palestinian state—yet that goal still remains elusive. And amid all this it remains an inescapable conclusion that the *intifada* has had a major, even fundamental, effect on the continuing conflict in the Middle East.

This volume represents an attempt to understand the repercussions of the Palestinian uprising and its implications for the future of Palestinian-Israeli and Arab-Israeli conflict. The book would not have been possible without the support of many people. Philip Mattar and Bill Young offered early encouragement and useful comments on the project. Alex Brynen, as usual, provided myriad forms of assistance. My research assistant, Adam Jones, also helped extensively with the volume. The contributors, of course, deserve my thanks both for their contributions and their suggestions along the way. Neil Caplan deserves special thanks, having not only collaborated in writing the various section introductions, but having also brought to our joint endeavors a mind sharp for historical meaning and constructive criticism. Barbara Ellington at Westview Press was as supportive and efficient as ever. Finally, I am grateful to the Social Science and Humanities Research Council of Canada for their financial support; and I am equally grateful to the Inter-university Consortium for Arab Studies (Montréal) and colleagues and students in the Department of Political Science at McGill University for providing an environment I have always found both productive and stimulating.

Rex Brynen
Montréal, Québec

INTRODUCTION

The Palestinian Uprising

Rex Brynen and Neil Caplan

On 5 June 1967 war once more erupted in the Middle East. Within a matter of days, the West Bank and Gaza Strip (controlled by Jordan and Egypt respectively since 1948) were occupied by Israel. Two decades later, in the summer of 1987, that occupation seemed as firmly entrenched as ever.

In the territories themselves, the status quo of twenty years seemed to have achieved a striking air of permanence. In addition to the constant presence of the Israeli Defense Forces, some 67,500 settlers now made their homes in more than one hundred and thirty settlements in what many Israelis had come to regard as "Judea," "Samaria," and "Gaza District."[1] To this end, over one-half of the land of the West Bank and almost one-third of that in the Gaza Strip had been appropriated by the Israeli authorities. Although divided on many issues of foreign policy, both main partners in Israel's "national unity" coalition government continued to oppose the principle of Palestinian self-determination. Prime Minister Yitzhak Shamir and the Likud Party emphasized Israel's historical claims to the territories, and hence rejected the principle of "land for peace" which seemed to flow from Israel's previous acceptance of UN Security Council Resolution 242 after the 1967 war. The Labor Party headed by Shimon Peres clung to hopes of a "Jordanian option" whereby the territories would pass under an Israeli-Hashemite condominium. Neither party seemed interested in taking political initiatives or risks over the future of the territories.

For the more than 1.7 million Palestinians in the West Bank and Gaza Strip, nothing in either Israeli position offered anything beyond the continued realities of occupation.[2] Indeed, if anything, those realities were growing ever more harsh. In response to growing levels of protest, the IDF had instituted a so-called "iron fist" policy in the territories since 1985. This, combined with increasing economic hardships, contributed to a widespread feeling (shared by 85% of Palestinians in a 1986 survey) that living conditions in the West Bank and Gaza had seriously deteriorated in recent years. In the same survey, more than nine out of ten Palestinian families reported incidents of harassment, arrest, physical abuse, land confiscation, curfew or collective punishment at the hands of the Israeli authorities.[3]

As 1987 came to a close, regional developments offered little hope of change. In the Arab world the salience of the Palestine issue seemed in slow but steady decline. Political coordination between the Palestine Liberation Organization and Jordan had broken down in 1986. The PLO itself, torn by bitter internal conflict since 1983, had only recently reestablished its own tenuous political unity in April 1987. It remained under attack in Lebanon, and embroiled in political disputes with both Jordan and Syria. Equally unpropitious was the November 1987 Arab League summit meeting in Amman, called to discuss the Iran-Iraq war. Quite apart from the offhanded treatment accorded members of the PLO delegation by their Jordanian hosts, most Palestinians were struck by the way the assembled Arab leaders appeared to relegate the Palestinian cause to a secondary status.

Finally, the Palestine question seemed in a state of increasing neglect at the international level too. Neither the Camp David accords of 1978 nor the short-lived initiative announced by US President Ronald Reagan in September 1982 had made significant progress towards meeting Palestinian national aspirations. On the contrary, both envisaged little more than limited Palestinian autonomy under Israeli or Jordanian sovereignty, with the Reagan plan explicitly rejecting the establishment of a Palestinian state. A "peace process" thus existed in name only; the Reagan administration continued to oppose direct discussions with the PLO, focussing instead sporadic diplomatic energies at Jordan. The Palestinian question also seemed absent from the agenda of improving East-West relations, a perception reinforced by the scant attention given to the issue by Reagan and Soviet leader Mikhail Gorbachev at their December 1987 summit.

Much of this was shortly to change, however—and to do so with stunning scope and rapidity. On 8 December 1987 an accident involving an Israeli truck left four Palestinians dead in Gaza. Many Palestinians considered the incident an act of premeditated murder, possibly in retaliation for the death of an Israeli there two days earlier. In the context of growing Palestinian frustration and anger generated by the absence of any progress towards an end to Israeli occupation, the incident provided the spark for massive demonstrations in Gaza on December 9. These soon spread to the West Bank. Israeli use of live ammunition in response did little to quell the unrest, nor did subsequent use of blanket curfews against Palestinian population centers, mass detentions, deportation, or systematic beatings of Palestinian protesters. Instead, the protests rapidly gained a momentum and a leadership of their own, mobilizing the bulk of the Palestinian population into a cohesive uprising against Israeli occupation—the most sustained and intense revolt by Palestinians against foreign rule in fifty years.[4]

Implications of the *Intifada*

As will become evident in the pages that follow, the *intifada* has had a profound effect on the course and dynamics of the Palestinian-Israeli conflict. Its implications have been greatest, of course, for Palestinians under occupation and the broader process of Palestinian nation-building, and for Israeli politics and Israel's own future course as a society. Yet the Palestinian uprising has also had wider repercussions than these, in the arena of regional and international politics. The Palestine Liberation Organization, by its declaration of independence and statehood in November 1988, signaled its hope that a diplomatic settlement to the conflict might be found. Within Israel, many have pointed to the need for a political, rather than military, solution to the Palestinian issue (however differently this may be defined). The *intifada* has created new regional pressures, constraints and opportunities, and an altered political environment for Egypt, Jordan, Syria and other regional actors. And the fact of the uprising has affected the foreign policies of the two global super-powers, just as hopes for a settlement will necessarily be shaped by US and Soviet policy and changes in East-West relations.

While the former aspect of the *intifada* has generated a number of insightful studies of Israeli occupation and the internal dynamics of the Palestinian protest,[5] the regional dimensions of the Palestinian uprising have not received the same degree of sustained attention. It is thus upon the latter areas that this volume focuses its attention. In Part Three the global dimension of the conflict is examined through case studies of US and Soviet policy. In Part Two, the repercussions of the uprising for Egyptian, Jordanian and Syrian policy are analyzed, as is the changing nature of the relationship between Palestinian/PLO diplomacy and inter-Arab politics. Before either of these areas can be addressed, however, analysis must first be directed to the roots of the conflict. Accordingly, Part One turns its attention to those most directly involved: Palestinians and Israelis themselves.

Notes

1. Meron Benvenisti, West Bank Data Base Project *1986 Report*, (Boulder: Westview, 1986). These figures exclude the more than 80,000 Israeli Jews living in East Jerusalem, also occupied by Israel in 1967 and subsequently annexed.

2. According to official Israeli estimates, 860,000 Palestinians lived in the West Bank and 560,000 in the Gaza Strip. The West Bank Base Data Project has suggested that these figures under-represent the actual size of the Palestinian population, which it put at 1.74 million at the end of 1987. *Jerusalem Post* (international edition), 26 March 1988, p. 6.

3. *al-Fajr* (East Jerusalem), 8 September 1986. The survey is reprinted in the *Journal of Palestine Studies* 62 (Winter 1987): 196-207.

4. For the context in which the uprising erupted, see Ann Mosely Lesch and Mark

Tessler, *Israel, Egypt, and the Palestinians: From Camp David to Intifada* (Bloomington: Indiana University Press, 1989); Raja Shehadeh, *Occupier's Law: Israel and the West Bank* rev. 2nd ed. (Wasington, D.C.: Institute for Palestine Studies, 1989).

5. On the first days of the uprising, see the special issue of the *Journal of Palestine Studies* 17, 3 (Spring 1988). For more detailed analysis, see also: Zachary Lockman and Joel Beinin, eds., *Intifada: The Palestinian Uprising Against Israeli Occupation* (Boston: MERIP/South End Press, 1989); Don Peretz, *Intifada: The Palestinian Uprising* (Boulder: Westview, 1990); Geoffrey Aronson, *Israel, Palestinians and the Intifada: Creating Facts on the West Bank* (London: Kegan Paul International, 1990).

PART ONE

Israel and Palestine: Implications of the *Intifada*

Since its first eruption on 9 December 1987, the Palestinian uprising has continued at an ever-increasing cost. Hundreds of Palestinians and dozens of Israelis have died; thousands have been injured; tens of thousands of Palestinians have been arrested or detained without charge or trial.[1] Confrontations between armed Israeli troops or settlers and rock-throwing Palestinian protesters have become a daily event throughout the territories, including East Jerusalem. At times, the violence has even extended to within Israel itself.

As dramatic as events in the occupied territories have been, however, it is not in their tragic violence that their greatest significance lies. Above and beyond this, in a fashion ill-suited to hurried analysis or the fleeting attentions of a typical television newsclip, the *intifada* has wrought deep and fundamental changes in the continuing Arab-Israeli conflict. The uprising has ushered in a new era in Palestinian mass mobilization; it has altered the structure and dynamics of occupation; it has reshaped regional diplomacy, and the possibilities for regional conflict resolution. In all these dimensions the most striking effect of the *intifada* has been clear: the extent to which the uprising has served to re-orient the Arab-Israeli conflict back to its historic Palestinian-Israeli core.

Palestine and Israel

The inevitable collision between the Zionist movement (later, the state of Israel) and the Palestinian Arab people traces its roots to the founding of political Zionism in the late 19th century among European Jews. Faced with continuing anti-Semitism in Europe, the Zionist movement sought to build in Palestine a Jewish National Home. Such intentions met with resistance, faint at first, from the indigenous Arab population of Palestine, whose own national awakening had begun amidst the gradual collapse of the Ottoman Empire.[2] Palestinian aspirations to construct their own national society were increasingly beset by the challenge of European/Zionist immigration and settlement.

Prior to the First World War, therefore, local communal tension and rivalry between native Palestinians and immigrant Zionists was the central feature of the emergent conflict. During the period between World War I and World War II, external factors served to accentuate and accelerate this clash. Britain, which in the Balfour Declaration of November 1917 had pledged itself to support Zionist aspirations, gained control of formerly Ottoman-ruled Palestine under a League of Nations Mandate. Later, the specter of European fascism lent new urgency to the Zionist endeavor. Faced with persecution and extermination in Europe, denied refuge elsewhere, tens of thousands of European Jews sought safety in Palestine. The Jewish population of Palestine grew rapidly, from perhaps 11 percent of the total in 1922 to some 31 percent by 1947.[3]

During the first decade of the British Mandate, the struggle remained a local conflict between Jewish national aspirations and Palestinian demands for self-determination. Major Palestinian protests and riots erupted in 1920 and 1921, and again in 1929 and 1933. From 1936 to 1939 a popular Palestinian rebellion was launched against the Zionist enterprise and British colonial rule. The rebellion, however, ultimately collapsed in the months prior to the start of World War II. After the war, this triangle of Palestinian-British-Zionist conflict was joined by the beginnings of serious US and United Nations involvement. The result was the UN partition resolution of 1947, the escalation of Arab-Jewish conflict, the establishment of the State of Israel on 14 May 1948, and a full-scale war involving Arab states.

This first Arab-Israeli war was ended by armistice agreements signed in the spring of 1949. The war itself had been decisively won by Israel. In its aftermath, construction of the Jewish state proceeded steadily in the three-quarters of historic Palestine that was now under Israeli control, and from which approximately three-quarters of a million Palestinians had been displaced. Two decades later, the June 1967 Arab-Israeli war saw the Gaza Strip and West Bank (including East Jerusalem) fall under Israeli occupation. A further 300,000 Palestinians were displaced from these territories. With this, all of historic Palestine came under Israel's control, and half the Palestinian people had now become refugees.[4]

Yet the scope of Israel's victories on the battlefield in 1948, 1956 and 1967 did little to resolve the Israeli/Palestinian dilemma. On the contrary, the conflict was only further sharpened.

For Palestinians, the dislocation, dispossession and exile that had befallen their society rendered it politically weak and physically divided. In the longer term, however, occupation at home and harassment abroad strengthened their socio-political identity, assuring the psychological and political foundations upon which continuing demands for self-determination would be based. In the Palestinian diaspora, shared bonds of national experience and the incentives and opportunities generated by political and economic marginality provided the essential ingredients for a resurgence of community and national organization during the 1950s and 1960s.[5] By the late 1960s the Palestine Liberation Organization had emerged both as the organizational umbrella for much of this activity, and as the leading vehicle for the expression and pursuit of Palestinian national aspirations.

For Israel, the realities of controlling a growing Palestinian population in the West Bank and Gaza Strip—however much the occupation may have enhanced its strategic position *vis-à-vis* regular Arab armies—locked it into a continuing effort to contain Palestinian aspirations for self-determination. A relatively modest military presence (and pervasive links of economic dependency) seemed, for two decades, sufficient to maintain physical control of the territories. For some Israelis, the apparent permanence of the occupation fueled hopes for Jewish settlement and annexation. For others, it raised the specter of a "demographic dilemma," namely, the contradiction between Israel's Jewish identity, its democratic character, and its rule over a growing disenfranchised Palestinian population.

But, in many respects, these Israeli debates were beside the point. However much military occupation could keep an intimidated Palestinian population in line, it was evidently not enough to prevent a revitalization of Palestinian political identity and nationalist institutions. Indeed, the fact of occupation generally had the reverse of its intended effect, serving to spur political mobilization. For those who doubted the process, ample proof was provided by the local activities of the PLO-affiliated Palestine National Front (PNF, 1973-78) and the National Guidance Committee (NGC, 1978-82), by the overwhelming victory of pro-PLO candidates in the Israeli-supervised 1976 West Bank municipal elections, and in repeated waves of popular protest and resistance. Such pressures could be contained only so long. In December 1987 they finally burst forth in the form of a major Palestinian uprising.

Palestinians and the Uprising

Perhaps the most far-reaching effects of the uprising have been not in the political or diplomatic realm, but rather within the Palestinian community itself. In the West Bank and Gaza, the *intifada* has hastened remarkable changes in the socio-political structure of Palestinian society under occupation. Virtually all age groups and social classes have been mobilized in its support. But the uprising and the twenty-first year of occupation also signaled the coming-of-age of a new generation of activists and activism amongst Palestinians in the occupied territories. They represent a potent social force, one with little respect for Israeli administrative authority and less responsive to Israeli coercive measures.

The uprising has also brought with it (and been hastened by) changes in the pattern of Palestinian nationalist leadership in the West Bank and Gaza. It is a new leadership rooted not in traditional Palestinian "notable" politics, but rather in the social mechanisms and institutions that have developed in the territories since 1967: youth and women's groups, student unions, trade unions, professional organizations, charitable associations, mosques and churches, and neighborhood popular committees. As Salim Tamari notes in his chapter on Palestinian strategy under occupation, these institutions have provided the "organizational crucible" for the uprising. They have also been a crucial element in its continuation, sustenance and survival. In the past, the high profile and individualism of Palestinian leadership in the territories—the PNF, NGC, and nationalist mayors—rendered it acutely vulnerable to deportation, detention, and other Israeli counter-measures. The current leadership of the *intifada* is more diffuse, and hence more effective and more resilient than its antecedents. The continuation of the uprising in spite of the detention of thousands is an indication that the *intifada* is a social movement rooted not in traditional patron-client politics but in a network of local community organization and activism.

Moreover, as Tamari also notes, the uprising has wrought considerable dislocation of the traditional structure of Israeli occupation within the Palestinian community. Some (if far from all) of the linkages of economic dependency have been weakened. Traditional conservative Palestinian notables, their political power already on the wane despite tacit joint Jordanian-Israeli sponsorship, have had their influence further undermined. All forms of collaboration with the Israeli civilian-military administration in the occupied territories have been severely curtailed. Through massive popular support and participation on the one hand, and local "strike forces" on the other, considerable levels of discipline have been maintained.[6] In essence, then, the uprising has witnessed the development of a new, more militant, political culture among the majority of Palestinians, one more conducive to sustained protest, civil disobedience, initiative, and resistance.

Overall leadership of the uprising has been provided since January 1988 by *al-qiyada al-wataniyya al-muwahhada li-l-intifada*—the "Unified National Leadership of the *Intifada*." The Unified National Leadership (UNLI) has acquired a powerful mantle of popular authority. Its periodic directives, issued through the uprising's periodic underground leaflets, have become the agenda of the *intifada*, accepted by Palestinians with a remarkable degree of unanimity.

What are the implications of this for the established leadership of the Palestinian nationalist movement, the Palestine Liberation Organization? At the outset it must be noted that the Unified National Leadership (consisting of representatives from the major nationalist/PLO groups)[7] proclaims itself the Unified National Leadership *of the PLO*, an identification it restates with every underground leaflet. Far from challenging the position of the PLO, the *intifada* seems to have reconfirmed its near-universal acceptance by Palestinians both under occupation and in the diaspora as the sole legitimate representative of the Palestinian people.[8]

Yet it is also clear that the uprising has catalyzed important changes within the PLO, accelerating a shift—already hastened by the 1982 war in Lebanon—in the movement's center of gravity from the diaspora to the occupied territories.

The November 1988 declaration of an independent Palestinian state by the Palestine National Council, PLO Chairman Yasir 'Arafat's statements before a special session of the UN General Assembly in Geneva in December, and months of formal US-PLO dialogue were all indicative of new directions assumed by the PLO under the impetus of the uprising. Certainly, much of this shift to an explicit two-state solution had already been underway, marked by a evolution of the PLO's goal from a secular democratic state in all of Palestine (1969-74), to that of establishment of a "national authority" (1974) or an independent Palestinian state (1977) on any liberated Palestinian soil (i.e., the West Bank and Gaza Strip). What the uprising did do, however, was to alter both the political balance of power within the Palestinian movement and in the inter-Arab, Arab-Israeli and international arenas—creating the conditions under which a more explicit and dynamic version of this program could be actively pursued.

The Impact on Israel

Although its immediate impact on Israeli society and politics has been less substantial, the long-term implications of the uprising for the Jewish state are also profound. The *intifada*, it is true, has not challenged Israel's ultimate preponderance of coercive power in the territories. It has, however, altered the dynamics of the Palestinian-Israeli conflict. For Israel, the uprising has rendered the occupation increasingly difficult and costly. Before the uprising, occupation seemed a relatively light burden to most Israelis. As Raja Shehadeh notes in his chapter on Palestinian human rights and the uprising, the cost of the Israeli civilian-military administration in the territories was more than matched by the "occupation tax" placed on its inhabitants, resulting in a net gain to the Israeli treasury. Additional economic benefits flowed to Israel in the form of water resources, trade, and especially access to a low-cost Palestinian reserve workforce.

As the *intifada* continued through its third year, Israel has had to confront the problems of fewer Palestinians working in Israel, a boycott of Israeli consumer goods, and a widespread (if only partially successful) campaign of non-payment of taxes in the territories. Israel is also faced with the increased expense of maintaining order amid the declining effectiveness of existing forms of social control. The consequent economic costs of the uprising to Israel's economy have been severe.[9] Moreover, as Shehadeh's analysis suggests, the violence of Israel's response to the uprising is indicative of the extent to which the occupation can no longer be maintained except through the greater application of force. It is a burden—physical, moral, political and economic—that is certain to continue as long as the occupation itself.

As Mark Tessler notes in his chapter on the impact of the uprising on Israeli political thinking, one effect of the *intifada* has been to sharpen the longstanding debate within Israel over the future of its relationship with the territories. To date, however, the uprising has failed to shift public opinion within Israeli decisively in favor of either proponents of territorial compromise or those who advocate a maximalist "Greater Israel" position. Instead, it has tended to polarize already-held ideological positions. The paralysis and eventual collapse of Israel's national unity government over the issue of Palestinian elections in the occupied territories in the spring of 1990 confirms his analysis, pointing to the continued existence of fundamental ideological and policy divisions within the Israeli polity.

The outcome of this debate will, of course, have important implications for the future. It is not simply among Israeli Jews, however, that the uprising has made itself felt within Israel. As Nadim Rouhana shows, Israeli citizens of Palestinian origin have also been affected by events across the Green Line. The eruption of the *intifada* has sparked a surge in sympathy and expressions of solidarity from Israeli Arabs. Despite their clear expressions of support across the Green Line, however, material support for (and involvement in) the uprising has been much more limited, reflecting the decades-old acceptance by Arabs in Israel of the reality of the Israeli political system. Moreover, the very orientation of the uprising—its efforts towards the establishment of a Palestinian state in the West Bank and Gaza alone—seems to confirm the status of Israeli Arabs as a permanent minority in a Jewish state. Rouhana concludes that the difficulties of the Arab-Jewish relationship within Israel, although long obscured by the broader Palestinian-Israeli conflict, remain unresolved—and that continuation of the *intifada* may well bring them increasingly to the surface.

All these changes must be weighed against any argument that the *intifada* has become "routinized" to a level of conflict that can be sustained indefinitely. It is undoubtedly true that, as the *intifada* has continued, Israel's ability to contain certain dimensions of civil protest has grown. It is true too that that uprising has become in many respects an accustomed feature of daily life for Palestinians in the occupied territories. Certainly press coverage of the uprising has tended to diminish over time. All the contributors suggest, however, that something quite fundamental changed in Palestine and Israel after December 1987. And it is unlikely that these changes—new levels of Palestinian mass mobilization and community organization, the substantial collapse of Israeli administrative authority, and the diplomatic and political ramifications of intensified Palestinian-Israeli confrontation—can ever be reversed.

Looking Ahead

What of the future trajectory of the conflict? The analyses that follow also suggest that, as the uprising enters its fourth year, Palestinians and Israelis are at a crossroads.

For its part, the Palestinian movement confronts important strategic choices. In the territories, Tamari suggests that the *intifada* must choose between differing views of its objectives and potentialities. Should it be directed towards institutionalization, furthering its rejection and replacement of Israeli authority through building the embryonic structure of a future Palestinian state? Or should it aim at more limited objectives, seeking to preserve its existing gains in the hopes that favorable external political conditions may one day lead to a political settlement?

How the Palestinian movement answers both of those questions will be shaped not only by its own internal dynamics, but also by the sorts of regional and international constraints and opportunities explored in Parts II and III. Palestinian responses will also be shaped by the political debate within Israel. Tessler's analysis of this debate suggests that, whatever strategy the Palestinian movement adopts, it must recognize that substantial shifts in Israeli political thinking—let alone the emergence of a political consensus in favor of territorial compromise and a negotiated settlement—will be a long time in coming. Certainly, the establishment of a new hard-line Israeli coalition government under Prime Minister Shamir in the summer of 1990 seemed to offer little hope of Palestinian-Israeli negotiations in the immediate future.

At another level, two important dynamics are underscored by the contributions to this section. On the one hand, the *intifada* has forced the Palestinian movement and Israeli political system to consider dealing with each other to an unparalleled extent. As Tessler notes, the *intifada* has spurred the emergence of greater political realism in Israel towards the Palestinian issue among important elements of both the Labor and Likud parties. A parallel shift is evident in the attitude of the mainstream Palestinian movement towards Israel. Although international diplomacy and mediation will still play a key role in shaping the forum and modalities for any future negotiating process, both parties' historic dependence on outside actors has, in many respects, become secondary to their maneuvering with each other as both adversaries and potential negotiating partners.

This in itself is an important development: with the struggle between the Palestinian movement and Israel more visibly at the core of the conflict, a future peace process may prove far more productive than that of the past insofar as it answers to the needs of Palestinians and Israelis more directly. At the same time, however, this process is neither stable nor cost-free. Continued confrontation and the absence of meaningful political progress towards a negotiated settlement only serve to stoke the level of frustration on boths sides. Political radicalization, a hardening of positions, and a further intensification of the violence and repression seem the likely result. More will be injured, detained, or die. Viewed in this light, the Palestinian-Israeli conflict is now as explosive—and urgent—as at any time in its long and tragic history.

Notes

1. The human rights organization *al-Haq*/Law in the Service of Man reports that 795 Palestinians were shot dead by Israeli soldiers and settlers, or died from beatings or tear-gassings, during the first two years of the uprising. A further 150 Palestinians were killed by other Palestinians as alleged collaborators, and 44 Israelis were killed in *intifada*-related incidents. *Middle East International*, 15 December 1989, p. 3.

2. See Muhammad Y. Muslih, *The Origins of Palestinian Nationalism* (New York: Columbia University Press, 1988).

3. Janet Abu Lughod, "The Demographic Transformation of Palestine," in Ibrahim Abu Lughod, ed., *The Transformation of Palestine* rev. ed. (Evanston, IL: Northwestern University Press, 1987), pp. 139-163.

4. By 1987, the total Palestinian population stood at approximately 5.1 million. Of these, 42 percent were to be found in historic Palestine (18 percent in the West Bank, 11 perecent in Gaza, and 13 perecent in Israel). In the diaspora, the largest Palestinian communities are to be found in Jordan (24 percent), Kuwait, Lebanon and Syria. *Middle East Report* 146 (May-June 1987), p. 10.

5. On the growth of Palestinian community and nationalist organization during this period, see: Laurie Brand, *Palestinians in the Arab World: Institution Building and the Search for State* (New York: Columbia University Press, 1988).

6. On the organization and discipline of the uprising, see Yezid Sayigh, "The *Intifada* Continues: Legacy, Dynamics and Challenges," *Third World Quarterly* 11, 3 (July 1989): 20-49. This process has not been without its excesses, as evident from the UNLI's concern at the number of Palestinians killed as collaborators through the second and third years of the uprising. Personal rivalries have played a role in this, as have problems of command and control. These events have also been indicative of the continuing struggle between the *intifada* (seeking to maintain its security) and Israel's security services (trying to reestablish the intelligence network that was so seriously disrupted in 1987-88). For an analysis, see Salim Tamari, "Eyeless in Judea: Israel's Strategy of Collaborators and Forgeries," *Middle East Report* 164-165 (May-August 1990): 39-44; Joost Hiltermann, "The Enemy Inside the *Intifada*," *The Nation*, 10 September 1990, pp. 229-234.

7. These comprise *Fateh*, the Popular Front for the Liberation of Palestine, the Democratic Front for the Liberation of Palestine, and the Palestine Communist Party. The Islamic Resistance Movement *Hamas* is outside the framework of the Unified National Leadership of the *Intifada*. Indeed, following its establishment in 1988 Hamas often clashed with the UNLI. Through 1989, however, such conflict declined as Hamas increasingly coordinated its actions with those of the mainstream nationalist groups.

8. In the 1986 *al-Fajr* survey cited earlier, 93.5 percent of Palestinians in the occupied territories declared their support for the PLO as the sole legitimate representative of the Palestinian people; *Journal of Palestine Studies* 16, 2 (Winter 1987): 200. For an insightful discussion of the relationship between the PLO and the *intifada*, see Helena Cobban, "The PLO and the *Intifada*," *Middle East Journal* 44, 2 (Spring 1990): 207-233.

9. One estimate by Israel's Bank Hapoalim put the costs of lost production and economic growth at $1 billion during the first two years of the uprising; *al-Fajr* (weekly) 19 February 1990, p. 2. See also Raja Shehadeh's chapter elsewhere in this section.

1

The Palestinian Movement in Transition: Historical Reversals and the Uprising

Salim Tamari

A persistent dynamic which has dominated Palestinian political discourse over the last twenty years has been the unspoken opposition between the struggle for a liberationist strategy and the territorial search for statehood. During the 1960s and early 1970s this dynamic was resolved almost overwhelmingly in favor of the liberationist strategy of the three main guerrilla contingents of the Palestinian movement. While a gradual shift away from this position was evident in the resolutions of the Palestine National Council after 1974, the mystique and rhetoric of armed struggle continued to dominate through the rest of the decade. During the 1980s, however, this dynamic has steadily shifted towards territorialism (the search for sovereignty) as the movement began to began to shift away from the diaspora and anchor itself in the political momentum of the occupied territories.

This shift has had immense consequences for the manner in which the Palestinian movement has articulated its direction over the last decade. The further Palestinian politics have moved from their liberationist-guerrilla dimension, the more they have articulated a political program that expresses the sentiments and needs of concrete social groups, as opposed to the vision of a bureaucratic military apparatus. This dynamic has often been described by the popular press as a conflict between the "internal forces" and the "external forces," or (more crudely) between the traditional elites of the West Bank and Gaza and the historic leadership of the Palestine Liberation Organization. There is a kernel of truth to this characterization, but one that has to be redefined. In the diaspora (and certainly in the Arab diaspora) Palestinian politics express the continued struggle of a *segment* of society to accommodate their survival within the contingencies of Arab politics. In occupied Palestine, however, a social formation has remained intact, despite Israeli attempts to fragment it. As a consequence, politics here express the battle between real social forces.

The "historical reversals" in the title above thus refer to the progressive demise of perceptions and strategies which governed the movement of

Palestinian nationalism among the "internal forces." They particularly refer to the reversal (through the intervention of organized politics) of assumptions about the deterministic consequences of Israeli control over Palestine. This chapter examines the manifestation of this dynamic in the conflict that took place in the occupied territories between two modes of resistance, based on the notions of steadfastness and popular mobilization respectively. It suggests that the demise of the strategy of steadfastness, premised on a "survivalist" ideology, took place not as a result of doctrinal shortcomings in that ideology, but because it was challenged on the ground by forces which saw the existing institutions of Palestinian nationalism as elitist and nepotistic. The demise of steadfastness constituted the reversal of a whole series of polemics which presumed Israeli rule to require long-range accommodations, ranging from specific development strategies to binationalism. At the same time, the rise of populism represented an unintended prelude to an escalation of political confrontations with Israel, culminating in the *intifada*—a confrontation that in turn has compelled populism to face its own limitations.

Polemic over Survivalism

The passage of two decades of Israeli occupation in June of 1987 was basically a non-event. There was a considerable amount of self-reflection on the part of Palestinian intellectuals who met in under-attended assemblies, and the usual manifestos were issued. But outside in the real world business went on as usual. Palestinian resistance was contained—to use the language of the Israeli *gendarmes*—at a "manageable" level, one that could be handled by the several contingents of the Israeli Defense Forces and the Border Police regularly stationed in the "territories." Arab workers continued to commute to their construction sites and the kitchens of restaurants in ever increasing numbers—the Israeli economic recession notwithstanding—and a new stratum of middlemen, contractors and sub-contractors (on both sides of the Green Line) was definitely adjusting to the situation. There was no indication of the brewing storm which would break at the end of the year.

One can delineate two major trends within the self-reflection mentioned above, both of which emerged in a number of conferences held locally and abroad (two in Jerusalem, one in Ramallah, another on the campus of Birzeit University and one at the St. Catherine's College, Oxford). One school of thought emphasized the meaning of Palestinian steadfastness and the proper strategy for its advancement. The second focused on the need to draw the proper lessons from the seeming irreversibility of Israel's mode of control over the territories. Both perspectives were permeated by pessimism: in the first, a political pessimism informed by the inability of the Palestinians (as well as the Arab regimes) to change the prevailing balance of power in the Middle East in the foreseeable future; in the second, a pessimism of structural determinism whereby the conditions of economic and infrastructural dependency created by Israel during the two decades were now seen as historically entrenched.[1]

The first trend can be gleaned from the theme of the most ambitious of these meetings, "Palestinian Development Under Prolonged Occupation."[2] The "prolonged occupation" in the title obviously presumed the endurance of the mechanisms of control established by the Israelis in the West Bank and Gaza. In response, the participants suggested a number of *survival strategies* which would help Palestinians to cope with the protracted period of struggle necessary to create new favorable conditions for the reversal of Israeli hegemony.[3] But these development strategies were seen as constrained, transient, and *ad hoc* given the nature of Israeli control over the economy and investment policies. Yusif Sayigh expressed this view most succinctly:

> ...meaningful and far-reaching development cannot be achieved, or even sought, under the conditions of dependency-cum-dispossession. "Dependent development" itself is not possible, since Israel's external-turned-internal colonialism blocks even capitalist transformation, which is claimed to be promoted by mature capitalist industrial countries in their relations with third world countries. Given present constraints, the viability of the economies of the West Bank and Gaza Strip can only be maintained at a low level of economic performance, even assuming the same volume of external financial support. But even this is predicated on the surrender of vital economic, sociocultural, and political desiderata.[4]

Until those political conditions on which this dependency is predicated are transformed, it was argued, Palestinians should devise survival programs that will make life tolerable and leave the fabric of community life intact. Only programs with limited objectives and a reasonable chance of success should be planned.[5]

The second perspective referred to above shared the assumptions of this analysis concerning the impact of Israel's economic and logistical control over the territories, but emerged with radically different political conclusions. At the twentieth anniversary symposium organized by the Jerusalem newspaper *al-Fajr* (June 1987), Sari Nusseibeh pointed to the consequences of Israeli integration as "the most salient feature the occupation has unfolded in the past twenty years."[6] Every seam of Palestinian daily life has been embedded over the years with the consequences of this integration, Nusseibeh argued. Israeli rule should not be seen only as a system of control, but also as the totalitarian adaptation of Palestinian life to the conditions of this control in every person's consciousness—or rather, in the Palestinian unconscious:

> Israel is not simply the Knesset. To think this is to be blind to the picture. Israel is... the long queues of women standing in front of the post office in Jerusalem to collect their social security... it is Zaki el-Mukhtar on Radio One at your service. Israel is the business licenses, the building permits, the identity cards. It is the Value Added Taxes, the income taxes, the television taxes.... It is also Dedi Zucker, Meron Benvenisti, Yehuda Litani and Amnon Zichroni commiserating with Palestinians at the National Palace Hotel. Israel is the Tambour [Israeli] paint used to scribble slogans attacking Hanna Siniora on the walls.[7]

It could not have been expressed better. The dilemma of this new dependency, in Nusseibeh's view, was that it proceeded at the same pace with the heightened articulation of Palestinian self-identity. This intense nationalism was not a phenomenon that was irreconcilable with the increased assimilation into the Israeli reality, but was seen by Nusseibeh as the appropriate consequence of that integration—"a direct response, at the mental level, to the increased immersion in the system on the behavioural level." However, since there was a lack of correspondence between the political consciousness of the Palestinians and their new social reality, one had to give way to the other. Given the nature of Israel's control over the territories, and the dispersal of the Palestinian movement after the Lebanese war, it was more likely that the Palestinians would have to accommodate themselves to Israeli hegemony rather than the other way round. Nusseibeh's solution is a restatement of the notion of democratic secularism, and an inversion, of sorts, of Meron Benvenisti's thesis: to overcome the existing system of apartheid we have to struggle not for two states (as already implicit in the PLO strategy) but for total enfranchisement in the context of a better national Israeli-Palestinian state.[8]

On the eve of the Palestinian uprising we have thus two trends of political thinking within the Palestinian movement (one explicit, the other implicit), in which contrasting conclusions emerge from the same assumption of dependency and socio-economic subordination to Israeli control. In the first account stress is placed on a strategy of steadfastness—a development strategy of survival and communal preservation until the unfavourable political conditions allow for an external intervention. In the second, the conditions of transformation are seen as irreversible and new political conclusions have to be drawn: the search for sovereignty has to be traded for equality with the Israeli polity.

Yet within the occupied territories new events were emerging on the ground that were to dramatically reshape the nature of this debate. Within a few months the uprising—unforseen by most—imposed a new trajectory for Palestinian political discourse, in which the notions of steadfastness, survival strategies, and integration (the keystones of the foregoing debate) had to be redefined or disposed of.

Steadfastness or Populism: Which Strategy?

Underlying the debate as to which strategy of liberation was to be followed by the Palestinian movement were important social transformations that had affected the West Bank and Gaza during the two decades of Israeli rule. The most salient of these changes (for the purpose of this analysis) was the emergence of new social groups and classes that had been generated by the political and economic linkages between Israel and the occupied territories.

Three of these groups are of particular significance: first, a class of urban entrepreneurs who mediated Israeli control over the economy (labor contractors, sub-contracting businessmen, and wholesale distributors of Israeli commodities, especially in the food, textile, and building sectors); second, a class of proletarianized peasants and refugee camp dwellers whose sole (or primary) source of livelihood was employment in the Israeli-Jewish sector, constituting about 40 percent of the Palestinian labor force; and third, a substantial grouping of unemployed or underemployed university graduates and dropouts, who (unlike previous generations that had benefitted from the oil boom in the Gulf states) could neither migrate nor find gainful employment at home. To this we must add a later, fourth class of energetic entrepreneurs centered around the townships of Nablus, Bayt Sahur, Ramallah, and Hebron who launched a successful campaign in the 1980s to capture the nationalist home market ("buy Palestinian") through the loopholes of Israeli control over markets and labor.[9]

Schematically, we can speak of the first and second of these classes as the primary beneficiaries of the territories' integration within the Israeli economy, with the third and fourth constituting the political and social basis (or the intellectual and bourgeois components, respectively) for the revival of Palestinian territorial nationalism in the 1980's. What created the illusion of national unity in response to Israel's strategy of control during the 1970's and the early years of the 1980s was the amorphous ideology of steadfastness (*sumud*)—the notion that all Palestinians suffer equally under the yoke of occupation, and that therefore they must postpone resolving their internal conflicts until the stage of deliverance.

But *sumud* has had a murky geneology in the idiom of the Palestinian national movement. It began as a form of passive resistance to Israeli rule in the early seventies and ended as a form of passive non-resistance (some would say as aggressive non-resistance) following the decision by the Arab states in Baghdad (1978) to aid the "steadfastness" of the West Bank and Gaza to the tune of $150 million annually.[10] The term *da'm sumud ahluna fi al-dakhil* ("in support of the steadfastness of our folks inside") became the official Arab "guilt money" for abandoning the confrontation with Israel. Behind this notion lies the assumption, as Edward Said has noted, that by merely staying on their land, Palestinians were asserting their nationhood—the *natural* expected behaviour from them being flight and exile. Conceptually, steadfastness was best expressed in a series of studies on the manner by which Palestinians adopted survival strategies to accommodate their traditional social and economic institutions to Israel control. Sharif Kana'na, for example, discusses how the extended patriarchal family in the Galilee (and by extension in the West Bank) adapted itself to the underclass conditions that Arab villagers have been subjected to.[11] The traditional family, by asserting its conservatism, became a conserving agent and a protector against attempts at manipulation and dismemberment.

In the West Bank, *sumud* also evolved as a form of asserting the traditional virtues of rural society (attachment to the land, the fecundity of Palestinian women, and self-sufficiency).[12] In effect there was something very retrogressive in this attitude. Attachment to the land took the form of an idealistic glorification of peasant society that never existed in reality. Fecundity was expressed as a parallel reaction to the Jewish nationalist mania with Arab demographic growth ("the procreation road to liberation"). And the search for self-sufficiency became a search for autarky—a perspective that was blind to the present economic realities of Israeli domination and market forces. Even today in the economic literature of the *intifada* we see the strong impact of this autarkic perspective in the discussion on the revival of the domestic economy.[13]

The Subversion of Steadfastness

The net effect of this conception of steadfastness was an assertion of traditionalism, both in the cultural domain and in the reinforcement of political hierarchies which were hegemonic prior to the Israeli rule (notable urban families and rural potentates). This reinforcement unwittingly corresponded to the Israeli onslaught against radical political forces of Palestinian nationalism (elected mayors, activists, trade unionists, and students) which reached a symbolic height after 1981 with the "rule of the *mukhtars*" exemplified by the collaborationist Village Leagues.[14] The failure of that attempt did not weaken the traditional forces it unleashed. On the contrary, traditionalism became a cultural core of Palestinian nationalism. This is indeed a case where conservative national forces played a role in defeating a reactionary (collaborative) political movement.[15]

Traditional steadfastness also engendered a parasitic tendency, one endemic to several Mediterranean societies that have experienced large-scale individual migrations early in this century. A considerable section of Palestinian society developed an addiction (also witnessed today in Turkey, Egypt, and Lebanon) to stipends sent by relatives abroad (Europe, America and the Gulf). This continuously undermined the development of the productive sector within the country, most notably in rural society. More important still, it created the psychological milieu for dependence on external aid and supported a lifestyle that exceeded the actual productive potential of society. In Palestinian society, these monetary injections affected the lives of a substantial section of the urban population, and (during the 1970s) a growing proportion of villagers.[16]

A study commissioned by the United Nations Conference on Trade and Development (UNCTAD) provide a concrete picture of the sources and dimensions of this dependence. Until 1978 remittances from Palestinians abroad were the chief external source of income available to Palestinians in the occupied territories, amounting to $55 million annually. By the early 1980s, these were overtaken by *sumud* funds, mostly money transferred by the Palestinian-Jordanian Joint Committee, amounting to an average of $110 million annually during the period 1980-1983, or roughly 35% of all transfers of funds from abroad (UNRWA aid to refugees excluded).[17] It was in this period that a conflict over aid appeared between a "developmental" strategy (favored by international agencies and private voluntary organizations) and the strategy of "steadfastness," the latter operationally translated as keeping people on the land.[18]

Yet these polemics were in fact deceptive. International aid to the territories in the 1980s was miniscule, and it was no more "developmental" than Arab funds channelled through the Joint-Committee.[19] *Sumud* money ostensibly was earmarked predominantly for infrastructural activities during the Committee's fertile years (1979-85), with the bulk of its aid going to agriculture, housing, education, and municipal activities.[20] In actual practice, however, the main beneficiaries of these funds were the big landlords of the Jordan Valley, the industrialists, the Jordanian civil service (in the West Bank), and professional groups who received generous housing loans.[21] At their height, *sumud* funds were readily manipulated by the traditional elites who were now equipped with the nationalist ideology of steadfastness, often with the connivance and active support of the Israeli military government under the guise of backing "moderate elements." The Israeli Civil Administration obviously stood to relieve their own budget with that portion of external aid which was earmarked for infrastructural activities (road building, rural electrification, and the introduction of potable water to villages).[22]

But aside from infrastructural investments, these funds served to buttress a most destructive and parasitic pattern of "economic development." During this period, the area witnessed the channeling of several million dollars towards building middle-class villas, subsidies to non-productive industrial firms, and a sizeable amount of handouts in the form of patronage money to nationalist institutions and personalities. The word *sumud* became a term of cynical self-denigration, often used as a mocking reference to the *nouveaux riches* recipients of patronage money.[23] Only to the external observer did it retain any positive content of glorification, thus enhancing its irony.

Populism and Factional Realities

It was against this degeneration of the ideology of *sumud* that a populist reaction arose. But populism itself, and the mass organizations it gave rise to, had its roots in an earlier illusion within Palestinian society. It can be traced to the period after 1976, when radical groups and social institutions saw their main task as building the embryonic basis of the future Palestinian state (and society) *as a parallel power to the occupation authority*. This strategy encompassed a wide array of movements and groups, from municipal councils at the top—ready for the seizure of power as administrative surrogates of the PLO—to university student circles and academics who conceived their role as the cadres of a technocratic intelligentsia of the future state. At the core of this movement were the few thousand members of clandestine Palestinian parties who were building mass, quasi-legal, popular groups (labor, student, and women's unions, among others) to widen their political base. This whole strategy was grounded in the perception of a new balance of power in the Middle East following the October War and preceding the Camp David agreement.

But the collapse of this political illusion about the impending realization of statehood did not end the dynamism of populism within the new Palestinian movement. On the contrary, it enhanced it by stripping it of its naive idealism and the retinue of political climbers that had joined the movement with the rise of the political (and financial) fortunes of the PLO. Populism became the ideology of a new radical and grassroots alternative to the elitist outlook of the nationalist movement. ("Elitism" is used here in a dual sense: first, in its espousal of a vanguardist organizational structure for its struggle; and second, in the sense that patronage and the adoption of notable personalities as leaders of the national movement became a *modus operandi* for the movement as a whole). The appearance of the mass organizations (*mu'assasat jamahiriyya*) in the early 1980s and their adoption of a populist ideology were seen as a necessary antidote to the limitations inherent in the nationalist movement.

Two studies by Taraki and Hiltermann shed significant light on the nature and structure of these groups.[24] In her work, Taraki traces the spectacular growth of mass organizations within the territories in this period, in part, to the organizational limitations of clandestine political activity by underground movements in the West Bank and Gaza.[25] The first two years of the 1980s saw the dismantlement of the National Guidance Committee (the "internal" wing of the PLO) and the mass crackdown on activists, trade unionists, and student leaders as a prelude to the invasion of Lebanon and the attempt to liquidate the PLO infrastructure physically. Thus the clandestine movement resorted to widening its political base through building a wider network of front organizations. Those would simultaneously create a semi-legal protective enclave around it, while mobilizing thousands of young people through popular committees—*lijan sha'biyya* (health, volunteer work brigades, women's groups, trade union blocs).

But it would be a mistake to view the mass organizations as performing a purely protective (or "frontist") function. Their importance lies in carrying the resistance movement to a new and critical plateau. They brought into the movement tens of thousands of young people who would have otherwise been reluctant to join clandestine organizations. They also incorporated marginalized social groups who, for class reasons, had been left out of the political arena. As a consequence the new movement, in Taraki's words, "mark[ed] the social and political enfranchisement of those sectors that had been traditionally excluded from Palestinian political and institutional life."[26] More significantly, these groups adopted an ideology of radical populism which challenged the traditional structure and perspective of the Palestinian movement.

What are the main features of this radical populism? At the institutional level, it was—as noted above—the rejection of the elitist and nepotistic character of the nationalist movement, whose *raison d'être* was *sumud* and survival. In the women's movement, it marked a rejection of the charitable and bourgeois orientation of the established women's societies in Palestine. In the student movement, it espoused (although never actually carried out) a democratic critique of the formalistic and degree-based university curriculum. In the labor movement it called for organizing and raising the consciousness of the most marginal and neglected of workers, those daily workers of refugee and peasant origin who commute to Israel, and who have hitherto been outside the domain of the official trade union movement. It was a *radical* movement in the sense that it challenged the established contours of political action set by the traditions of the nationalist movement. (It should be added, however, that the radicals too often resorted to traditional forms of patronage when they sought shortcuts in political action.) And it was *populist* in the sense that it involved all sectors of the population in its organized political activities, rather than making them the *target* of these activities. Ideologically, the marks of populism were evident in the amorphous overarching thrust of the movement and its lack of a specific class perspective.[27]

Nevertheless, the new movement remained factionalized to the core, with its populism reinforcing at the mass level the same partisan boundaries that typified its parent political groupings. Often zeal for the recruitment of new members overrode ideological considerations, making it hard for observers to distinguish the programs of various leftist groups or even the difference between socialist (those who identified with the Palestine Communist Party, Democratic Front for the Liberation of Palestine, and the Popular Front for the Liberation of Palestine) and nationalist (those allied with Fateh) mass organizations.[28] There was also a tendency, particularly among the leftist groups, to de-emphasize socially progressive positions which might hamper their recruitment drives in traditional circles. Lisa

Taraki notes, for example, that all groups avoided raising the issue of the status of women in the domestic sphere:

> No women's organization has been willing to challenge prevailing legislation governing the personal status of women, especially in matters concerning inheritance rights and divorce. Disputes within families over such issues, when they do come to the attention of the committees, are generally dealt with on an individual level, and rarely are conflicts in the domestic sphere made public.[29]

But when all is said and done, it is difficult to conceive of factionalism exclusively as a divisive issue in the national movement, although it often was. Factionalism (i.e., organizational sectarianism) was ultimately the most effective mechanism, especially during the uprising, for mass mobilization of groups, neighbourhoods, and popular committees. It created an institutional framework, and made available to individual members the proper incentive to "belong" and act within a familiar, and exclusive, concrete identity. It also set the parameters for each organization's sphere of influence and political mobility. And it was this competing network of ideological and organizational struggle that created the political infrastructure which sustained and propelled the national uprising of December 1987.

The Intifada *and the Limitations of Populism*

There seems to be agreement on the part of the Israeli security establishment, as well as within the Palestinian national movement, that the popular committees (and the mass organizations that preceded them) provided the organizational crucible for the uprising.[30] But this agreement did not emerge without controversy, most of it centering on the role of spontaneity in guiding the mass action of the *intifada*. In the first month of the uprising, an article in *Filastin al-Thawra* (the organ of the PLO Central Council) declared:

> ...in no great revolt does the organized side of mass action prevail over the spontaneity of the people. Revolutions are not manufactured, and any capable leadership (which constitutes the disciplined component of the revolt) is tested severely during these critical watersheds of history. The events and new contingencies of the *intifada* compel the political leadership to reconsider many of its slogans, forms and tactics in light of these new realities.[31]

In response, Jamil Hilal writing in *al-Fikr al-Dimukrati* accused the editorial writer of underestimating the accumulated organizational experience of the resistance movement in the territories:

> But the most striking feature of the current popular uprising, which is also the greatest modern Palestinian revolt, is that it occurs against the background of unprecedented *widescale organizing activity*. The claim that the spark that

> ignited the current uprising had a specific form and occurred at a specific time should not lead us to assume that the revolt was a spontaneous act, but that the subjective conditions which made the *intifada* possible were ripe. Whatever delay we witnessed in the organized forces of the national movement assuming control of events... was due to the absence of the *appropriate form of unified organized formation* for the movement [since] the elimination of the National Guidance Committee in the eighties [by the military government]. The speed with which the Unified National Leadership was formed attests to the necessity of this framework as a condition for the continuity and escalation of the popular revolt...[32]

This historical intervention, according to Hilal, would have been impossible without the mass organizations of the syndicates, women's and youth groups, labor committees, and their "strike forces."[33] One could, of course, criticize Hilal himself for exaggerating the organized element of the *intifada* to the exclusion of any element of spontaneity, which was obvious in the first weeks of the uprising.[34] In addition, one could dispute the conceptual utility of the distinction between the "organized" and "spontaneous" categories as if they were opposites. Every mass movement exhibits (in various proportions) both a disciplined, "led" component as well as voluntarist, unplanned tendencies—both being essential features of a popular revolt. Nevertheless, Hilal's emphasis is well taken in this instance, given the recent tendency to explain the uprising ahistorically—attributing its origins to such factors as mass frustrations, generational conflicts, cultural gaps, and the like—without specific reference to the structural conditions of the occupied territories.

It is also important to note that this view of the role of popular committees and the mass organizations which established them is not the conspiratorial perspective held by the security establishment. Rather, it is a position that is acknowledged by the political leadership of the national movement in the occupied territories. Confirmation of this appears in the pronouncements of five prominent cadres of the clandestine movement who were deported in 1988 for membership in the Unified National Leadership of the uprising.[35] Discussing their experiences in the 19th Palestine National Council meeting in Algiers in November 1988, they differed in assessing the immediate "causes" of the uprising. But there was a consensus among the five leaders (representing the four major political factions of the PLO) that the mass committees constituted the institutional foundation upon which the *intifada* was built, so that (in the words of deportee Ghassan al-Masri) "revolt became a patterned activity."[36]

This is not the place to discuss the uprising as a process, nor its immediate consequences for the occupied territories. Elsewhere, I have defined the main features of the *intifada* in terms of its negative achievements: namely, that it has succeeded in undermining (it is premature to speak of *dismantling*) the apparatus of Israeli political control over the

Palestinian population. During the past two decades of Israeli rule, those direct control features rested on the "unseen" subordination of Palestinian society through the mechanisms of market, labor, and infrastructure.[37] In effect, West Bank and Gazan societies became ungovernable, thus compelling the Israeli ruling elite to rethink its attitude towards Palestinian sovereignty. Any attempt to assess this process in terms of positive achievements (i.e., in terms of actual fixed consequences) at this historical juncture must remain tentative. That it is difficult to go further in this assessment can be appreciated by comparing the responses made by five deported "UNL leaders" in response to the question: "What in your view is the main accomplishment of the uprising?"[38]

> L.A. (Fateh): "It has transformed revolt into a daily pattern of life."
>
> G.M. (Fateh): "Dismantled military rule, and reconstituted people's authority."
>
> J.Z. (DFLP): "The construction of a Palestinian society of a new type."
>
> A.N.A. (PFLP): "Dismantled the foundation of the occupation authorities (police, municipalities) and replaced them with the nucleus of an alternative power."
>
> A.Z. (PCP): "Created the conditions for Jordan's legal and administrative disengagement from the West Bank."

What is striking in these responses is their radically different characterization of what constitutes the single most important achievement of the uprising, on the eve of its first anniversary. Clearly, this stems from the difficulty of summarizing the effects of a revolutionary situation that is itself in flux. To the extent that there is a modicum of consensus, it is a highly idealized and visionary perspective ("building the embryonic units of future Palestinian society" and "the replacement of Israeli colonial authority with the people's national authority"). There is on the other hand a consensus on the historic role of the mass organizations and their later manifestations, the popular committees, in bringing about this revolutionary situation.[39]

The main tasks of the popular committees, however, remain ahead. If serious thought is to be given to the claims of the movement that it is building the embryonic institutions of the future independent state,[40] then obviously a more concrete program of action would be required from the popular committees. The withholding of taxes, boycott of Israeli produce, work stoppages during strike days, and the mass resignations of the police force and tax collectors, are all essential features of the process of the withdrawal of Palestinian society from two decades of dependence on the Israeli colonial state apparatus.[41] The Unified National Leadership has exhibited a great deal of skill and flexibility in coordinating these acts of civil disobedience among the rural, urban, and refugee segments of the population, and in translating them into a collective national act of rebellion. But they all remain acts of *disengagement*. To transform them from a process of disobedience to a process of affirmation requires that the committees devote themselves to the task of forging alternative economic, social, and administrative structures. So far a great deal of myths have arisen around popular neighborhood teaching (including the planning of alternative curricula), home gardening, cottage industries, rural co-operatives, and many other arenas of popular organization.[42] But many of these activities remain more expressions of revolutionary *élan* than substantive programs of social change. The popular committees succeeded in creating a vast organizational network, enhancing the communal solidarity of what used to be segmented and atomized neighbourhoods, and mobilized thousands of people in the ranks of the nationalist movement: that has been the fundamental achievement of the *intifada*. What remains is to narrow the gap between the radical rhetoric of the committees, and their declared objectives for revolutionary change.

There is, of course, another possible strategy—one based on a different reading of current Palestinian populism. That would be to regard the popular committees, in conjunction with the political network of the PLO inside the territories, as constituting *not* the embryonic foundations of a new society, but as *the nascent organs of an alternative power base*. In this perception, the historic function of the popular committees (if they are to survive the Israeli onslaught against them) would be confined to performing its negative role as defined above: namely, to undermine and erode the basis of Israeli colonial rule until the external political conditions are met for the PLO to establish itself as a state power in the occupied territories. In that case, a disciplined retreat would compel the decision-makers in the movement to adjust their revolutionary idiom to this more pragmatic objective.[43]

As the *intifada*—already the most sustained rebellion in the history of the modern Middle East—approached its fourth year, such a disciplined retreat seemed very much in order. The declining tempo of street warfare and the temporary eclipse of the Palestinian issue from the international agenda during the Gulf crisis will doubtless compel the leadership of the Palestinian uprising to make a difficult choice between two alternative visions.[44]

Notes

1. Meron Benvenisti was among the first writers to advance the view that Israeli policies had created patterns of interaction and structure which had become quasi-permanent in nature, creating a process of integration that had passed the point of no return. However very few commentators, Arab or Israeli, agreed with the political conclusions he drew from this process.

2. Actually, the conference was held 3-5 January 1986 at Oxford University in

anticipation of the second decade anniversary. The proceedings appeared in George Abed, ed., *The Palestinian Economy: Studies in Development under Prolonged Occupation* (London: Routledge, 1988).

3. See Abed, ed., *The Palestinian Economy*, especially the contributions of Ibrahim Dakkak, Harold Dick, and (for Israeli Arabs) Raja Khalidi.

4. Yusif Sayigh, "The Palestinian Economy Under Occupation," *Journal of Palestine Studies*, 15, 4 (Summer, 1986): 63-64. Also published in Abed, ed., *The Palestinian Economy*, pp. 259-286.

5. Sayigh, "The Palestinian Economy Under Occupation," p. 64; see also Ibrahim Dakkak, "Development from Within: A Strategy for Survival," in Abed, ed., *The Palestinian Economy*.

6. Sari Nusseibeh, "The continuation of the status quo," *al-Fajr* (Jerusalem), 9 August 1987.

7. Nusseibeh, "The continuation of the status quo."

8. The space given here to Nusseibeh's paper is not meant to indicate widespread approval of his views in national circles, but because it presents the sharpest and clearest expression of a political stand that was implicit in much of the pre-*intifada* literature.

9. We do not have any comprehensive work analyzing the class transformations of the Palestinians under Israeli rule. The reader might benefit from consulting the following works: Jamil Hilal, *The West Bank: Economic and Social Structure* (Beirut, 1975) [in Arabic]; Pamela Ann Smith, *Palestine and the Palestinians, 1876-1983* (New York: St. Martin's Press, 1984); Joel Migdal, *Palestinian Society and Politics* (Princeton: Princeton University Press, 1980); and this writer's "Building other People's Homes: the Palestinian Peasant and Work in Israel," *Journal of Palestine Studies*, 2, 1 (1981). On proletarianization, see also, M. Semyonov and N. Lewin Epstein, *Hewers of Wood and Drawers of Water: Non-citizen Arabs in the Israeli Labor Market* (New York: ILR Press 1987).

10. In the end only a portion of the promised aid actually materialized. For a discussion of this dimension of *sumud* see Samir Abdallah Salih, *Jordanian Economic Policies towards the Occupied Territories*, (Jerusalem, 1988), pp. 51-59 [in Arabic].

11. Sharif Kana'na, "Survival Strategies of the Arabs in Israel," *MERIP Reports*, 53 (November 1976).

12. The main organ of this assertion was (and continues to be) *Society and Heritage*, the journal of the Palestine Folklore Society in al-Bireh.

13. See, for example, "The Thousand Mile Journey Begins with the Domestic Economy," *al-Biyader al-Siyasi* (Jerusalem), 12 November 1988 [in Arabic].

14. See Salim Tamari, "In League with Zion: Israel's Search for a Native Pillar," *Journal of Palestine Studies*, 12, 4 (Summer, 1983).

15. This is not to belittle the role of radical nationalist groups in the defeat of the Leagues, which was substantial, but to point out the cultural role of rural conservatism in resisting Israeli attempts to foster collaborationist groups.

16. For West Bank and Gaza income generated from emigrant stipends see, UNCTAD, *The Palestinian Financial Sector Under Israeli Occupation* (New York, 1987), pp. 132-139.

17. UNCTAD, *The Palestinian Financial Sector Under Israeli Occupation*, 155-158.

18. UNCTAD, *The Palestinian Financial Sector Under Israeli Occupation*, p. 147; see also Abed, ed., *The Palestinian Economy*, pp. 1-12.

19. See A. Qassim, *Funding Sources Development in the Occupied Territories* (Jerusalem: Arab Thought Forum, 1986).

20. UNCTAD, *The Palestinian Financial Sector Under Israeli Occupation*, pp. 151, 155.

21. cf. Salih, *Jordanian Economic Policies towards the Occupied Territories*, pp. 51-59.

22. A good critique of this aspect of aid is Meron Benvenisti, *U.S. Government Funded Projects in the West Bank and Gaza* (Jerusalem: West Bank Data Project, 1984), pp. 14-15.

23. Next to the main road between Ramallah and Nablus, there is a hill-top neighborhood known as *Jabal al-Sumud* (The Hill of Steadfastness), mocking the patronage money spent in building a housing cooperative there.

24. Lisa Taraki, "Mass Organizations in the West Bank," unpublished manuscript; Joost Hiltermann, *Before the Uprising: The Organization and Mobilization of Palestinian Workers and Women in the Israeli-Occupied West Bank and Gaza Strip*, Ph.D. thesis, University of California, Santa Cruz, June 1988. For an examination of the subsequent role of workers' organizations in the *intifada*, see Joost Hiltermann, "Mass Mobilization and the Uprising: The Labor Movement," in Michael Hudson, ed., *The Palestinians: New Directions* (Washington, D.C.: Center for Contemporary Arab Studies, 1990), and Joost Hiltermann, "Work and Action: The Role of the Working Class in the Uprising," in Jamal Nassar and Roger Heacock, eds., *Intifada: Palestine at the Crossroads* (New York: Praeger Publishers, 1990).

25. Taraki, "Mass Organizations in the West Bank," p. 12

26. Taraki, "Mass Organizations in the West Bank," p. 32.

27. See Hiltermann, *Before the Uprising*, for the 'nationalist' ambiguities of the class perspective of the trade union movement (pp. 336-341) and the class-feminist dilemmas of the women's committees (pp. 469-488).

28. This claim can be substantiated by comparing the programs of the four main women's committees and workers' blocs in Hiltermann's excellent discussion, *Before the Uprising*, pp. 291-326, 469-488. See also Taraki, "Mass Organizations in the West Bank," p. 31. Taraki notes, however, that there is a tendency on the part of leftist women's groups "to de-emphasize the domestic function. This is done primarily through mobilizing women for political activism and creating contexts very removed, both physically and socially, from the traditional meeting places of women."

29. Taraki, "Mass Organizations in the West Bank," p. 29—but see note 28 above for a modification.

30. See the crucial analysis made by three Israeli leaders and military commanders, Yizhak Rabin (Minister of Defense), Ihud Barak (Deputy Chief of Staff) and General Dan Shomron (Chief of Staff): "Rabin sets his sights on local People's Committees of the areas," *Jerusalem Post*, 8 August 1988; "Nothing in the territories will revert to what it was prior to December 1987," *Yediot Ahronot*, 4 December 1988; "Shomron: *Intifada* can't be eradicated," *Jerusalem Post*, 11 January 1989. See also Bashir al-Barghouti's "Year of the *Intifada*: meanings and connotations," *al-Ittihad* (special supplement), 9 January 1989.

31. *Filastin al-Thawra* 21 January 1988, p. 25.

32. Jamil Hilal, "The Uprising and the Needed Change," *al-Fikr al-Dimukrati* 3 (July 1988): 6 [emphasis added].

33. Hilal, "The Uprising and the Needed Change," p. 6.

34. The most vivid description of this early spontaneity appeared in a Hebrew article by Makram Makhoul in the Tel Aviv newspaper *Ha'Ir*, "This is not a revolt, it's a war," 18 December 1987; translated and reprinted in *Journal of Palestine Studies* 17, 3 (Spring 1988): 91-99.

35. Bashir al-Bakr, "Five deportees discuss their field experiences," *al-Yawm al-Sabi'* (Paris), 5 December 1988.

36. *al-Yawm al-Sabi'*, 5 December 1988.

37. "What the Uprising Means," *Middle East Report* 152 (May-June 1988): 24-30.

38. *al-Yawm al-Sabi'*, 5 December 1988. I have used inverted commas around "UNLI leaders" because this is the term used by the Israeli authorities to justify (in part) their deportation. In the interview, however, none of them rejected this identification.

39. Reflecting their importance in the uprising, on 18 August 1988 the Israeli Ministry of Defense banned the popular committees, making membership in such a committee a security offence punishable by up to ten years in prison (*al-Fajr,* 21 August 1988). The new measures did not have much effect in restricting the the committees' activities, however. Joost Hiltermann, "Human Rights and the Mass Movement: The First Year of the Uprising," *Journal of Palestine Studies* 18, 3 (Spring 1989): 130-132.

40. This sort of terminology has appeared in several communiques of the Unified National Leadership. Communique 59 (July 1990), for example, noted: "in the field, the UNLI, proceeding from a consistent strategy of developing the fabric of the national authority of our independent state, once again urges all our masses to seriously involve themselves in building popular and specialized committees."

41. For details, see Information Committee (Jerusalem), *Toward a State of Independence*, September 1988, pp. 16-19; see also the collection of UNL directives in Zachary Lockman and Joel Benin, eds., *Intifada: The Palestinian Uprising Against Israeli Occupation* (Boston: South End Press/MERIP, 1989), pp. 327-394.

42. There is considerable unevenness in the achievements of these committees. Mention should be made of the considerable success achieved by women's productive cooperatives in several refugee camps (in Gaza) and villages (in the West Bank), especially in marketing processed foods. See *Shu'un Tanmawiyya* [*Development Affairs*, published by the Arab Thought Forum in Jerusalem] 2 (December 1988), a special issue on the women's movement; *al-Fajr* (weekly edition), 12 March 1990, pp. 8-9.

43. Some evidence of this language can already be found in the communiques of the UNLI. Leaflet 54 (27 March 1990), for example, called on the population "to continue forming, building, and developing the popular committees in every camp, village, district, and city so that these committees will constitute the *alternative popular authority for the occupation's collapsing organs and departments* (emphasis added)."

44. For further analysis of the internal crisis of the *intifada* as it has affected both particular social groups and the national movement as a whole, see: Salim Tamari, "The Revolt of the Petite Bourgeoisie," in Nassar and Heacock, eds., *Intifada: Palestine at the Crossroads*; and "The Uprising's Dilemma: Limited Rebellion and Civil Society," *Middle East Report* 164-165 (May-August 1990): 4-8.

2

Israel and the Palestinians: Human Rights in the Occupied Territories

Raja Shehadeh

To understand the current Palestinian *intifada*, it is necessary to understand the nature of the Israeli-Palestinian relationship established during more than two decades of Israeli occupation of the West Bank and Gaza Strip. During this period, it has become clear that Israel's actions in the territories have been aimed at changing the status quo in order to make permanent the acquisition of the areas seized in 1967. East Jerusalem and the Golan Heights have been formally annexed, while the West Bank and Gaza are being gradually absorbed. In violation of internationally accepted conventions and norms, Israel has introduced far-reaching legal, material, and administrative changes through more than 1,303 military orders. Palestinian land has been expropriated on a massive scale, water resources have been monopolized, settlements have been created in a pattern aimed at fragmenting the Palestinian population, and the local government and the judiciary have been restructured.

Israel's explanation of the nature of its occupation has changed several times. In the beginning, it acknowledged its status as an occupying force,[1] even while claiming the occupation had been forced upon it by a war it had not sought and insisting that the occupation was "the most benevolent in history." Somewhat later it stated that the occupation would continue until a final settlement was reached according to which land would be exchanged for peace. Next, Israel announced that since the occupied areas were of strategic importance to its defense, land would be expropriated for settlements that would serve Israeli security interests.

In a subsequent stage, marked by the advent of a Likud government, the possibility of an exchange of "land for peace" was dropped. The territories were now held to belong to Israel by right, indeed, by divine right: there could be no question of expropriating or occupying what was rightfully Israel's. Use of the words "West Bank" was discontinued, with "Judea" and "Samaria" the only officially recognized terms. The word "occupation" was also dropped. The territories were now "administered," as were their 1.8 million Palestinian inhabitants. With the rightful ownership of the land now deemed to be Israeli, the Palestinians, by implication, were reduced to the status of squatters, who were fortunate to benefit from Israel's presence and whose periodic outbursts were generally dismissed as the work of sinister forces from the outside. For more than twenty years, then, Israel's policy has been based on a specific view of itself, its adversary, and its future. Underlying all these successive positions is Israel's insistence that the Palestinians are merely "resident"[2]—not a people with a national identity, but rather an amorphous mass of individuals who happen to be living in a given area. It is this assumption that enables the Israeli government seriously to insist that its occupation has benefited the Palestinians; indeed, that the harsh methods used during the current uprising—the use of live ammunition against protesters, indiscriminate beatings, mass arrests, deportations—were undertaken, as a Foreign Ministry spokesman declared, "for safeguarding the security of its inhabitants."[3] In other words, the harsh measures benefit the population insofar as they defend it against terrorism and enable it to lead a "normal life."

This chapter will examine the nature of Israeli administrative, physical, and economic control over the occupied territories, and its cost in terms of Palestinian human rights. In this context, it will show how the severity of such measures and recourse to coercive means of control have intensified as a consequence of the Palestinian uprising, and how the economics of occupation have also changed. In doing so it will indicate the unacceptability of present conditions—and hence the need to forge a new Palestinian-Israeli relationship.

Occupier and Occupied

In the years prior to the *intifada*, several major trends could be observed in the nature of Israeli control over the occupied territories. One of these was a pattern of ever more pervasive control over the lives of Palestinians through the application of an increasing number of military orders. This "officially sanctioned illegality" (that is to say, Israeli military orders and actions in violation of international law) was complemented by "unofficial illegality"—acts carried out by overzealous settlers impatient with the rate of "Judaisation" effected through official channels. Although officially condemned by the authorities, this latter type of action has in fact been tolerated, if not encouraged.[4]

A second trend has been a broadening of the interpretation of what constitutes security. From the beginning of the occupation, successive Israeli governments have justified their activities—land seizures, the building of settlements, changes in the legal system, or harsh treatment of Palestinians—on the grounds of state security. Increasingly, however, the Israeli authorities condoned on security grounds excesses and practices at odds with international law. A clear indicator of this attitude could be found in the October 1987 report of the Landau Commission, established by the Prime Minister to examine the interrogation methods of the Shin Bet [General Security Services]. While voicing concern that "breach of the law [might] lead to a relaxation of standards whereby interrogators become a law unto themselves," thus damaging the image of the state to the point that "we could come to resemble those regimes which give their security services unrestrained power," the report went on in effect to condone the very breach of the law whose effects caused it concern, thereby negating the entire system of checks and balances for curbing such excesses.[5] As Rabbi Haim Druckman of the National Religious Party stated: "When it comes to Arab suspects, the Shin Bet must have a completely free hand."[6]

While reserving for itself the right to be the exclusive arbiter of what is legal, what constitutes security and what actions are needed to safeguard it, Israel has nonetheless always insisted that despite the threat under which it lives, it has upheld the highest standards of law and human rights for the inhabitants of the occupied territories. Charges of excesses have been vigorously and routinely denied. In an official letter dated 4 February 1987 to the president of the United Nations Commission on Human Rights, Israel's permanent representative to the UN in Geneva cited numerous examples of how Israel has not only upheld the Fourth Geneva Convention Relative to the Protection of Civilian Persons in Time of War, but has gone beyond it. He asserted that the legal protection accorded the local population, whose situation Israel is determined to improve, "far exceeds" that required by the convention and "assures this population the same rights as those granted to Israeli citizens by Israeli administrative law."[7]

This evaluation, long accepted by Israel's friends in the West and challenged mainly by human rights organizations and Palestinian advocates and in forums of the United Nations, has had to be modified. It must be emphasized that the methods used to quell the *intifada*—mass arrests, beatings, use of live ammunition, and summary trials, extensive curfews, deportations and so on—are no different from those that have been used since the beginning of the occupation. Nor are they being reported for the first time.

What is new, in addition to the scope, is the prominence and relentlessness of the coverage following the start of the uprising and the fact that major stories were carried by mass circulation newspapers and magazines which have traditionally been strong defenders of Israel, such as the *New York Times*. The impact of this coverage has undoubtedly left its mark. Faced with revelations that cannot convincingly be denied—official and categorical denials of the use of tear gas in mosques were reported even as television footage clearly documenting such episodes was shown—Israel has adjusted its official position as regards both morality and law. Claims of superior morality do continue: Shimon Peres (then foreign minister) declared on 8 February 1988, after more than fifty Palestinians had already been killed, that Israel was "hampered in dealing with the protests because of its moral constraints."[8] But such statements have been somewhat muted over the past few years. Instead, the emphasis has shifted from an insistence on humane and ethical behavior as the norm, to the justification of measures taken on the grounds of regrettable necessity in the face of international and local terrorism. Israel's Justice Minister, Dan Meridor, said on 25 September 1989 that Israel must take extraordinary measures of deterrence, including collective punishment, to deal with the *intifada*, since this is a "war" that Israel must win.[9]

Security has thus become the ultimate justification: for the use of live ammunition, for throwing tear gas canisters into mosques, for breaking bones, for house demolitions and deportations, for a security service that can beat alleged terrorists to death with impunity and lie under oath in the courts.[10] In the atmosphere that now prevails, it is tempting to focus on the brutality and excesses at the expense of the less dramatic methods used in controlling the population, i.e. the permanent infrastructure of repression. But it is at least partially these "quieter means" that led to the uprising in the first place and that will doubtless continue if the current unrest at least temporarily abates.

Nothing is more representative of these quiet means than the Shin Bet itself. Its power is in many ways symbolic of Israeli power over the inhabitants of the territories: it is immune to supervision, not answerable to public scrutiny, not accountable to the law. Administrative detention orders, deportations, house demolitions and sealings, and other such administrative measures all ultimately depend on recommendations made by this secret organization. Moreover, it is in fact Shin Bet, and not the Civil Administration, that has the real power to decide on the applications for permits for the large number of activities requiring military approval. Such applications are routinely submitted to the Shin Bet, and when a rejection is appealed by a lawyer, the matter is simply referred once again to the security service for a second review. The High Court of Justice in Israel also accepts the determinations of the secret service and basis its judgments on it. When one considers that permits are required for opening businesses, obtaining or renewing cars and drivers' licenses, obtaining or transferring telephones, obtaining travel documents, importing and exporting, growing crops, joining a professional union, seeking employment in the public sector, and practicing such professions as law, accounting, pharmacy, and surveying (all considered to have security implications), one has some idea of the pervasiveness of the Shin Bet's power over Palestinians' lives.

One important development that has abetted this process of absolute control is the computerization of the records of the military government in the West Bank. This was described by Meron Benvenisti in the 1987 report of the West Bank Data Base Project as "the ultimate instrument in population control, a computerized carrot-and-stick operation." According to Benvenisti, "By pressing a key on a computer terminal, any Civil Administration official will gain access to name-lists of 'positives' and 'hostiles,' and decide on the fate of their applications... The Data Bank might develop... into a sinister 'big brother' control apparatus in the hands of an administration that already possesses absolute power and is free of any checks and balances... The computerization project, if allowed to attain its stated goals, may prove to be a milestone in the institutionalization of the ultimate police-state in the territories."[11]

Under the impetus of the *intifada*, all these features of the occupation have intensified. During the first two years of the uprising, an estimated 48,000 Palestinians were arrested and detained for three days or more. Of these, some 7,900 were placed in administrative detention, without charge or trial. Another 61 persons were deported during this period.[12]

Moreover, the power of the security services was further reinforced by Military Order 1262 of 17 December 1988, which makes it necessary to obtain the approval of six different departments on almost any application for which the approval of the military is required. Computerized controls were extended in 1989 with the introduction of new magnetically-coded identification cards in the Gaza Strip.[13] Throughout the occupied territories, Palestinians are regularly stopped at checkpoints and made to wait while a soldier consults a computer terminal or computer print-out. If the name of the Palestinian who has been stopped is found in the computer files, Israeli soldiers have been heard to announce victoriously: "bingo." "Super bingo" means that the name of the Palestinian is on a hit list. The number of dead "super bingos" has been mounting.

Violence and Brutality

Israel's control of the West Bank and Gaza Strip has, of course, always rested ultimately on physical coercion. Live ammunition has always been used against demonstrators: between 1 January 1986 and early December 1987, for example, 116 West Bank Palestinians were wounded by bullets fired by the Israeli army. Of these, 18 died of their wounds.[14] Beatings and other violence were also frequently used to control unrest.[15]

Nonetheless, this pattern of violence has increased sharply since the eruption of the *intifada*. At no other time in more than two decades of occupation has the brutality of Israeli methods been more concentrated and intensive than in the period since December 1987. From 9 December 1987 until 10 December 1989, 795 Palestinians died in the occupied territories at the hands of Israeli soldiers and civilians. There were 32 deaths in July 1989 alone. The victims ranged in age from newborn infants to the elderly and included women; nonetheless, the vast majority were in their teens or early twenties. Tens of thousands of others have been injured both from bullets and clubbings, the latter especially as of mid-January 1988 when

Defense Minister Yitzhak Rabin announced his new policy of "force, might and beatings," declaring, "we have to drive home to their mind and hearts 'by violence you'll gain nothing.'"[16] Prime Minister Shamir elaborated on this idea shortly after the policy was instituted: "Our task is to recreate the barrier [of fear] and once again put the fear of death into the Arabs of the areas so as to deter them from attacking us anymore."[17] In addition to the didactic function of the beatings, the fracturing of particular bones in strategic places was thought to be effective in keeping youngsters from throwing stones "for at least several months." According to three medical faculty members from Harvard and one from the City University of New York, members of the Boston-based independent monitoring group Physicians for Human Rights, thousands of Palestinians (3,500 would be a "conservative estimate," according to one member of the team) suffered bone fractures and other injuries from beatings by soldiers during the first three months of the uprising alone. An examination of X-rays and medical records during their week-long stay in the territories indicated a pattern of "mid-shaft" fractures showing deliberate breakage. This policy of "force, might and beatings" continued into the second and third year of the uprising, with dozens of Palestinians being killed and thousands of others suffering injuries (some of them permanent).[18]

Other forms of army brutality have included intimidation of civilians after imposing curfew, as happened in the town of Bayt Sahur in late September 1989 when troops beat up old women and men, causing some to suffer heart attacks and then refusing to allow families to call an ambulance. Several villages and refugee camps have been placed under a continuous curfew for up to forty continuous days, as happened in March-April 1988 in the Jalazun refugee camp near Ramallah. Food sent by the UN and other relief agencies has been seized and destroyed, probably on the assumption that hungry people are more likely to submit.[19] Another form of collective punishment has been the sealing or demolition of houses. During the first two years of the uprising some 250 houses were sealed or destroyed for "security" reasons, and another 750 homes demolished for lack of appropriate building permits.[20]

Instances where army "excesses" (if this is indeed what they are) have been checked and the perpetrator(s) brought to justice are very rare. Despite claims that every killing by army gunfire is investigated, the number of officers and soldiers courtmartialed between December 1987 and October 1989 was, according to figures announced by the office of the Military Advocate-General, only 86. The highest sentence given was two years, which has not yet been served since the sentence was appealed.

Supplementing the violence of the army is that of the settlers, who, like many Israeli citizens, are in possession of firearms of all types (including automatic weapons) and other military equipment.[21] Indeed, an excessive resort to violence on the part of the Israeli army is sometimes instigated by the settlers, who constitute a veritable lobby, with no counter-lobby to act as a restraining force. Vigilante squads and retaliatory attacks by settlers have become a regular feature of life in the territories, particularly during times of unrest. On 28 February 1988, for example, settlers from the West Bank settlement of Halamesh, accompanied by Israeli soldiers, attacked the village of 'Abbud near Ramallah. Soldiers illuminated the area while the settlers opened fire on the villagers, killing two.[22] What is particularly disturbing about these sorts of incidents is the apparent coordination between the settlers and the army. A pattern has become apparent whereby the army imposes a curfew, and the settlers go on a rampage. Nor is the destruction always gratuitous: at times such occasions have enabled settlers to initiate the implementation of "development" plans which would not have been possible otherwise, such as the creation of settlements and roads in disputed areas, the destruction of vegetation in preparation for land seizure, and so on. In most such cases, the army, although capable of putting a rapid halt to the settlers' actions, has delayed until the settlers have achieved their goals. It was through such tactics that the Jewish settlement inside the Palestinian city of Hebron was expanded.

There have also been reported cases of over-zealous settlers staging what the Israeli police have described as "*intifada* attacks" against other settlers, in an attempt to provoke them to action. One such incident was the petrol bomb attack on Avraham Shalev, a resident of the settlement of Ginot Shomron. According to the *Jerusalem Post* of 26 September 1989, "following the attack, enraged Ginot Shomron residents went on a rampage, damaging Arab-owned cars in the area." The North District Police spokesman Gideon Arbel said that an investigation was launched following the receipt of intelligence information that two petrol bomb attacks and a number of stoning incidents in January and February of 1989 near the settlements of Ariel and Ginot Shomron were carried out by settlers to incite demonstrations for increased security on the roads in the area.

While attacks against settlers (whoever is responsible for them) are investigated, the police rarely question the victims of the settlers' attacks when these are Palestinians. As Israeli Army Chief of Staff Dan Shomron admitted, the legal system appears to grind at a more leisurely pace with Jews than with Arabs.[23] He was, of course, putting it mildly. In the very exceptional cases where Israeli settlers have been charged for attacks committed against Palestinian Arabs, the punishment meted out has been light. On 1 May 1990, for example, the Jerusalem District Court sentenced Rabbi Moshe Levinger (who lives in the Jewish settlement of Kiryat Arba in Hebron) to five months in prison and a seven-month suspended sentence after convicting him of killing a Palestinian shopkeeper, Kayid Salah, and causing grievous bodily harm to a customer, Ibrahim Bali, in Hebron on 30 September 1988.[24] Given the settlers' powerful and growing support within Israel, it is politically risky to impose what would be considered "fair" sentences. As one settler has remarked: "Arabs are much, much more afraid of the settlers than they are afraid of the army and the police because they know the army is limited by the politicians... The settlers are not. They can do whatever they want."[25]

The Economics of Occupation

Defenders of Israel's occupation of the West Bank and Gaza Strip frequently cite statistics on the number of refrigerators and television sets in the occupied territories today, as compared with 1967, to show how beneficial the occupation has been to the inhabitants. The rise in the standard of living is supposed to compensate for whatever inconveniences may have resulted from Israeli "administration." Such benefits—the famed "carrot"—are, in fact, dubious at best. Even if such statistics, provided in isolation, were valid indices of an overall improvement in living standards, they take no account of the passage of years or of what would have been the case over the past two decades if the occupation had not occurred.

In fact, not only has the population not benefited from the occupation, it has been economically exploited. The occupied territories have represented to Israel a pool of cheap labor and an unrestricted export market for its own goods. In 1986, Israel exported US$780 million worth of goods to the West Bank and Gaza, making the territories Israel's second largest export market after the US. Israeli goods, meanwhile, represented 89 percent of the occupied territories' imports both in 1985 and 1986. Indeed, the territories are virtually obliged to import from Israel because they have been cut off from their traditional sources in the Arab world. Fees levied on imports from Jordan are so high as to make them uncompetitive. Direct imports from other countries are either entirely banned or heavily taxed, with import duties reaching 200 and 300 percent.[26]

Moreover, while Israeli exports to the occupied territories are unrestricted and competition from goods from other sources virtually eliminated through duties and other controls, Palestinian access to Israeli markets has been sharply limited. Palestinians cannot sell their agricultural produce in Israel without permits, the issuance of which is severely restricted in order to prevent competition with Israeli farmers. Nonetheless, 73 percent of the territories' exports in 1986 were to Israel, most of them for re-export. Indeed, Israel totally controls the export of agricultural products from the territories by requiring that they be channeled exclusively through Israel's own export marketing board, Agrexco, which sells the produce under an Israeli brand name and with profits accruing to Israel. This marketing program seems to have been largely responsible for a sharp decline in the citrus production in the Gaza Strip. According to Hashim Shawa'a (chairman of the Society of Citrus Growers in the Gaza Strip) production has fallen from 250 thousand tons per annum in the mid-1970s to 110 thousand tons today.[27]

In order to maintain the benefits of this situation and to ensure that the West Bank and Gaza Strip continue to be economically dependent captive markets, industry in the territories has been "encouraged" to remain underdeveloped, small-scale, and traditional. According to the West Bank Data Project the "contribution of industry to the West Bank GDP (value added), which was about 8 percent in 1986, was still lower than at the beginning of the occupation (9 percent)."[28] Permission for business projects is frequently withheld by the military government if it is believed that the proposed project could compete with an Israeli business.[29]

In the absence of a published budget (and none has ever been available, contrary to the law in force) it is difficult to know exactly how the balance of payments stands between Israel and the territories it occupied in 1967.[30] Until the *intifada*, however, it could be stated without reservation that the occupation in no way constituted an economic burden for Israel. Indeed, the occupied territories have provided a source of revenue through direct and indirect taxation that has gone directly into the Israeli treasury to be used for Israeli public consumption. Meron Benvenisti has estimated that the so-called "occupation taxes" paid to the occupation authorities (excluding local taxes) by West Bankers and Gazans over the first twenty years of occupation stood at "a conservative figure of US$800 million." In 1987 alone, at least $80 million of this was directed to *Israeli* public expenditures. In addition, during the first twenty years of occupation some $1 billion was deducted from the wages of Palestinians working in Israel for employee benefits for which they are not eligible, since they are not residents of Israel. According to Benvenisti, significant amounts of this "deduction fund" have been used directly for Israeli public consumption and the remainder used to subsidize the civilian administration in the occupied territories.[31] There are also exorbitant fees imposed by the authorities for crossing the bridges to travel to Jordan, for transferring land, and for a large number of other transactions. Hisham Jaber has estimated that the travel tax collected for the year 1986 at the two bridges crossing the Jordan River was $31,893,834—to which must be added about $3,000,000 per year in permit fees paid by taxis and trucks that operate between bridges and the cities.[32]

Despite these various revenues derived from the occupied territories, the overall level of civilian government annual spending in the West Bank and Gaza Strip remained constant between 1984 and 1987 at $250-280 million —a sum which the Civilian Administration declared to be the "maximum" that could be utilized in the territories. Per capita public consumption in the territories was $185 in 1985, compared to $1,350 in Israel. It should further be noted that slightly under 40 percent of total public expenditures in the territories comes not from Israel, but from Jordan, other foreign governments, and UNRWA (the United Nations Relief and Works Agency for Palestine Refugees in the Near East).[33]

Economic conditions in the West Bank and Gaza have deteriorated still further since the onset of the *intifada*. Despite their support for such activities, the boycotts, strikes and other activities associated with the uprising do constitute a significant economic burden for Palestinians. The Israeli authorities have intensified their economic pressure on the population, in an apparent attempt to sap its will to resist. The administrative and tax hurdles facing local businesses have multiplied, in an effort to inhibit economic self-sufficiency and reestablish Israeli administrative authority.[34] Finally, Palestinian access to the Israeli and export markets has been further curtailed. Despite special regulations passed by the European Community in 1986 granting favored treatment to goods from the occupied territories, only 2 percent of the produce of 1989 was exported to the EC due to various bureaucratic obstacles erected by the Israeli authorities. As a result, 50 percent of the produce had to be sold to Israeli juice factories at reduced prices.[35] Bans on the export of West Bank agricultural products to Israel have been imposed. In addition, all factories in the West Bank and Gaza Strip that do business in Israel are now required to label their products in Arabic. This directive, issued jointly by the Industry Ministry and the Civil Administration, was said to be "aimed at cracking down on what the government regards as a worrisome increase in the flow of imports from the territories." The labeling "will make it easier for consumers to differentiate between Israeli and Palestinian products."[36]

At the same time, however, the uprising has reshaped some important economic dimensions of the Israeli-Palestinian relationship. According to the Bank of Israel, the *intifada* cost Israel $650 million in 1988 in export losses and "caused further incalculable losses by creating a climate of uncertainty that deterred investors and consumers—both foreign and Israeli—from putting money into the economy." This figure included $280 million in lost tourism. The *intifada* reduced the business sector's production by 1.5 percent. Exports fell by 4.2 percent, and Israeli exports to the occupied territories fell by about 40 percent. Israel's "trade surplus" with the West Bank and Gaza decreased by 76 percent to $42 million. Sporadic Palestinian strikes have caused a 25 percent decrease in the effective supply of workers. By one estimate, the damage caused by arson "apparently motivated by anti-Israel feeling" was estimated at over $180 million. According to Director of the Defense Ministry's budget department, Brig. Gen. Michael Navon, the immediate military cost of fighting the Palestinian uprising in the territories was expected to reach approximately $1.8 billion—more than $2 million per day—by the end of fiscal year 1990.[37]

Conclusion

Some Israelis continue to deny Palestinians the status of a people. They cling to the hope that control can be maintained indefinitely over a docile population which is content to till its remaining land, while purchasing ever-increasing quantities of television sets and washing machines. In reality, however, the uprising has called into question some of the basic assumptions underlying the occupation. The intensity and duration of the general uprising that began 9 December 1987 has been remarkable, spreading from refugee camps to remote villages and engulfing all segments of society, all classes and groups. It has undermined the administrative control that the authorities once enjoyed, requiring even greater recourse to violence and force. It has also affected the low cost—indeed, the profitability—of the occupation, which amid continuing unrest can no longer be taken for granted. Most important of all, the *intifada* has underscored the Palestinians' insistence upon their identity as a people. Barring mass expulsion of the population to neighboring states,[38] this continued assertion of Palestinian identity guarantees continuing challenges to Israeli occupation.

In many ways, it is still too soon to predict the ultimate effects of the uprising. It is unclear, for example, what effect economic factors may have on future political developments (although as long as US economic aid to Israel remains guaranteed, it cannot be assumed that it will be a determining factor). The impact of large-scale Soviet Jewish immigration to Israel—and their possible settlement in the occupied territories—is also uncertain.[39] What *is* clear is that even if the current unrest eventually subsides, new waves will follow, and with increasing frequency: over half of the Palestinian population is under the age of twenty-one, and the uprising has shown the young people to be far less compromising than their parents.

Among the Palestinians of the occupied territories, over twenty years of Israeli occupation have only intensified the will to exercise self-determination in their land. There are no changes or improvements that can make the occupation tolerable. Expropriation of land, the establishment of settlements, economic exploitation, and the repression of Palestinian society and institutions—all these attest that there can be no justice under occupation.

This is perhaps stating the obvious. What has been less obvious—at least until the current uprising—is that two decades of more or less open borders between Israel and occupied territories have *not* increased the chances of co-existence and peace between the two nations. The Palestinians have experienced only oppression and injustice under Israeli rule. The continuation of this rule can only result in increasing bitterness and hatred. If peace is to come, a new relationship has to be forged.

Notes

1. Article 35 of Military Proclamation 3, issued on 7 June 1967, states that the military courts and their officers "must apply the provisions of the Geneva Conventions of 13 August 1949 regarding the protection of civilians during war as to all which pertains to legal proceedings. If there should be any contradiction between the provisions of the order and the Geneva Conventions, the provisions of the Conventions should apply." Published in Volume One of the official publication of the Israeli Army's West Bank Command, *Proclamations, Orders and Appointments*, 11 August 1967, p. 12.

2. For a further discussion of the resident alien status of Palestinians under Israeli occupation, see Raja Shehadeh, *Occupier's Law: Israel and the West Bank*, 2nd edition (Washington, D.C.: Institute of Palestine Studies, 1989), pp. 113-115.

3. *Los Angeles Times*, 7 January 1988.

4. For example, then-Vice-Premier Yitzhak Shamir was quoted as saying that when it came to "land redemption," the police force "even when it investigates criminal acts, must consider the national interest." He was also reported as having said that it was never simple to buy land from Arabs, and that in many cases the process was accompanied by threats and murders. Shamir added: "sometimes tricks and schemes were needed and unconventional means used to purchase land." *Jerusalem Post*, 18 August 1985.

5. The Landau Commission was established after the Israeli Supreme Court ruled that the Shin Bet had framed 'Izzat Nafsu, an Israeli Druze officer, for espionage. Specifying that the "means of pressure should principally take the form of nonviolent psychological pressure," the Landau Report allowed that "when these do not attain their purpose, the exertion of a moderate measure of physical pressure is not to be avoided. The General Security Services should be guided in setting clear boundaries in this matter, in order to prevent the use of inordinate physical pressure arbitrarily administered by the interrogator." Thus, despite its conclusion that agents of the secret service had "routinely" used illegal methods of interrogation, the commission ruled that the agents singled out in the 'Izzat Nafsu case had been acting according to "established norms" and recommended that they not be punished. The same held true for the 1984 beating deaths of two Palestinian youths who had hijacked a bus in Gaza, since the guerrillas had forfeited the "moral right to demand [that] the state safeguard normally accepted civil rights." And even though the commission found that agents had "systematically" lied in the courts to convict suspects, it recommended that no charges be filed or other steps taken against security agents who had committed perjury in the past.

6. *Jerusalem Post*, 29 December 1987.

7. These claims about applying higher standards are not new. In 1969, Meir Shamgar, now president of the Israeli High Court of Justice, said: "I do not pretend that Israel has attained perfection and furthermore I have no tendency to find solace in comparison with other systems of law and government, because we do not content ourselves with the norms followed by others..." "The Observation of Law in the Administered Territories," in the *Israeli Yearbook of Human Rights* (1971), p. 277.

8. *New York Times*, 2 February 1988. This was confirmed by senior infantry and paratroop commander Shumuel Arab, who said: "There is no absolute military solution to the current unrest in the West Bank and Gaza Strip because the people of Israel will not allow it." Defense Minister Yitzhak Rabin also claimed that the violence could be ended within three days if ruthless measures were taken. *Jerusalem Post*, 1 April, 4 May 1988.

9. *Jerusalem Post*, 26 September 1989.

10. In one respect, however, some Israeli officials have de-emphasized security considerations: with regard to Jewish settlement in the occupied territories. Yitzhak Rabin said on 2 March 1988: "Between one-third and one-fifth of the troops now deployed to quell the unrest in the occupied territories are being used to protect traffic and roads leading to the West Bank settlements... For now, the settlements do not contribute to our

security—but they are our responsibility." Similarly, Israeli Army Chief of Staff Dan Shomron stated on May 10, 1988: "The presence of Jewish settlers in the West Bank creates continual tension there." Israeli right-wingers, however, generally reject this view. Ron Nahman, chairman of the local council of the Jewish settlement of Ariel, responded: "If the settlers are indeed a source of tension, then Israel's entire existence is a source of tension in the Middle East." *Jerusalem Post*, 11, 12 May 1988.

11. Meron Benvenisti, *West Bank Data Project 1987 Report* (Jerusalem: Jerusalem Post, 1987), p. 35.

12. *al-Haq* data bank and annual reports; *Middle East International*, 15 December 1989, p. 3.

13. According to *Middle East International* (3 November 1989), "The Defense Minister announced on 17 May that all workers from the Gaza Strip would henceforth require special permits to enter Israel. The new permits, which supplement rather than replace the identification papers that all Gaza residents over the age of 16 are already obliged to carry, consist of plastic cards with the worker's photo on the front and a magnetic strip on the back. Designed to be read by computers connected to the centralized information system maintained by the security services, they allow the army to monitor and thus maintain strict control over the movements of the workers into and out of the Gaza Strip."

14. *al-Haq* data bank and annual reports.

15. Pre-uprising examples took place on 18 September 1987 in Balata refugee camp near Nablus and on 21 September in the town of Halhul. The sworn statements given by the victims to the West Bank human rights organization *al-Haq* referred to clubbings by a rod with a nail driven into it, severe beatings that resulted in the breaking of the victim's limbs, and in one case urination in the mouth of a 22-year old by an Israeli soldier. The ages of these victims ranged from 12 to 24. Despite the fact that more than one soldier was involved in these activities and the victims were at one point taken to military headquarters, no investigation was undertaken by the army.

16. *New York Times*, 24 January 1988.

17. *The Nation*, 13 February 1988.

18. *The Casualties of Conflict: Medical Care and Human Rights in the West Bank and Gaza Strip*, Report of a Medical Fact-Finding Mission by Physicians for Human Rights, 30 March 1988. According to a January 1990 report by the Swedish branch of the Save the Children Fund, 159 children aged 16 or less were killed in the first two years of the uprising. An estimated 50,000-63,000 others required medical treatment for injuries from Israeli army gunfire, tear gas, and beatings. For excerpts from this report, see the *Journal of Palestine Studies* 19, 4 (Summer 1990): 136-149.

19. For further details, see *al-Haq* briefing paper of 26 October 1989 on the Bayt Sahur tax raids; *Punishing a Nation: Human Rights Violations During the Palestinian Uprising, December 1987-December 1988* (Ramallah: *al-Haq*, 1988); and *al-Haq*'s second annual report, *Nation Under Siege*, chapter 11.

20. *al-Haq* data bank and annual reports; *Middle East International*, 15 December 1989, p. 3.

21. Military Order 378 prohibits residents of the West Bank from carrying arms without permission from the military. In practice, only Israeli soldiers and settlers as well as some Palestinian collaborators are given such permission.

22. *al-Haq*, *Punishing a Nation*, p. 117.

23. *Jerusalem Post*, 11 May 1988.

24. *Jerusalem Post*, 2 May 1990.

25. *New York Times*, 9 February 1988.

26. Benvenisti, *West Bank Data Project 1987 Report*, pp. 10-11.

27. *al-Quds* (East Jerusalem), 26 September 1989.

28. Meron Benvenisti and Shlomo Khayat, *The West Bank and Gaza Atlas*, (Jerusalem: The Jerusalem Post, 1988), p. 42.

29. A case in point is the attempt of some West Bank entrepreneurs to establish a cement factory in the Hebron region. After a feasibility study (carried out at great expense) yielded very promising results, the project could not get a license on the explicit grounds that it would compete with the Israeli cement industry. Similarly, in 1987 a group of Palestinians imported a machine from Italy for the manufacture of folding boxes used by Palestinian agricultural producers. When they applied for registration of the design, an Israeli firm (which had hitherto enjoyed a monopoly on selling such boxes in the West Bank, and which had never bothered to register its product as the law requires) moved to stop them. When the Israeli firm belatedly attempted to register the design, it found that the Palestinians had already applied. Nevertheless, the Israeli firm immediately received a certificate of registration signed by the head of the Civil Administration himself, thus bypassing the normal channels. At the same time, the Israeli producers obtained an injunction against the Palestinian manufacturer through an Israeli court—which legally has no jurisdiction in this matter over the West Bank. But the aim of stopping the Palestinians was achieved.

30. Pressed to justify the Military Government's refusal to publish a budget, a government official told BBC radio (23 October 1989) that the refusal was due to security reasons!

31. Benvenisti, *West Bank Data Project 1987 Report*, p. 32.

32. See Hisham Jaber, "Financial Administration in the Israeli-occupied West Bank," a paper submitted to a conference organized by *al-Haq*, Ramallah, 22-25 January 1988. For a discussion of taxation under Israeli occupation see Marc Stephens, *Taxation in the Occupied West Bank, 1967-1989* (Ramallah: *al-Haq*, 1990).

33. Benvenisti, *West Bank Data Project 1987 Report*, p. 31.

34. Military Order 1262 of December 1988, for example, complicated the procedure for obtaining and renewing licenses for industrial projects as well as for imports and exports by requiring the applicant to get stamps from six different departments (including tax, police, and security) before the application can be considered. The same is true for registering companies or trademarks or applying for any transaction concerning these (including affecting any change in the company's shareholding or capital or any other matter that the law requires to be notified to the Registrars of Companies or Trademarks).

35. The authorities have, for example, searched up 20 percent of containers bound for export, causing serious damage to the fruit; see *al-Quds*, 26 September 1989. The situation improved significantly in 1990, in large part because of pressure on Israel by the European Community. *Middle East International*, 3 August 1990, p. 13.

36. *Jerusalem Post*, 7 November 1989.

37. *Jerusalem Post*, 11 April, 1, 12 June, 27 September 1989.

38. According to a survey by Israeli pollster Hanouch Smith, the number of Israelis supporting the mass expulsion of Palestinians rose from 38 percent to 52 percent in the latter part of 1989. Reported in *al-Sha'ab* (East Jerusalem), 11 November 1989.

39. It had been estimated that by the year 2012 there would be parity between Arabs and Jews in the entire area of mandatory Palestine. Although the immigration of Soviet Jews will undoubtedly affect this demographic balance, most analyses suggest it will only postpone the eventual date of demographic equality. It is also too early to predict the effect that this influx of new immigrants will have on the Israeli economy, on settlement in the territories, or on Israel's relations with countries which oppose the settlement of Soviet Jews in the Gaza Strip, West Bank, and East Jerusalem.

3

The Impact of the *Intifada* on Israeli Political Thinking

Mark Tessler

In thinking about the Israeli response to the Palestinian *intifada*, it is necessary to distinguish between what Israelis regard as short-term and long-term issues respectively. The former involve matters bearing on containment, on the suppression of the uprising so that Israelis, and others, can get back to their debates about the final status of the West Bank and Gaza. This is sometimes described as the restoration of "normalcy," although many in Israel would acknowledge that there is nothing normal about occupation. In any event, even Israelis opposed to their country's occupation of the West Bank and Gaza for the most part believe that order must be restored before there can be progress toward territorial compromise and an exchange of land for peace, and most are thus prepared to differentiate between their ideas about how Israel should deal with the *intifada* and their views about the future of the territories more generally. How should Israel seek to bring an end to the Palestinian uprising, and to what extent and under what conditions should the state use violent means to achieve this objective? These are central questions relating to the short-term issue of containment.

Long-term issues, by contrast, involve questions about the eventual disposition of the occupied territories, about the final status of the West Bank and Gaza. Should Israel relinquish these territories as part of a peace settlement? If so, what should be the extent of Israel's withdrawal, and to whom should control be given? These are familiar questions about which political opinion in Israel has long been deeply divided. They are also questions of great importance; indeed, many Israelis regard them as existential matters, with serious implications for the future of the Jewish state itself. But while it might be thought that there is nothing new to say about issues that have been the focus of such extensive and passionate debate, the *intifada* has in fact had a significant impact on Israeli thinking about the West Bank and Gaza. Moreover, this impact is discernible among advocates both of territorial compromise and of territorial maximalism.

Most Palestinians are not persuaded by this Israeli distinction between the short-term and the long-term. They see the two as inextricably linked, arguing that were the uprising to stop there would be little pressure on Israel to deal with final status issues and, accordingly, progress toward peace would be less likely rather than more likely. They suggest that although Israelis may claim to be addressing the short-term issue of containment, they are in reality advancing positions that bear directly on the long-term issue of occupation. Furthermore, this analysis continues, Israel can bring an end to the *intifada* any time it wishes, easily and without violence: it need only indicate that it is prepared to accept a peace formula involving territorial compromise. In sum, say the Palestinians, there is only one question: whether there will be continued occupation or whether, alternatively, there will be liberation and self-determination. This is both the short-term and the long-term issue.

To a degree, this analysis put forward by Palestinians and some others may be accurate so far as the Israeli political right is concerned. Those committed to Israel's permanent retention of the West Bank and Gaza would probably agree that control of the territories is the only meaningful issue, and their desire to see an end to the *intifada* undoubtedly reflects a wish to continue deepening Israel's demographic presence in the territories and, thereby, to make progress toward eventual annexation of the West Bank and Gaza. Yet even these Israelis participate in debates about containing the *intifada* in which final status issues are at best only background and contextual considerations. Furthermore, as noted, Israelis committed to solving the Israeli-Palestinian conflict, most of whom recognize that this requires an end to occupation, quite routinely distinguish between the short-term and the long-term, between conditions that are necessary for peace talks on the one hand and the desired outcome of such talks on the other. More specifically, Israelis who acknowledge Palestinian political rights, and who claim to seek mutual recognition between their country and the Palestinians, in most cases insist that efforts to negotiate a settlement cannot go forward so long as the *intifada* continues.

There are thus two distinct sets of debates taking place in Israel. They are related, of course, but they are nonetheless analytically distinguishable. Indeed, it is not unusual for each to be pursued with only limited reference to the other.[1]

The Issue of Containment

As soon as they recognized the coordinated and sustained character of the Palestinian uprising that began in December 1987, Israeli leaders declared their intention to restore order and addressed themselves directly to the containment of the *intifada*. Primary responsibility for achieving this objective fell to Yitzhak Rabin, the minister of defense in the national unity government that had been established after the inconclusive parliamentary elections of 1984. The centrist Labor Party and the right-wing Likud Union were the principal factions in this coalition government, and under a rotation agreement between the two parties the prime minister in December 1987 was Yitzhak Shamir of Likud. Rabin, by contrast, was from Labor. As a former military commander who was unaffiliated with any of Labor Zionism's internal ideological camps, he had long been regarded as a moderate and a pragmatist. Further, in prior service as Israeli ambassador to the United States and then as his country's prime minister (1974-77) he had earned a reputation as a centrist and an advocate of territorial compromise. For example, Rabin maintained—and still maintains—that Israeli acceptance of United Nations Security Council Resolutions 242 and 338 commits his country to withdrawal from most of the West Bank and Gaza. This is in clear opposition to the position of Shamir and Likud, who assert that Resolution 242 does not apply on all fronts and that its requirements have already been satisfied by Israel's withdrawal from the Sinai Peninsula.[2]

Yet Rabin, who had been minister of defense since 1984, had already established himself as a tough-minded guarantor of order in the occupied territories. Even as he continued to profess commitment to an exchange of land for peace (the official position of the Labor Party), he presided over a military administration of the West Bank and Gaza that regularly took actions designed to suppress expressions of Palestinian nationalism. Palestinian universities were frequently closed, for example, on the grounds that instead of pursuing their education students were engaging in political activities and organizing opposition to the occupation. Other Israeli actions, which by the summer of 1985 were routinely described as an "iron fist" policy, included deportations, press censorship, and such forms of collective punishment as curfews and the demolition of homes. Rabin saw no contradiction between his support for territorial compromise and his opposition to political agitation in the territories, however. The one is a matter for meticulous negotiation between Israeli representatives and a Jordanian-Palestinian bargaining team, in which discussion and decision-making should be marked by careful deliberation and thorough consideration of vital national interests. The other, by contrast, is emotional and distracting, creating pressures that work against the hard-headed calculations that all parties must undertake if a durable peace is to be achieved.

Guided by this logic, Rabin instructed the Israel Defense Forces (IDF) to take vigorous action to bring the *intifada* to an end. If the uprising continued, he declared, Palestinian violence would be met by force on the part of Israel, including whatever military measures were necessary to assure that order was maintained. Thus, in addition to detaining and deporting suspected activists, Israel undertook to suppress Palestinian protests, and when necessary it dispersed demonstrators by firing live ammunition. Rabin and most other Israeli leaders justified these actions by saying that the Palestinians had left them no alternative. In defending his policy, Rabin also predicted that Israel's use of force would bring an end to the uprising within a matter of weeks, perhaps even sooner.[3] Yet the *intifada* continued and, if anything, grew more intense, even as the number of Palestinian demonstrators shot by Israeli soldiers increased.[4]

In late December, the UN Security Council (with the US abstaining) passed a resolution deploring Israeli actions and calling for an end to the use of live ammunition against unarmed Palestinian civilians. The following month Rabin announced a new policy under which the use of live ammunition would be limited to situations where the lives of Israeli soldiers were at risk. This policy—which the defense minister publicly characterized as "force, might and beatings"—was less lethal than the one it replaced, but brutal nonetheless.[5] Israeli troops used clubs to subdue protesters, often beating demonstrators indiscriminately, even when they were attempting to flee. Moreover, Israeli soldiers were encouraged to break the bones of young Palestinians, to break either their legs so they would be unable to run or their hands to prevent them from throwing stones. Hundreds of Palestinians were subsequently injured, many insisting that they had been rounded up and beaten not while attending protest rallies or engaging in any other illegal activity but solely for the purpose of intimidation. In the two months following the introduction of Rabin's new policy, about a dozen Palestinians died from beatings administered by Israeli soldiers. CS tear-gas was also widely used by the IDF. When canisters were utilized in closed alleyways or tossed into homes, exposure sometimes resulted in death.[6] The use of live ammunition to put down demonstrations continued as well. This occurred with less frequency than in the past, but roughly 25 young Palestinians were nonetheless shot while participating in demonstrations during February and March 1988, and almost twice that number were shot by Israeli soldiers while inside their homes or walking in the street. Taking together these various categories of *intifada*-related deaths, the number of Palestinians killed by Israelis since the beginning of the uprising had reached 160 by the end of March 1988. By August, according to Palestinian sources, the total number of deaths had climbed to 323.[7]

In the fall of 1988, as the number of Palestinian deaths continued to rise, Israelis troops began to use plastic bullets. Israeli military spokesmen claimed that these bullets (which have an aluminum core) are not lethal when fired at seventy meters or more. Further, their use was in principle restricted to officers, who were instructed to use them only for self-defense or against the ring-leaders of demonstrations involving violence. Claims about the non-lethal character of these bullets were disputed, however, in Israel as well as among Palestinians, and there were also charges that regulations governing their use were often ignored.[8] Moreover, these regulations were officially relaxed early in 1989, use of bullets now being authorized against fleeing demonstrators and against Palestinians building barricades or burning tires who did not heed a warning. In addition, NCOs were now permitted to fire plastic bullets. Thus, the number of Palestinians shot by the Israeli military did not diminish during the course of 1989. By June of that year, as the intifada entered its nineteenth month, the Palestinian death count stood at 574.[9] During this period, the uprising also resulted in seventeen Israeli deaths.

This violence was in addition to the severe administrative measures which Israel employed in its effort to contain the *intifada*. Universities were closed by Israeli authorities; many primary and secondary schools were also shut for prolonged periods. Hundred of homes were demolished, usually because it was believed that a young man who lived there had thrown stones at Israeli soldiers. Entire communities were placed under curfew—sometimes for a week or more at a time—preventing people from leaving their homes at any time, even to obtain food. The deportation of suspected activists was another administrative measure designed to suppress the uprising. Despite a December 1988 UN resolution condemning these deportations (adopted unanimously), about thirty-five Palestinians were deported during the first year of the uprising. Other Israeli actions included the censorship of Arabic-language newspapers published in East Jerusalem, closure of a number of Palestinian charitable societies, and the imposition of restrictions on the transfer of currency into the occupied territories. Finally, thousands of Palestinians have been arrested and detained, some for prolonged periods and the overwhelming majority without trial. In August 1988, Rabin announced that 18,000 Palestinians had been detained since the beginning of the *intifada* and that 2,600 were being held in administrative detention at that time. Under military regulations in force in the occupied territories, an individual suspected of illegal activities (such as membership in an organization supporting the uprising) can be held without trial for a period up to six months, and administrative detention is also renewable without trial at the end of this period. Six months later, in February 1989, Rabin reported that the total number of detainees had grown to 22,000 and that 6,200 of these Palestinians were now in detention. Palestinian sources put the figures even higher.[10]

For the most part, these actions have been defended vigorously by Israeli officials. Moreover, this defense has been mounted not only by those affiliated with Likud but by many Labor Party leaders, who see no contradiction between their harsh posture toward the *intifada* and their declared moderation on the question of eventual territorial compromise. Although they deny some of the charges levied against their country (especially those alleging that regulations have not been enforced and that military authorities take no action when regulations are violated), both civilian and military officials readily acknowledge that hundreds of Palestinians have been killed and, more generally, that Israel has responded to the violence of the *intifada* with violence of its own. What they add is that Israel's actions are justified; they are a legitimate response to an extreme and threatening provocation. As expressed by Zvi Poleg, IDF Commander in Gaza Strip, "In a confrontation with a 12-year old boy with a stone and a 20 year old soldier with a rifle, sympathy naturally goes to the boy. But it is not justified, because a stone thrown by a boy of 12 can kill." Further, Poleg continued, "The local people ask me why the soldiers hit. I ask them the opposite question: what is your purpose when you throw stones or metal bars or petrol bombs at me? They're not embarrassed to say 'in order to kill you.' They're not embarrassed to say that."[11] Israeli spokesmen also point out that those who are unhappy with Israel's response to the *intifada* should remember that Palestinians can easily remove themselves from harm's way. As the Chief of General Staff, Dan Shomron, told the Knesset Foreign Affairs and Defense Committee, "[Only] Arabs who deliberately choose to go out and demonstrate are getting injured." The violence will stop when, eventually, these Palestinians "realize that it is not in their interest to get involved in riots."[12]

Many Israelis also defend the assertive as well as the responsive character of efforts to contain the uprising. In this connection, Israeli forces have not only sought to disperse demonstrations and apprehend protest organizers, they have also attempted to establish the IDF's authoritative presence in all parts of the occupied territories. Indeed, it is part of Israel's test of wills with the Palestinians that the IDF seeks to prevent or suppress expressions of protest even when they take place in remote areas or do not inconvenience Israeli Jews. For example, military patrols are on the look out for barricades of stones or burning tires even when these are across urban alleyways utilized only by Palestinians or in the streets of out-of-the-way villages. In these cases, as elsewhere, Israeli soldiers usually confiscate the identify cards of anyone in the vicinity, even if it is obvious they are not responsible for the offending action, and then hold these cards until their owners have removed the barricade. Similar methods are used to force Palestinians to remove political graffiti and Palestinian flags. Although these expressions of nationalism are not violent, they are regarded as part of an effort to mobilize support for the *intifada*. They are thus intolerable from the Israeli point of view. As Shomron told the Knesset Foreign Affairs and Defense Committee when asked about the advisability of withdrawing the IDF from major Arab centers, "If the soldiers leave, the rioters will take over... We cannot exercise remote control. With the army gone, terror would move outward toward Israel."[13]

Some Israelis believe that the way to end the *intifada* is to seek a political accommodation with the Palestinians. In this, their analysis approaches that of the Palestinians, who insist that the uprising will continue until Israel agrees to negotiate a definitive end to its occupation of the West Bank and Gaza. Shomron himself said as much in a series of highly visible newspaper and television interviews in January 1989, declaring that the *intifada* is a genuine popular resistance movement and explicitly comparing it to the Algerian revolution and other anti-colonial struggles in the Third World.[14] Similar sentiments were expressed by Gad Ya'acobi, a Labor Party minister in the national unity government. According to Ya'acobi, negotiation with the Palestinians is the only way to end the uprising. Indeed, he added, "If Labor were in power now, we would be in the middle of peace negotiations and the disturbances in the territories would not have taken place."[15] This being the case, the proper response to the uprising must be political rather than military. Other civilian and military leaders have made this point, too. Rabin himself declared early in 1988 that "I've learned something over the past two and one-half months. You can't rule by force over one-and-a million Palestinians." A week later he stated that "You cannot saddle the IDF with a mission that is outside its proper function. The unrest in the areas reflects a problem that can only have a political solution." Speaking early in 1989 about Palestinian grievances and the need for territorial compromise, Rabin suggested that the riots in the West Bank and Gaza "express a sense of frustration that no one in the Arab world, in the international community or in Israel had created any expectation of a political settlement."[16]

But this is not to say that Rabin, Shomron and others are willing to see the *intifada* continue until a political accommodation is reached. Obviously they are not. If territorial compromise is the key to solving the problem of the West Bank and Gaza, the key to negotiations aimed at achieving this goal is, in their view, the restoration of order—by military means if necessary. They may agree with the former member of the Israeli military establishment who wrote that "The Palestinians do not need to throw any more stones to convince us. They have made their point and sensible people in Israel and the rest of the world have got the message."[17] Nevertheless, as long as there are disturbances in the occupied territories, these Israeli leaders will advocate the use of force against the Palestinians; and the fact that they accept the need for a political solution does not lead them to embrace the view that progress toward this must be made *before* the uprising can end.

The uprising is thus seen as an obstacle to peace in Israel, even by most who favor territorial concessions and claim to be ready to recognize Palestinian rights. It is worth noting in this context that some hard-line Likud politicians, who are unwilling to relinquish any part of the West Bank and Gaza, also include in their denunciations of the *intifada* the complaint that it hinders peace talks. Likud's Moshe Arens, for example, stated that while Israel is willing to negotiate a "regional peace" with its neighbors, the time is not right in large part because "riots, stones... [and] petrol bombs are not appropriate musical accompaniment for negotiations in which the most vital subjects are on the agenda."[18] This sentiment is almost exactly that expressed by Rabin, even though, in the Israeli context, the two men have very different conceptions of negotiation and peace.

Such thinking persisted as the *intifada* entered its third year, there being no indication that Israel's approach to the short-term issue of containment was about to change. The government of Shamir and Rabin remained determined to crush the Palestinian uprising. "The nation can bear the burden no matter how long the revolt goes on," Rabin declared in December 1989. Further, he specified that "we will continue with all the measures that we used for the first years, including the confrontations, the hitting, the arresting, the introduction of the plastic bullet, the rubber bullet and the curfews on a large scale."[19] At the time Rabin made this statement, at least 615 Palestinian had been killed by Israelis since the beginning of the *intifada*. Moreover, about twenty percent of these deaths had occurred within the last four months, indicating that the defense minister was being true to his word about continuing to use violence against Palestinian demonstrators. Injuries, as opposed to deaths, also remained high. IDF figures reported that 15,000 to 20,000 Palestinians had been wounded in incidents related to the uprising, and arrests and imprisonments associated with the *intifada* totaled about 50,000 by the end of the uprising's second year. Of the latter figure, roughly 13,000 Palestinian remained in detention in December 1989.[20] In concluding his assessment, Rabin acknowledged that the IDF had thus far failed to suppress the *intifada* but asserted that his government's policies would eventually succeed. "We have reached a war of attrition," he stated, "but I think they feel more attrition than we do."[21]

Ends Versus Means

There is broad agreement in Israel on the desirability of ending the *intifada* as soon as possible. From the Israeli point of view, it is an extremely unpleasant business, in which only a few fanatics of the far right take any pleasure. It is also extremely costly, both in economic and in political terms. With respect to the former, it is estimated that the uprising costs Israel roughly $900 million dollars a year, divided between increased military expenses ($225 million) on the one hand and lost revenue from tourism ($400 million) and reduced exports to the West Bank and Gaza ($275 million) on the other.[22] With respect to the latter, it has brought world-wide condemnation, deepening the Jewish state's diplomatic isolation and even introducing new strains into its important relationship with the United States. Thus, regardless of their views on the long-term issue of territorial compromise, most Israelis support the government's declared objective of suppressing the Palestinian uprising. Even among those few who would be willing to enter into negotiations before order is restored, most would want the IDF to make an effort to suppress any continuing agitation designed to put pressure on would-be peace-makers. Only a tiny handful would favor negotiations while allowing Palestinian activists in the territories to organize and protest without interference.

This broad consensus on the goal of bringing the *intifada* to an end does not mean, however, that there has been agreement about the means it is appropriate to utilize in pursuit of this objective. On the contrary, there has been intense debate about the means by which the IDF has sought to suppress the uprising, and there are strongly-held differences of opinion about the extent and kind of violence that should be used against the Palestinians. There have been consistent calls from some right-wing politicians for the use of greater force in the suppression of the *intifada*. One of the most vocal of these has been Ariel Sharon of Likud, an established contender for the leadership of his party. Sharon frequently denounced Rabin for timidity and misplaced moderation. While it may seem to Israel's critics that the IDF has been authorized to employ too much, not too little, brutality and violence against the Palestinians, Sharon frequently declared that if he were defense minister the Palestinians would know that Israel is serious and the *intifada* would be brought to a swift conclusion.[23]

Right-wing criticism of Rabin's policies intensified as the 1988 elections approached. The defense minister frequently came under attack at cabinet meetings, such as the time in September 1988 that Shamir demanded sterner measures and waved a letter from 170 reserve soldiers asking the government to take a stiffer line against Palestinian activists in the territories. Many officials in Likud and parties further to the right also used public speeches and statements to the media to disseminate as widely as possible their contention that the *intifada* was continuing because the defense minister and the IDF were unwilling to take the measures that were needed. Indeed, an important theme in Likud's election campaign against Labor was that Rabin should have been dismissed as defense minister months ago for failing to put down the Palestinian uprising. When Chief of General Staff Shomron noted that IDF operations must remain scrupulously within the law, Sharon charged that this was precisely the problem: "The law should have been changed if it does not empower the IDF to take sufficiently effective measures." He added that he had personally prepared and given to the Justice Ministry "a comprehensive set of proposals for dealing with rioters and terrorists."[24] Similar statements were made by officials of parties to the right of Likud. For example, Geula Cohen, a leader of the right-wing Tehiya [Renaissance] Party, complained that Israel should have deported "not just dozens," but hundreds of Palestinian activists, and that this should have been done years ago.[25]

Such pronouncements were not restricted to the election campaign. Nor should they be understood as rhetorical excesses prompted by the election. Calls for using greater force to suppress the *intifada* continued to be issued by right-wing politicians and others throughout 1989. For example, Rafael Eitan of the small Tsomet Party demanded the expanded use of collective punishment, telling the Knesset Foreign Affairs and Defense Committee in January 1989 that this would take care of the Palestinian uprising. A few weeks later, a prominent intellectual associated with the settler movement echoed the calls for the deportation of more Palestinians. Shubert Spero, a professor of Jewish thought at Bar Ilan University, wrote that "henceforth anyone found guilty of throwing stones or gasoline bottles should be deported, regardless of his age or the success of his efforts, [and] minors should be accompanied by their parents."[26]

Rabin and his supporters responded to these demands and criticism, of course. For example, Shevah Weiss of the Labor Party replied to Eitan's comments about collective punishment by asserting that the increased use of collective punishment would be counter-productive and "merely prompt more [Palestinian] civilians to join the ranks of the *intifada*." Rabin himself has lashed out at his critics, such as the time during the 1988 election campaign that he was asked by reporters to comment on the assertion by Likud's Yitzhak Moda'i that a homogeneous right wing coalition would be able to suppress the uprising within one week. Rabin sarcastically answered that at least Likud leaders had become a little less unrealistic. They have "made progress from when they were going to solve the terrorist problem in Lebanon in 48 hours," he quipped, adding that "six years later the problem [of Lebanon] is still with us."[27] The Labor Party also worked to prevent the government from adopting policies which would make clashes in the occupied territories even more violent. For example, in the fall of 1988, with the Knesset election campaign in high gear and the atmosphere highly charged, Labor headed off an effort by Prime Minister Shamir to have the cabinet discuss the possibility of authorizing soldiers, and possibly even settlers, to fire on Palestinian stone-throwers, thereby extending the "open-fire" policy that was already in effect against those who throw petrol-bombs. Labor minister Moshe Shahal stated in a cabinet meeting that this policy would be against the law and would "in effect constitute a license to kill," bringing "something resembling the Phalangist anarchy of Lebanon." Shamir eventually backed away from the idea.[28]

The election of 1988 was a virtual standoff. Likud won 40 seats in the Knesset and Labor won 39. Both parties actually lost ground relative to their performance in the election of 1984, reflecting an increase in the number of voters who supported parties to the left of Labor and the right of Likud respectively. The broad division of opinion that had already been visible for a number of years thus remained as characteristic of Israeli political life as it had before the *intifada*. Indeed, if anything, this division had increased, indicating that the distribution of political attitudes had become even more polarized. After a period of prolonged and intense bargaining following the inconclusive election, another national unity government was formed, this time with Likud as the senior partner. Shamir retained the premiership, without the requirement of rotation that had forced him to share the position with Shimon Peres of Labor after 1984. Peres (who moved to the finance ministry) was replaced as foreign minister by Moshe Arens, a Likud hard-liner and close political ally of Shamir. Rabin retained the position of defense minister. Although they disagreed on the long-term issue of territorial compromise, Shamir recognized that Rabin had aggressively sought to suppress the Palestinian uprising and, in this area, policy differences between the two men were not as large as the rhetoric of the election campaign sometimes made them appear. In addition, Shamir found it politically advantageous to have criticism by those who want to see greater IDF restraint in the territories focused on a politician from Labor rather than Likud.

As the political divisions reflected in the 1988 election results suggested, there are some Israelis who believe the government has been insufficiently aggressive in seeking to suppress the uprising in the West Bank and Gaza, and others who are deeply disturbed by some of the methods employed by the IDF. While the number who believe that less force should be used against the Palestinians is much smaller than the number who support current policies or favor greater use of force, the number calling for restraint is not insignificant and appears to have grown since the beginning of the *intifada*. Moreover, criticism often comes from intellectuals, journalists and well-known public figures, giving their voice an influence disproportionate to their numbers. For example, Abba Eban, an elder statesman who for many years served as Israel's foreign minister, was a bitter and visible critic of Rabin's policies for dealing with the *intifada*. Although he and the defense minister are both members of the Labor Party, Eban strongly denounced what he called the "ugly ideas" that guide Israel's actions and rhetoric in the West Bank and Gaza.[29]

An opportunity to observe the internal Israeli debate about methods of dealing with the *intifada* was provided by the expressions of concern that accompanied the introduction of Rabin's policy of "force, might and beatings" in January 1988, and by the outcry that met some of the abuses associated with this policy. In February 1988, for example, several IDF reservists described an incident in Halhul in which a group of men were bound and made to sit on the road while soldiers beat them with rifles and truncheons. When they were severely bruised and could no longer walk, the reservists asserted, "fifteen of the bound youngsters were loaded onto a lorry and driven to a wadi filled with refuse and dumped into the valley... [and] it was only after argument and discussion among the soldiers that the prisoners' hands were unbound." The letter containing this testimony was given to two MKs, Chaike Grossman of Mapam and Ran Cohen of the Citizens Rights Movement, who praised the reservists for speaking up and released their letter to the press. A few days later another leader of the leftist Mapam Party, Yair Tsaban, told a Peace Now rally that "orders to beat in order to break bones are unlawful and should be refused," adding that his quarrel was not with the soldiers serving in the territories but "with Rabin and the government for having put the IDF in an impossible position." Tsaban's comments brought a sharp rebuttal from Geula Cohen of Tehiya, who accused him of inciting soldiers to disobey orders and promised to see that he was politically neutralized.[30] That same month, a CBS News film (a portion of which was aired on Israeli television) showed four soldiers beating two Palestinians whose hands were tied behind their backs. This, like the incident in Halhul and others, produced an outcry among some intellectuals and leftist politicians. Rabin expressed concern over some of the IDF actions reported in the press but stated that these were isolated incidents. "There are no beatings for beatings' sake," he insisted, asserting that beatings were employed only to break up demonstrations, not for purposes of intimidation or harassment. Yet many found these statements unconvincing. For example, MK Yosef Sarid of the Citizens Rights Movement called Rabin a liar, stating that "grave incidents have taken place, involving extreme cruelty and violence against persons and property. The violence was not the result of soldiers defending themselves, but was applied as a punishment." Concern about the accuracy of Rabin's denials was also expressed by Attorney General Yosef Harish, who said that the number of reports of beatings cast doubt on Rabin's claim they were isolated incidents. Harish wrote a letter to the defense minister in which he demanded that it be made clear to soldiers that it is illegal to beat demonstrators after they have been arrested, and that "it is forbidden to use force to punish or humiliate."[31]

Criticism of Rabin's policies was also articulated by some within the military. Some soldiers said they were deeply disturbed by the orders they were expected to carry out. One example is the previously mentioned reservists' testimony about the IDF's behavior in Halhul in February 1988. Another is the complaint by a group of reservists, delivered to Rabin and passed on to leftist politicians in October 1988, about the brutal behavior of an IDF tank unit in the village of Qalqiliya. The medic in the group said he had been threatened at gun point not to reveal that beatings of Palestinians by the unit's officers and soldiers were routine, that he had been prevented from giving aid to Palestinians who were badly beaten, and that some detainees were kept in "dehydration facilities."[32] In response, Rabin acknowledged that while some soldiers implemented the government's policies with considerable enthusiasm, perhaps accounting for some of the unintended abuses, others were indeed distressed by the actions they had witnessed or in which they had taken part. In another denunciation by soldiers that received wide public attention, Shamir was told by troops serving in Nablus in January 1989 that they were very disturbed by the IDF's behavior. Accompanied by reporters, which military officials had tried in vain to convince the prime minister not to invite along, Shamir was inspecting IDF operations in the northern West Bank city and stopped to talk to a group of soldiers. To his consternation, he was told in extremely strong terms that young Israelis were not raised on universal values and respect for human rights only to be sent to the occupied territories to commit violence unrestrained by the rule of law. The political and military establishments "have no idea what really goes on in the territories," one soldier told the prime minister, while another stated, with reporters present, that he had to "beat innocent people" every day. As one of the reservists serving in Nablus later wrote, "the sunny morning Mr. Shamir visited our unit in Nablus, I would have liked to scream and cry about how our army is being sullied, corroded and undermined by the impossible task the government has given it."[33]

Expressions of concern were also heard from senior officers, such as General Amram Mitzna, the commanding officer of Central Command. In February 1988, in the wake of incidents following the introduction of Rabin's policy of force, might and beatings, Mitzna spoke out forcefully against abuses. In one of the worst incidents, soldiers buried four Palestinians alive in Salim village near Nablus. Further, the action was defended by some extremists. As a resident in the West Bank settlement of Elon Moreh, near Nablus, stated, "If only we could bury all the Arabs... In our country, they kill us, throw stones at us... they do what they feel like. So we should do what we feel like. They are unnecessary here." But Mitzna and other officers stated that it was unthinkable to defend such actions. Speaking of the incident, he declared that "even in my worst dreams, I couldn't imagine it," promising that officers would do everything possible to prevent such incidents from recurring in the future.[34] Yet, reflecting the breadth and the intensity of the debate over IDF actions, Mitzna himself was strongly criticized by Israelis who believe he has not done enough to oppose harsh containment policies. Indeed, an article published in June 1989 charged that he had "surrendered to the longings of Jewish settlers to prove who is boss [in the occupied territories]," and deplored the fact that he could be praised for fairness by a prominent settler leader.[35] Shortly thereafter, Mitzna left his position.

Debates about the use of beatings, allegedly for purposes of intimidation and punishment, were replayed throughout 1988 and 1989 in relation to other IDF policies designed to contain the *intifada*. For example, MK Dedi Zucker of the Citizens Rights Movement criticized the use of tear-gas in closed spaces and commissioned a study of the effects of this policy. In the study, released in June 1988, a team of Israeli doctors and toxicologists confirmed charges that the use of tear-gas in closed spaces was extremely dangerous and could even be fatal, especially to babies, children, the elderly and persons with heart and respiratory diseases.[36] In the wake of this study, the IDF General Staff issued orders limiting the use of tear-gas to open areas. There were also condemnations of the IDF's use of plastic bullets against Palestinians, a policy that was instituted in the fall of 1988. Rabin and some military leaders stated that they were not concerned about the number of persons wounded by the bullets, "as long as they were wounded as a result of being involved actively [in the *intifada*], by instigating, organizing, and taking part in violent activities." Indeed, the defense minister went on to state, injuries to the rioters "is precisely our aim." But some politicians in Labor and parties further to the left strongly denounced the policy. In addition, some, including Yosef Sarid of CRM, Aharon Nachmias of Labor and Benyamin Ben-Eliezer of Yahad, charged that plastic bullets were being employed for purposes of harassment as well as for the control of demonstrations, thereby turning non-involved Palestinians into enemies. Another protest came from the Association for Civil Rights in Israel, which called on the attorney-general to issue specific guidelines for the use of plastic bullets. According to ACRI chair, Judge Eli Natan, "There is no doubt that opening fire for purposes of deterrence is an illegal act."[37] In response, the Attorney General stated that plastic bullets were not intended for use as a deterrent and that he had already reviewed and approved guidelines to this effect. To this Natan offered a comparison with the beatings policy introduced nine months earlier: regardless of the initial intent, he contended, both beatings and plastic bullets were in fact widely used not only for riot control but for punishment and deterrence as well.

Most complaints and criticism about the excessive use of force have focused on human rights violations and a disregard for the rule of law, which are seen as undermining Israeli democracy and the country's commitment to universal humanistic values. Although the IDF's actions in the West Bank and Gaza are obviously injurious to Palestinians, they are seen as also doing serious damage to Israel. This theme runs through the statements and denunciations that have been made by leftist political leaders and others since the beginning of the *intifada*. In making this argument, those who advocate greater restraint assert that the end does not justify the means. They state that the goal of order in the territories, however desirable and necessary, fails to provide a justification for many of the actions that have been taken in pursuit of this objective. Indeed, although they rarely express their views in precisely this manner, these critics of the government move toward a position that rejects a distinction between means and ends. Preserving (or restoring) the moral integrity and civilized character of the State of Israel is the only true goal, and if this is lost in the pursuit of some more instrumental objective, such as the restoration of order in the West Bank and Gaza, then it is meaningless even to ask whether the end justifies the means. Seen from this perspective, the end and the means are one and the same. The most important objective of all is to be a country that refuses to sanction the use of inappropriate means: in other words, to be a society that scrupulously respects human rights, refuses to depart from the rule of law, and imposes on itself a civilized code of conduct, no matter what might be the provocation to which it is exposed.

A striking indication of this concern, expressed in terms that carry special weight in Israel, was a discussion in May 1989 of the differences and similarities between the Nazi persecution and annihilation of Jews during World War II and the repressive measures being carried out by Israel in the occupied territories. The discussion took place at a Holocaust Memorial Day program organized by the Center for Holocaust Studies of Ben Gurion University.[38] Many speakers, and the majority in the audience, found the comparison not only unconvincing but offensive as well. "There is no room for spurious and idiotic comparisons between Auschwitz and the suppression of the *intifada*," declared one scholar, even though she herself was actively involved in opposition to Israel's occupation of the West Bank and Gaza. On the other hand, referring to the "dehumanization of the enemy" and to the different value systems that govern IDF behavior in Israel and the occupied territories, another speaker told a silent audience that "the *intifada* helps us to understand the human infrastructure that made Nazism possible." And still another speaker warned that the occupation of the territories could eventually go so far as an Israeli Auschwitz.

That such a discussion could take place is highly significant. Breaking a taboo, it was tolerated by the audience and reported in the press, being called "an amazing evening" by veteran journalist Tom Segev.[39] In his account of the program, Segev offered his own view, that the attempt to draw an analogy between the Holocaust and Israel's suppression of the *intifada* is "unintelligent and... infuriating, and for these reasons ineffective." Yet, Segev continued, "The attitude of Israeli society toward the repression in the territories, and the repression itself, are terrible and horrid... [so] perhaps I am mistaken." That Segev and others could entertain such thoughts, even though it is hard to disagree with their conclusion that Nazi behavior and IDF action in the West Bank and Gaza are in fact radically different, shows just how deeply disturbing and morally offensive some Israelis consider their government's policies to be.

The sorts of divisions and debates outlined above are fully reflected in national public opinion polls. One survey conducted in April 1989 indicated that a clear majority favored an increase in the use of force to contain the *intifada*. In response to the question, "Are you in favor of the use of greater military force to suppress the uprising the territories," 54.6 percent replied in the affirmative, 36.6 percent were opposed, and 8.8 percent had no opinion.[40] While this poll supported the conclusion that most Israelis take a hard-line position on the short-term issue of containment, it is also significant that greater use of force is opposed by over one-third of those interviewed. In particular (and although the poll is subject to competing interpretations on this point) it appears that most who do not favor increased force do not support the current policy either. Instead, they believe that greater restraint is needed. This interpretation is suggested by responses to a related question, which asked about the effectiveness of military action in dealing with the uprising. In response to the question, "Do you think it is possible or impossible to suppress the uprising in the territories by military force," only 53 percent thought it possible, whereas 38.1 percent said it is impossible, and 8.9 percent had no opinion. This suggests that there is considerable support for a political rather than a military response to the *intifada*. Add to this the fact that public opinion in Israel is known to be volatile and, as elsewhere, swayed by events, and one is left with the conclusion that both the political right and the political left are articulating views that strike a responsive chord among substantial segments of the population.

Thinking About the Occupied Territories

In addition to arguing about how their country should attempt to contain the *intifada*, Israelis are debating the future of the territories themselves. This is the long-term issue and, although thinking about it has clearly been influenced by the Palestinian uprising that began in December 1987, the considerations involved were well-known and much-discussed long before the current disturbances in the occupied territories. Since Israel took control of the West Bank and Gaza in 1967, and especially since Likud came to power in 1977, there have been heated exchanges between advocates of territorial compromise and territorial maximalism. The former, who for the most part vote for Labor or parties further to the left, assert that withdrawal from the West Bank and Gaza, or at least from most of these territories, is a fair price to pay for peace with the Arab world. Thus, although these territories should be retained until the Arab world is ready to exchange land for peace and proper guarantees for Israeli security, their status and character should not be altered. The occupied territories should be held in escrow, as it were, belonging to the Arabs but controlled by Israel until suitable peace arrangements have been agreed to and implemented.

Advocates of territorial maximalism, on the other hand, who for the most part vote for Likud and parties further to the right, reject the proposition that peace requires territorial concessions. They assert that once the Arabs are convinced that there is no possibility of Israeli withdrawal, they will resign themselves to the territorial status quo and eventually conclude that peace is in their interest, even if it is not based on a return to the pre-1967 borders. Further, most advocates of territorial maximalism assert, the West Bank and Gaza should be retained by Israel even if the Arabs do not eventually sue for peace. If it comes to a choice, in other words, land is more important than peace; the exercise of Jewish sovereignty over as much of the historic Land of Israel as possible is more important to these Israelis than is a resolution of the Arab-Israeli conflict and the establishment of peaceful relations between the Jewish state and its Arab neighbors. Some supporters of Likud and parties further to the right believe that retention of the territories is a religious obligation. Indeed, some among them believe that the messianic era has arrived and that Israel's territorial gains in 1967, like the birth of the modern Zionist movement and the creation of Israel in 1948, reflects the unfolding of God's plan for the Jews and mankind, an important part of which is the return of the Jewish nation to the Holy Land. Others take a more secular approach, basing their advocacy of territorial maximalism on what they regard as the Jewish people's historically legitimated rights in the Land of Israel. In both cases, however, there is a militant commitment to Israel's permanent retention of the West Bank ("Judea" and "Samaria") and Gaza.

In political debates about the final status of the West Bank and Gaza, supporters of territorial compromise not only call attention to the obstacles to peace created by Israel's retention of the West Bank and Gaza, they also place emphasis on the danger to the Jewish state that would be posed by the incorporation of these territories. In this context, they assert that there is an inverse relationship between the quality and the extent of the Jewish-Zionist state. Referring to what they describe as the "demographic issue," they argue that permanent retention of the West Bank and Gaza would threaten either the Jewish character of the State of Israel, the democratic character of Israeli political life, or both the country's Jewish and its democratic character.[41]

So far as Israel's Jewish character is concerned, there can be no meaningful Zionist state without a Jewish majority. This proposition has been central to modern political Zionism since the early days of the movement. Yet this majority, achieved with so much effort, would be placed in jeopardy by redefining Israel's borders so as to add to its 750,000 Arab citizens the more than 1.5 million Palestinians who live in the West Bank and Gaza Strip. This would bring the non-Jewish population of "Greater Israel" to about 40 percent of the total, and the higher birth rate of these Arabs could well make them the majority within a generation or less. Indeed, in Israel and the occupied territories taken together, there is already an approximately equal number of Jewish and Arab children under the age of five. Thus, annexation of the territories would have the effect of making Israel a bi-national rather than a Jewish state. At the very least, this situation would exist on a *de facto* basis. It would also exist *de jure*, if Palestinians from the territories were given the same political rights as Arab citizens who already live in pre-1967 Israel. In this case, the Arabs would translate their growing demographic weight into political strength, and within a few years would simply use the ballot box to undermine Israel's Jewish character.

Advocates of territorial maximalism usually respond by denying that a demographic issue exists. They contend that holding the territories will simultaneously stimulate Jewish immigration from abroad and encourage Arab emigration. But those who oppose retention of the territories convincingly reply that seven years of territorial maximalism under Likud, and subsequent years of stalemate under the national unity government, did not increase Jewish immigration or even, for that matter, diminish the serious problem of Jewish emigration. They also point out that the notion of "steadfastness" is fundamental to Palestinians in the occupied territories, meaning that they are determined to remain in their homeland no matter how harsh the conditions of occupation (or annexation) and that it is an illusion to believe these Palestinians will voluntarily surrender the remainder of their country. Thus, unless Israelis are prepared to use force to remove the Arab inhabitants of the territories, retention of the West Bank and Gaza does indeed involve a demographic threat to the Jewish character of the State of Israel. Should the territories be annexed, they reiterate, it would only be a matter of time before Israel would lose its Jewish majority.

The argument that preservation of Israel's Jewish majority requires withdrawal from the occupied territories has been somewhat weakened by increasing Jewish immigration from the Soviet Union, which began to assume significant proportions in late 1989 and early 1990. Tens of thousands of Soviet Jews arrived in Israel during this period and some projections suggest that the number of new immigrants will reach several hundred thousand within a few years. Advocates of territorial maximalism see this as additional evidence that there is no demographic threat confronting the Jewish state. On the other hand, supporters of territorial compromise are quick to point out that there is no connection between the arrival of Soviet Jews and retention of the occupied territories. The circumstances that have brought these new immigrants to Israel do not include the fact that the West Bank and Gaza are under Israeli control. Indeed, in the view of those who support territorial compromise, the need to devote attention and resources to the absorption of Soviet Jews constitutes an additional reason for seeking an accommodation with the Palestinians. In addition, and most important, these Israelis insist that the presence of new immigrants from the Soviet Union, while most welcome, is not a solution to the demographic challenge facing the country. Unless Palestinians are forcibly removed from the West Bank and Gaza, it will push back by no more than a decade or so the point at which the Arabs would become the majority in Greater Israel.

So far as the issue of democracy is concerned, if the Arab inhabitants of Greater Israel were not given citizenship they would not be able to vote the Jewish state out of existence. Instead, their incorporation into Israel would undermine the country's democratic character. While Israel's critics have often claimed that Zionism is racism and compared Israel to South Africa, freedom of political expression and participation for Israeli Arabs has made it possible to show the fallacies of such propaganda. How tragic it would be, advocates of territorial compromise insist, if Israel's policies toward the occupied territories and their inhabitants led to governance on the South African model. In other words, Israel's incorporation of the West Bank and Gaza would require it to rule permanently over an involuntary and subject Palestinian population possessing few if any political rights—a situation incompatible with democracy.

Those favoring retention of the territories contend that most Palestinians from the West Bank and Gaza do not want Israeli citizenship, and if offered it would refuse. Most observers agree that this is correct, and to this extent an enlarged Jewish state would be relieved of responsibility for the disenfranchisement of these Palestinians. If these analysts are wrong and the Arab inhabitants of an annexed West Bank and Gaza were to demand Israeli citizenship (as some of their leaders have occasionally proposed as a means to force Israel to recognize the contradictions inherent in its policies), the Jewish state would either have to deny equal political rights to a large segment of its population, or face the prospect of having the Jewish state voted out of existence by Palestinians working through its democratic political system. But even if Palestinians did not claim Israeli citizenship (in the unlikely event that it would in fact be offered to them), it does not follow that Israel's democratic character would be preserved. It is hardly consistent with democratic principles that 60 percent of the population should rule over 40 percent against the will of the latter, or, whatever the reason, that the former but not the latter should enjoy full political rights.

In response to these challenges posed by retention of the West Bank and Gaza, many supporters of territorial compromise advocate a partial withdrawal, which they characterize as significant but which in fact is unlikely to accommodate the Palestinians' minimal requirements. This is the position of the Labor Party, for example, which calls for a withdrawal from Gaza and the heavily populated central highlands of the West Bank, but which recommends that Israel retain the Jordan Valley and the western slopes of the West Bank. This would leave Israel in possession of about one-third of the latter territory. Moreover, Labor has been reluctant to surrender control of the territories to their Palestinian inhabitants, arguing that lands relinquished by Israel should instead be given over to Jordan. Asserting that a fuller withdrawal will be necessary if is peace is to be achieved, these limitations on the territorial concessions proposed by Labor lead some observers to assert that the party's compelling analysis of the demographic issue is not matched by comparable wisdom so far as its proposed solution is concerned.

As noted, supporters of Likud and parties further to the right for the most part reject these arguments put forward by advocates of territorial compromise. In the period leading up to the outbreak of the *intifada*, Prime Minister Yitzhak Shamir and other leading figures of the political right asserted that continuing occupation of the West Bank and Gaza was without significant costs from the Israeli point of view. Shamir and others insisted that the Palestinian inhabitants of these territories did not constitute a serious obstacle to their development in accordance with the design of those committed to territorial maximalism. Indeed, these hard-line Israeli leaders often asserted that many and perhaps most Palestinians in the West Bank and Gaza were actually quite content to live under Israeli hegemony. While they might be reluctant to say so publicly, these Palestinians were said to recognize and appreciate the improvement in their standard of living that had accompanied occupation—and hence sought no more than local or regional autonomy under continuing Israeli rule. To see the basis for these claims, territorial maximalists insisted, one need merely travel through the territories. The Palestinians had never lived better. Television antennas were everywhere, there were more new cars than ever, and many new homes had been constructed. In addition, available data showed an increase in the import of refrigerators and other consumer durables. Finally, there had been significant improvements in education, health care and other areas. For example, whereas there were no universities in the occupied territories prior to 1967, five had been established under Israeli occupation. All of this, according to Likud and parties further to the right, had led Palestinians to appreciate and welcome the benefits of Israeli rule, and this in turn meant that few inhabitants of the West Bank and Gaza had any desire to create problems for the country that had done so much to help them.

It is impossible to determine with precision the degree to which Shamir and like-minded Israeli leaders believed their own rhetoric. Certainly there were numerous indications that their characterizations of Palestinian political sentiments were wide of the mark. Prominent among these pre-*intifada* indications were the sustained and sometimes violent protests that took place in the winter and spring of 1982. Israel responded to these not only by confronting demonstrators in the streets but also by disbanding the National Guidance Committee (formed several years earlier to protest the Camp David autonomy proposals), and by dismissing elected, pro-PLO mayors and dissolving the municipal councils of various West Bank towns.[42] Another clear indication of Palestinian attitudes toward Israeli rule in the West Bank and Gaza was provided by the failure and eventual abandonment of the "Village League" policy instituted by the government in the early 1980s.This policy sought to fill the gap left by dismissed mayors and dissolved municipal councils and, more generally, to bring to power a compliant local leadership that would accept limited autonomy under Israeli sovereignty.[43] The March 1986 assassination of Zafir al-Masri, the Israeli-appointed mayor of Nablus, gave further evidence of broad Palestinian backing for the mainstream nationalist consensus. Al-Masri's appointment had been approved both by the PLO and Jordan; his death (apparently at the hands of Syrian-based Palestinian rejectionists) was an occasion for widespread nationalist demonstrations. A few months later, in the summer of 1986, a public opinion poll conducted by a Palestinian political scientist provided broader and more systematic evidence for Palestinian attitudes. The survey found that there was no support whatsoever among West Bankers and Gazans for Palestinian autonomy under continuing Israeli rule and that only 3.7 percent favored return of the West Bank to Jordan and of the Gaza Strip to Egypt, whereas 93.5 percent regarded the PLO as the sole legitimate representative of the Palestinian people and supported the creation of an independent Palestinian state.[44]

While it might seem that these indications of Palestinian political sentiments would make it difficult to attach much credibility to the contention that the inhabitants of the West Bank and Gaza would willingly accept autonomy under permanent Israeli rule, such views were articulated with conviction by the Israeli political right, and prior to the *intifada*, they appear to have been accepted at face value by substantial segments of the country's Jewish population. As expressed by an Israeli journalist critical of such thinking, "prior to the *intifada*, the illusion was that Palestinian docility under occupation would go on forever."[45]

The Intifada *and the Green Line*

On the eve of the *intifada*, the "Green Line"—the pre-1967 border separating Israel from its Arab neighbors—had become nearly invisible to many Israelis. Even as the debate between supporters of territorial compromise and territorial maximalism continued and intensified, Israelis became increasingly familiar with the West Bank and Gaza, to which they had had unrestricted access for two decades. They felt increasingly at home in the occupied areas. The number of Israelis living there rose steadily, reaching more than 70,000 (excluding East Jerusalem) on the eve of the *intifada*. Other Israelis also frequently found themselves in the territories, traveling through the West Bank to get from one part of Israel to another, taking their cars to garages in Gaza, driving to Jericho for a casual meal in one of the city's oasis restaurants, and much more. These contacts, as well as the many important economic and institutional linkages established between Israel and the territories since 1967, gave many (and perhaps most) Israelis a feeling that there was a natural connection between their country and these areas. Indeed, by the end of 1987, a majority of Israel's population was too young even to remember a time when the West Bank and Gaza were not under their country's control. Thus, while the West Bank and Gaza were not quite seen as Israel itself, neither did they appear to be part of another, foreign country. As one Israeli commentator explained, "For young Israelis born around 1967, it was as normal and easy to travel from Tel Aviv to Nablus (West Bank) as it was to travel from Tel Aviv to Nazareth (Galilee). In their eyes, both were Arab cities under Israeli rule, and they did not stop to ponder over distinctions."[46]

This situation, however, changed rapidly after December 1987: an important early consequence of the Palestinian uprising was the resurrection of the Green Line in the consciousness of most Israelis. The territories are now zones of insecurity, which Israeli civilians avoid as much as possible and where even soldiers would prefer not to serve. Rabin himself made this point in September 1988, when asked to comment on the fact that the number of Israelis killed in the territories had actually declined since the beginning of the uprising. "Jews simply don't visit the territories as they used to," the defense minister stated. "No one's wandering around the garages of Gaza any more these days."[47]

Likud and other parties of the right would like to convince Israelis that this is not the case. During the 1988 election campaign, for example, they organized bus trips to the West Bank in an attempt to show that the situation was normal. They convinced very few, however. Their convoys attracted few participants, a disproportionate number being children and elderly persons, and the presence of armed guards probably reminded travelers more of the danger than the tranquility and normalcy of a visit to the territories. In any event, Likud's propaganda notwithstanding, few Israelis, even those who advocate territorial maximalism, would seriously contend that Israelis travel to the West Bank and Gaza with the frequency or the lack of self-consciousness that they did before the *intifada*. As summarized by an Israeli journalist, "Perhaps the most conspicuous result of the *intifada* has been the restoration of Israel's pre-1967 border, the famous Green Line, which disappeared from Israeli maps and consciousness as early as 1968.... [Today] the West Bank and Gaza are seen as foreign territories inhabited by a hostile population, whose stone-throwing youngsters are ready to die—and do—in their quest for freedom."[48]

One clear illustration of this situation—and one that sends a particularly strong signal to most Israelis—is the effective redivision of Jerusalem. Israel has worked since 1967 to isolate East Jerusalem from the rest of the West Bank. It has also sought an accommodation with the city's Palestinian residents, offering reduced interference in their political affairs in return for the absence of major protest demonstrations and other organized disturbances. Prior to the *intifada*, this strategy was largely successful. It produced a *modus vivendi* that was satisfactory from the Israeli point of view, permitting Jews to frequent all parts of Jerusalem without hesitation and enabling them to think of their country's capital as a unified city. Now, the current uprising has made East Jerusalem, like the rest of the West Bank and Gaza, an area where Israelis no longer feel comfortable. A general strike has been maintained since the beginning of the *intifada*. Some businesses are open on a limited basis, at times set by the leadership of the uprising; but commercial life remains far from normal and many shops and restaurants normally frequented by Israelis or tourists now do almost no business at all. Even more important, East Jerusalem has been the scene of numerous (sometimes violent) clashes between Israeli police and Palestinian demonstrators. Thus, the Israeli capital has in effect become two cities, with its Arab residents participating in the *intifada* and its Jewish inhabitants increasingly reluctant to visit Palestinian neighborhoods. As Yehuda Litani (Middle East correspondent for the *Jerusalem Post*) noted barely two months into the uprising, "both Jews and Arabs living here know that for the last few weeks [Jerusalem] has been practically redivided. Many ask themselves if it was ever united. Jews are going out of their way to avoid passing through Arab neighborhoods, and fewer Arabs are shopping in [the Jewish areas of] Talpiot and Rehov Jaffa." Similar sentiments were expressed by an authority on walking tours in Jerusalem, who stated that "Before the *intifada*, all the routes of the hikes I wrote about were over the Green Line.... [but] today the Green Line is my map of fear."[49]

Resurrection of the distinction between Israel and the occupied territories, in Jerusalem and more generally, offers powerful evidence that the message of *intifada* is getting through to many Israelis. Public ignorance about the territories has been shattered, as has the apathy which was surprisingly common in spite of the passion that attended debates between politicians of the left and right. In the elections of 1984, for example, the current and future status of the territories was but a secondary issue, even though both Labor and Likud had established platforms based on territorial compromise and territorial maximalism respectively. It would be going too far to say that most Israelis were uninterested in the West Bank and Gaza. But many saw little urgency in addressing the issue, apparently concluding that decisions about their final status could be deferred for the time being and that, in the short run at least, Shamir and Likud were perhaps correct in their assertion that occupation was relatively cost free. Such views may have been held even by many who found Labor's concern with the demographic issue persuasive, and who accordingly were willing to see the West Bank and Gaza traded for peace. Despite these views, many who held them may have seen this as requiring action only in the future, at some distant point when the Arabs were truly ready for peace, and therefore concluded that Israel had no special or pressing need to hasten the peace process along.

The *intifada* has forced Israelis to recognize certain truths about the occupied territories. The uprising communicates that Palestinians are unwilling to live under continued occupation, that they demand that their right to self-determination be recognized, and that they are in a position to make Israel pay a price if it insists on retaining the territories. In short, Palestinians are determined to let Israelis know that occupation is not cost free so far as the Jewish state is concerned, and that political leaders who state otherwise are either ignorant of or deliberately lying about Arab grievances and demands. This message is getting through to the Israeli public, and it is in this connection that the tour organizer quoted above declared that "I've reached an understanding attained by the government, the army, and every sane person in Israel—that the Green Line was never abolished, that our presence in the occupied territories was never accepted as a necessary evil that could be lived with."[50]

Evidence of this change in the way that Israelis look at the occupied territories comes from a variety of sources. For example, the price of housing in Jewish settlements in the West Bank has declined since December 1987, indicating a diminishing demand that is largely due to the fact that fewer Israelis consider it possible to lead a normal life in the territories. The contrast between the elections of 1984 and 1988 is also instructive. In 1988, with the election held roughly eleven months after the outbreak of the *intifada*, the situation in the territories was by far the most important issue. Indeed, in a poll commissioned by the *Los Angeles Times* and conducted by Dahaf about two months before the election, 54 percent said the most important issue facing the country was the future of the West Bank and Gaza and the Arab-Israeli conflict more generally. The next most frequently chosen issue was the economy, which only 21 percent judged to be the most serious problem facing the country. In a second poll taken about the same time, conducted by the Decima polling agency, 80 percent expressed the view that the territories, peace and security was the most important issue on the Jewish state's political agenda.[51]

To report that Israelis are getting the message is not to say that they have necessarily drawn the conclusion that Palestinians would wish. It is one thing for Israelis to recognize that what they have been told about Palestinian political sentiments and the cost free character of occupation is incorrect. It is another for them to conclude that this requires their country to withdraw from the territories and accommodate itself to Palestinian nationalism. In fact this is only one of the conclusions that Israelis can draw, and are drawing, from their heightened recognition that occupation is not a normal and benign state of affairs and that something fundamental is amiss in the West Bank and Gaza. While those who believe that Israel should seek to trade the territories for peace have had their convictions strengthened, and have begun to exchange their patience (or apathy) for a belief that movement in this direction can no longer be deferred, those committed to the permanent Jewish sovereignty over the West Bank and Gaza are drawing very different conclusions. Overall, the resurrection of the Green Line, and the *intifada* more generally, have reinforced and intensified existing ideological divisions. On long-term issues concerning the future of the West Bank and Gaza, both supporters of territorial maximalism and advocates of territorial compromise find confirmation of their views in the current Palestinian uprising.

The Intifada *and Territorial Maximalism*

Advocates of territorial maximalism frequently argue that the uprising is actually not about the West Bank and Gaza at all. Rather, they assert, it is an expression of the unwavering opposition of the Palestinians, and of Arabs in general, to the existence of a Jewish state in any part of Palestine. In other words, the uprising is not a struggle for Nablus and Hebron, but for Haifa and Jaffa; it is a struggle for the Palestinians' historic and continuing objective, the end of the Jewish state. In advancing this argument, Likud and parties further to the right use their pre-*intifada* assessment of conditions in the territories as a point of departure and as the logical foundation for the case they now seek to make. Reaffirming their belief that occupation has brought a significant improvement to the lives of most inhabitants of the West Bank and Gaza, they assert that these Palestinians are ungrateful; and, since the Palestinians have no logical reason to oppose Israeli rule in the territories, the only possible motivation for the uprising is an unshakable Arab commitment to Israel's destruction.

These notions are often expressed by ordinary citizens, whose fear of the Arabs is encouraged and exploited by advocates of territorial maximalism. This does not mean that the latter are insincere. They may indeed believe that occupation has been beneficial for the Palestinians, and even if they recognize that this is not the case, or at least not the whole story, they may in fact be convinced that the Palestinians oppose not only occupation but Israel itself. In any event, so far as these judgments find an echo within the public at large, it is not unusual to hear Israelis complain that "if the Palestinians want to riot after all we have done for them, what can it mean except that they hate us now and will always hate us, so long as our state exists." Or, expressed differently, "the uprising shows that no matter how much we do for them, there is really no hope for peace." A possibly hopeful sign is the addition by some that the Palestinians "could have the West Bank and Gaza if they would only settle for that and leave us alone, but of course we know this is impossible."[52] This is hopeful in that it suggests that at least some Israelis who support the political right do so out of fear, and not because of an ideological commitment to territorial maximalism. But so far as an assessment of responses to the *intifada* is concerned, the lesson to be drawn is that many Israelis have had their fears and suspicions of the Arabs heightened by the uprising and, as a result, have become not more but *less* willing to consider making concessions.

Palestinians and others who are knowledgeable about conditions in the occupied territories will wonder whether Israelis could seriously entertain such views, based as they are on an assumption that occupation is beneficial and should logically be welcomed by the inhabitants of the West Bank and Gaza. Commenting on this matter, a Palestinian participant in a symposium on the psychological effects of the *intifada*, held at the Hebrew University in June 1988, stated that only someone remarkably ignorant of the humiliation and degradation associated with occupation could contend that the uprising shows the Palestinians to be ungrateful, or that it must be about something else since rational men or women would not disrupt their lives so thoroughly and sustain such significant losses simply to bring an end to occupation.[53] But in fact most Israelis have been ignorant about life under occupation, a fact which, as noted, made it possible for Likud to contend that retention of the territories posed no problems for Israel and for Labor to attach no urgency to its calls for an exchange of land for peace. And it is a consequence of this ignorance that many Israelis, and certainly those who identify with the political right, conclude from the message they are now receiving from the Palestinians that what is at stake is the very existence of the Jewish state.

Widespread international condemnation of Israeli attempts to suppress the *intifada* reinforces these views in the minds of many Israelis. Government spokesmen and some propagandists have frequently claimed that the extent of IDF violence against the Palestinians is greatly exaggerated by the international news media. In addition, many Israelis complain that the media have focused on Israel's efforts at containment without giving equal weight to the Palestinians' violent and provocative behavior. Finally, even Israelis who acknowledge that there have been excesses by the IDF often state that, deplorable as they may be, these actions are insignificant in comparison to the brutal and repressive measures that some Arab and other governments have carried out against their own citizens, and which are scarcely mentioned in the international press and or condemned in international gatherings. Not only does this reflect what Israelis see as a lamentable double standard, it also adds to Israeli fears by reinforcing a sense of isolation. Many Israelis believe their country is in danger of being abandoned by the world community. The world is indifferent, even hostile to the Jewish state, which means that the Arab struggle against it, represented and spearheaded by the *intifada*, is all the more worrisome.

Again, Arabs and others may wonder about these Israeli perceptions. The Jewish state has never been militarily stronger. It enjoys a stable peace with Egypt, its most powerful Arab neighbor. Syria, the most bellicose Arab state on its border, is receiving reduced military assistance from its principal international patron, the Soviet Union. The PLO has issued increasingly clear statements that it wants to end the conflict on the basis of a two-state solution. Nevertheless, although such considerations have led to differing views among some sectors of the Israeli public (with the possibility that alternative perceptions will become more widespread in the future), it is in fact the case that a significant number of Israelis consider their country more vulnerable and isolated than ever and believe that the *intifada* has placed it on the defensive. All of this means that these Israelis are indeed receiving the message sent by the Palestinians and that they do not see the West Bank and Gaza in the same way they did before December 1987. But it also means that many Israelis are coming to the conclusion that it will be impossible for Jews and Arabs to live together in the territories, as Likud and the political right have always insisted was possible, and that plans for the future of the occupied territories must take this into account.

With the issue posed in these terms, territorial maximalists are beginning to think about the ultimate solution, removal of the Palestinians from the West Bank and Gaza. This is a logical response to the perceptions and judgments of the Israeli political right. If Israel is indeed to retain the territories, and if it is true, as the *intifada* itself proclaims, that the Palestinians will never submit to Israeli rule, then it is not a very big logical step to the conclusion that the Palestinians will have to be removed from the occupied areas. This is the policy of "transfer," and though it is not the official position of Likud or any other established party of the political right, the notion is no longer considered outside the bounds of legitimate political discourse, as it was before the current uprising.[54] The *intifada* has thus brought the idea of transfer from the lunatic fringe of the extreme right to the arena of established partisan politics. In the 1988 election, for example, it was the principal plank in the platform of a new party, Moledet (Homeland), which captured two Knesset seats. Although Moledet is a small party which is substantially to the right of Likud, or even Tehiya, its campaign and (success) broke an important political taboo. In the past, the idea of transfer was considered too outrageous to be discussed, even though it was undoubtedly on the minds of a few fanatics. In 1988, by contrast, it was placed before the voters and debated in the election campaign. It was also endorsed by the more than 50,000 Israelis who voted for Moledet.[55]

Typical of the support for transfer that is now being articulated with increasing militancy and frequency by advocates of territorial maximalism is the following statement given to an interviewer in 1989 by a Jewish resident of Kiriyat Araba, a large Israeli settlement near Hebron:

> A few years ago, the ideas of Rabbi Kahane (leader of the ultra-nationalist Kach Party and an advocate of transfer) were looked down upon and his followers were ostracized, but now things are different and people see the Arab problem more vividly. People say you can't live with the Arabs and you can't keep so many soldiers [in the West Bank and Gaza] permanently, so the solution is to remove the Jews and you don't have to worry about coexistence. I say the land belongs to us and the Arabs don't belong to us, so the land we should keep and the Arabs we should let go. I think it's feasible today. Militarily it's no problem.... As Westerners, it seems very cruel, very unrealistic, very barbaric to do this, but you have to realize that the Arab mind is not the Western mind. They are a cruel people. They are a people who want to spill blood. I don't feel toward a people like this that we have any obligations.[56]

Similar statements, and those which seek to establish an ethical foundation for the transfer of Palestinians, can be found in the settler press. For example, a March 1988 article entitled "The Fear of Employing Force Stems from Moral Weakness," states that "If [in 1967] we had expelled all the residents of Judea, Samaria and Gaza to the other side of the Jordan, to the king who rose up against us to kill us, it would have been a righteous and just act.... A nation which tears asunder a stranglehold of aggression has the moral right to defeat its enemies and banish them."[57]

Public opinion polls show that support for the notion of transfer extends far beyond those Israelis who voted for Moledet or who live in Jewish settlements in the West Bank and Gaza. For example, a poll conducted for the *Jerusalem Post* in August 1988 by the Israel Institute for Applied Social Research found that fully 49 percent of those interviewed leaned toward transfer as a solution to the long-term problem of the occupied territories. Moreover, about thirty percent of those supporting this option expressed an intention to vote for Labor, rather than Likud or another party of the right, in the approaching election. The results of such polls should be interpreted with caution. Opinions about such issues are unstable, being effected by events and prone to rapid swings of substantial proportions. Further, the August 1988 poll placed the question about transfer in a particular context, with respondents being asked what Israel should do to preserve its democratic character should it retain the occupied territories. (Other possible responses included giving rights to the Palestinians, and hence endangering Israel's Jewish character, and the view that it is acceptable to compromise Israeli democracy.) But while the poll may inflate the support for transfer among Israeli Jews, it is nevertheless a powerful indication of the impact of the *intifada* that so many Israelis consider the transfer option plausible. As the *Jerusalem Post* wrote when reporting the results of its poll, "Virtually unmentionable (and unaskable) until a few months ago, except by the tiny minority that supports Rabbi Meir Kahane's Kach Party, the subject of transfer is no longer taboo; it has gained legitimacy, become a focus of public discussion and swept through the right."[58]

So far as the political right is concerned, what all this means is that the *intifada* has solidified existing orientations, reinforcing the view that Israel should retain the occupied territories. Although their interest in the West Bank and Gaza does not stem only, or even principally, from considerations of security, the uprising leads advocates of territorial maximalism to conclude that conflict with the Arabs will continue and that Israel should therefore retain the military advantages associated with control of the occupied territories. Indeed, since Israel is already at war with the Palestinians, what would be the sense of giving inhabitants of the West Bank and Gaza, who are clearly committed to the Jewish state's destruction, the possibility of organizing their anti-Israel campaign without IDF interference? Equally important, the views of many have shifted further to the right, meaning that they are not only held with greater conviction but are substantively more hard-line and extreme than they were before the *intifada*, thereby intensifying the polarization of the Israeli political spectrum. This is shown in the serious interest in the notion of transfer, an extreme but nonetheless logical strategy for responding to the demographic consequences of retaining the West Bank and Gaza.

The Intifada *and Territorial Compromise*

This, however, is only part of the story. The *intifada* has also strengthened and solidified the views of advocates of territorial compromise. The arguments put forward by Israelis holding these views are not new ones, associated as they are with the demographic issue that Labor and the left has been raising for some time. Nevertheless, the underlying rationale for these arguments is seen as more compelling than ever, and the demographic issue itself is articulated with an immediacy and urgency that was infrequent in the past. A typical example is the following opinion by Gad Ya'acobi (considered middle-of-the-road, or even to the right of Labor's ideological center of gravity), expressed only a month after the beginning of the uprising:

> Already today, in 1988, over half the children born in the territory under Jewish control are not Jewish. In the absence of a peace settlement, the number of Jews and Arabs living in Israel at the turn of the century will be approximately equal, and just a few years later, the Arabs will outnumber the Jews... We will become either a non-democratic bi-national state, in which approximately half of the population does not enjoy full political rights, or a bi-national democratic state that will lose its Jewish character. This is not an apocryphal vision of the end of the world, but a development which will take place during the lifetime of most of the citizens alive in the country today, unless a way is found to reach a settlement.[59]

In another article, written about a year later, Ya'acobi stated that "the long *intifada* has produced a new Middle Eastern reality... All of a sudden it's an entirely new ball game. In the wake of this transformation, we must ask ourselves if we truly wish to retain the territories indefinitely and, if so, whether we are willing to accept the consequences."[60]

Similar sentiments are discussed in *Writing on the Wall*, a book published in 1988, after the outbreak of the *intifada*.[61] The author, Arye Naor, conceives of the problem as a triangle, the sides respectively being the territories, democracy, and Israel's Jewish character. Any two of these three sides can coexist, Naor observes, but there is no way the triangle can rest on all three side simultaneously. And since Israel must accordingly make a choice, the author argues that Israel's interests are best served by relinquishing the occupied territories and preserving the state's democratic and Jewish character. Among the other Israelis who have articulated these sentiments with particular urgency is Yehoshafat Harkabi, a Hebrew University professor who is former director of Israeli military intelligence and one of the country's foremost authorities on Palestinian political attitudes. In an important book published a year before the *intifada*, and in articles and speeches after December 1987, Harkabi offers an apocryphal vision of Israel's future if it insists on retaining the West Bank and Gaza.[62] Speaking and writing with great passion, and carrying out what he regards as an urgent mission to save his country from itself, Harkabi describes Israel's attachment to territorial maximalism as "suicidal." He contends in this context that religious nationalism and political extremism threaten the survival of a Jewish and democratic Israel far more seriously than any external challenge from the Arabs could ever hope to do.

Public opinion polls show the degree of support for each possible solution to the dilemma associated with control of the occupied territories, as symbolically represented by Naor's triangle. There is nearly unanimous support for preserving Israel's Jewish character. The *Jerusalem Post*/ Israel Institute for Applied Social Research poll conducted in August 1988 found that 75 percent of those surveyed considered the preservation of Israel's Judaism to be very important, another 22 percent judged it important, and only 3 percent considered it to be unimportant.[63] In addition, there was widespread, although somewhat weaker, support for preserving Israeli democracy: 49 percent said it was very important, 33 percent considered it important, and 18 percent judged it to be unimportant. Faced with a choice, about 20 percent were willing to sacrifice either the country's democracy or its Jewish character, most of the former being supporters of the right and most of the latter being supporters of the left. Also, a few on the political right rejected the formulation of the problem, asserting that it will be possible to find a formula that both gives the Palestinians meaningful political rights and involves no threat to Israel's Jewish character. The vast majority, however, accepted the dilemma posed by the demographic issue and, preferring to compromise neither the state's democracy nor its Judaism, concluded that the country must either transfer large numbers of Palestinians to other areas or withdraw from the occupied territories. The latter solution, territorial compromise, was selected by about one-third of all respondents, by about two-thirds of those identifying themselves as Labor Party supporters, and by almost all of the 10 percent or so expressing support for a party to the left of Labor.

Other polls, which did not ask questions within the restricted context of solutions to the demographic issue, also shed light on the degree of support for territorial compromise. In addition, these polls indicate that such support has increased since the beginning of the *intifada*. For example, a March 1989 survey conducted for the *New York Times* by the Hanoch Smith Research Center in Jerusalem found that 54 percent of all Israelis would be willing to give up at least some territory in return for suitable guarantees.[64] The *New York Times* poll is conducted annually, and in April 1987, before the current uprising, only 41 percent of those interviewed expressed such a willingness. Thus, even though advocates of territorial maximalism will argue that by attaching conditions to territorial compromise most Israelis are actually indicating that they oppose withdrawal from the West bank and Gaza, it is clear that a willingness to withdraw, with or without conditions, has increased since the beginning of the uprising. Moreover, this trend appears to have continued in the months since the *New York Times* survey was conducted. According to one Israeli journalist, writing in December 1989, "public opinion polls in Israel show that there is a steady movement among the mainstream toward a peace settlement."[65]

Many of the Israelis who advocate territorial compromise reject implicitly, or even explicitly, the assertion of the political right that the *intifada* is part of a continuing Arab effort to bring an end to the Jewish state. Acknowledging that occupation is an unnatural and undesirable state of affairs, and that it is therefore logical and reasonable for Palestinians in the West Bank and Gaza to seek its end, they do not attach to the uprising any goals associated with the destruction of Israel. Indeed, although there are some respects in which living standards in the territories have improved since 1967, these Israelis recognize that occupation has not only brought humiliation, political insult, and harsh and arbitrary rule, it has also been accompanied by poor and deteriorating living conditions for hundreds of thousands of Palestinians. As expressed by Aaron Hart, a former member of the Israeli security establishment:

> The spontaneous outbreak of unrest in the occupied territories is understandable and to some extent even forgivable... A youth born in a squalid refugee camp in Gaza or Nablus does not need much encouragement or incitement to lift a stone against the only visible symbol of the hopelessness of his situation and his future. He has nothing to lose and everything to gain. Indeed, the recent outbreaks of unrest are less surprising than the relative docility of the Palestinians for the last twenty years.

Further, Hart continued, although the Palestinians "should not expect any understanding from Yitzhak Shamir and his friends... the rest of us have taken notice and are in agreement: the Palestinians want to be left alone, to rule their own destiny, in their own homeland."[66] Such analyses are in stark contrast to those offered by advocates of territorial maximalism. They dispute the latter's assertion that since occupation has benefited most Palestinians, the *intifada* cannot be a struggle for the West Bank and Gaza alone but must instead be motivated by an unswerving Arab determination to control all of Palestine.

The *intifada* has also deepened the understanding of Israelis that their conflict is not with the Arab world in general, or the Arab states, but with Palestinians who are seeking control over some part of their homeland. The *intifada*, and the resurrection of the Green Line, have broadened Israeli recognition of this basic truth, to which Palestinians and others have been calling attention for some time but which even many advocates of territorial compromise have tended to ignore. Indicative of this new realism in the thinking of many Israelis is criticism of the traditional platform of the Labor Alignment, which advocates territorial compromise within the framework of a "Jordanian option." So, too, are recent statements by Alignment leaders acknowledging that the Palestinian dimension is the core of the Arab-Israeli conflict and calling for negotiations between Israelis and Palestinians.

Prior to December 1987, many in Labor considered the Palestinians to be of secondary importance; the official position of the party was that territory surrendered by Israel should be turned over to Jordan. More recently, however, even though formal change in Labor's platform has been slow in coming, there has been an evolution in the thinking of many Labor Alignment supporters. On the one hand, some have urged the party to clarify its position and adopt a more realistic platform. It is in this context, for example, that some complained during the 1988 election campaign that Labor's advocacy of peace "as if there were no *intifada*" was "misleading and damaging."[67] On the other hand, despite the continuing ambiguity of Labor's official position, many leaders of the party acknowledge that the *intifada* has changed their outlook. As noted, Gad Ya'acobi wrote in January 1989 that "the long *intifada* has produced a new Middle Eastern reality."[68] Even Defense Minister Yitzhak Rabin, architect of Israeli efforts to suppress the *intifada*, acknowledged in September 1989 that Israel's conflict is with the Palestinians, not with the Arab world in general, and accordingly that there will be no peace "without starting some sort of process between us and the Palestinians."[69] More precisely, Rabin declared that whereas he had formerly believed "the best path for Israel was to keep the conflict and the solution within the framework of Israel's relations with the Arab states... the reality today is that the only partner with whom Israel can, perhaps, enter into a political process is the Palestinians... and whoever does not see this is not reading the map correctly."

Committed to territorial compromise and confronted by the *intifada*, many in Israel are moving toward the conclusion that it will be necessary to negotiate with the Palestine Liberation Organization. This is an important new development, comparable in some respects to the emergence of the notion of transfer on the right side of the political spectrum. In the past, talks with the PLO were not quite as much an idea of the political fringe as was the notion of transfer, but they were nonetheless favored by relatively few Israelis and were considered unthinkable by a substantial majority of the population. Indeed, actual contact with the PLO, as opposed to advocating negotiations, was (and continues to be) prohibited by law. But interest in holding talks with the Palestinian organization has assumed significant proportions since the beginning of the current uprising, reflecting yet another aspect of the *intifada's* impact on the thinking of Israelis oriented toward territorial compromise.

Increased Israeli willingness to consider talks with the PLO undoubtedly reflects the evolution of that organization's attitude toward Israel, including its declarations in the fall of 1988 accepting United Nations Resolutions 242 and 338 and expressing support for a two-state solution to the Israeli-Palestinian conflict. It is the *intifada*, however, which has been at the foundation of a new constellation of forces producing substantive attitudinal change among advocates of territorial compromise.[70] The uprising has demonstrated to many Israelis that there is a high price to be paid for retention of the West Bank and Gaza, not only in terms of hostility from the Arab world but also in the form of a threat to Israel's Jewish and democratic character. In addition, the *intifada* has increased recognition that Israel's conflict is with the Palestinians, not with the Arab world in general. Thus, while declarations by the PLO have helped to convince Israelis that it is possible to negotiate with Palestinians about the future of the West Bank and Gaza, it is the *intifada* which has persuaded many that it is desirable and important to take advantage of this option. In other words, while recent PLO statements are telling at least some Israelis that there is an alternative to continued conflict with the Palestinians, the uprising is sending the message that it is in the interest of the Jewish state to pursue this alternative by, among other things, negotiating with the Palestine Liberation Organization.

Opinion polls taken since the beginning of the *intifada* document the new willingness to consider talks with the PLO. For example, in the previously-mentioned poll conducted for the *New York Times* in April 1987, before the *intifada*, only 42 percent of the respondents were in favor of negotiations with the PLO. A year later, with the *intifada* in its fifth month, a replication of the *Times* survey found that 53 percent of those interviewed favored such talks; and in another replication of the annual poll, in March 1989, the proportion expressing such support had grown to 58 percent.[71] In addition, the results of the latter survey were corroborated by a Dahaf poll carried out a month later, which reported that 59 percent of Israeli Jews favored talks with the PLO.[72] Furthermore, the 1989 *New York Times* survey showed that support for negotiations between Israel and the PLO was particularly high among advocates of territorial compromise. Such talks were favored by 78 percent of the respondents identifying themselves as Labor supporters, and by 94 percent of those identifying with parties further to the left. In fact, even 49 percent of those indicating a preference for Likud said Israel should talk to the PLO.

All of these findings indicate that the salience and legitimacy of the PLO as a negotiating partner, or at least a potential partner, has increased dramatically since the beginning of the uprising. Admittedly, it must be acknowledged that the polls did not inquire about unconditional support for talks with the PLO. For example, the *New York Times* survey asked about negotiations with the PLO if that organization recognizes Israel and ceases terrorist activity. Moreover, since these are conditions that most Israelis believe the PLO has not yet fulfilled, there is some basis for the claim of the political right that the results of these polls should be interpreted with caution. Nevertheless, the important point is that a shift in Israeli public opinion has taken place since the beginning of the Palestinian uprising. With the same conditionalities attached, the proportion of Israelis expressing support for talks with the PLO was found to be much higher in 1988 and 1989 than in the years before the *intifada*.

Other indications of a willingness to negotiate with the PLO come from the statements of many politicians and intellectuals. Moreover, among them are even a few individuals affiliated with parties of political right. An example of the latter is Shlomo Lahat, mayor of Tel Aviv and a prominent Likud politician. Lahat told an interviewer during the 1988 election campaign: "I believe a Palestinian state is inevitable. I believe, unfortunately, that the PLO represents the Palestinian people. I know that the price of peace and real security is withdrawal." Although Lahat added that "I advocate voting Likud, because only the Likud will be able to advance such a peace process," his remarks nonetheless indicate some growth even on the political right in the view that the Palestine Liberation Organization is Israel's natural bargaining partner in negotiations about peace.[73]

Equally significant are the increasing clarity of statements to this effect by leftist politicians and the fact that public support for parties to the left of Labor appears to be increasing. For example, during the 1988 election campaign the leader of the Citizens' Rights Movement, Shulamit Aloni, expressed support for holding peace talks with the PLO and even indicated that an appropriate outcome of such talks might be the creation of a Palestinian state alongside Israel. Although Aloni's remarks brought sharp condemnation from advocates of territorial maximalism, her party did well in the elections. Whereas the CRM had won only three Knesset seats in the elections of 1984, it captured five in the balloting of 1988. In addition, a Modi'in Ezrachi poll conducted in April 1989 found that if elections were held at that time the CRM would have captured nine Knesset seats, and the seats held by two like-minded parties committed to territorial compromise, Mapam and Shinui, would have increased from five to eight.[74]

Aloni's statements and her party's performance in the 1988 election are indicative of general trends on the left side of the political spectrum. The broad movement of opinion often described as the peace camp, which includes the CRM and other groups and parties, has experienced a strong revival since the beginning of the *intifada*. Many of these groups operate within the loose organizational framework provided by Peace Now, which offers a measure of institutional and structural unity to the Israel political left; and by the end of 1988 there were roughly fifty different groups working under the Peace Now umbrella. Peace Now had been largely moribund for five years prior to the outbreak of the *intifada*, having done little since Israel's invasion of Lebanon in 1982. In 1988, however, it sprang back to life, holding rallies, symposia, petition drives and more.[75] In January 1988, for example, 80,000 Israelis took part in a Peace Now demonstration in Tel Aviv, and in March, on the eve of a trip by the prime minister to the United States, it organized another rally that attracted an equal number of sympathizers. Another activity was a petition drive seeking support for territorial compromise among military officers. Conducted in March 1988, it produced 1300 signatures in favor of withdrawal from the West Bank and Gaza. So far as talks with the PLO are concerned, Peace Now and many of its affiliated groups have modified their earlier position, which was deliberately vague and declared that the matter of a suitable negotiating partner should be resolved in the future. Most have now embraced the view that Israel must deal directly with the Palestine Liberation Organization. This important change in the thinking of the peace camp is reflected in numerous speeches and articles by its leaders, such the statements by Shulamit Aloni discussed above. In addition, in November 1988, Peace Now kicked off a new campaign to "Speak Peace with the PLO Now."[76] The campaign opened with a symposium at which there were speeches by leading political figures and intellectuals, followed in December by a rally in Tel Aviv that attracted 50,000 supporters. The activities planned for the campaign included "peace visits" between Israeli Jews and Palestinian villagers, symposia with Israeli and Palestinian leaders, a media campaign, demonstrations, vigils, and parliamentary lobbying.

Growing Israeli interest in talks with the PLO was also reflected in some well-publicized meetings between Israeli politicians and PLO leaders and, equally, in the increased public and political tolerance that characterized reactions to these meetings. For example, in January 1989, four Israeli MKs joined PLO officials in Paris for a discussion-debate on Middle East peace, which both sides characterized as a step toward formal and high-level dialogue. Furthermore, the Israelis attending the session included not only MKs from parties of the political left, namely Shulamit Aloni of CRM and Yair Tsaban of Mapam; other participants were Lova Eliav and Ora Namir of the centrist Labor Alignment. The Israelis in Paris addressed their remarks to the audience rather than the Palestinians in order to respect a 1986 Knesset law making contact with the PLO illegal, but subsequent criticism of this law provides yet another indication of movement toward a dialogue with the Palestine Liberation Organization. Namir, one of the participants, called the 1986 law "shameful," and several Labor Party officials who did not attend the Paris meeting told the press the time had come to amend the law prohibiting contact with PLO representatives. In a related and equally significant development, the Knesset failed to pass a bill proposing that the parliamentary immunity of the MKs who went to Paris be lifted, making them liable for prosecution under the 1986 law. The bill was introduced by right-wing politicians but opposed by Labor, as well as the left, and failed on a tie vote. These and other recent developments make it clear that the PLO has become a central focus in Israeli thinking about peace in a way that differs dramatically from the situation before the *intifada*.[77]

This is not to say that opponents of talks with the PLO are necessarily on the defensive. No bill permitting contact with the PLO has yet been introduced in the Knesset, meaning that Israelis without parliamentary immunity remain liable to prosecution if they meet with representatives of the PLO. Also, in response to proposals to hold elections in the occupied territories, which were introduced by Prime Minister Shamir in April 1989 and subsequently amplified in election plans presented by both the Egyptian and American governments, Likud opposed all formulas that would require Israel to talk to the PLO. Despite differences between Likud and Labor on the issue of elections, Likud (and the party's right wing in particular) was able to impose on all these plans conditions that aborted any possibility of Israeli-PLO negotiations. Finally, advocates of territorial maximalism assert that opposition to a dialogue with the PLO is evident in the domain of public opinion, as well as in the arena of partisan politics. For example, some insist that a proper reading of opinion poll data shows that most Israelis would support talks with the PLO only were that organization to revise its charter and give other evidence of a sincere desire for peace; and since the PLO has not taken such action, and is deemed incapable of doing so by the Israeli political right, it is argued that what opinion polls actually reveal are the conditions Israelis attach to negotiations and the public's continuing distrust of the PLO.

While the actions and analyses of advocates of territorial maximalism are an important part of the Israeli political equation, and should thus be taken seriously, differences between the present situation and that prevailing before the *intifada* are nonetheless clear and pronounced. If resistance to change and doubts about PLO intentions reflect a measure of continuity, changes in Israeli thinking about the place of the PLO in an eventual peace settlement are no less dramatic. An Israeli intelligence report discussed in the news media in March 1989 concluded that Israel has no choice but to talk to the PLO if it wishes to end the uprising and make progress toward peace, and the report also concluded that the Palestinian organization is sincere in its calls for an accommodation with the Jewish state.[78] It is significant in this context, too, that the March 1989 *New York Times* poll found that 58 percent of all Israelis, and 80 percent of those supporting Labor, disagree with the proposition that the Palestinians want "a Palestinian state plus all of Israel in the long run," suggesting that much of the public agrees there is a basis for negotiating with the PLO. In the same poll, 62 percent of all Israelis (including 75 percent of Labor supporters and even 55 percent of those identifying with Likud) foresaw talks between Israel and the PLO within the next five years. Remaining doubts about the change taking place in Israeli political thinking should have been dispelled in July 1989 when Yossi Beilin, Deputy Finance Minister and aide to Labor Alignment leader Shimon Peres, acknowledged that "for two and a half months, clear, official and unequivocal negotiations have been under way between [the PLO and] the Israeli government headed by Yitzhak Shamir, via the Americans." Addressing his remarks to Israeli hard-liners, Beilin stated further that "whoever doesn't admit or recognize this, whoever tries to ignore it, is like a small boy who closes his eyes and thinks the world doesn't see him."[79]

The Intifada *and Israeli Security*

Debates between advocates of territorial maximalism and supporters of territorial compromise place heavy emphasis on considerations of military security. On the one hand, even though many of the former urge retention of the West Bank and Gaza for ideological rather than strategic reasons, their position is enhanced to the extent that control of the territories would give Israel an important military advantage in any renewed hostilities with its Arab neighbors. In other words, if it can be shown that the territories are important for the defense of the Jewish state, even those who do not believe that retention of the West Bank and Gaza can be justified on historic or religious grounds may judge the risks associated with withdrawal to be high and hence make common cause with advocates of territorial maximalism. On the other hand, if the West Bank and Gaza do not have major military significance, then territorial compromise appears much more attractive. In this instance, the demographic arguments advanced by Labor and the left are not offset by strategic disadvantages and, accordingly, will be more persuasive to the Israeli public. Indeed, some with Likud connections assert that even Israelis who vote for right-wing parties might accept territorial compromise if their concerns about security were answered. For example, former Likud central committee member Moshe Amirav declared that "nine out of ten Likudniks will compromise on territory if their questions about security are satisfied."[80] Strategic considerations thus figure prominently in the thinking of Israelis who calculate the costs and benefits of territorial compromise and territorial maximalism.

Ever since Israel captured the West Bank and Gaza in 1967, there have been clear differences between Likud and Labor regarding the strategic significance of the occupied territories. Not surprisingly, Likud has traditionally asserted that control of the West Bank and Gaza makes Israel more secure, thus arguing that ideological and military considerations converge in support of territorial maximalism. By contrast, Labor, the party of territorial compromise, has traditionally taken the position that withdrawal from Gaza and much of the West Bank can be undertaken with little or no important military costs. Familiar debates between Likud and Labor have been replayed since the beginning of the *intifada* and were sharper than ever in the elections of 1988. In one typical exchange, Likud's Benjamin Netanyahu declared that withdrawal from the West Bank would enable Palestinians to use hand-held Stinger missiles to attack planes landing at the country's major international airport near Tel Aviv. Yitzhak Rabin responded that this statement was "complete gibberish." Noting that attacks could be launched across any border, and thus the important Israeli cities of Tiberias and Eilat were vulnerable from Stinger missiles in Jordan, Rabin asked, "Shall we therefore occupy the East Bank, too?" [81]

Although the differences between Likud and Labor are substantial within the Israeli political context, it should be noted that Labor does favor retaining parts of the West Bank for security reasons, most notably the Jordan Valley along the eastern edge of the territory. Since the late 1960s, the Alignment has argued that the Jordan Valley could serve as an important buffer, which would reduce the chance of an attack from Jordan and give Israel a military advantage should such an attack nonetheless occur. From the Palestinian and Arab point of view, this limitation which Labor has traditionally placed on its advocacy of territorial compromise constitutes a significant obstacle to peace, and even some within the Alignment have suggested that the party will have to go farther if the the Arab-Israeli conflict is eventually to be resolved on the basis of a formula involving the exchange of land for peace. Be this as it may, however, Labor's platform differs markedly from that of Likud. While the two parties may agree that control of the Jordan Valley is of military value, they differ fundamentally, and passionately, about the overall strategic significance of the occupied territories.

Those who attach military significance to the occupied territories, beyond the Jordan Valley's potential utility as a buffer, point to their proximity to Israel's most important population and industrial centers. In addition, with respect to the West Bank in particular, they emphasize those geographic factors that are said to render Israel particularly vulnerable.[82] The narrow coastal strip between Tel Aviv and Haifa (the most important part of the country from a demographic and an economic point of view) shares a long border with the West Bank, is dominated by the mountain ridges in the center of the latter territory, and is less than ten miles wide at its narrowest point. Thus, some argue, the Arabs could use these territories to inflict considerable damage, either in the form of a ground attack or by shelling Israel from the hills overlooking the country's coastal plain. Most express confidence that, once mobilized, Israel would defeat its Arab attackers decisively. In the meantime, however, in the event of a surprise attack, losses sustained by the Jewish state could be heavy. Further, in a related argument, it is asserted that control of the hilly areas of the West Bank are important as observation posts, permitting the use of equipment that is essential if Israel is to detect hostile Arab intentions in advance.

Yet many knowledgeable Israelis discount the importance of the West Bank and Gaza from a security point of view, asserting that the conditions of modern warfare have greatly reduced Israel's need to control the occupied territories and charging that most who state otherwise are in reality motivated by ideological considerations. Claims that withdrawal from the West Bank and Gaza will not endanger Israeli security have been put forward with increasing frequency by specialists in the fields of military science and strategic studies, including many in the IDF. For example, an important study by an Israeli scholar at Tel Aviv University's Center for Strategic Studies, published in 1983, examined the implications of withdrawal from the West Bank and Gaza and the creation of an independent Palestinian state in these areas and then concluded that this would "probably leave Israel in a better overall position than would a continuing political stalemate or any of the other potential outcomes." Like most other advocates of territorial compromise, the author of the study stated that withdrawal from the occupied territories should be accompanied by various risk-minimization measures, including temporary demilitarization and other arrangements dictated by Israeli security needs. These measures respond to the arguments of those who acknowledge that the Jewish state's ability to defeat its enemies does not depend primarily on territorial considerations but who believe that Israel must nonetheless have enough strategic depth to absorb a surprise attack or the opening of a second front. But, the study goes on to conclude, "If this [independent Palestinian] state were created with appropriate risk-minimization provisions for Israel and within the context of a broad Israeli-Arab detente, it would probably result in a significantly less tense and dangerous environment for Israel."[83]

An eloquent statement in support of this position was put forward by former Israeli foreign minister Abba Eban in an article written about a year after the *intifada* began. Eban begins by summarizing some of the arguments of those who believe the West Bank and Gaza are essential for Israel's defense, citing primarily American supporters of the Jewish state rather than knowledgeable Israelis. Some, according to Eban, see the creation of a Palestinian mini-state in the West Bank and Gaza as a formula for disaster: "with battles raging fifteen miles from Israel's population centers and with the Palestinians flanking Jerusalem on three sides and Tel Aviv on two, and attacking along a line nine miles from the sea... Israeli casualties could reach as high as 100,000."[84] Such visions are ludicrous, according to Eban. On the one hand, Israel is more than capable of defending itself. "The Israeli defense system is one of the wonders of the world. Never in history has so small a community been able—and ready—to wield such a vast capacity of defense, deterrence and reprisal." On the other, the PLO, which would control the Palestinian state alongside Israel, has no such capacity. Citing figures from the Center for Strategic Studies at Tel Aviv University, Eban noted that Israel has a mobilizable manpower of 540,000, with some 3,800 tanks and 682 aircraft. The PLO, according to the same study, has "8,000 men in scattered places, zero tanks and aircraft, a few guns and no missiles, but a variety of hand grenades, mortars, stones and bottles." Thus, he concludes, "it takes a great effort of imagination to envision this array of forces flanking our cities from five sides and the sea, while inflicting 100,000 casualties."

In recent years, and especially since the start of the *intifada*, many IDF officials have begun to speak out on the issue of territorial compromise and have lent support to the assertion that retention of the West Bank and Gaza is not essential for Israeli security. The opinions of a number of military leaders and other specialists who share this view were collected by Peace Now in Summer 1988.[85] Among the opinions quoted were the following:

> Chief of Staff Dan Shomron: "Israel has had different borders throughout its short history and the IDF has provided security accordingly."

> Former Chief of Military Intelligence Aharon Yariv: "I, like others, am anxious about a Palestinian state, but I believe we can deal with it."

> Hirsh Goodman, military correspondent of the *Jerusalem Post*: "Weapons currently in the development pipeline will, without a doubt, make it easier for Israel to give up territory and retain a high degree of security."

The prevalence of such sentiments in Israeli military circles is reflected in the fact that early in 1988 a group of senior reserve officers formed the Council for Peace and Security, which advocates territorial compromise and maintains that withdrawal from the West Bank and Gaza is acceptable from a military point of view. According to Moshe Amirav, one of the Council's co-founders, "We want to promote a general understanding about the real value of the territories." More specifically, one of the planks in the Council's platform is that "the development of military technology, including missiles, precision-guided munitions and combat helicopters, can give the IDF a relative edge over the Arab armies and will lessen the need for continual and full occupation of the territories."[86] Composed of roughly three hundred generals and other high-ranking officers, as well as prominent scholars and business leaders, the Council for Peace and Security seeks to influence both government policy and public opinion by issuing position papers and organizing conferences and seminars. So far as the public is concerned, there is evidence that the Council's message will fall on receptive ears. Agreeing with those military and civilian leaders who do not see unacceptable risks associated with withdrawal from the West Bank and Gaza, 78 percent of those interviewed in a Dahaf Institute public opinion poll in the spring of 1988 stated that Israel would be able to defend itself were it to withdraw from the occupied territories.[87]

Much of the impetus for the creation of the Council for Peace and Security, and for intensified discussion of the military value of the occupied territories more generally, is to be found in the *intifada*. Founders of the Council, who identify themselves as non-political, readily admit that their efforts were speeded up by the uprising. Further, according to an Israeli journalist who attended a gathering of retired army officers shortly before some of them established the Council, the conversation focused on the *intifada* and the damage it was causing Israel at home and abroad. "We have to cut ourselves loose [from the West Bank and Gaza] quickly," said a veteran officer whose political orientation was described as middle-of-the-road. "So even let there be a Palestinian state on the other side of the border. If they make trouble, we can always move back in and establish order as we are now doing in Lebanon." And according to the journalist who reported these conversations, the most surprising aspect of this scene was that "even the last point provoked no disagreement among those present."[88]

Senior officials associated with the Council for Peace and Security, as well as some others, have been widely quoted in the Israeli and international press since the beginning of the *intifada*. Not only have these officials insisted that Israel is fully capable of compensating for the loss of the West Bank and Gaza, but some have gone further and declared that the military value of the territories is in fact quite limited. For example, Brig. General (res.) Ephriam Sneh, former head of the Civil Administration in the West Bank, asserted that three AWACS radar aircraft would provide Israel with better early warning than its current stations on the mountain ridges of the West Bank.[89] Former Air Force Commander Amos Lapidot stated that "from the standpoint of Israel's defense, the territories have no value."[90]

Indeed, some military leaders and strategists go so far as to call the West Bank a security liability. According to Major General (res.) Uri Orr, "I think we should all agree that the occupation should end because maintaining it does more damage to our security than ending it."[91] Similarly, General (res.) Shlomo Gazit was quoted in the fall of 1988 as saying that "although the territories have some strategic value, in the end they are a burden."[92] That such sentiments are at present widespread within the military is suggested by an informal survey conducted by *Yediot Aharonot*, a prominent Israeli daily. According to the paper, on the basis of this survey "one can estimate that among the current general staff a clear majority of 75 to 80 percent believe that the security risks associated with Israel's continuing to rule the territories are greater than the security risks which Israel will assume if it relinquishes the territories."[93] The survey does not make a careful distinction between those who believe the territories have little strategic value (who are probably in the minority) and those who attach military significance to the West Bank and Gaza but, as a result of the *intifada* and other factors, have concluded that this is outweighed by the cost of continuing conflict with the Palestinians. Nevertheless, the survey, like formation of the Council for Peace and Security, is a strong indication that those with the greatest military experience favour territorial compromise.

Arguments that the occupied territories are a security liability derive much of their logic from Israel's experience with the current Palestinian uprising. For one thing, the *intifada* is said to have transformed the IDF into a police force charged with keeping order in the West Bank and Gaza and, in the process, undermined military preparedness. According to this view, operations in the occupied territories have lowered morale, disrupted training and undermined the IDF's organizational coherence, thereby making Israel weaker *vis-à-vis* Syria and other external challenges, the only real military threats to its security. As stated in the platform of the Council for Peace and Security, the continuation of the occupation will "lessen the motivation among recruits to the army and increase the emigration of high quality veterans," trends which are said to be under way already. Also, more specifically, continued occupation "will devour our resources and divert the army from its main mission, preparation for war"[94]

A related consideration is the psychological damage that service in the occupied territories may be doing to Israeli soldiers. Military service is compulsory in Israel, with young men and women entering the army upon graduation from high school, and it is these new recruits who are particularly vulnerable to psychological problems as a result of their efforts to suppress the *intifada*. Concerned with the impact of the uprising on its troops, the IDF has sent a number of psychologists into the field. Among their findings are that confrontations with Palestinian demonstrators frequently produce extreme and essentially pathological reactions. On the one hand, frustration sometimes leads to "moral apathy," which encourages Israeli soldiers to resort to violence without discrimination or military purpose. On the other, it can also lead to "inner agonies," which in turn give rise to depression, nightmares and a propensity to disobey. Both reactions are injurious to morale, military discipline and effective combat, to say nothing of their psychological consequences for the individual soldier. They erode the soldier's respect for military authority and his (or her) willingness to do neither more nor less than what has been ordered by superior officers. They may also erode long-term public support for the military, especially if turns out that the *intifada* cannot be dealt with through military means and that the sacrifices of young soldiers have been in vain.[95]

Among those who have articulated these concerns is a group of soldiers calling itself The Order of the Day, composed of men who met with President Chaim Herzog in July 1988 in order to express their worries. They later established a loosely-knit organization in the spring of 1989. The group charges that daily confrontations with Palestinians have produced confusion about which orders to follow and how they should be implemented, and, sometimes, a loss of confidence in commanding officers. As expressed by one of the group's members:

> The problem that we raised in our July meeting with the president, and which has been exacerbated since that time, is that the army is being used for non-military purposes, in direct and day-to-day contact with a civilian population. This is very costly. Operationally, since it comes at the expense of training, especially for reservists, it directly harms our preparation for war. But the greatest toll affects that which is customarily referred to as the unit's morale. There is a lack of discipline and readiness to carry out orders, which in the past were supreme values of the Israeli army.[96]

A particularly forceful statement of these issues, especially as they relate to Israel's security and military preparedness, has been put forward by Martin Van Crefeld, a military historian at the Hebrew University of Jerusalem. Crefeld asserts, with hyperbole, that the Israeli army is in danger of falling apart. Indeed, according to Israeli news reports, Crefeld has stated that "Israelis are living in an illusion that they still have an army. But that's a mistake. It's a disintegrating structure that has totally lost its deterrent capability." Charging that Israeli soldiers in the territories feel abandoned, he argues that they increasingly operate not as a unified structure seeking to carry out an assigned mission but as isolated "bands that try to protect themselves and to cover up their acts so that the high command and the media don't discover [what they've done]." In addition, he cites historical precedents, including the American army in Vietnam and French forces in Algeria, and notes that "in both places the army was sent in to suppress a civilian uprising in which it could not but fail." Finally, therefore, making his case in the strongest possible terms, Crefeld asserts that "the Israeli army is growing weaker day by day.... The situation is impossible... and refusal to serve in [the occupied territories] does not harm the army and is the only way to save it."[97]

Yet another important argument related to security, also made more persuasive by the *intifada*, is that ruling over a large and hostile population within the country's borders poses a much greater security threat than does a peace settlement based on borders that are less than ideal from a purely military point of view. Indeed, in the long run, this internal challenge may be even more injurious to Israeli security than problems of discipline and morale that undermine the IDF's effectiveness. As expressed by Yehoshafat Harkabi, former Chief of Military Intelligence, "With difficulty a state can defend poor borders, of the kind we will have after withdrawing from the West Bank and Gaza. But it cannot defend itself if half the population is loyal to the enemy."[98] And again, according to Shlomo Avinieri, former Director General of the Foreign Ministry:

> Israel indeed can be defended within pre-1967 borders—the Six Day War proved that. What is much more difficult is to defend Israel from 1.5 million people living within the present territory. This is the paradox: the West Bank and Gaza do indeed pose security dilemmas for Israel—not when they are outside Israel's control, but when they are inside it.[99]

While available evidence suggests that such views are held by a clear majority of those in the military and strategic studies communities, there is nonetheless a small but noteworthy collection of IDF officers and specialists in strategic affairs who believe that it is in Israel's interest to retain control of the West Bank and Gaza. This group includes Ariel Sharon (former general and minister of defense, who resigned as minister of industry and commerce in the national unity cabinet in protest against proposals for

Palestinian elections, and was later appointed minister of housing in Shamir's new hard-line government), former Chief of Staff Rafael Eitan, and former Air Force chief Beni Peled. Sharon and Eitan were the architects of Israel's war against the PLO in Lebanon in 1982. Sharon is also a powerful figure within Likud and, as noted earlier, has vigorously denounced Yitzhak Rabin and the IDF for failing to use enough force to bring the *intifada* to a definitive end. Indeed, many who agree with Sharon about the occupied territories believe that talk about security has become more widespread primarily because Israel has been too timid to take the steps necessary to suppress the Palestinian uprising. In any event, military and other figures who judge the West Bank and Gaza to be necessary for the security of Israel assert that "it is impossible to concede the strategic and tactical depth which the territories provide, precisely because of the balance of forces and the development of military technology in the area."[100] In addition, they tend to view withdrawal from the occupied territories as appeasement rather than compromise and argue that concessions will only provoke more demands from the Arabs. Finally, many insist that an accommodation with the Palestinians can be reached on the basis of Likud's autonomy proposals. According to Beni Peled, "The Arabs in the territories are able to become loyal citizens if we just give them the chance and convince them that we have no intention of evacuating the territories."[101]

Though put forward with passion and conviction, this kind of thinking is apparently embraced by only a minority of those with important military and strategic studies connections. Counterarguments are made more persuasive by the *intifada* and also, according to one Israeli journalist, "the doves [supporters of territorial compromise] among senior officers have a great advantage in having concrete answers to their right-wing counterparts' claims."[102] Thus, as noted, polls show that a substantial majority of senior military officers believe that the risks of retaining the occupied territories are greater than the risks of withdrawal. Most also apparently disagree with the proposition of Sharon and Eitan which asserts that territorial compromise will be taken as a sign of weakness and will provoke the Arabs to demand additional concessions. On the contrary, planks in the platform of the Council for Peace and Security proclaim that "Our presence in the territories increases the Arabs' motivation for war against us," whereas territorial compromise will lead to a secure peace because "The Arabs honor agreements which they sign with us and therefore we can depend that they will also honor future agreements."

Conclusion

The *intifada* sends a powerful message about Palestinian demands and desires, and about the way that Palestinians will respond to a continuing abridgment of their right to self-determination. In response to this message,

Israelis are arguing about the costs and benefits of various policies toward the West Bank and Gaza and their Palestinian inhabitants. On the one hand, focusing on the short-term issue of containment, they are debating whether it is possible to suppress by force the Palestinian uprising. Questions of human rights are central to such debates, with some Israelis advocating an increase in the use of force and collective punishment and others insisting that such actions are politically damaging to the Jewish state and above all, whether effective or not, morally unacceptable. On the other hand, with the Green Line resurrected in the political consciousness of most Israelis, there are also debates about long-term issues pertaining to the final status of the West Bank and Gaza. Focusing on both political and security considerations, Israelis are arguing about the costs and benefits of territorial maximalism and territorial compromise and asking how their country's vital interests will be affected by policies associated with each of these competing orientations. The issues that arise in these debates and discussions are familiar ones in Israeli political discourse, predating the *intifada* by a decade or more. Nevertheless, they have acquired much greater urgency since December 1987.

Israelis of differing political and ideological orientations disagree about whether the *intifada* has done more to strengthen the right or the left, and a case can be made for each position. But available evidence suggests that much more substantial than the number of Israelis who have moved from one political camp to the other is the number who have had their pre-existing convictions strengthened, who believe that the current uprising shows the correctness of their basic views about the future of the West Bank and Gaza. So far as the final status of these territories is concerned, it is clear that while the *intifada* sends a message that is getting through to Israelis of all political persuasions, the content of that message, and the implications attached to it, differ radically among those who favor territorial maximalism and territorial compromise respectively. The results of the *intifada* thus include a deepening of existing ideological divisions and an increasing polarization of political opinion in Israel. The uprising has given ammunition to, and shaped the thinking of, both the political right and the political left. Moreover, it is likely that the difference between these two ideological camps will grow even wider in the future—a judgement that would seem to be supported by the collapse of the national unity government in March 1990.

Advocates of territorial maximalism see the uprising as part of a continuing Arab struggle to end the existence of the Jewish state, and this makes them less willing, not more willing, to consider withdrawal from the occupied territories. They also believe that control of the West Bank and Gaza enhances Israeli security and, judging future wars with neighboring Arab states to be likely, this reinforces their opposition to territorial concessions. With the *intifada* thus intensifying their determination that

Israel must retain the West Bank and Gaza, many advocates of territorial maximalism are concluding that they should not shy away from the implications of their political commitments. If the territories are to remain under Israeli control, and if the Palestinians who live in these territories are determined to resist occupation, then the Jewish state must face up to the need to remove a significant number of the Palestinian inhabitants of the occupied territories. Though radical and extreme, this is a program for dealing with territorial questions that, as a result of the *intifada*, has gained acceptance and legitimacy on the right side of the political spectrum.

Alternatively, supporters of territorial compromise see the uprising as an indication of the costs and burdens that Israel will have to bear if it insists on retaining the West Bank and Gaza, and they are accordingly more determined than ever to deflect their country from this disastrous course. In their view, retention of the territories threatens both Israeli democracy and the state's Jewish character, and it also poses serious risks to Israeli security from a purely military point of view. Thus, reflecting a symmetry between their response to the *intifada* and that of the political right, supporters of territorial compromise are accepting the logical implications of their commitments and, motivated by a growing sense of urgency, displaying an increased willingness to do whatever needs to be done to implement their program. For the left this means talking to the PLO, a policy which, like that of transfer, has moved from the political fringe into the realm of acceptable political discourse.

It follows from the preceding that the *intifada* has added an important measure of realism to the thinking of both the left and the right. More and more Israelis are seeing Palestinian political sentiments and the circumstances of occupation in a less distorted way. It is this realism that drives both advocates of territorial maximalism and supporters of territorial compromise to embrace prescriptions that were once marginal to political thinking in Israel. This is not to say transfer itself is realistic. Palestinian resistance, international pressure and the good sense of a majority of Israelis are likely to preclude any attempts to implement this policy, at least for the foreseeable future. But the policy is a response—and a logical one at that—to a much more realistic assessment of what it will take for Israel to hold on to the territories, and it stands in marked contrast to the political right's naive pre-*intifada* claims that most Palestinians welcomed Israeli rule and that occupation was cost-free to Israel. This realism is also evident on the left, where there is growing recognition that an accommodation can be reached only by talking to the Palestinians and to their chosen representatives, rather than to the foreign Arab leaders of Jordan or Egypt. This, as well as the notion that a solution will probably require the creation of a Palestinian state alongside Israel, are conditions for peace which have long been obvious to most of the international community but which even advocates of territorial compromise in Israel found it possible to dismiss before the *intifada* sent the message that this was totally unrealistic.

While outside observers should not look for any near-term resolution of the deep divisions in Israeli political life, several important developments that took place in the spring and summer of 1990 have the potential to introduce changes into Israeli debates about both the short-term issue of containment and the long-term issue of the future of the occupied territories. Moreover, while it is still too early to speak with confidence about the implications of these developments, they raise the possibility of increased Israeli public support for the retention of the West Bank and Gaza.

First, collapse of the national unity government in March 1990 led to the formation of a right-wing coalition and the replacement of Labor's Yitzhak Rabin by Likud's Moshe Arens as minister of defense. However, although many on the political right had called for the use of greater force to suppress the *intifada*, Arens has sought to deal with the uprising by pursuing the opposite strategy. He has sought to limit confrontations between the IDF and the Palestinian population of the territories. In addition, he has reduced some forms of collective punishment, permitting some colleges and universities to reopen, for example. Palestinians insist that these and other measures have not undermined the *intifada*, and it is indeed the case that life in the occupied territories remains far from normal. Also, IDF harassment of Palestinians remains widespread. On the other hand, fewer Palestinian deaths and fewer casualties being received by hospitals in the territories suggest that there is at least somewhat less of the violence and abuse that produced criticism of Rabin and the IDF during the first two years of the uprising. Welcome as this is, a reduction in the number of IDF confrontations with the Palestinians has the potential to make it more difficult for the Israeli left to argue that an important cost of territorial maximalism is the abridgement of those human rights to which the Jewish state claims commitment. Should the Israel indeed find a less violent way to carry forward its campaign against the *intifada*, the Israeli public might become less receptive to arguments about the high moral cost of retaining the West Bank and Gaza.

Second, Palestinian support for Iraqi president Saddam Husayn and his country's August 1990 invasion of Kuwait has had a number of important effects on political debates in Israel. The Israeli right believes that its analysis has been confirmed by events: in their judgment, the Palestinians have shown their true colors and indicated once again that they remain committed to the recovery of all Palestine. The Israeli left, by contrast, has been placed on the defensive. Some prominent advocates of territorial compromise admit feeling betrayed by Palestinian endorsement of an Arab leader who, in their view, presents himself as a modern-day Saladin and calls for the banishment of non-Arabs from the Middle East. Such sentiments have found expression, among other places, in an open letter published by Peace Now in the *Jerusalem Post*. Other advocates of territorial compromise point out, however, that Israel still has no choice but to seek an accommodation with the Palestinians if it wishes to achieve peace and avoid the high costs of occupation. Accordingly, they continue to advocate a dialogue with the PLO and recognition of Palestinian political rights. At the same time, they acknowledge that their arguments are now meeting resistance not only from the political right but also from some in Labor and parties of the left. More generally, receptivity to their views is—for the time being, at least—diminishing among the general public.

Even if it does turn out that these developments strengthen the position of those who advocate territorial maximalism, fundamental divisions will continue to characterize Israeli political life for the foreseeable future. Indeed, as reflected by the collapse of the national unity government and the narrowness of the coalition with which it was replaced, political polarization is, and is likely to remain, the most salient feature of Israeli political life. So far as the *intifada* is concerned, the uprising has succeeded in changing the way that most Israelis look at the occupied territories. It has not, however, turned out to be a catalyst for broad political realignment within the Jewish state. On the contrary, it has thus far reinforced and deepened existing political divisions—and, despite recent developments, this is likely to be its impact in the future as well.

Notes

1. For example, addressing a question that is central to the short term issue of containment, an April 1989 poll by the Dahaf Institute asked Israelis whether they were "for or against the use of greater force to suppress the uprising in the territories." Addressing the long-term issue, the same poll asked a different question about support or opposition to the principle of Israeli withdrawal from the occupied territories. *Yediot Aharonot*, 28 April, 1989. Polls conducted in 1988 similarly distinguished between short-term and long-term issues. This includes a poll conducted for *Newsweek* in January 1988 and reported in "Israel's War at Home," *Newsweek*, 25 January 1988; a Hanoch Smith Institute poll conducted in March and reported in *Davar*, 1 April 1988; and a Modi'im Ezrachi poll conducted in March and reported in *Ma'ariv*, 1 April 1988.

2. For discussion of Labor and Likud attitudes toward the West Bank and Gaza see Real Jean Isaac, *Party and Politics in Israel: Three Visions of a Jewish State* (New York: Longman, 1981); Ann Lesch and Mark Tessler, *Israel, Egypt and the Palestinians: From Camp David to Intifada* (Bloomington: Indiana University Press, 1989), pp. 140-173.

3. For a discussion of Rabin's statements during the early weeks of the *intifada*, see Mordechai Bar-On, "Israeli Reactions to the Palestinian Uprising," *Journal of Palestine Studies* 17, 4 (Summer 1988): 46-65, especially pp. 49-50. Bar-On, an Israeli Member of Knesset, notes that Rabin's statements about suppressing the *intifada* demonstrated that he failed to understand the utterly novel nature of the Palestinian uprising.

4. Between 9 December 1987 and 15 January, 1988, for example, Israeli security forces killed at least 37 Palestinians taking part in protest activities, more than half of whom were under the age of twenty. The name, age and cause of death of those killed are given in Ann Lesch, "Uprising for Palestine," *Journal of South Asian and Middle Eastern Studies* 11 (Summer 1988): 11-13. A summary of relevant information through

the summer of 1988 is also provided in Ronald R. Stockton, "*Intifada* Deaths," *Journal of Palestine Studies* 18, 2 (Winter 1989): 101-108.

5. Rabin's new policy was actually introduced on 4 January 1988 but was not made public until several weeks later. According to the *Jerusalem Post*, 26 January 1988, the defense minister stated that the use of force was necessary "to instill fear of the IDF [among Palestinians]."

6. According to one report, 34 Palestinians died in tear-gas related incidents between the beginning of the *intifada* and March 1988. Lesch, "Uprising for Palestine."

7. *al-Fajr* (weekly edition), 28 August 1988, p. 1. Stockton, "*Intifada* Deaths," gives somewhat lower figures, reporting that "at least 287 Palestinians had been killed by October 31, 1988." According to Israeli figures reported in *Yediot Aharonot*, 25 April 1988, over two hundred Palestinians were killed between December 1987 and April 1988.

8. For example, strong complaints about the policy were registered by the Association for Civil Rights in Israel (ACRI). *Jerusalem Post*, 30 September 1988.

9. *al-Fajr* (weekly) 12 June 1989, p. 1. Israeli sources give lower figures, indicating that 450-475 Palestinians had been killed by June 1989.

10. Many of these measures (such as curfews) constituted a form of collective puniushment that affected not only protesters but also men, women and children who had not taken part in protest activities: the 55,000 residents of Jabaliyya refugee camp in Gaza, for example, spent about 200 days under curfew between the beginning of the *intifada* and June 1989. *New York Times*, 24 June 1989. On deportation, see Judith Gabriel, "Israel's Policy of Deportation," *The Return* 1, 3 (October 1988): 6-10, 30. The US State Department estimated that 154 houses were demolished during the first year of the uprising;*Country Reports on Human Rights Practices for 1988: Report Submitted to the Committee on Foreign Relations of the US Senate and the Committee on Foreign Affairs of the US House of Representatives* (Washington, D.C.: US Department of State, February 1989). Palestinian sources put the figures as high as 550 houses; Judith Gabriel, "Israel's Use of House Demolitions: Collective Punishment on the Rise," *The Return* 1, 11 (July 1989): 16-19.

11. *Jerusalem Post*, 8 September 1988.

12. *Jerusalem Post*, 5 October 1988.

13. *Jerusalem Post*, 6 January 1988.

14. See, for example, Asher Wallfish, "Shomron: *Intifada* can't be eradicated," *Jerusalem Post*, 11 January 1989. Similarly, Colonel Nehemia Dayan, chief education office of the IDF, was quoted in a *Voice of Jerusalem* newscast on 10 April 1988 to the effect that "the defense forces cannot handle the root of the matter [in the occupied territories], since the Israeli-Palestinian conflict requires a political, not a military, solution." A comparison between the *intifada* and the anti-colonial nationalist struggles in Algeria and other countries was also made by Israeli scholar Emmanuel Sivan; "Israel's Decolonization Crisis," *New Outlook* (December 1989): 16-19.

15. *Jerusalem Post*, 29 February 1988.

16. *Jerusalem Post*, 22, 29 February 1988; 12 January 1989. During the latter speech, Rabin also expressed his belief in the eventual creation alongside Israel of a Jordanian-Palestinian state.

17. Aaron Hart, "The Unrest that Makes Peace More Remote," *Jerusalem Post*, 28 January 1988. Aaron Hart is a pen-name.

18. *Jerusalem Post*, 16 February 1988.

19. Quoted in Joel Brinkley, "Israeli Defense Chief Sees Failure in Quelling Uprising," *New York Times*, 5 December 1989.

20. All figures are quoted in *New York Times*, 5 December 1989, which notes that 45 Israelis had also lost their lives as a result of the *intifada*. Palestinian sources again put the number of deaths higher. According to *al-Fajr* (weekly), 13 November 1989, 716

Palestinians had been killed by Israelis since the beginning of the uprising. See also Anita Vitullo, "A Third Year of Death and Living in Slow Motion," *Washington Report on Middle East Affairs* 8 (December 1989): 5.

21. *New York Times*, 5 December 1989.

22. Some information is provided by Arye Avneri, "The *Intifada*: The Economic Aspect," *Yediot Aharonot*, 13 May, 1988; Shlomo Maoz, "Paying for It: The Economic Costs of the Uprising for Palestinians and Israelis," *Jerusalem Post*, 10 June 1988, pp. 5 and 20; Greer Fay Cashman, "Tourism Sector in Worst Crisis Ever," *Jerusalem Post*, 24 January 1989; and Nabil Kukali, "The Impact of the *Intifada* on Israel's Economy," *The Return*, 2, 2 (October 1989): 20-24. See also *New York Times*, 13 February 1989.

23. See, for example, Sharon's statements in the *Jerusalem Post*, 29 February 1988.

24. *Jerusalem Post*, 22 August 1988. For a discussion of the tactics Sharon would employ to suppress the *intifada*, unrelated to the 1988 election campaign, see Uri Milstein, "Sharon's Iron Fist," *Hadashot*, 25 March 1988.

25. *Jerusalem Post*, 21 August 1988. In the same statement, Cohen also complained about the Association for Civil Rights in Israel, which opposes the deportation of Palestinians. She called ACRI "a racist political organization working mainly for Arabs' rights under the guise of working for civil rights in general."

26. Shubert Spero, "Losing the '*Intifada*' Game," *Jerusalem Post*, 24 January 1989.

27. *Jerusalem Post*, 11 September 1988.

28. *Jerusalem Post*, 5 September 1988.

29. *Jerusalem Post*, 24 February 1988. Eban made his comments at a conference held at the Jerusalem YMCA. Asked during questions whether Rabin should resign, Eban replied that "If I were going to ask him to resign, I would not say it in the YMCA. But there must be a change in policy and rhetoric."

30. *Jerusalem Post*, 11, 15 February 1988.

31. *Jerusalem Post*, 27 January, 23 Februaray 1988.

32. *Jerusalem Post*, 17 October 1988.

33. Asher Wallfish, "The Perils of Talking to the Troops," *Jerusalem Post*, 23 January 1988; Ami Dar, "Shooting and Defecating," *Jerusalem Post*, 21 February 1989. Earlier expressions of such views by reservists include Ronit Mitlon, "The Wild West: A Reservist's Monologue," *Ha'Aretz* (weekly supplement), 11 March 1988; and Dan Sagir, "This Isn't the Way to Suppress the Uprising," *Ha'Aretz*, 26 August 1988.

34. *Jerusalem Post*, 16 February 1988.

35. Yehuda Meltzer, "Mitzna As A Parable," *Hadashot*, 8 June 1989.

36. *Jerusalem Post*, 6 September 1988.

37. *Jerusalem Post*, 28, 30 September 1988.

38. Tom Segev, "The Comparison," *Ha'Aretz*, 5 May 1989.

39. *Ha'Aretz*, 5 May 1989.

40. The poll was conducted by the Dahaf Institute late in April and reported in *Yediot Aharonot*, 28 April 1989.

41. For an introduction to these "demographic" issues, see Mark Tessler, "Thinking about Territorial Compromise in Israel," *Journal of South Asian and Middle Eastern Studies* 11 (Summer 1988): 38-53. See also Lesch and Tessler, *Israel, Egypt and the Palestinians*, pp. 272-284.

42. See Ann Lesch and Mark Tessler, "The West Bank and Gaza: Political and Ideological Responses to Occupation," *Muslim World* (July/October 1987): 229-249.

43. The intellectual foundations of the Village League policy were provided by Israeli scholar Menachem Milson; see his "How to Make Peace with the Palestinians," *Commentary* (May 1981), and "The Palestinians in the Peace Process," *Forum* 42/43 (1981). For fuller discussion of the Village League program, see Howard M. Sachar, *A History of Israel: From the Aftermath of the Yom Kippur War* (New York: Oxford

University Press, 1987), p. 160; and Lesch and Tessler, *Israel, Egypt and the Palestinians*, pp. 243-244. Israeli support for the Village Leagues was withdrawn during the latter part of 1983, with the Defense Ministry's coordinator for the occupied territories acknowledging that the policy had attracted only "quislings." The Federation of Village Leagues was formally disbanded in March 1984. *Ha'Aretz*, 12 March 1984.

44. The survey was sponsored by *al-Fajr*, *Newsday* and the Australian Broadcasting Corporation; see Mohammed Shadid and Rick Seltzer, "Political Attitudes of Palestinians in the West Bank and Gaza Strip," *Middle East Journal* 42, 1 (Winter 1987): 16-32.

45. Uri Avnery, "The *Intifada*: Substance and Illusion," *New Outlook* (December 1989), p. 13. Similar sentiments were expressed several months after the beginning of the *intifada* by Ze'ev Schiff, one of Israel's leading military commentators. See Ze'ev Schiff, *Security for Peace: Israel's Minimal Security Requirements in Negotiations with the Palestinians* (Washington, D.C.: The Washington Institute for Near East Policy, 1989), pp. 14-15. Schiff writes that "for a number of years, some Israeli policy-makers viewed the territories as though they were unpopulated. They viewed local Palestinians as either lacking political aspirations or lacking any desire to fulfill them.... The possibility that they might one day rebel against Israeli rule was completely discounted."

46. Victor Cygielman, "The Impact of Two Years of the *Intifada*," *New Outlook* (December 1989), p. 5.

47. *Jerusalem Post*, 11 September 1988.

48. Cygielman, "The Impact of Two Years of the *Intifada*."

49. *Jerusalem Post*, 8 February 1988; Neri Livneh, "Border of Fear," *Hadashot*, 29 September 1989.

50. *Hadashot*, 29 September 1989.

51. Findings are summarized in the *Jerusalem Post*, 30 August, 1 September 1988.

52. Such sentiments were expressed to the author in many conversations held during his four visits to Israel since the beginning of the *intifada*. So far as politicians on the political right are concerned, an example of this thinking is a January 1989 speech by Prime Minister Shamir to a convention of the Israel Hotel Association, meeting in Jerusalem. As on other occasions, Shamir stated that the Arabs want what they have always wanted: destruction of the State of Israel. See *Jerusalem Post*, 26 January 1989.

53. The program, attended by the author, took place on 6 June 1988. It was attended by more than one hundred Israelis and Palestinians.

54. For several years prior to the *intifada*, a few declarations and statements by personalities of the extreme right had sought, largely without success, to give legitimacy to the notion of transfer and to initiate a national debate on the subject. See Shabtai Teveth, "The Evolution of 'Transfer' in Zionist Thinking," *Occasional Papers of the Dayan Center for Middle Eastern and African Studies*, 107 (May 1989); Israel Eldad, "Transfer as a 'Zionist' Solution," *Ha'Aretz*, 9 July 1987; and Avishai Erlich, "Is Transfer an Option?" *Israeli Democracy* 1 (Winter 1987): 36-38.

55. Rehavam Ze'evi, the founder of Moledet and author of its platform, spelled out his views in *Ha'Aretz*, 17 August 1988. For a general account of the 1988 elections, see Don Peretz and Sammy Smooha, "Israel's Twelfth Knesset Election: An All-Loser Game," *The Middle East Journal* 43, 3 (Summer 1989): 388-405.

56. Dr. Baruch Goldstein; quoted in *The Report of the American-Israeli Civil Liberties Coalition*, 9 (Summer 1989), p. 1.

57. Yitzhak Shilat, "The Fear of Employing Force Stems from Moral Weakness," *Nekuda*, March 1988.

58. *Jerusalem Post*, 12 August 1988.

59. *Jerusalem Post*, 10 January 1988.

60. Gad Ya'acobi, "A Path out of the Bunker," *Jerusalem Post*, 15 January 1989.

61. Arye Naor, *Ktovet Al Hakir* [Writing on the Wall] (Tel Aviv: Idanim, 1988).

62. Yehoshafat Harkabi, *Hahlatot Goraliot* [Fateful Decisions] (Tel Aviv: Am Oved, 1986); published in English as *Israel's Fateful Hour* (New York: Harper & Row, 1988). See also Yehoshafat Harkabi, "A Policy for the Moment of Truth," *Jerusalem Post*, 13 February 1988.

63. *Jerusalem Post*, 12 August 1988.

64. *New York Times*, 2 April 1989.

65. Avnery, "The *Intifada*: Substance and Illusion."

66. *Jerusalem Post*, 28 January 1988.

67. Yael Dayan, "Viewpoint," *Jerusalem Post*, 17 October 1988. Dayan, daughter of the late Moshe Dayan, is a Member of Knesset from the Labor Party.

68. Ya'acobi, "A Path out of the Bunker."

69. Interview published in *Davar*, 29 September 1989. See also Schiff, *Security for Peace*, pp. 1, 3-4. According to Schiff, the *intifada* "removed any lingering suspicions that the Palestinians could be sidestepped in the search for an Arab-Israeli settlement. It has led to the unavoidable conclusion that there can be no end to the Arab-Israeli conflict without a resolution of the conflict between Israel and the Palestinians."

70. For a useful discussion, see Schiff, *Security for Peace*, pp. 1-3. According to Schiff, "the Palestinian uprising against Israel has shattered a static situation that Israel has consistently sought to preserve... Because of the *intifada*, the possibility of Israeli-Palestinian negotiations is immeasurably closer than it was before December 9, 1987, the day the uprising began. The uprising, after all, has opened a new chapter in the political relationship between Israelis and Palestinians." Schiff also credits PLO initiatives in late 1988 with creating a new opportunity for Israel-Palestinian negotiations; but he states as well that "it was only as a direct result of the uprising that the Palestine National Council met in Algiers in November 1988, to adopt resolutions reversing a more than 40-year-old rejection of UN resolution 181. This resolution calls for the establishment of two states—one Jewish, one Arab—on land west of the Jordan River. And it was only as a result of the uprising that PLO chairman Yasir Arafat, at a press conference in Geneva, formally renounced terrorism and extended virtual recognition to the state of Israel." For similar conclusions by a Palestinian scholar, see Philip Mattar, "The Critical Moment for Peace," *Foreign Policy* 76 (Fall 1989): 141-159. Mattar reviews PLO diplomatic moves during the fall of 1988 but makes the point that, "Unquestionably, the *intifada*, or uprising, in the West Bank and Gaza is responsible for the new situation."

71. *New York Times*, 2 April 1989. This article also discusses earlier polls.

72. *Yediot Aharonot*, 28 April 1989.

73. *Jerusalem Post*, 14 September 1988. There are even some indications that moderate Jewish settlers, such as those in Gush Etzion, are beginning to talk about negotiations with the PLO. See Dan Margalit, "The Settlers—Confusion Sets In," *Ha'Aretz*, 12 May 1988.

74. *Hadashot*, 28 April 1989; "A Two-State Solution is the Only Way Out: An Interview with Shulamit Aloni," *al-Fajr*, 12 June 1989.

75. See Edy Kaufman, "The Intifadah and the Peace Camp in Israel," *Journal of Palestine Studies* 17, 4 (Summer 1988): 66-80, especially pp. 79-80. See also Bar-On, "Israeli Reactions to the Palestinian Uprising," p. 54. Both Kaufman and Bar-On are active in the Israeli peace movement.

76. See Aryeh Dayan, "PLO Now," *Kol Ha'ir*, 25 November 1988.

77. An account of the January meeting appears in M. Zlotowski, "MKs, PLO Nearly Together," *Jerusalem Post*, 15 January 1989. At the time, Labor chairman, Haim Ramon also stated publicly that the time had come to amend the law prohibiting meetings with PLO representatives. Another meeting took place several weeks later, when seven Israelis, including politicians and academics, traveled to the Netherlands to participate in a conference with PLO representatives and other Palestinians. One of the Israelis was Abba

Eban, veteran Labor politician and former foreign minister (1966-74). Again, because of Israeli law, the Israelis did not talk directly to the PLO members. Nevertheless, Eban stated that "Israel should accept the PLO for talks." *New York Times*, 3 February 1989.

78. *New York Times*, 9 March 1989.

79. Quoted in *New York Times*, 13 July 1989. For additional discussion, see Mark Heller, "The Middle East: Out of Step with History," *Foreign Affairs* 69 (1990), p. 157.

80. Quoted in Ron Ben-Yishai, "What do the Generals Think about Territorial Compromise," *Yediot Aharonot* (supplement) 10 June 1988, pp. 6-7.

81. The exchange is quoted in the *Jerusalem Post*, 9 September 1988.

82. For example, see Yuval Ne'eman, "A Foundation for Israel's Security," *Ma'ariv*, 10 April 1981. The most detailed study of the military significance of the West Bank is by Brigadier General (res.) Aryeh Shalev, *The West Bank: Line of Defense* (New York: Praeger, 1985). Although this balanced account is frequently cited by those who believe that military considerations require retention of the occupied territories, Shalev himself advocates territorial compromise. See also Aharon Yariv, "Strategic Depth," *Jerusalem Quarterly* 17 (Fall 1980); and, more recently, Schiff, *Security for Peace*, pp. 36-41.

83. Mark Heller, *A Palestinian State: Implications for Israel* (Cambridge: Harvard University Press, 1983), p. 147-148. Similar arguments are advanced by Ze'ev Schiff (the military affairs editor of *Ha'Aretz*) and Ehud Ya'ari (the Middle East correspondent for Israel Television), who have outlined the security arrangements that should accompany an Israeli withdrawal from the West Bank and Gaza and the establishment there of a Palestinian political entity. See Ze'ev Schiff and Ehud Ya'ari, *Intifada: The Palestinian Uprising—Israel's Third Front* (New York: Simon and Schuster, 1990), pp. 331-337; see also, Schiff, *Security for Peace*.

84. Abba Eban, "Israel: Hardly the Monaco of the Middle East," *New York Times*, 2 January 1989. The quotation cited by Eban is from an article in *New York Post* by Norman Podhoretz, a prominent American supporter of Israel.

85. The statements are reprinted in an article entitled "Machiavellian Doves," in the *Newsletter of Peace Now*, 4, 1 (Summer 1988): 5. Some of these individuals were interviewed by Peace Now. Other statements are taken from the Israeli and international press.

86. *Jerusalem Post*, 25 October 1988. The initiative for formation of the Council was taken by General (res.) Aharon Yariv of the Institute for Strategic Studies at Tel Aviv University. For a discussion of the Council, including the April 1988 press conference at which its establishment was announced, see Bar-On, "Israeli Reactions to the Palestinian Uprising," p. 58. See also *Yediot Aharonot* (supplement) 10 June 1988; "Generals Dismiss the Security Value of the West Bank," *Ha'Aretz*, 31 May 1988.

87. Cited in "Machiavellian Doves."

88. *Yediot Aharonot* (supplement) 10 June 1988.

89. *Yediot Aharonot* (supplement) 10 June 1988.

90. Quoted in Dore Gold, "The Generals and the Areas," *Jerusalem Post*, 10 June 1988.

91. Quoted in "Machiavellian Doves."

92. *Jerusalem Post*, 25 October 1988.

93. *Yediot Aharonot* (supplement) 10 June 1988.

94. *Yediot Aharonot* (supplement) 10 June 1988.

95. Ronit Matalon, "Without a Norm," *Ha'Aretz* (supplement), 19 February 1988. See also Bar-On, "Israeli Reactions to the Palestinian Uprising," pp. 51- 52; and Ayala Pines, "Israeli Burnout and the *Intifada*," *New Outlook*, December 1989, pp. 35-36.

96. *Hadashot*, 18 March 1989; Shlomo Slutsky, "They Don't Believe the IDF Spokesman," *Hadashot*, 18 March 1989.

97. Roli Rozen, "The Era of Conventional Wars Has Come to an End, and the Future

Battlefield is the *Intifada*," *Ha'Aretz* (weekend supplement), 12 May 1989.

98. Quoted in "Machiavellian Doves."

99. Quoted in "Machiavellian Doves." For a fuller discussion, see Schiff, *Security for Peace*, pp. 14-17. Schiff writes that "As a result [of the *intifada*], for the first time since 1967 many Israeli strategists have reoriented their approach to West Bank and Gaza security concerns. Israel has learned that the strategic importance of the area is not only a function of territorial depth, but also of the activities of the populace. The uprising has taught Israel that ruling the West Bank and Gaza does not automatically provide greater security to the rulers. What was once considered a security belt may now be a security burden. Israel has learned that one nation, particularly a small one, cannot rule another nation for long; that 3.5 million Israelis cannot keep 1.5 million Palestinians under perpetual curfew" (p. 15).

100. *Yediot Aharonot* (supplement) 10 June 1988.

101. *Yediot Aharonot* (supplement) 10 June 1988.

102. *Yediot Aharonot* (supplement) 10 June 1988.

4

Palestinians in Israel: Responses to the Uprising

Nadim Rouhana

The Palestinian uprising in the occupied territories and the political program adopted in its wake by the Palestine Liberation Organization both have direct bearing on the political future of the Palestinians in Israel. To date, both Israelis and Palestinians have tended to view the Palestinians in Israel as a marginal segments of their respective societies. Neither has shaped any serious vision of their future relationship to this group. But for Palestinians in Israel, the nature of their relationship to both Israel and the Palestinian people touches on the essence of their political future and collective identity. The new circumstances generated by the *intifada* have forced them to think out their relationships with both the Jewish state and the Palestinian people.

Both the Palestinians and Israelis have shown considerable misunderstanding of the way the Arabs in Israel have reacted to and dealt with the uprising. While the Palestinian response has been colored with romanticism, the Israeli public has displayed fundamental shortcomings in comprehending the political behavior of their Arab compatriots. This chapter will examine, and seek to explain, the influence of the uprising on Arab political beliefs and thinking, and the relative extent of their sentimental identification with, and behavioral involvement in, the *intifada*. It will also survey Israeli Jewish perceptions of the response of Arabs in Israel. Finally, the differential involvement of the Palestinians in Israel and the occupied territories in the Israeli system—proposed as the basis for understanding the former's political response to the uprising—will be used to delineate the limits of their potential involvement should the *intifada* continue for a prolonged time.

Responses to the Uprising

Even prior to the uprising, the Arab citizens of Israel had settled on a political consensus that had three main elements: first, a demand for full equality as citizens of Israel; second, unequivocal support for the establishment of a Palestinian state in the West Bank and Gaza led by the Palestine Liberation Organization; and third, agreement that all forms of political activity be conducted within the limits allowed by Israeli law.[1] After the uprising, support for this consensus broadened to include—in addition to the supporters of the Democratic Front for Peace and Equality (DFPE) led by the Israeli Communist Party, the Progressive List for Peace (PLP), and the Arab Democratic Party (ADP)[2]—many of the Arabs who vote for (and represent) Zionist parties, and those who fall to the left of the DFPE. This tripartite consensus forms the core of the present Arab political platform in Israel, although the various parties and factions are still distinguished by different emphases and priorities.[3]

The uprising and the ensuing political program adopted by the PLO at the 19th session of the Palestine National Council in November 1988 consolidated all three elements of this consensus. Arabs in Israel had expressed overwhelming support for a Palestinian state in the occupied territories long before the uprising, a fact frequently documented by social researchers.[4] Agreement on this element of the consensus was achieved, to a large extent, due to the consistent and unrelenting political program of the DFPE, which has emphasized the need to establish a Palestinian state in the occupied territories next to Israel as the core of its political program since the mid-1970s. Although there was some public discussion of that issue, Arabs in Israel have never openly debated the desirability of different options for their collective future, or whether the two-state solution best addresses their aspirations. In the limited discussions that did take place, Rakah (the Israeli Communist Party), unmatched by others, outweighed all opponents. The more the PLO leaned towards a two-state solution, directly or indirectly, the more Rakah's position—a mainstay since the mid-1970's—garnered popular support.

The PLO's explicit endorsement of a two-state solution in November 1988 fortified this element of consensus throughout the political spectrum, and disarmed the minority that had argued for a secular state in all Palestine. All significant segments of the political spectrum in the Arab community now openly support the Palestinian program of a two-state solution, albeit for different reasons.[5] By recognizing Israel, declaring a Palestinian state in the West Bank and Gaza, and foreclosing on the option of a democratic secular state as a political program, the PLO leadership had sent the Arabs in Israel a message of profound importance: that they would remain under Israeli control as citizens of Israel if any permanent political settlement were achieved. Their political status is not on the agenda of any possible negotiations between Israel and the Palestinians. Therefore, achieving equality with Israeli-Jewish citizens—the second element of the consensus—has now taken on a strategic meaning. If the shape of the final settlement is to be two states, equality is indispensable and urgent for the Arab's political future in Israel. This element of the consensus is now being given higher priority by all Arab political factions, grassroots organizations, and the Arab public at large.

As for the agreement that all forms of political activity be conducted within the limits allowed by Israeli law, this is not new for the Arabs in Israel, even if it previously went unannounced. Whether out of complete conviction in that position—as is the case for the DFPE—or out of acceptance of the reality of absolute Jewish control, the outcome was the same: no political faction supports, directly or indirectly, any form of illegal collective or individual action. But prior to the *intifada*, the Arabs were not often faced with situations that required taking a public stance on this issue.[6] On the infrequent occasions when a Palestinian from Israel was involved in a "security violation," the formal, public reaction from the Arab leadership was condemnatory.[7] If some individuals believed otherwise, they kept their views to themselves.

Once the uprising was underway in the territories, the issue of avoiding illegal activity had to be openly addressed by the Arab community. When some incidents of stone-throwing or tire-burning were reported during a national strike in support of the uprising on 21 December 1987, Arab political groups unanimously condemned the incidents. Great pressure was exerted on the Arab leadership by the Jewish public and the authorities to assure that open violence would not ensue; thus, although the Arab leadership believed this danger was nonexistent in any case, they repeatedly stated publicly that only pre-defined "peaceful" activities would be allowed during demonstrations or strikes. The calculated effort that all Arab factions exerted to communicate this element of the consensus made it explicit and indisputable. Moreover, through various channels, the Palestinian leadership in the occupied territories and the PLO both demonstrated an awareness of what they called the "special circumstances" and constraints of the Arabs in Israel, which lent this third element further legitimacy.

Sentimental Identification

The reaction of Arabs in Israel to the *intifada* can for the most part be described as one of *sentimental identification*: that is to say, expressions of solidarity with the uprising, including forms of expression such as the arts and literature. In contrast, *behavioral involvement*—defined to include overt and publicly observable organized manifestations, such as material support or organized political behavior—has been much more limited.

Identification with the uprising is reflected across the Arab political spectrum. It encompasses the broadest segments of Arab society, even extending to some sectors of the Druze and Bedouin communities[8]—most of whom do not identify themselves as Palestinian. A survey of the only Arabic daily in Israel, *al-Ittihad,* shows that from the outbreak of the uprising in December 1987 to mid-September 1989 (the end of the survey) the paper reported in a detailed and systematic manner on the events in the occupied territories.[9] Except in the rare case of unusual events among the Arabs in Israel,[10] news of the uprising monopolized the headline; at the least, it was always on the front page. A special reporter—the only assigned reporter—was sent to cover the Palestinians and the behavior of the Israeli army in the territories; almost daily, a picture of a Palestinian and the "heroic story of his or her martyrdom" appeared. The terminology of the articles—"heroism," "martyrdom," "massacres of occupation," "soldiers of occupation," and so forth—was virtually indistinguishable from that used in the occupied territories. Analysts and reporters made clear their solidarity with, pride in, and sympathy and support for the people in the territories, and did not hide their rage over the behavior of Israeli military. The paper emphasized news of solidarity with the Palestinians, international criticism of Israel, and signs of restlessness in various sectors of Israeli society. Editorials frequently discussed the inevitability of Palestinian victory, and the paper began using terms such as "occupied state of Palestine," "President of the State of Palestine," and "the flag of the state of Palestine" almost consistently after the declaration of independence by the PNC.

The paper also provided a stage for Palestinians from the occupied territories to express their views. Many letters written by Palestinian prisoners have been smuggled out (particularly from the Ansar III detention camp) and published in *al-Ittihad*. Reports prepared by Palestinians from the territories on the prevailing conditions there also appear often. The paper has run a weekly column by a Palestinian journalist from the West Bank. Given the censorship on Palestinian journalism in the territories, *al-Ittihad* has provided an alternative outlet for news and expression.[11]

In addition to news items, an abundance of uprising-centered literature has appeared in the paper, written by Palestinians from Israel, the occupied territories and the diaspora. Short stories, poetry, and folk songs are published on a weekly basis in the literature sections—praising the courage of the "children of the stones," portraying the suffering of the people, denouncing the cruelty of the military, describing the savagery of the occupation, promising victory, and admiring the spirit of the people.

The sentimental identification discussed herein is matched by other manifestations in Palestinian society in Israel. Arab cultural, social, and political discourse has to some extent become dominated by the sentiments of the uprising. For example, the *intifada* dominates social discussions. In contrast to mainstream Jewish society (which copes with the uprising by trying to deny it in various ways), Arabs talk about it, follow its news, circulate stories, read its literature, sing its songs, recite its poetry, and learn its folklore. While people have done this spontaneously, organizations have also followed suit, a trend best reflected in the conference on the folklore of the uprising held in Nazareth in the summer of 1989.

Such sentimental identification, however, should be placed in its proper context. On the one hand, it could be seen as representing more than mere support; to some extent, it reflects psychological participation that requires psychic energy to cope with the never-ending flow of information about the daily suffering of the Palestinians in the territories and evolving political developments. Yet, as profound as it might be, sentimental identification has not been strong enough to disrupt the course of daily life among the Palestinians in Israel. Their political, social, and economic life continues, largely unchanged by the uprising or by their sentimental identification with it. Social occasions for celebration, for example, remain undisturbed by their feelings for the uprising. In contrast to Palestinians in the territories (who have drastically curtailed their wedding and other ceremonies), Palestinians in Israel still host enormous weddings, a focus of the social milieu, whose receptions, banquets, parties, and bands grow ever more elaborate and complex. This is only one of many indications that the sentimental identification with the uprising is not being followed through behaviorally.

Behavioral Involvement

The Arabs in Israel and their leadership—represented in the Follow-up Committee on the Concerns of Arab Citizens (FCCAC)[12]—were among the first Palestinian communities to respond to the uprising. They did so in two main ways: material assistance was sent to the territories, and a number of demonstrations and strikes were organized to show support. During the first weeks of the uprising, local committees were organized in many Arab towns and villages to collect material support such as money, food, medication, and clothes. The shipments were sent to Gaza and the West Bank, sometimes through the facilitation of UN agencies. While the FCCAC often supported and encouraged the effort, it was actually initiated by local activists from all political affiliations.

The flow of support to the territories has continued since the beginning of the uprising, although it has fluctuated. The real value of the support, and the amount of aid, is arguably modest.[13] Among sixty Arab leaders interviewed by the author, all but a few (representing Likud and, to a lesser extent, Labor) agreed that the absolute value of the support is minimal, and it falls below what the Arabs could and should be offering.[14]

Organized public protest against Israel practices in the territories and solidarity with the uprising began within two weeks of the eruption of the *intifada*. A one-day national strike was declared on 21 December 1987. The strike was held to show support for the efforts of the Palestinians to free themselves of the occupation, and to protest Israeli measures taken against the population. Its political message was unequivocally clear: support for an independent Palestinian state in the occupied territories, living in peace with

Israel. The strike was met by surprise in Israeli society, and indeed rage from some, who issued veiled threats against the Arab leadership.[15] Nonetheless, the Arab leadership, in a show of unity, led one of the largest national demonstrations ever organized in Nazareth on 23 January 1988. It was followed by another national strike on Land Day (March 30) in 1988.

Based on the survey of *al-Ittihad*, during the first eighteen months of the uprising Arabs in Israel held thirty-five national, regional, and local strikes and demonstrations in support of the *intifada*. Most of these were organized locally (rather than regionally or nationally) by either the DFPE or, to a lesser extent, the PLP. A list of the major (defined as taking place in a city or in more than one town) mass political activities during this period is presented in Table 4.1. From it, one can see that through mid-1988 internal issues began to eclipse the *intifada* as the focus of protests. Whereas nine major events of solidarity, two related to internal issues and one related to both were organized during the first nine months of the uprising, in the following nine months only three events were concerned the uprising, while four were related to internal issues (and one event to both).

Table 4.1
Major Palestinian Mass Political Activities, December 1987-June 1989

Date	Place	Organizer	Activity	Issue/Slogan	Participants
19/12/87	Nazareth, Umm al-Fahm	FCCAC	demonstration	pre-Peace Day in support of uprising; *intifada*-related slogans	10,000 in Nazareth; thousands in Umm al-Fahm
21/12/87	national	FCCAC	strike ("Peace Day")	in support of uprising; against govt. policy; *intifada*-related slogans	majority of Arab population
23/01/88	Nazareth	FCCAC	demonstration	in support of uprising; against govt. policy; *intifada*-related slogans	10,000
13/02/88	Haifa	FCCAC	demonstration	in support of PLO's "Ship of Return" and the *intifada*	5,000
28/02/88	Shafa 'Amr	DFPE	demonstration	in support of uprising; protesting Shultz visit	1,000+
18/03/88	Nazareth	local Rakah youth	demonstration	commemorating 100 days of uprising; in support of planned strike for March 30	about 5,000
25/03/88	Nazareth	Rakah	demonstration	against closure of *al-Ittihad*; slogans on "free press"	thousands
30/03/88	national	FCCAC	strike and four regional gatherings	Land day and *intifada*; slogans on uprising and equality	strike observed by majority; 10,000 at gatherings
18/07/88	Jerusalem	Committee of Local Arab Councils	demonstration	protest policy of demolition of homes of Arab citizens; for equality in municipal budgets	tens of representatives of local councils

Date	Place	Organizer	Activity	Issue/Slogan	Participants
20/08/88	Umm al-Fahm	local committee in support of uprising	demonstration	protest govt. policy in the territories; support for uprising and independent Palestinian state	thousands
14/09/88	Nazareth and Majd al-Kurum	DFPE	demonstration	support for uprising; against govt. policy in the territories; *intifada*-related slogans	thousands
15/11/88	national	FCCAC	strike	demolition of 15 homes in Tayiba; slogans on uprising and equality	majority of Arab population
09/12/88	Kafr Yasif, Sakhnin, Tayiba, Nazareth	DFPE	demonstration	commemorate first anniversary of uprising; slogans on equality and *intifada*	thousands
13/12/88	Jerusalem (Knesset)	FCCAC	demonstration	demolition of homes; slogans against demolition and for equality	hundreds
24/03/89	Majd al-Kurum, Acre region	DFPE	demonstration	*intifada*-related slogans	thousands
30/03/89	national	FCCAC	strike and four regional gatherings	Land Day and *intifada*; slogans on uprising and equality	strike observed by majority of Arab population; thousands at each gathering
19/05/89	Nazareth	Nazareth municipality	demonstration	protest of police action against local football team	thousands
10/06/89	Sakhnin, Shafa 'Amr, Umm al-Fahm, Tayiba, Rahat	FCCAC	strike and demonstrations	decrying "national Israeli mood of hostility and racism;" slogans on equality and *intifada*	strike observed by majority of Arab population; thousands at each demonstration

In keeping with the third element of the national consensus, organizers always obtained prior approval from the Israeli authorities for the strikes and demonstrations. Except for a few incidents in four localities during the first strike in December, there were no disorderly incidents in more than 120 cities, towns, and villages. Indeed, some Arab observers argued that one of the leadership's goals for the strike in March 1988 was to show the Israeli authorities that the Arabs are law-abiding citizens, and that the incidents in December were an exception, not the rule. It has not always been easy to accomplish this goal: as will be shown later in this chapter, Israeli Jews have shown considerable misunderstanding of the way Arabs in Israel have responded to the uprising.

Palestinians in Israel and the Israeli Political System

The preceding survey has suggested that while the sentimental identification of Arabs in Israel with the uprising is profound and manifested in numerous ways, their behavioral involvement has been limited in scope and frequency. It includes a few organized strikes, demonstrations and assemblies, some donations and other material support. It does not include the activities that have become the hallmark of the uprising in the territories. Interviews with leaders representing all political parties and factions indicate that, on the whole, Palestinians in Israel are convinced that they can do much more within the limits of Israeli law. Interviews also show that even in the case of increased future support, their behavioral involvement in the uprising will be limited to showing solidarity and increasing material support, but not participating or joining it. Their pattern of response to the uprising—profound sentimental identification and limited behavioral support—is inextricably related to their political status as Palestinian nationals, and Israeli citizens. Their status within the Israeli system and their involvement in it is totally different than that of the Palestinians in the occupied territories. Those differences are the critical factor in explaining their dual reaction to the uprising.

Differential Status: Citizenship and Occupation

The status of Palestinians in Israel as theoretically equal citizens before the law has neither been challenged nor resisted by the Arabs themselves or by the Jewish majority since 1948. They are involved in the Israeli system to a considerable degree: they participate in Israeli politics; they use legitimate political means to achieve collective gains; they vote and get elected to the Israeli Knesset; they are full members in the Histadrut (the Israeli workers' union); they receive their social services from the Israeli authorities. They have been educated in the Israeli education system (in separate Arab schools) and attend Israeli universities; they are completely conversant in Hebrew; they know intricacies of the Israeli political system, and feel more or less comfortable maneuvering within it.

Indeed, although Arabs in Israel charge the government with a deliberate policy of discrimination, and though they may oppose the exclusive ideology of the state and not identify with its goals, they nonetheless see themselves as citizens of Israel. They have not resisted that status, nor have they challenged Israel's sovereignty. This does not mean that Arabs grant legitimacy to the Zionist claim of having the moral right to establish a Jewish homeland in Palestine, nor does it mean that they accept Jewish exclusivity in Israel. It does mean that the legitimacy granted by the international community to Israeli sovereignty over the part of Palestine that became Israel is generally accepted. This is the distinction between Israel's right to be there in the first place, in contrast to Israel's right to exist *ex post facto*. Not only do they not question their citizenship, but they demand full equality like *other* Israeli citizens. This persistent demand for equality makes sense only if one assumes that they do not question their status. On the contrary, they want to enhance it. In short, the goal of the Arabs in Israel is to achieve full equality within the framework of the Israeli system, not to disentangle themselves from that system.

By contrast, Palestinians in the occupied territories reject the legitimacy of Israeli rule altogether. Their rejection is fully supported by all segments of the Palestinian people, by all Arab peoples, and by the broadest sectors of the international community. The Israeli system has not considered granting the Palestinians in the territories citizenship, nor have they considered requesting citizenship or any of the legal rights that accompany it. Palestinians in the occupied territories have no vote and no voice in Israeli political debates. Their experience with the Israeli judicial system is with military courts, where "due process" is an altogether alien term. They have not charged discrimination or demanded equality. They have not asked for improved services from the Israeli system, nor for any further involvement in that system. For them, that system is a military occupation that exists to control them and their resources, not to serve their needs in any way. Compared to those across the Green Line, this Palestinian population is far more instrumentally involved in the Palestinian (and, until July 1988, the Jordanian) system, which has provided financial and moral support for services, education (particularly higher education), and public and political institutions. Palestinians in the occupied territories generally do not care to know Hebrew or to follow Israeli politics or media reports beyond their immediate relevance to the Palestinian question; their social frame of reference is entirely Palestinian in the local sense and a larger national sense.

The *intifada* represents an expression of a collective demand by Palestinians in the occupied territories to secede entirely from the Israeli system. Their prolonged, unwavering, total commitment to that effort is being pursued by means that are considered illegitimate by the Israeli system. Their goal is for national liberation, not for equality under Israeli rule.

International recognition of Israel's sovereignty over the territories it occupied in the 1948 war, and its extension of citizenship to the Arab population in those territories thus created the foundation for a new dividing line between the two peoples in Palestine: Israeli citizens versus non-citizens. When the West Bank and Gaza were occupied in 1967 and citizenship was not extended to their residents, this dividing line assumed a particular future significance for the country. It put the Arabs in Israel and the occupied territories in completely different positions vis-à-vis Israel in terms of both their involvement in the legal-political system and the degree of legitimacy granted to it. The traditional dividing line in Palestine of Arab versus Jew—although not overridden—was confounded. In many ways, the uprising has provided a historical test for the validity of each dividing line.

Differential Means: Popular Uprising and Political Solidarity

Differential involvement in the system and the differential legitimacy accorded to it affects both the means adopted by each group to achieve its goals and those goals themselves. Therefore, the strikes and demonstrations held by Arabs in Israel are of an entirely different nature and have totally different goals than those held in the occupied territories. In Israel, strikes and demonstrations are always held with official permission, and carefully preplanned and organized. Often the organizers encourage police not to interfere or enter Arab towns in order to avoid tension. Jewish participants are invited to speak at public assemblies, and the whole atmosphere —though sentimentally charged—is relaxed with regard to possible clashes with the police. There are no spontaneous clashes with the security forces; indeed, there is rarely any sign of open violence on either side.

The contrast is striking if one compares the 1989 Land Day events on either side of the "Green Line" dividing pre-1967 Israel from the occupied territories. The day was commemorated by both Palestinian groups by a national strike. In the occupied territories the strike was called by the Unified National Leadership of the uprising (the underground leadership of the *intifada* affiliated with the PLO), but in Israel by the FCCAC (a committee of mostly elected representatives of the community, including Knesset members in Zionist parties). In the main demonstration that the Palestinians in Israel held in Dayr Hanna (one of three regional demonstrations), thousands of marchers from all over Galilee and the northern part of the country walked from two adjacent villages (Sakhnin and Arrabe) chanting slogans in support of the uprising and its political program of two states, and in favor of full equal rights for the Arabs in Israel. While Arab and Jewish speakers gave their speeches, participants could buy cold drinks, coffee, sandwiches, and barbecued meat giving the event the coloring of a festive "happening". Parents, confident that no clashes with police would ensue, carried children on their shoulders. All slogans were in complete adherence with the first two elements of the Arab political consensus described above. The only violation to third element was the picture of a small Palestinian flag next to an Israeli flag—raised by a Jewish participant. People were more conscious of tension arising from internal divisions[16] than by possible clashes with Israeli police, who remained outside the villages.

By contrast, the army completely sealed the West Bank, and Gaza was placed under prolonged curfew. Despite the heavy military precautions, curfews, arrests, and sealing off, here is a description of what took place that same day, as it described in the *Jerusalem Post*:

> Troops shot and killed two Palestinians yesterday and wounded at least 50 during heavy clashes that swept the West Bank as Palestinians demonstrated solidarity with Israeli Arabs on Land Day. Palestinians said a third man was killed in the

> Gaza Strip... the entire Strip remains under curfew. Clashes were reported in scores of villages and towns throughout the West Bank, where the casualty toll was one of the highest in months.[17]

In addition to being qualitatively different, the demonstrations and strikes held by each group differ in frequency. Assuming for the sake of argument that they are accurate, figures provided by the office of the Minister for Arab Affairs suggest that the total number of incidents attributed to Arab citizens of Israel for the entire year of 1988 would probably fall short of the number registered on some single days in the occupied territories during the *intifada*.[18]

The differential legitimacy each Palestinian group grants to the Israeli system thus determines the means they choose in their efforts to achieve their goals. By challenging the legitimacy of authorities, regulations, and the system itself, the Palestinians in the occupied territories inevitably use means judged illegitimate by the system. No such challenge has been either articulated or posed by the Palestinians in Israel.

In the West Bank and Gaza, the daily protests enjoy the broadest support and participation of the entire population. By contrast, the few confrontational acts undertaken by Arabs inside Israel do not enjoy such support. Before all demonstrations, Arab leaders have called on the public to act according to the FCCAC instructions, which limit the activities to a general strike and four regional assemblies. Thus, before the "Peace Day" strike in December 1987 Nimr Murkus, mayor of Kafr Yasif, noted that the Arab leaders had called on the public not to demonstrate or create any disturbances on a day that had been designated as a national strike day. And just before Land Day in 1988, Ibrahim Nimr Husayn, the chairman of FCCAC, "stressed that the general strike would be peaceful and orderly, and urged members of the Arab community to act with restraint and not to commit any illegal acts."[19]

When violence has taken place at demonstrations, Arab leaders have been quick to deplore it and to assert it is the work of "individual hotheads," not the community as a whole.[20] In an article in *Washington Jewish Week*, journalist Walter Ruby noted: that "in questioning the Arab leaders and people from a wide variety of political stripes, including communists, Islamic fundamentalists, and persons who declaimed any party loyalty—this reporter found no one who advocated that Israeli Arabs undertake acts of rock throwing and other forms of violence along the lines of the Palestinians of the West Bank and Gaza."[21] Illegal incidents have been repeatedly publicly condemned. Thus, for example, when a petrol bomb attacked a bus in Baka al-Gharbiyya, the local council head, Samir Darwish, said the vast majority of the residents were appalled by what had happened. He said: "This is the first time we have had an incident of this nature, and we hope it will be the last."[22] Likewise, when petrol bombs were hurled at a truck near the entrance to Shafa 'Amr, the towns' leaders roundly condemned the incidents. The mayor of Shafa 'Amr declared that: "incidents of this kind only harm the cause of peace and coexistence. We have had a meeting of the town council at which it was unanimously agreed to denounce these incidents and to make it clear that those responsible acted on their own and did not have the support of any residents here."[23]

The uprising—with its symbols, its bloodshed, the sacrifice of its people and their collective suffering—is unlike anything that the Arabs in Israel have been through since the establishment of Israel, even in the period of the military government.[24] The uprising has required Palestinian residents of the territories to demonstrate at risk to their own lives; to organize in underground popular committees and take charge of local affairs at the risk of near-certain incarceration without charge; to comply with strike orders from the underground leadership, at great economic loss and personal inconvenience; to boycott certain Israeli products and produce their own substitutes, also at great personal inconvenience; to refuse to pay taxes or serve in or in any way legitimize Israeli institutions; to hoist Palestinian flags, throw stones, and take other kinds of protest actions. And above all, the uprising has required that they find the will to endure the inevitable military response—shooting, killing, wounding, demolishing houses, curfews, and all the rest. None of that is requested by the Arabs in Israel. The only commitment shown by large segments of their society (not all of it) is to *support* the uprising in the modes described above.

Jewish Perceptions of the Arab Response

As suggested earlier, most Arabs and Jews seem to hold divergent views on the nature of the Arabs' reaction to the uprising, and the extent to which they have supported it. Although the prevalent feeling among Arabs in Israel is that Arabs are demonstrating insufficient support, the Israeli media has been giving credence to a view in Israeli security and political circles that the Arabs are on the verge of joining the uprising.

The Israeli media, in particular, has given a great play to the notion that the uprising is creeping over the Green Line. In the summer of 1989, news analyses and reports about the "creeping uprising" appeared constantly.[25] Reportedly, the Israeli cabinet discussed the assessment of specialists that the intifada might expand from the territories to the Arabs in Israel.[26] The possibility that the security system might lose control over the Arabs in the country has likewise been discussed.[27] Assessments by the Ministers of Police and Defense that incidents involving Arabs in Israel were on the rise have been widely quoted.[28] Following protests and a strike in May 1990, Prime Minister Shamir warned Arab citizens of Israel that such activities "passed the limit of what is allowed."[29] Some of the most seasoned journalists have shared the assessment that Arabs in Israel are showing signs of extremism[30] or that they may join the *intifada*.[31] These analyses and reports have been almost exclusively based on security sources. With minor exceptions,[32] Israeli academics and researchers have not provided empirical evidence or analytical support for such an assessment.

Accounts that the Arabs were joining the uprising have been accompanied by reports about incidents within the Green Line: arson, stone throwing, flag raising, uncovering of underground cells, fights between Arabs and Jews, uprooting of trees, graffiti in Arab towns and many other incidents.[33] Even some children's summer camps were implicated by the media and the police as uprising related activities.[34]

To back up this analysis, the security establishment provided its own "evidence," namely the rise in the number of "hostile incidents" perpetrated within the Green Line relative to the years preceding the uprising. But, on close scrutiny, the evidence seems far from solid. For example, *Davar* Hebrew daily reported in July 1989: "The *intifada* inside the Green Line: in 1988, 3,200 hostile incidents."[35] The figure was based on the annual police report. The article listed the incidents as follows: about 1,900 molotov cocktails, about 600 incidents of arson, and 230 other acts. According to the report, 43 people were killed, and 420 wounded in these acts. The report terms this increase in hostile acts "unprecedented." One year earlier, in July of 1988, *Ha'Aretz* reported a decrease in the number of incidents in the first half of 1988, based on figures provided by the Minister of Police.[36] According to that report, 110 suspects were arrested in 1988, half of them from the territories. The peak month for incidents, March, saw a total of 46; in June, the number was 22. The article gave a total of 208 hostile acts inside the Green Line for 1988 (versus 69 in the previous year). These figures were quoted in other papers as well.[37] During the first eight months of 1989, according to *Ha'Aretz*, there were 265 incidents, "indicating a rising trend" in hostile Arab activity, according to the paper.[38] Ehud Olmert, the Minister for Arab (meaning Arab citizens') Affairs told the Knesset that security sources had reported 508 incidents of political subversion within the Green Line in 1988.[39] The minister neglected to differentiate between Palestinians from territories and from Israel, and, moreover, he included in his totals the Golan Heights and East Jerusalem. Nonetheless, none of these sources even came close to the figure quoted by *Davar*.

According to Elon Cohen, deputy minister in charge of Arab Affairs, the number of allegedly Arab-perpetrated violent incidents inside Israel has indeed risen since the *intifada* began. Specifically, he said, for 1988, 210 acts of sabotage were recorded (including throwing molotov cocktails, arson, knife attacks and grenades), although most suspects were from the occupied territories. In addition, 507 nationalist-motivated incidents were recorded, "such as raising the PLO flag, writing slogans on walls, stone throwing, and burning tires."[40] However, despite this increase, he was of the view that there was no uprising within the Green Line.

In contrast to this impression of impending doom among much of the Israeli establishment, there is unanimity across those members of the Arab political elite in Israel interviewed that the *intifada* is not creeping across the Green Line, and that the Arabs in Israel should not join the uprising. Different views are given, but two are acceptable to representatives of all factions: joining the uprising is strategically wrong for the Palestinian cause because it confuses the basic issue of independence in the occupied territories, and it harms the interests of the Arabs in Israel. The distinction is made between increasing material and moral support within the framework of Israeli law (acceptable), and active participation in the uprising that involves violating the law (unacceptable).[41] These views, which are stated unanimously and unequivocally, somehow do not find their way to the mainstream media.

Erroneous Israeli media reports and analyses are not necessarily the result of irresponsible journalism only. They are also a genuine reflection of the larger Jewish-Israeli societal perceptions of Arab citizens. They are an indication of Israeli society's shallow understanding of the relationship of Arab society to Israel on the one hand, and to the Palestinian people on the other. The Israeli media, like Israeli society itself, generally sees Arab citizens first and foremost as a potential security threat. It is not surprising that they willingly adopt the definitions, reports, and assessments of security sources. Because the media naturally plays that role, it actually becomes an integral part of the security mechanism itself by conveying the concerns of Israeli society and the security establishment to the Arabs. For example, by overplaying the aspect of "preserving law and order" on strike days, the media sends a message to the Arabs that the authorities are concerned by their activities. It also sends a message to the Jewish public that the "preservation of law and order" is the only thing that matters about such strikes. Thus the political and social motives behind strikes are dismissed, and existing views are reinforced. The Arabs are then compelled to dispel the image that they are citizens who intentionally disrupt law and order. In doing so, they often paradoxically find themselves leaving the opposite impression because the media again fixes on these calls, blows them out of proportion, and creates the erroneous impression among the Jewish public that mass Arab unruliness would have resulted, had not the leadership made such a concerted effort.

Conclusion

Psychological and Political Resurrection of the Green Line

The uprising has raised the awareness of Palestinian communities on both sides of the Green Line to the fact that the Arabs in Israel have very different status, goals, and future than do their compatriots in the territories.

Prior to the *intifada*, these differences remained submerged. In the climate of passive resentment (without mass, active resistance) to a seemingly perpetual occupation, it was the things the two groups held in common that were most salient: common cultural heritage and customs, common oppressive experiences under military rule, common frustration at their inability to control gradual seizure of land and resources, common identification with larger abstract Palestinian dreams of self-determination and an end to the oppression. The more Israel built settlements and moved settlers into the territories, the more the Green Line seemed to fade in significance, if not disappear. The importance of the traditional dividing line of Jew versus Arab was gradually taking precedence over that of citizen versus non-citizen, laying the psychological grounds for two nations in one state. But when the Palestinians in the territories opted for a more active resistance, and when the PLO announced its formal adherence to the two-state solution, the nature of the relationship changed substantially. Indeed, the *intifada* actually reversed a slow-growing trend towards increasing interaction between the two communities, and created (or recreated) powerful divisions between the two populations: it brought the differences in status, collective goals, and collective future into sharp focus. In that sense the *intifada* not only ended at the Green Line, it resurrected the Green Line in the consciousness of both Palestinian communities.

For the Palestinians in Israel, the PLO's new policy meant that the Palestinian problem would be resolved next door, not at home. Thus, however much they may support the PLO's decision, they also understand that it will not resolve *their* problems. As Palestinians they may share many of the same insecurities and existential dilemmas as Palestinians at large, but as Israeli citizens who do not intend to leave their homes their problem is of a profoundly different nature.

The questions that the uprising and the Palestinian political program raise are existentially grave. In the short run, the Arab community must find ways to cope with dissonance between their profound sentimental support for the uprising, and the fact that they have done so little to act on this sentiment. It is not clear whether some sectors of Arab society (particularly the consolidating middle class) are willing to risk losses by showing more support in the form of commercial strikes, demonstrations or acts that instigate tension with the Jewish public (including employers and clients).

But even if such willingness to translate the feelings into actions existed, there are many reasons for restraint. The first is the deeply seated feeling among many in the Arab leadership—particularly those who experienced the 1948 trauma—that some in the Israeli establishment might be interested in provoking the Arabs into exactly such behavior, in order to use it as an excuse for massacres, expulsion, or legitimizing the concept of transfer.[42] The trauma of 1948 is a powerful internal deterrent against provoking the Israeli authorities. As indicated above, Arabs are usually well aware that the

Israeli establishment, media, and society in general looks at them through the colored lenses of "security." It is clear to them that their support for the uprising will increase the alienation with Israeli society that has reached unprecedented levels during the uprising.[43] What gives this dilemma a dimension of acuteness is that Arabs see their future as part of Israel as being increasingly finalized and legitimized by all concerned. So rising alienation does not serve their future relationship with Israel.

The Arabs in Israel realize that the time has arrived to determine the desired nature of their relationship with the state of Israel. They never considered or publicly debated this issue, because it was always contingent upon what would happen with the Palestinian question. As the goal of achieving equality within Israel gains prominence, the Palestinians have to consider the meaning of being Israeli. It is true that Israel has never offered the Arabs the choice of being full Israelis in the sense of sharing the land as a common homeland, and sharing the state as an instrument of two nations. But it is also true that Arabs have never actively pursued that possibility until recently.

Once they do, Arabs will face the crux of Israel: how to achieve equality in an ideologically exclusive state. Genuine full equality is not on the agenda of most Zionist parties. The real meaning of equality for Arabs is a basic transformation of Israeli state and society: a state in which they are full and equal partners, a state for all its citizens, a state whose character, ideology, policy and priorities they will contribute to shaping. In that sense, the Palestinians in the occupied territories have an easier goal—disentanglement from the Israeli system—because it does not directly threaten the tenets of Zionism, though it might weaken it. But complete equality is tantamount to de-Zionising Israel, an idea which meets wall-to-wall, fierce resistance among most Israeli Jews. But many among the present leadership of the Arabs in Israel believe that the peaceful establishment of a Palestinian state in the territories would reduce interethnic tension in Israel; in the wake of such a solution, they believe, their rights could be addressed more effectively. But if a Palestinian state is ultimately established, then one more Jewish counter reaction would likely follow in the face of persistent Arab demands for full equality: "there is a Palestinian state, this is not it, this is a Jewish state, if you want full equality you can achieve it in the Palestinian state just across the borders."

The Arabs will have to face the reality that their homeland is not really regarded as theirs by the majority of the Jewish public, and the state of which they are citizens does not want to include them in its goals. They have to confront the present reality of being strangers in their own homeland and challenge it as a final political destination. If they do not accept it, they might demand a different arrangement, such as institutional autonomy. That way, the self-fulfulling prophecy of some Israeli right-wingers will be realized. But Palestinian autonomy in Galilee, on the heels of a traumatic disentanglement from the occupied territories, would be fiercely resisted by Israel.

Arabs will be faced with other hard questions that are beginning to arise now. They, for example, will have to find a new definition for their Palestinianism. How are they to be Palestinians within the new arrangement if only the West Bank and Gaza is Palestine? In what sense are those in Galilee Palestinians when their origins are not from Palestine, as it is newly redefined. What attachment could they possibly have to the West Bank and Gaza state?

In their support for the *intifada* and the political program of an independent Palestinian state in the West Bank and Gaza, Arabs, in a sense, are identifying with the national Palestinian goal without due consideration for the complexity of their own predicament. This complexity is now being suppressed by the larger Israeli-Palestinian conflict. However, the *intifada*, as it continues, threatens to bring it to the surface for both Arabs and Jews.

Notes

1. See Nadim Rouhana, "The Political Transformation of the Arabs in Israel," *Journal of Palestine Studies* 18, 3 (Spring 1989): 38-59.

2. These three parties support the establishment of an independent Palestinian state in the West Bank and Gaza as a central part of their political platform. The DFPE, PLP, and ADP received 33.4%, 13.7%, and 10.8% of the valid Arab vote respectively in Israel's 1988 national elections.

3. The PLP, for example, emphasizes the Arabs' Palestinian identity and gives first priority to general Palestinian issues. While the ADP doesn't challenge Palestinian identity, it gives higher priority to the question of equality for Arabs inside Israel. The DFPE manages a balance between the two.

4. A summary of some findings is presented in Murad A'si, *Israeli and Palestinian Public Opinion*, Occasional Paper No. 5 (Kingston: Near East Cultural and Educational Foundation of Canada, 1986).

5. For those in the DFPE, who internalized this position as a political imperative determined by their ideological system, the PLO's program only proved to them that they had been right all along, since 1947, when they were isolated in their acceptance of the partition plan for Palestine. Emile Habibi (the editor of the Israeli Communist Party organ *al-Ittihad* at the time the PNC program was presented) and other columnists frequently reminded the readers of the communist position in support of partition in 1947, and made historical accounts with the "nationalistic elements," particularly the communists' competitors among the Palestinians in Israel, who had considered that support to be unwise or "defeatist."

Those who held that position solely out of identification with the Palestinian people and because they interpreted the PLO moves to mean approval of the two-state solution found their interpretation and identification greatly strengthened by the new position. Those who adhered to a program based on a secular democratic state, with equality for Arabs and Jews in all of historic Palestine, complied reluctantly with the two-state political program as the only realistic, practical, and internationally defensible program. So all in all, most Arabs in Israel greeted the PNC political program as a wise, realistic, and defensible position.

6. The policy of open adherence only to political activity permitted by law gained some saliency after the meticulous scrutiny of the Progressive List for Peace—as individuals and a political platform—by the security establishment (including a meeting with the then-Defense Minister, Moshe Arens) and the Hebrew press, before the PLP first ran for the Knesset elections in 1984. Public debates on the issue were launched in both Jewish and Arab society after the Central Elections Committee decided that the PLP should not be permitted to run and the List responded by taking the case to the Supreme Court. The debate in the Jewish community served as an unusual reminder to the Arab public of the Israeli legal system's limits. The Arab political elite was always aware of the Israelis' extreme sensitivity to "security violations," a term which, if applied loosely, could always provide a ready pretext for outlawing political activity.

7. Meetings with PLO leaders were a rare exception; Arabs who went ahead with these meetings usually tried to protect themselves by either attending the meeting with Jewish colleagues or by using their parliamentary immunity as Knesset members. Such meetings were never condemned by the Arab public or leadership. To the contrary they have been often used as an act that would increase a groups' or individual's legitimacy in the eyes of their Arab constituency.

8. The Hebrew press published frequent reports on "increased extremism"—usually a misnomer for increased national and political consciousness—among the Bedouin community. See, for example, Uzi Benziman in *Ha'Aretz*, 28 July 1989, "An Extremist Spirit in the Tent [Fly]," in which he argues that the Bedouin are not separate tribes any more, and that they are developing a sense of community and Arab Palestinian identity. When isolated incidents of stone throwing or distribution of political pamphlets were recorded by the police in the Negev, the Israeli press began talking about a "Bedouin *intifada*" and saying that the uprising had arrived in the Negev. See, for example: "Commander of the Negev Region: The *intifada* arrives in the Negev: Foresee a hard future" by E. Rabin in *Ha'Aretz*, 17 July 1989; "The *intifada* of the Bedouin expands almost to all the Negev," by W. Sofer in *Maariv*, 8 May 1989; "Bedouin *Intifada*, blue and white" by O. Lipfshitz in *Al-Hamishmar*, 26 May 1989.

Among the Druze community, the Druze Initiative Committee—the only organized Druze group that consider the Druze community to be Palestinian—has shown unmistakable support for the uprising. A Follow-up Druze Committee was established by people mostly associated with the Zionist establishment but disturbed by reports that Druze soldiers were involved in brutalities against Palestinians in the territories. The committee initiated meetings with representatives of the Palestinian press in Jerusalem, condemned the brutalities and, in some cases, declared support for an independent Palestinian state. See detailed reports in *al-Sha'ab*, 13 June 1989; *al-Fajr*, 13 June 1989; *al-Ittihad*, 14 June 1989; *al-Quds*, 14 June 1989.

9. The paper is the organ of the Israeli Communist Party; it is a dependable candidate for such a survey because it is located at the center of the political spectrum. Moreover, *al-Ittihad* reflects a particularly sound measure of that "center" when it comes to sentiments and feelings among Palestinians, which are less subject to editorial manipulation by the ideological line of the party (to which the paper strictly adheres). One would probably find some variation within the publications of the PLP and ADP, with the former showing even more open sentimental identification with the *intifada* and the latter somewhat less.

10. After the Israeli Minister of Interior closed the paper for a week just before Land Day (March 30), 1988, *al-Ittihad* ran an additional page to cover the daily reports about the uprising during the period of its closure.

11. The distribution of the paper is prohibited in the occupied territories except for East Jerusalem. Thus its effectiveness as an alternative channel of communication is seriously curtailed.

12. For a description of this committee's composition and role, see Rouhana, "The Political Transformation of the Arabs in Israel."

13. See, for example, Attallah Mansur in *Ha'Aretz* from 14 June 1989. He gives examples, all of which reflect a low level of material support.

14. The interviews were held in July and August of 1989 with leaders representing eight political factions encompassing the whole political spectrum of Arab political thinking. The interviews are part of continuing research on the collective identity of the Arabs in Israel and the desirable form of relationship with Israel. They included a section on Arab involvement in the uprising and their response to it. Some preliminary findings from this research are reported in this paper.

15. Defense Minister Yitzhak Rabin, for example, told an Arab Knesset member, in explicit reference to the demonstration: "You have known tragedy in the distant past, and it would be better for you, and for us, that you not return to that tragedy." *Jerusalem Post*, 22 December 1987. See some examples of other reactions in Rouhana, "The Political Transformation of the Arabs in Israel."

16. One day earlier, in Kafr Kanna, 10 people were wounded in an internal feud between the Islamic movement and other factions; a year earlier, MK Meier Willner (DFPE) was continuously heckled by supporters of the Islamic movement in a meeting in the triangle.

17. *Jerusalem Post*, 31 March 1989.

18. For a breakdown of alleged incidents, see note 40. It should be kept in mind that the quantitative difference, as sharp as it is, gains significance only in the light of the disparity in the nature and motivation of the incidents in the communities. Without such disparity, the difference in frequency of incidents could not be validly considered to indicate support for, rather than participation in, the uprising.

19. *Jerusalem Post*, 21 December 1987, 21 March 1988.

20. *Jerusalem Post*, 22, 24 December 1987; 14 January 1988.

21. Walter Ruby, "Israel's Arabs: Will they Join the Uprising?" *Washington Jewish Week*, 20 July 1989.

22. *Jerusalem Post*, 3 March 1988.

23. *Jerusalem Post*, 27 October 1988.

24. Of course this does not include the 1948 war which, in any case, was of a different nature. The closest experiences of Arabs in Israel to the uprising were the Kafr Qasim massacre and the first land day strike of 1976. In the massacre of Kafr Qasim committed in 1956 by the Israeli army against Arab workers, the victims were passively mowed down by soldiers upon their return to their town—in one incident. Like the Palestinians in the territories they were unarmed, but they were not—as in the territories—people who willingly chose to face an army in a continuous confrontation in which they know that they might die, be injured, or detained. In the 1976 Land Day, six people were killed in confrontation with the army.

25. For example, the headlines "Has the *intifada* crossed the green line?" *Jerusalem Post*, 19 May 1989, or "Intifada within the family," *Al Hamishmar*, 24 April 1989 and "The intifada is creeping into Galilee," cover story of *Yediot Aharonot* (weekly supplement), 28 July 1989.

26. *Al Hamishmar*, 24 April 1989.

27. *Maariv*, 23 April 1989; *Hadashot*, 21 April 1989.

28. *Maariv*, 21 July 1989.

29. *New York Times*, 23 May 1990. The protests followed the shooting deaths of seven Gazan laborers near Tel Aviv by a "deranged" Israeli gunman.

30. See Reuven Pedhezar in *Ha'Aretz*, 24 November 1989; he argues: "Extremism is engulfing all sectors of Arab society in Israel." Accordingly, he advises the security system to get ready to cope with the Arabs' aspiration to secede from the state. See also

Uzi Binziman in *Ha'Aretz*, 4 April 1989. he describes events on Land Day 1989 as follows: "Even without dead and wounded, this was a depressing scene that heralds great dangers: the Arab minority, citizens of Israel, raises the flag of the PLO, calls slogans against the state and actually expresses desire not to be under its sovereignty. In contrast to the protest of other civic groups, the demonstrations of the Arabs in Israel carry a message of basic challenge to the condition that was imposed on them to be under the control of Israel."

31. See, for example, a news analysis by Yehuda Litani, the editor of the *Jerusalem Post*'s Middle East page at the time, entitled "Intifada violence could blur the Green Line." In it, he claims that the PFLP "is trying to mobilize the Israeli Arabs to join the uprising," and he warns of a hot summer inside Israel. *Jerusalem Post*, 3 May 1989.

32. One of the few academic "prophets" of Arab participation in the uprising was Arnon Sofer of Haifa University; (see *Kol Haifa*, 18 November 1988). Sofer (a geographer) argues that the Arabs are building the infrastructure for an Arab state in Galilee; see his arguments in Roman Frister's "In Galilee without illusions," *Ha'Aretz*, 15 September 1989; and in an interview with Amos Gilboa "Has the Intifada reached the Arabs in Israel?" *Maariv*, 6 June 1989. See also Alexander Bligh, who argued that "if the local [Arab] leaders, along with us, do not make a special effort to dismantle the seeds of terrorism, we may see a situation in which the [Arab] mainstream could be persuaded to throw stones" "Community at a crossroad," *Jerusalem Post*, 16 March 1989.

33. At one point, an Arab physician in a hospital in Beersheba was accused by staff members of refusing to treat a soldier wounded by a stone in the territories; this caused a public storm in the country. In other versions, Dr. Samuel Da'ud told the soldier: "Whoever shoots Palestinian children deserves a stone." See *Davar*, 23 November 1988. The physician was given a dismissal note within a month, but later a committee that reviewed the case and found no evidence for the accusation recommended that he be returned. See also *Yediot Aharonot*, 11 November 1988.

34. In the summer of 1989, stories about "intifada children's camps" in Arab towns in the Galilee and the Triangle received wide coverage in Israeli press. Following these reports, police swept two camps in Shafa 'Amr, arrested organizers and reported finding PLO symbols and children singing the Palestinian nationalist song *Biladi Biladi*. *Yediot Aharonot* (weekly supplement), 13 July 1989. Ariela Ringle-Hofman reported that the Abna' al-Balad camp in Shafa 'Amr was divided into groups, each with names such as "children of the stones," "hero children of Nablus," and "for every child who dies—a child will be born." *Zou Haderech*, 2 August 1989 (Rakah's Hebrew weekly) provided a description of what took place in Rakah-run camps. The organizers were particularly meticulous in abiding by the law. Following the debate in the Knesset about the legality of the song *Biladi Biladi*, the DFPE provided a Hebrew translation to the Knesset. The song is a modified version of the old Egyptian song *Biladi*—modified by Palestinian poet Samih al-Qasim, himself a member of Rakah—to celebrate the victory of the DFPE in the 1974 Nazareth mayoral elections. The DFPE wanted the Israeli public to see that "the song doesn't include nationalistic or anti-Israeli intentions."

Many of the media depictions of the summer camps left little doubt but that they were illegal, however, and related to the *intifada*. For example, *Hamodia* reported the events as follows: "Another nationalistic children's camp was uncovered in Shafa 'Amr" and "Intifada children's camp was uncovered in the Shafa 'Amr region" on 21 and 24 July 1989 respectively. Similarly, "Shafa 'Amr: A children's camp in the spirit of the *intifada*," *Maariv*, 21 July 1989; "Police sweep Rakah's intifada children's camp in Shafa 'Amr," *Yediot Aharonot* 24 July 1989; "Where do children go? To the *intifada* children's camp," *Davar*, 21 July 1989.

35. *Davar*, 12 July 1989.

36. *Ha'Aretz*, 19 July 1988.

37. *Hadashot*, 4 April 1989; *Jerusalem Post*, 28 March 1989.
38. *Ha'Aretz*, 27 September 1989.
39. *Detroit Jewish News*, 28 April 1989.
40. Interview arranged by the author, 2 August 1989. The figures of incidents provided by Cohen break down as follows:

Sabotage

	1987	1988
bottle throwing	6	49
arson	3	96
sabotage (such as wrecking cars)	1	26
clashes	1	5
knife attacks	4	9
bomb attacks	51	20
grenade attacks	3	3
shootings	0	2
TOTAL	69	210

Expressions of nationalism

	1987	1988
stone throwing	20	133
raising PLO flag	21	135
slogans	34	145
sabotage (burning Israeli flag)	7	16
setting barricades	7	48
burning tires	7	12
telephone threats	-	10
fake bombs	5	8
TOTAL	101	507

Examples of "nationalist slogans" include "we support the PLO," "yes [to the] Palestinian state," " 'Arafat is our leader," "down with the occupation," and "hurrah to the PLO." These figures exclude the Golan Heights.
41. Interviews, July-August 1989.
42. A strong argument to that effect appeared in Emile Habibi's column in *al-Ittihad*, 24 March 1988. The theme is recurrent in his political analysis. It is also clear in the response of many Arab mayors in answering questions about "*intifada*–related incidents." See, for example, the explanation of Nimr Murkus (mayor of Kafr Yasif, representing the DFPE) to Uzi Binziman in *Ha'Aretz*, 16 September 1988.
43. Of the 60 interviews with leaders mentioned earlier, 46 believed that relations between Arabs and Jews in Israel have worsened, and only two believed they have improved; 42 thought that the Jewish society had become more extreme, whereas only 3 thought it had become more moderate, and 10 saw signs of both extremism and moderation. On the other hand, 35 thought that Arab society had become more moderate in its political attitudes, 15 thought it had become more extreme, and 5 thought it had gone in both directions. Two factors seem to cause increasing alienation, even on the interpersonal level: Arabs are angry with the practices of Israel in the territories and disappointed with Israel public reaction to the army's excessive and inappropriate use of force; and Jews are angry with the support that Arabs are offering to the uprising and interpret it as willingness to join it.

PART TWO

Regional Repercussions of the Uprising

The intensification of the Palestinian-Israeli conflict represented by the *intifada* has had broad repercussions throughout the Arab world. Despite the apparently declining salience of the Palestinian issue in the Arab world, the *intifada* has generated a broad wave of Arab popular support.[1] The uprising has also spurred a flurry of regional diplomatic activity, including Jordanian disengagement from the West Bank (July 1988), a series of mediatory initiatives by Egypt, and emergency summits of Arab League heads of government and state in June 1988 (Algiers), May 1989 (Casablanca) and May 1990 (Baghdad).

Moreover, as argued earlier, the uprising has had the profound effect of refocusing the regional Arab-Israeli conflict back to its intrinsic Palestinian-Israeli core. Viewed from the perspective of the 1990s—at a time when events in the occupied territories figure frequently in the news, and when the term "*intifada*" itself has entered the world's political vocabulary—the centrality of this latter dimension may well seem self-evident. For the better part of half a century, however, the dominant external conceptualization of the struggle was *not* that of Palestinian-Israeli confrontation, but rather that of a military and territorial conflict between Israel and the surrounding Arab states.

The Regionalization of Palestinian-Zionist Conflict

Historically, the political roots of the connection between the Palestinian cause and broader Arab world can be traced to the emerging Arab nationalist movement before World War I. After the war, some Palestinian nationalist leaders linked their hopes for independence to those of Amir Faysal bin Husayn, who in March 1920 was declared King of independent Syria. Until Faysal was forced to flee from an invading French army, these nationalists viewed Palestine as a southern province of an independent Arab Syria.

Following this abortive episode, it would be almost a decade before another opportunity would arise for Palestinians to link their local struggle with other nationalist and anti-colonial forces in the region. This came in

1928-29, when Muslim fears of a Zionist threat to the holy places of Jerusalem marked the start of serious pan-Islamic interest in the local Zionist-Palestinian conflict, an interest which many Palestinian leaders encouraged. A more significant step was the pan-Arabizing of the Palestinian struggle against Zionism and British rule, alongside the gradual loosening of British and French colonial bonds in the region. By the mid-1930s British Mandatory Palestine remained the only territory not advancing towards any semblance of self-government. As their struggle erupted into anti-British demonstrations and riots in 1933 and a full-fledged anti-British and anti-Zionist revolt during 1936-39, Palestinians appealed for moral, political and practical support from nationalist forces in the surrounding countries, thereby changing considerably the structure and dynamics of the original conflict. Arabization of the conflict was also evident in the "Greater Syria" ambitions of Transjordan's King 'Abdallah; in the brief halt to the Palestine Revolt of 1936 brought about by Iraqi, Transjordanian and Saudi diplomatic intervention; and at the 1939 St. James conferences on Palestine, where the Palestinian Arab delegation was overshadowed by those of Iraq, Transjordan, Saudi Arabia, Egypt and Yemen. Through the 1930s and 1940s, therefore, Palestine occupied an increasingly important position in the political geography of the region.

The interlacing of the central Zionist-Palestinian dispute with the interests of neighboring Arab countries became even more evident in 1947-48. Indeed, Transjordanian and Egyptian military intervention in May 1948 was motivated as much by domestic politics and the desire to limit each other's territorial gains from a dismembered Palestine as by concern for the fate of the Palestinians.

The Arab-Israeli Conflict and Inter-Arab Politics

The "disaster" (*al-nakba*) of 1948 assured the position of Palestine in inter-Arab politics (and hence the continuation of Arab-Israeli conflict) for decades to come. Within the Arab world, the establishment of the state of Israel was widely seen as a direct political, economic and strategic threat. Hundreds of thousands of Palestinians had sought refuge in Arab countries. Moreover, the loss of such an important part of the Arab's cultural heritage to Zionism and its Western supporters raised agonizing questions about the Arab political "awakening" which had been underway since the nineteenth century. As an indirect result, the collapse or overthrow of the *anciens régimes* in Egypt, Syria, and Iraq followed. For the nationalist governments which emerged from their wreckage, Palestine became the leading Arab issue of the day, legitimizing state policy at home and abroad. For conservative regimes too, the Palestinian issue was used to reinforce their internal and external legitimacy. Thus, throughout the 1950s and 1960s, the Palestine question dominated Arab political discourse. It also, for these very reasons, became an important weapon in inter-Arab politics and political competition.

Many of these factors served to obscure the Palestinian/Israeli core of the regional conflict. The very status granted *al-qadiyya al-filastiniyya* ("the Palestinian cause") in the Arab nationalist pantheon rendered expression of distinct Palestinian identity a deviation from pan-Arabism, to be rejected accordingly. So too, conservative Arab-Islamic conceptions of the Palestinian Question tended to gloss over the Palestinians *per se* in their emphasis on the universality of the struggle. And Jordan, of course, represented a special case. After the annexation by Transjordan (now Jordan) of the West Bank in 1950, the unity of the two banks of the Jordan River constituted an ideological pillar of the state—and any expression of a distinct Palestinian identity became a serious threat to the existence of the Hashemite regime.

Meanwhile, with the displacement of the bulk of the Palestinian population from within Israel's borders, the conflict was also obscured in the Israeli consciousness: the Palestinians all but disappeared from a psychological equation in which Israelis perceived themselves as a beleaguered Jewish society surrounded by hostile Arab states. There was, in Golda Meir's oft-cited statement, "no such thing as Palestinians."[2] This attitude—whatever its moral or ideological implications—was based, at least in part, on contemporary military realities. Palestinian society and politics had been seriously dislocated by the defeat of 1947-49. Later, despite its revitalization during the 1950s and 1960s, it remained weak in the face of Israeli power. Instead, the major military threat to Israel at this time was that posed by Arab regular armies.

Arab-Israeli inter-state conflict thus began to assume a momentum of its own. Skirmish led to skirmish, and raid to retaliation. Opposition to the growing profile of Egypt under Nasir on the part of both Israel and a decaying European colonial order led to the Suez war of 1956. Eleven years later, the escalatory pressures of inter-Arab politics and Israel's propensity to make assertive use of its own strategic power produced a third Arab-Israeli war in June 1967.

The 1967 war was to prove a watershed in several respects. With the capture of the Sinai, Golan Heights, West Bank and Gaza by Israel that June, territories claimed by Egypt, Syria and Jordan now came under occupation. For these countries issues of territorial integrity, sovereignty and national security soon overshadowed all else. A number of indicators signaled the growing entrenchment of the logic of *raison d'état*: United Nations Security Council resolution 242, which emphasized state security and characterized the Palestinians as a "refugee" problem; Nasir's acceptance of the Rogers plan in 1970 to end the war of attrition; King Husayn's efforts to regain the West Bank. The rise to power of Hafiz al-Asad in Syria and Anwar al-Sadat in Egypt marked general decline of ideological warfare in inter-Arab politics and the advent of more pragmatic leadership. Finally, the October 1973 Arab-Israeli war—initiated by Egypt and Syria in pursuit of territorial state interests—confirmed the apparent eclipse of the original Palestinian core of the conflict.

Such trends were reinforced by a fragmented inter-Arab balance of power, marked by the decline of Egypt's leadership role and the simultaneous rise of the Arab petroleum-exporting states. The political coordination attained during the October war and 1973-74 Arab oil embargo rapidly dissipated, giving way to the shuttle diplomacy of the mid-1970s and a series of separate bilateral disengagement agreements between Israel and the two chief Arab confrontation states. The apparent essence of the conflict seemed no longer the issue of Palestinian national rights, but rather narrow technical questions of border demarcation, demilitarized zones, limitation of military forces, and so forth.

One effect of all this was to sustain parallel changes within the Palestinian movement itself. First founded under Arab League auspices in 1964, the Palestine Liberation Organization had emerged from the wreckage of the 1967 war as an independent and revitalized representative of Palestinian national aspirations. And, for all its complaints about the inadequate support given its cause by Arab regimes pursuing their own agendas, the PLO would follow a similar political trajectory. Repeated confrontations with Arab regimes —with Lebanon in 1969 and 1973; with Egypt in 1970, 1975 and from 1977; its confrontation with Jordan in 1970-71 and thereafter; the civil war in Lebanon from 1975, and Syrian intervention against it in 1976—reinforced the Palestinians' inclination (already intrinsic in the shared identity upon which the modern Palestinian movement had been founded) to try to set their own independent course. The problematic nature of Palestinian relations with the Arab world, as much as the continued reality of Israel's strength and existence, encouraged the PLO's gradual shift to a two-state solution in the latter half of the 1970s. With this, the diplomatic weight of the PLO—already reflected by the Arab League's formal acceptance of it as the "sole legitimate representative of the Palestinian people" at Rabat in 1974, and the attainment of observer status at the United Nations later that year—was further enhanced.

The Camp David Order

The ascendancy of the geopolitical logic of the Arab territorial state over the ideological force of pan-Arabism was unmistakably signaled (and further reinforced) by Egyptian foreign policy in the mid-1970s. Weighted under a heavy military burden, and believing that the imperatives of liberal economic development required both peace and a realignment of Egyptian foreign policy towards the West, Anwar al-Sadat made his historic trip to Jerusalem in November 1977. The initiative set the stage for a flurry of new diplomatic activity, culminating in the US-mediated Camp David accords of

17 September 1978. Six months later, on 26 March 1979, the leaders of Egypt, Israel and the United States placed their signatures on a formal Egyptian-Israeli peace treaty, bringing an end to 31 years of war between Israel and the most powerful of the Arab confrontation states.

Despite the proclamations of their preambles, neither the Camp David Accords nor the Egyptian-Israeli peace treaty brought either "comprehensive peace" or a settlement of the Arab-Israeli conflict "in all its respects." The Camp David process did, however, bring about a fundamental shift in the regional balance of power. Egypt—the only Arab state posing a serious military threat to Israel—was removed from the coalition of confrontation states. In doing so, the treaty assured Israel of unchallenged regional strategic superiority.

Moreover, the Camp David process also left the Palestinian issue unresolved, treating it as little more than an irritant to Arab-Israeli inter-state relations. True, the treaty's signatories had pledged themselves to implement the autonomy provisions of the Accords. But Israeli Prime Minister Menahem Begin clung to a "functionalist" definition of autonomy which envisaged control of local services devolved to municipal councils in the West Bank and Gaza, while Israel retained security control and maintained its claim of sovereignty. For Palestinians in the territories, the Camp David process seemed little more than an invitation to participate in the legitimation and facilitation of their own continued occupation. In the territories "autonomy" was overwhelmingly rejected, while the PLO continued to press its case for independence and self-determination—with growing effectiveness—before the international community.

Thus the Camp David process, while vastly strengthening Israel's regional position, did not resolve or eliminate the basic issues of Palestinian -Israeli conflict. Israel increasingly deployed its new-found power in the regional Arab-Israeli arena to "resolve" these core issues in what, in the 1980s, had become the two primary sites of Palestinian-Israeli confrontation: the occupied territories and Lebanon. In the occupied territories, the aftermath of the Camp David accords and Egyptian-Israeli peace treaty saw the Likud government redouble its efforts to change the face of the West Bank and Gaza through land expropriations and the accelerated construction of new settlements. The number of Jewish settlers in the territories, which had doubled between 1977 and 1979, further quadrupled by 1984. The National Guidance Committee, like the Palestine National Front before it, was banned. Nationalist mayors were removed from office and deported. In their place, the new "Civil Administration" established for the occupied territories in 1981 attempted to promote—albeit with little success—a client leadership (the so-called "Village Leagues") that would collaborate with Israeli rule.

The effects of Camp David were also evident in Lebanon, where the institutional infrastructure of the Palestinian nationalist movement had taken root and developed since the PLO's expulsion from Jordan in 1970-71. Israel had long-standing foreign policy and security interests north of its border, and since the late 1960s had responded to Palestinian cross-border raids from Lebanon with increasingly severe punitive attacks. These attacks against the PLO in south Lebanon had also been used as a means to provoke the PLO and to undermine the movement's improving image and rising international profile. Now, with the treaty signed, Egypt's neutralization afforded Israel a decisive strategic advantage *vis-à-vis* both Syria and the PLO in Lebanon.

The result was escalating confrontation between the PLO and IDF in south Lebanon in 1979-81, culminating in Israel's massive June 1982 invasion of Lebanon. The motives behind the 1982 war extended far beyond the security of Israel's northern border, however. They also represented a broad vision (most explicitly voiced by then Defense Minister Ariel Sharon) of how the conditions of post-Camp David strategic balance could be translated into further Israeli gains. In this view, an invasion of Lebanon would serve several objectives: it would demonstrate Israeli military power, deterring Arab states from future confrontation; it would facilitate the installation of a pro-Israeli regime in Beirut; and it would strike a humiliating blow at Syria, halting its drive for strategic parity. Most important of all, Israeli strategic power would be used to restructure the very Palestinian-Israeli core of the regional conflict by depriving the PLO of its territorial base, destroying its institutional infrastructure, and weakening its credibility and influence among its own West Bank and Gaza population. This would produce a weaker, more fragmented PLO vulnerable to the cross-pressures of Syria, Jordan, and other Arab states. Such a PLO would likely grow more radical and less effective. In the meantime, Palestinian leaders in the West Bank and Gaza would be stripped of external support and left to their own devices—and hence be more vulnerable to Israeli pressures to accept a functionalist definition of limited autonomy.[3]

Initially at least, the 1982 invasion seemed to have achieved many of these objectives. Deprived of its territorial base, the PLO found itself beset by both external pressures and its own internal centrifugal tensions. Disagreements over the PLO's future political direction provided the motive force for a rebellion by Syrian-supported Fateh dissidents from 1983. In Lebanon, Palestinian refugee camps found themselves under attack by the Syrian-supported Lebanese Shi'ite Amal militia in 1985-87. Meanwhile, the political coordination established between 'Arafat and Jordan's King Husayn in the Amman accords of February 1985 had, by 1986, come unraveled. A series of Jordanian counter-measures against the PLO followed, as Husayn sought to strengthen Hashemite influence in the occupied territories. Within the West Bank and Gaza, Israel responded to growing levels of local protest with its "iron fist" policy, announced by Defense Minister Yitzhak Rabin in August 1985.

Ironically, the very intensity of these pressures ultimately engendered a defensive unity of sorts among the major Palestinian groups. They thus provided the catalyst for the reunification of the PLO at the 18th session of the Palestine National Council meeting in Algiers in April 1987. Military and political pressure against the PLO had been able to limit it only in the short run: the importance of the PLO lay not in its organizational existence but rather as a manifestation of a continuing and fundamental Palestinian desire for self-determination.

Such developments signaled the ultimate failure of the strategic vision that had informed Israel's post-Camp David strategy. The continued regional significance of the PLO and Palestinian issue, however much Arab leaders tried to side-step it at their November 1987 summit in Amman, would be restated with unmistakable clarity and regional resonance one month later with the eruption of the *intifada*.

The Uprising and the Arab World

Among Arab states, the foreign and domestic political repercussions of the uprising have been most strongly felt Jordan, the country with the closest relationship to the Palestinian issue. In addition to the special historic ties between the East and West Banks, much of Jordan's population is of Palestinian origin.[4] Serious tensions over political representation of the West Bank (and, more generally, custodianship of the Palestinian cause) have plagued Jordanian-PLO relations since the latter's founding in 1964—tensions that neither the PLO-Hashemite showdown of 1970-71 nor the Rabat Arab summit declaration of 1974 ever really resolved. Indeed, as already noted, tensions between the two were once more in evidence on the eve of the *intifada*.

As Lamis Andoni shows, the uprising itself amplified the resulting pressures on Jordanian policy to an unacceptable level. The result was King Husayn's historic speech of 31 July 1988 severing administrative ties to the West Bank. In the wake of that announcement, the Jordanian government embarked on a strong drive to "Jordanize" the political process. Far from ending the potential challenge of suspected Palestinian "dual loyalties," however, the government's restriction of already limited press and political freedoms only served to further alienate Jordan's Palestinian citizens while simultaneously angering native Transjordanians. Moreover, this occurred at a time when declining levels of Arab aid and remittances from expatriate workers were threatening a financial and economic crisis. Retrenchment measures announced to deal with the latter were, in the context of the former, sufficient spark to ignite economic and political protests in many areas of the country in April 1989.

These incidents led to the replacement of the government of Prime Minister Zaid Rifa'i with a caretaker administration, and the relaxation of some previous government restrictions. But more fundamentally, Andoni argues, events rocked the basis of the Hashemite regime's domestic and international legitimacy. This, in turn, rendered it imperative that the regime establish the foundations for a new Jordanian-Palestinian relationship, both at home and internationally. The improved state of PLO-Jordanian relations and Jordan's November 1989 parliamentary elections (the first since the 1967 Arab-Israeli war) have both been important steps along this route.

In Egypt the situation has been rather different, but no less complex. Alone among Arab states, Egypt's relationship with Israel and hence its attitude toward the Palestinian-Israeli and Arab-Israeli conflicts has been constrained by a formal peace treaty: the Egyptian-Israeli treaty of 1979, together with the legal obligations and political constraints embodied therein. As Bahgat Korany argues in his analysis of this issue, one result has been to create contradictory cross-pressures on Egyptian policy, between Egypt's inter-Arab relations and the pro-Palestinian sympathies of the bulk of Egyptian society on the one hand, and its relationship with Israel (and the US) on the other. In the case of the *intifada*, Korany reviews Egypt's official stance towards the uprising and performs a content-analysis of the Egyptian press, contrasting the present situation with another comparable period of potential strain (Israel's 1982 invasion of Lebanon). He finds that the incongruities between the state and civil society are markedly less than in 1982. Tensions have not vanished, however—and will not, as long as the Palestinian issue remains unresolved and Egypt's commitments to Israel and the US remain operative. As a result, Egyptian policy is likely to find refuge in passive ambiguity or in a mediatory role which attempts to extricate Egyptian leaders from the contradictory pressures they face. The ten-point proposal put forward by President Mubarak in the summer of 1989 (designed to bridge the gap between the positions of the PLO and Israel) provided confirmation of this latter inclination, as did Egypt's efforts to promote and preserve direct US-PLO dialogue. While the ascent of a hard-line Likud coalition in Israel, the collapse of the US-PLO dialogue in June 1990 and Iraq's invasion of Kuwait in August all served to abort immediate hopes for diplomatic progress, Egyptian policy is likely to reassert a mediatory role whenever Palestinian-Israeli conflict intensifies or diplomatic prospects brighten.

For Syria, the intensification of Palestinian-Israeli conflict has also had a direct (if lesser) impact on both domestic and foreign policy. For Syria's Ba'thist rulers, pan-Arabism and Palestinian liberation have always been important elements of domestic legitimacy. Moreover, Syria has important national security concerns at stake in the conflict, whether these relate to its suspicion of what it perceives as an aggressive and expansionist Israel, or the more tangible goal of recovering the Golan Heights (annexed by Israel in 1981). One result of this has been Syria's desire to establish for itself a leading role in the Arab-Israeli conflict, whether through its quest for inter-

Arab leadership, pursuit of strategic military parity with Israel, or failed attempts to exert hegemonic control over the Palestinian movement.

In all these areas, however, the effect of the *intifada* has been problematic. As the PLO moved towards closer contact with the US and a negotiated settlement with Israel, Damascus clearly feared the possibility of being excluded by another "separate peace." If this were to pass, Syria's leverage on the Golan issue would quickly fade. It is this fear (among other issues) that has reinforced a Syrian antipathy to the mainstream PLO, an antipathy already founded upon the latter's political independence. In turn, Syrian-PLO conflict has often served to exacerbate the regional isolation Damascus has suffered as a consequence of its actions in Lebanon and its support for Iran during the Iran-Iraq war.

At the same time, however, President Asad clearly believed through the first two years of the uprising that the diplomatic approach adopted by the PLO was doomed to eventual failure, and that as a consequence Syria need not assume an assertive role in Arab-Israeli diplomacy. Instead, a more pressing threat to Syrian interests seemed to lie in the Lebanese arena. Indeed, as Fred Lawson suggests in his chapter on Syrian policy, the primacy of the latter and the linkage between the two was evident throughout the first two years of the uprising. Not only has Syria's response to the *intifada* been muted, but whenever Syria's position in Lebanon has been challenged, the uprising has been implicitly deemphasized as a subordinate concern. Continuing conflict with Yasir 'Arafat's Fateh organization (often manifest in Lebanon) has also underwritten Syrian attitudes, limited only in part by the clear support given to the mainstream PLO by the bulk of the Palestinian population.

As Lawson observes, Syria has sometimes (notably at the May 1989 Arab summit in Casablanca) given ground on the Palestinian issue so as to protect its position in Lebanon. How long Damascus can continue to pursue this course remains open to question. Should the costs of its Lebanese involvement grow, and should the prospects for Palestinian-Israeli negotiations and settlement make a significant advance, Damascus may ultimately be forced to confront difficult policy choices—choices that it has thus far been able to postpone. How it resolves these may well depend on the extent to which it feels that Syrian interests will be taken into account in any negotiation process. As the eventual collapse of the US-sponsored 1983 Lebanese-Israeli troop withdrawal agreement demonstrated, Damascus cannot be expected to participate meekly in a regional arrangement which it has no part in shaping. When and if the negotiating process moves forward, this is a point that all concerned would do well to remember.

For the PLO, the regional repercussions of the uprising have brought with them new political and diplomatic opportunities. As Paul Noble demonstrates in his chapter on the PLO in regional politics, the first months of the uprising saw a significant strengthening of the PLO's position in inter-Arab politics (most notably in the form of Jordanian disengagement). Thereafter, the PLO's attention increasingly turned to international diplomacy, with the declaration of Palestinian independence and the political program adopted by the 19th session of the Palestine National Council in November 1988, 'Arafat's December 1988 appearance before the United Nations, and the subsequent opening of a direct dialogue between the PLO and the United States. Eventually, however, the Palestinian initiative began to stall. With this, the PLO has once more had recourse to Arab diplomacy—specifically, a mediatory role by Egypt—in its attempts to break the diplomatic deadlock generated by Israel's reluctance to accept the PLO as a negotiating partner (and American unwillingness to press the issue). It also sought, notably at the Casablanca and Baghdad summits, to mobilize continued Arab support for its political platform.

The summer of 1990 also demonstrated that limits exist in the extent to which mediation or the mobilization of Arab support can overcome Israeli rejectionism or other obstacles. Moreover, the PLO's regional position was significantly damaged by the eruption of the crisis in the Gulf. The PLO's close ties to Iraq angered both Egypt and the conservative Gulf states, threatening a marked reduction in political and economic support for the Palestinian cause from these countries. As Noble notes, this change in the regional conditions shifted the PLO's energies from promoting its faltering peace initiative to frantic efforts at political damage control.

In the broader context of the Palestinian-Israeli conflict, issues such as Egypt's role in PLO diplomacy, Syria's concerns as to the possible course of a regional settlement, Jordan's sensitivities to events across the river, and the myriad repercussions of the crisis in the Gulf, collectively underscore both the dangers of the Palestinian-Israeli conflict and the importance of regional conflict resolution. As events have made clear, the absence of meaningful progress towards a negotiated settlement of this conflict only serves to stoke general frustration and anger in the region to potentially explosive levels.[5] As argued in Part One of this volume, negotiations between Israel and the Palestinians/PLO are clearly an essential prerequisite to any progress towards peace. The contributors of Part Two, however, remind us that such negotiations—while necessary—may not in themselves be sufficient. Developments through the second and third years of the uprising pointed to the important role that regional actors have to play in any potential resolution of the Palestinian-Israeli conflict, whether as potential supporters, mediators or "spoilers." Regional negotiating processes are therefore important too, in order to address very real interests of other regional actors. However much the *intifada* has focussed attention to the Palestinian-Israeli roots of the Arab-Israeli conflict, continued regionalization of the conflict remains inescapable.

Notes

1. Mass sympathy for the uprising in many Arab countries has sometimes been coupled with implicit or explicit criticism of the inadequacy of Arab support for the Palestinian cause, however. As a result, initial media coverage of the uprising was limited in some countries, and popular protests suppressed in favor of carefully-controlled official demonstrations of solidarity. For initial reaction to the *intifada* in the Arab world, see MERIP, "Repercussions in the Middle East," *Middle East Report* 152 (May-June 1988): 45-52.

2. *Sunday Times* (London), 15 June 1969.

3. Avner Yaniv, *Dilemmas of Security: Politics, Strategy and the Israeli Experience in Lebanon* (Oxford: Oxford University Press, 1987), pp. 100-101.

4. The Palestinian proportion of the Jordanian population has long been a matter of contention. In a widely-cited analysis Valerie Yorke has suggested that, contrary to to the conventional view, Palestinians make up only about 40% of the Jordanian population; *Domestic Politics and Regional Security: Jordan, Syria and Israel* (Aldershot: Gower, 1988), pp. 33-35. This view was later officially echoed by King Husayn in his 31 July 1988 speech severing administrative links to the West Bank. Such calculations are based on a quite restricted notion of "who is a Palestinian," however, and most evidence continues to suggest that a majority of Jordanians are of Palestinian origin.

5. Despite the apparently declining salience of the Palestine issue in the Arab world and the unlikelihood of a "classic" Arab-Israeli confrontation on the model of the 1948, 1956, 1967 and 1973 wars, the tensions generated by the Arab-Israeli conflict continue to shape regional politics. This was clearly evidenced even by the otherwise unrelated crisis in the Gulf. Although Iraq's invasion of Kuwait had little to do with the Arab-Israeli conflict (and, indeed, seriously weakened the PLO's political position), Baghdad's threats against Israel and widespread public anger at continued US support for the Jewish state played a major role in enabling Iraqi President Saddam Husayn to mobilize significant Arab public support (particularly in Jordan and among Palestinians). See Edward Said's insightful essay "Behind Saddam Hussein's Moves," and Lamis Andoni, "US Intervention Spawns Arab Reaction," both in the *Christian Science Monitor*, 13 August 1990.

5

The PLO in Regional Politics

Paul Noble

The Palestinian uprising that erupted in December 1987 has had a profound impact on regional politics in the Middle East. In a relatively short period of time it transformed the position of the Palestinian community and of the Palestine Liberation Organization. In so doing, it modified the basic parameters not only of the Palestinian–Israeli conflict, but also of Palestinian relations with Arab states and the broader international system.

This chapter will examine how the *intifada*, and the PLO diplomatic program sustained by it, have reshaped the PLO's position in regional politics. In particular, it will focus on how these developments have affected inter-Arab politics, and how the PLO sought to use the Arab arena to further its political objectives during the first three years of the uprising. Finally, the chapter will assess how recent developments—particularly continued diplomatic stalemate and the Iraqi invasion of Kuwait—have affected the PLO's position and policies.

The Shaping of PLO Policy

Before examining the changing regional setting and the PLO's position therein, it is useful to first outline the various spheres of PLO activity and their role in PLO policy.[1] There are, broadly speaking, four major areas of concern. The *Palestinian sphere* has been the area of most immediate concern to the PLO leadership throughout its history. Given the dispersed and fragmented character of the Palestinian community—striving to achieve national status, but everywhere subject to the jurisdiction of others—the PLO leadership has understandably been preoccupied with the promotion of Palestinian national consciousness, the mobilization of support among Palestinian populations, and the strengthening of links between Palestinians of the diaspora and those under occupation (as well as promoting the steadfastness of the latter). The PLO has also been concerned to expand PLO capabilities, maintain cohesion among constituent groups, and promote support for the organization's policies at any given time. In short, the principal preoccupations of the PLO leadership have been internal in nature.

Externally, the *Israeli sphere* is ultimately the most fundamental in terms of the achievement of Palestinian national objectives. However, Israeli policy has consistently been characterized by intense opposition and rejectionism both toward the PLO and the Palestinian community as a whole. Consequently, there has been little or no prospect of movement in this area. Since the situation in this sphere has been relatively constant and unchanging, it has not been of as much immediate concern as other dimensions of the external setting—except when Israel has stepped up its offensive pressure either against the Palestinians in the occupied territories or against the PLO.

The *major power sphere* has been another significant area for the PLO. Here the US has been the key actor. Its support has been considered crucial to Israel, enabling it to maintain a rigid policy toward the Palestinian community. The US has thus been seen as a major obstacle to the achievement of Palestinian national aspirations. The US has also been regarded, however, as a key to any change in Israeli policy insofar as an easing of its unqualified support for Israel might force the latter to reassess its position. The major power sphere has therefore been almost as fundamental to the PLO as the Israeli sphere, and has received even greater Palestinian attention in the belief that changes in Israeli policy are more easily wrought in Washington than in Israel itself.

In all these contexts—Palestinian, Israeli, and major power, the *Arab sphere* has played a particularly important role in PLO policy. First, recognition by the Arab world of Palestinian national aspirations and the PLO's role as sole, legitimate representative of the Palestinian community has been seen as essential for gaining recognition from the US and Israel. Second, since the Palestinian community has generally lacked an autonomous territorial base of its own, it has been important to obtain sites where the PLO could function in a relatively unhindered manner. In particular, the PLO eagerly sought bases of activity which enjoyed direct access to the occupied Palestinian territories or Israel. These were useful both for inflicting damage on Israel and for providing assistance and encouragement to Palestinians under occupation. Third, the PLO has sought material support from the Arab states to fund its activities and expand its capabilities. It has also been anxious to acquire diplomatic support to press the Palestinian case at the international level. Finally, the PLO sought to obtain this assistance while still preserving its autonomy, in other words maximizing Arab support while minimizing Arab tutelage.[2] The Arab sphere has thus been important both positively and negatively. It has provided a vital supportive environment in which the Palestinian community could organize, mobilize, and develop its strength and cohesion to the point where it could successfully press its case for national status. At the same time, it has posed serious challenges to the strength, cohesion, autonomy, even survival, of both the PLO and Palestinian national aspirations.

As a result, conditions in the Arab sphere have not only been important for the success of the Palestinian cause, but have also been a continuing preoccupation. In contrast to the positions of Israel and the US—which, although hostile, have generally been stable—the Arab sphere, while nominally supportive, has been characterized by frequent change and unpredictability. This was particularly true of the frontline states, whose policies toward the PLO have frequently shifted from support to challenge within a short space of time. Small wonder then that, apart from the Palestinian sphere itself, the Arab sphere has normally been the area of most immediate concern to PLO leaders.

From Camp David to the Eve of the *Intifada*

In the years prior to the *intifada* the PLO was confronted with a worsening political and strategic situation. The blockage on the Israeli and major power fronts remained as serious as ever, while the situation on the Arab front had become ever more precarious.

On the Israeli front, the PLO and Palestinian community had been subjected to increased pressures in the years following the 1978 Camp David accords. These included accelerated settlement activity in the occupied territories, the official annexation of East Jerusalem, and intensified military operations in Lebanon culminating in the invasion of 1982. The latter was successful in eliminating the PLO's only autonomous base of military and political activity on the frontline, thereby depriving the organization of any viable military option against Israel (if indeed one had ever existed). With the advent of a Labor-Likud coalition in 1984, Israeli policy became more cautious and a little less rigid. Labor leader Shimon Peres explored the possibility of a diplomatic opening, but this flexibility was limited to the pursuit of a "Jordanian option". At the same time, in the occupied territories the government pursued an "iron fist" policy designed to repress opposition.

During this same period the situation in the major power sphere was almost as discouraging. After several years of relative inactivity, the US had embarked on a new initiative (the Reagan plan) in the wake of the Israeli invasion of Lebanon.[3] While the proposal displayed some flexibility on the Palestinian question, the US remained committed to the Jordanian option and sought to circumvent both the PLO and Palestinian national aspirations. The eventual failure of both the Reagan plan and the US-brokered Lebanese-Israeli peace agreement led the Reagan administration to adopt a relatively passive stance toward the conflict in subsequent years. In effect, it decided not to undertake any further initiatives on its own but rather to await overtures from the parties concerned.

As the superpowers embarked on a process of detente in the mid-1980s there were expectations that they might cooperate in the resolution of regional conflicts. Whatever hopes the PLO may have had in this regard were dimmed by the US-Soviet summit in December 1987.[4] It became clear that the two powers were preoccupied with bilateral relations, especially arms control issues, and other regional conflicts. The US in particular appeared to believe that the situation on the Arab-Israeli front, unlike that elsewhere in the region, was relatively stable for the foreseeable future. It therefore did not require any special attention or effort, especially since there seemed to be such a wide gap between the parties on both substantive and procedural issues. Given the absence of any sense of urgency and the fact that the US was about to enter a presidential election year, there appeared to be little immediate prospect of any serious superpower effort to resolve the Palestinian-Israeli conflict.

As a result of these blockages and pressures in the Israeli and major power spheres, the Arab sphere assumed added importance for the PLO. Here, however, it also confronted increasingly serious difficulties, especially on the frontline. The PLO tended to be on the defensive, with relatively limited options during most of this period. As a result, it was forced to conduct a diplomacy of mobility, shifting from one alignment to another to promote Palestinian interests and preserve PLO autonomy. Indeed, by 1987 it found itself increasingly isolated and vulnerable, lacking any effective support and facing challenges and pressures from two key states (Syria and Jordan).

On the Syrian front, relations had consistently been difficult due to conflicting national interests and policies. Syria continued to seek a sphere of influence in its immediate area both to strengthen its hand in the regional arena and to present a common front toward Israel. It therefore expected other frontline actors to coordinate policies with it and allow it a decisive say on crucial issues. In particular, it wished to bring the PLO and Palestinian community under its tutelage and assume the role of dominant partner in a strategic alliance.[5] The conflict came to a head after the Israeli invasion of Lebanon, when Yasir 'Arafat sought to diversify the PLO's relations and pursue a more independent approach to the Arab-Israeli conflict.[6] This encouraged President Hafiz al-Asad to support a rebellion within 'Arafat's own Fateh organization, which soon widened into an open split in the PLO itself. The conflict escalated further as Syria supported Fateh/PLO rebels in a successful campaign to drive loyalist forces from Syrian-controlled areas of Lebanon. From here on, Syria worked actively to weaken and paralyze the mainstream PLO, seeking to bring it to terms or change its leadership. In addition to political and subversive pressures, Syria stepped up the physical pressure on the PLO in Lebanon. Here its local Shi'ite allies (Amal) moved to forcefully eliminate the independent Palestinian politico-military presence which Fateh had sought to rebuild. In the resulting "camps war" (spring 1985 until early 1988), Fateh and its allies found themselves constantly under siege. Matters were carried a step further when the Lebanese parliament, presumably with Syrian encouragement, canceled the 1969 Cairo Agreement which constituted the legal basis of the PLO's presence.

The PLO's problems were compounded during this period by renewed pressures from Jordan. In the wake of the Israeli invasion of Lebanon, 'Arafat had moved to lessen the PLO's dependence through a diversification of ties, and in particular developed links with Jordan with a view to exploring a diplomatic opening to the US.[7] It was not until February 1985, however, that an accord was reached, providing for a Palestinian-Jordanian delegation to any peace talks and an eventual Palestinian-Jordanian confederation.[8] In spite of the agreement and the continuing efforts at policy coordination, a climate of competition and mutual suspicion prevailed in PLO-Jordanian relations.[9] By early 1986, faced with continued blockage in its settlement efforts due to deep-seated Israeli and US hostility toward the PLO and the latter's unwillingness to make the concessions insisted upon by the US, King Husayn decided that Jordan's ties with the PLO constituted a liability. He therefore moved to suspend political cooperation. He also took steps to undermine the position of the organization, suggesting to Palestinians that they might do well to develop an alternative leadership. Jordan sought further to strengthen its position in the occupied territories through the establishment of a development fund to channel aid and investment to the area. At the same time, quiet cooperation apparently developed between Jordan and Israel to hinder pro-PLO elements in the territories. In short, Jordan was attempting to weaken and marginalize the PLO in order to substitute more cooperative Palestinians from the territories as negotiating partners, or else force the PLO leadership to come to terms.[10]

Two other elements in Jordan's policy were worrisome to the PLO. One was Jordan's increasing rapprochement with Syria. The two countries had been involved in bitter conflict since the late 1970s. Now, however, Jordan sought an ally in its campaign against the PLO as well as political cover for a potential opening to Israel. Syria, seeking to reduce its isolation and eager to detach Jordan from the PLO, responded favorably to these overtures. From late 1985 on there were regular discussions and some attempt at coordination of policy regarding the Arab-Israeli conflict. By emphasizing an international conference as the mechanism for negotiations, Jordan sought to reassure Syria that all segments of the conflict would be linked and that no attempt would be made to achieve a separate settlement at Syria's expense. There also appears to have been an increasing alignment of positions concerning the PLO and the Palestinian question. By 1987, Syria was quietly supporting Jordanian efforts to undercut the PLO, establish a joint Jordanian-Palestinian delegation and reassert a Jordanian role in the occupied territories.[11]

The PLO's other main concern centered on King Husayn's efforts to reach an agreement with Israel regarding a mechanism and procedures for initiating negotiations. This initiative culminated in a secret agreement between the King and Israeli Foreign Minister Shimon Peres in April 1987 (the London agreement) to work for a loose international conference within which negotiations would be conducted largely on a bilateral basis.[12] This was not implemented due to opposition from the Likud half of Israel's coalition government. Nevertheless, the PLO remained worried about Israel's attempts to bypass it, as well as the possible collusion of one or more frontline states in this regard.

This shift in alignments left Egypt as the PLO's only potential frontline supporter—but even this relationship was seriously strained by the spring of 1987. In the mid-1980s, as part of his effort to diversify the PLO's ties, 'Arafat had moved to restore relations with Cairo. This step was also a logical extension of the PLO's overtures to Jordan: given its connections with the US, Egypt could be helpful in reinforcing the PLO-Jordanian initiative and encouraging a favorable US response. An Egyptian link would also enable the PLO to avoid excessive dependence on Jordan. In other words, Egypt could serve as a counterweight should Jordan attempt to press the PLO too hard. This connection had been useful to the PLO, although Egypt had by no means been an unconditional supporter. While Cairo generally supported the PLO and Palestinian national rights, the PLO leadership became concerned that as the balance of forces between it and Jordan tilted in the latter's favor, the center-of-gravity of Egyptian policy was also shifting towards Amman.[13] Relations were further complicated by developments during the 18th session of the Palestine National Council in April 1987, when a resolution was passed reaffirming earlier PNC support for opposition forces in Egypt. This angered the Egyptian government and led to a closure of PLO offices in Cairo.

On the eve of the *intifada*, therefore, the PLO found itself in virtual isolation on the frontline, estranged from all the neighboring Arab states and faced with a joint Jordanian-Syrian effort to undermine its position. The situation in the larger Arab system was not much better. During the 1980s, the Arab world found itself under mounting pressure on its eastern flank. The new Islamic regime in Iran had emerged as an ideological, internal security, and military challenge for many Arab regimes. Due to the immediacy and multi-dimensional character of the threat, the Iran-Iraq conflict and developments in the Gulf came to overshadow the Arab-Israeli conflict in the minds of most Arab decision-makers. Consequently, the attention and resources of the states of the eastern Arab world were concentrated on the eastern front, making it difficult to mobilize much support on behalf of the Palestinian cause.[14]

All these developments were reflected in the proceedings of the Arab summit held in Amman in November 1987. At the summit, the Iran-Iraq war was clearly the major topic of concern, with the Arab-Israeli conflict accorded a much lower priority.[15] Moreover, in discussion of the

Palestinian issue the PLO found itself faced with a working paper prepared by Jordan (in conjunction with Syria) which sought to dilute the PLO's role and assign greater responsibilities to Jordan both in the negotiating process and any eventual settlement. In the end, 'Arafat was able to secure enough support from other Arab states (notably Iraq, Algeria and South Yemen) to sidetrack the Jordanian-Syrian attempt to undercut the PLO and Palestinian national aspirations.[16] Still, there could be no overestimating the extent to which, as 1987 approached its close, the PLO found itself in difficult circumstances on all fronts.

Impact of the *Intifada*

In the midst of what was, from a Palestinian viewpoint, a rather bleak situation, the *intifada* erupted in December 1987. Encompassing all parts of the occupied territories as well as all segments of the population, the uprising constituted a landmark event in Palestinian history. The uprising restored the Arab–Israeli conflict to the forefront of regional and global politics at a time when both Israel and the major powers believed that it was declining in importance. It activated, for the first time since 1948, a distinct Palestinian front, thereby obliging Israel and the US to take Palestinian nationalism more seriously. It demonstrated that the situation in the occupied territories was an unstable one, and gave the Palestinians new leverage in their struggle. In creating an active Palestinian front, the *intifada* gave the PLO and the Palestinian people enhanced standing as a party to the conflict. This new standing placed added responsibility on the PLO to spell out its position regarding the conflict and address itself directly to its opponents. At the same time, the success of the *intifada* created a new sense of self–confidence among the PLO and Palestinian community. This enabled them to be more flexible in their policy and to make the compromises necessary to initiate a peace process. In short, the *intifada* seemed to perform many of the same functions for the PLO that the 1973 war had performed for Egypt.

While less noticeable perhaps, the *intifada* also had a strong impact in the Palestinian and Arab spheres. In the Palestinian sphere, the uprising served to strengthen the links between Palestinians of the interior and those of the diaspora, thereby contributing to further integration of the Palestinian political system.[17] By increasing solidarity at all levels, it also reduced the penetrability of Palestinian society and politics. This "hardening" of the Palestinian political system strengthened the community vis–à–vis both its Arab rivals and Israel. The *intifada* altered the balance of forces between the Palestinian community and Arab states in other ways as well. The intensity of Palestinian national consciousness undercut any claims neighboring states may have had to Palestinian territories or to tutelage over the PLO. Moreover, by opening their own front, the Palestinian community could now promote their cause by their own actions and no longer had to depend so heavily on others. This increased sense of self–reliance extended to the diplomatic sphere. With their newly enhanced standing obliging adversaries to take them more seriously, the PLO now felt less need of Arab sponsors or intermediaries.

These tendencies did not manifest themselves all at once or with equal force. In terms of the impact on the PLO's position and policies, one can discern three phases in the era of the *intifada*.

Breakthrough in the Arab Sphere

Whatever the ultimate effects of the *intifada* on Israel and the US, the PLO's most immediate challenges and opportunities lay in the Palestinian and Arab spheres. In the Palestinian sphere there were several urgent tasks. The first was to sustain and intensify the uprising, since this constituted the most powerful weapon available to advance the Palestinian cause. Parallel to this, the PLO sought to ensure its overall authority over the uprising. Internal cohesion was another key concern therefore. Matters were helped, however, by the substantial reunification of the PLO which had taken place several months prior to the *intifada,* as well as by a determination among all groups that the uprising should succeed.

Apart from its activity on the internal front, the PLO leadership paid considerable attention to the Arab sphere during this initial phase. Before the uprising could be translated into political gains at the international level, the PLO was faced with two major tasks: first, to overcome challenges from frontline states; and second, to refocus Arab attention on the Palestinian–Israeli conflict and mobilize Arab support for the Palestinian cause. Unless these tasks could be accomplished, it would be difficult to convince the US and Israel to take Palestinian national aspirations seriously.

Among the frontline states, the initial breakthrough occurred with Egypt. This sector posed the least problems since Egypt appeared to have no particular ambitions regarding Palestinian territory or tutelage over the PLO. Attempts had already been made during the summer of 1987 to persuade Egypt to disregard the offending PNC resolutions and renew relations with the PLO. The Amman summit improved the atmosphere by legitimizing the restoration of diplomatic relations with Egypt. Shortly afterwards, Egypt responded to PLO overtures by allowing the reopening of the organization's Cairo offices.[18] Relations improved steadily thereafter. In fact, Egypt seemed determined to work toward a settlement of the Palestinian problem—in part to prove that the Egyptian–Israeli treaty had not been a separate peace, and in part to demonstrate its importance to the Arab world and thus expedite its full reintegration into the Arab system.

Seeking to capitalize on the momentum generated by the *intifada,* Egyptian President Husni Mubarak moved at an early stage to encourage a

US initiative to address the Palestinian problem. While many in the Palestinian movement objected to some of Egypt's initial suggestions (particularly the notion that a truce should be called in the *intifada* to create a satisfactory climate for negotiations), this move was successful in securing the first US peace initiative in five years.[19] And, although Secretary of State Shultz's proposals were a disappointment (in that the US government continued to try to bypass the PLO and pursue a modified Jordanian option), Egypt did prove helpful in insisting on the need to deal with the PLO and to accept Palestinian self determination, albeit within the framework of links with Jordan. Egypt also sought, unsuccessfully, to promote direct US contacts with the PLO. Nevertheless, the efforts of Egypt and others were successful in securing some symbolic modification of the US position, notably the description of the conflict as a clash between two national movements and the need to secure the legitimate political rights of the Palestinian people.[20] From this point on, Egypt emerged as a major focal point of diplomatic activity on the Palestinian issue and the PLO's closest associate among the frontline states.

Of all the frontline states, the *intifada*'s impact was greatest on Jordan. As noted earlier, Jordan had been working to undermine the influence of the PLO and to position itself to play a major role in negotiations over the West Bank and Gaza. For the US government and an important part of the Israeli political elite (notably the Labor party), such a "Jordanian option" was clearly a preferred solution. In this initial phase, therefore, Jordan constituted the principal frontline challenge to the PLO.

Initially the PLO leadership sought to capitalize on the *intifada*, and the sympathy which it generated, to achieve a normalization of PLO–Jordanian relations. Amman felt obliged to respond to PLO overtures, renew contacts and reactivate the PLO–Jordanian joint committee.[21] It also sought, however, to limit any organized manifestations of support within Jordan itself. As the uprising continued and intensified, Jordan found itself increasingly on the defensive. Developments in the territories left absolutely no doubt as to where the loyalties of the population lay. The uprising's intense display of Palestinian national consciousness—and periodic expressions of opposition to Jordanian tutelage—seriously undermined the credibility of any Jordanian claims to the occupied territories or to representation of their Palestinian inhabitants.[22]

With the momentum shifting in its favor, the PLO leadership became more insistent on its exclusive right to represent the population of the territories and on the right of Palestinians to self–determination and an independent state. At the same time, 'Arafat and his advisors saw the advantage of good relations with Jordan in terms both of access to the occupied territories and the need to find an acceptable formula for a settlement. It was felt that links with Jordan would facilitate US, if not Israeli, acceptance of Palestinian self–determination. Jordanian cooperation could also be useful in the process leading to a settlement. Hence, while a climate of competition and mutual suspicion continued to prevail in PLO–Jordanian relations, the PLO leadership sought to avoid overplaying its hand. 'Arafat adopted a tactic of restrained assertiveness, seeking to maneuver Jordan into dropping its claims rather than attempting to provoke an outright rupture.[23]

The success of the *intifada* in undermining Jordan's position was reflected in the latter's response to the Shultz initiative during the first half of 1988. Jordan was initially encouraged that the uprising had galvanized the US into action after several years of relative passivity.[24] It may also have been satisfied that the US proposals envisaged a significant role for Jordan both in the peace process and in an eventual solution. Whatever Jordan's hopes, however, the forceful expression of Palestinian nationalism in the occupied territories and the PLO's refusal to assume a role of junior partner made clear that Jordan's room for maneuver was limited. Israeli policy contributed substantially to this by demonstrating that there was no real possibility of an honorable settlement even if Jordan decided to act unilaterally. Hence, King Husayn was obliged to affirm that Jordan had no intention of trying to substitute for the PLO and that it continued to support the right of self–determination of the Palestinian people. These views were expressed in a series of talks during the spring of 1988 as well as in the King's speech to the Algiers summit in June.[25] This was followed shortly afterward by the King's decision to sever Jordan's legal, administrative, and financial ties to the West Bank.

If the PLO was able to make substantial headway in overcoming the Jordanian challenge, this was much less true in the case of Syria. To improve its precarious position on the frontline, the PLO had made overtures for a normalization of relations prior to the Amman summit. Syria did not respond. After the outbreak of the *intifada*, however, it made a few gestures to improve relations. A number of PLO officials were released from Syrian prisons. More importantly, in Lebanon, Syria's Amal allies proclaimed an end to their siege of Palestinian camps as a gesture of support for the *intifada*. These steps were followed by contacts between Syrian and PLO officials. The assassination in April 1988 of the PLO's second-in-command, Khalil al-Wazir ("Abu Jihad"), generated new opportunities for detente. 'Arafat's visit to Damascus after the funeral and his meeting with President Asad appeared to set the stage for a further improvement in relations. Some officials of the Popular Front for the Liberation of Palestine and Democratic Front for the Liberation of Palestine who had been involved in PLO reunification efforts at the Algiers PNC meeting the previous spring were now allowed to return to Damascus and resume their activities.[26]

While these moves toward normalization were occurring, Syria was also attempting to enhance its influence in the Palestinian movement. Its position had been weakened when the PFLP, DFLP and Palestine Communist Party had decided to rejoin the mainstream PLO. The uprising, however, appeared to provide Syria with new opportunities. A Syrian–backed group, the PFLP–General Command, had played a role in triggering the *intifada* through a spectacular glider raid into northern Israel in late November.[27] Moreover, the uprising itself fitted in well with Syria's approach to the conflict. According to this view, no progress toward an honorable settlement would occur until the unfavorable regional balance of forces had changed: it was not by gratuitous concessions but rather by keeping the pressure on Israel that the occupied territories would be recovered.[28] The *intifada* appeared to be an excellent expression of this approach and, in President Asad's view, a suitable contrast to the strategy pursued by Yasir 'Arafat. Hence Syria gave strong verbal encouragement to the *intifada*. It also provided facilities for *al–Quds* radio, which played an important role in informing and mobilizing the population of the territories in the early months of the uprising.

Syria, however, soon discovered that its potential for influence in the Palestinian movement was still limited. For one thing, as the focus of Palestinian activity shifted to the occupied territories, Syria's leverage weakened. Syrian–backed Palestinian dissident groups carried some weight in Lebanon (where they functioned under a Syrian umbrella) but they were weak to non–existent in the West Bank and Gaza. More generally, by heightening Palestinian national consciousness and underlining the need for national unity, the *intifada* had made it more difficult for external actors to penetrate the Palestinian political system and acquire allies within the movement. Finally, the uprising generated an increased sense of confidence and self–reliance among Palestinians which made them feel less dependent on others. Thus the *intifada* altered to some degree the balance of forces between the PLO and Syria and created new obstacles to Syrian influence.

In spite of attempts at detente, conflicting national ambitions and deep–seated animosities proved difficult to overcome. A new round of conflict between the PLO and Syria was set off by developments in Lebanon and intra–Palestinian rivalries. Shortly after 'Arafat's talks with President Asad, fighting broke out in Beirut area Palestinian camps between Fateh forces and groups allied with Syria.[29] The conflict persisted at a low level until after the Algiers summit in June. Then Syria moved quickly to support its Palestinian allies and prevent Fateh from posing a challenge to its control over the Beirut area. Under strong Syrian pressure, Fateh and its allies were forced to withdraw to the south of Lebanon. This was accompanied by sharp attacks on the PLO leadership and its direction. Thus the latter not only found itself under serious pressure in Lebanon once again but also embroiled in a new cold war with Syria.[30]

While the role of the frontline states was crucial, PLO diplomacy did not stop there. At this key juncture it also sought to refocus Arab attention on the conflict and mobilize broad Arab support for the Palestinian cause. Such a show of support was necessary to strengthen the hand of the PLO vis-à-vis not only Israel and the US but also its frontline Arab rivals. The importance of this support was further accentuated by the need to counteract the impression conveyed by the Amman summit that the Palestinian question was of secondary concern (compared to the Gulf war), and by challenges posed by the newly-declared Shultz initiative.

In response to PLO appeals, an Arab foreign ministers' meeting was held in January 1988. This established a seven nation committee to coordinate Arab diplomatic activity in support of the uprising.[31] The PLO kept pressing, however, for a full Arab summit devoted to the *intifada*. These efforts were rewarded when the leaders of the Arab states met for this purpose in Algiers in June 1988. The Algiers summit accomplished several things from a Palestinian viewpoint. To begin with, the very holding of the conference signaled that the Palestinian question was once again a prime concern of the Arab states. Furthermore, the conference strongly reaffirmed its support for Palestinian national rights, including the right to self-determination and an independent state, as well as recognition of the PLO as the sole, legitimate representative of the Palestinian people. It also endorsed an international conference attended by all the parties to the conflict, including a Palestinian delegation participating on an equal footing, as the proper mechanism for resolving the conflict. In short, Arab leaders stated clearly that the Palestinian option constituted the only acceptable solution to the conflict and that the PLO had to be a full participant in the settlement process.[32] Finally, the summit agreed in principle to provide a significant amount of financial support to help sustain the uprising.[33]

Yasir 'Arafat was also able to use the weight of Arab opinion, as expressed at the summit, to bolster the PLO's position vis-à-vis Jordan. Realizing that Jordan's position had weakened significantly, King Husayn acknowledged in his speech to the conference that the PLO constituted the sole, legitimate representative of the Palestinian people and stressed that Jordan had no intention of substituting for it. He also recognized the right of the Palestinians to determine their own future. If the Palestinians wished to form a joint delegation to the proposed international conference and develop eventual confederal links with Jordan, Jordan would be prepared to cooperate. If they decided in favor of an independent delegation and an independent Palestinian state, that was fine also. Whatever they wanted, Jordan was prepared to support. The King did advise the PLO privately, however, not to insist on agreement to an independent Palestinian state as a precondition for the conference, since this would mean that no conference would be convened.[34]

While insisting on clear-cut recognition of Palestinian national rights and of the PLO's right to sole representation of the Palestinian people, 'Arafat displayed some awareness of Jordanian sensitivities. This may have been encouraged by rumors circulated immediately prior to the conference that

Jordan was considering ending its financial and administrative involvement in the occupied territories.[35] For whatever reason, 'Arafat was conciliatory in his meeting with King Husayn and agreed to modify certain PLO proposals (notably one omitting reference to Jordan as a channel of assistance to the occupied territories) to which Jordan took exception.[36]

The Algiers summit substantially reinforced the PLO's position and led King Husayn to further reconsider Jordan's role in the conflict. The *intifada* had demonstrated the depth of both Palestinian national consciousness in the territories and their opposition to any reassertion of Jordanian authority. The uprising had also caused unrest among Palestinians resident in Jordan. Moreover, Arab states had once again clearly recognized the PLO as the embodiment of Palestinian national aspirations. King Husayn and his advisors were stung by the constant questioning of Jordanian motives and by the opposition to a renewed Jordanian role in the territories. Resentment of the alleged ingratitude of the population of the territories gave rise to strongly-held sentiments that the Palestinians should be allowed to fend for themselves.[37]

Since continuing rivalry with the PLO appeared to jeopardize Jordan's regional relationships and possibly its domestic stability as well, King Hussayn decided on a dramatic move. On 31 July, 1988 he announced that Jordan would disengage from its legal, administrative, and financial ties with the West Bank, placing these responsibilities squarely on Palestinian shoulders.[38] While presented as a definitive step, it is possible that the King initially viewed this as a tactical move to jolt the PLO and the residents of the territories into rethinking their options. The calculation may very well have been that the sharp reduction in Jordanian assistance and the prospect of assuming full responsibility for the territories on short notice would force both the PLO and the local population to turn to Jordan once again.[39]

The far–reaching steps envisaged and the speed with which they were to be implemented caught the PLO off-balance. There was considerable initial concern about the impact of the disengagement measures on the well–being and resolve of the population of the territories.[40] After two or three weeks of uncertainty, the PLO leadership concluded that the potential damage was not as great as first feared. More importantly, the steps taken by Jordan and the abrupt manner in which they were implemented strengthened Palestinian determination to prove that they could manage on their own. This determination, together with the belief that Jordanian disengagement constituted an historic opportunity, enabled the PLO leadership to regain its balance and take up the challenge. The PLO now asserted confidently that events had demonstrated that the Palestinian option was the only viable one.[41] Those seeking a solution to the conflict would have to address themselves to the Palestinian people and its representative, the PLO. Whatever the King's original intent, disengagement intensified the Palestinians' drive for self–reliance and ultimately independence.

The Peace Initiative

By late summer 1988, the *intifada* had produced significant improvement in the PLO's position within the Arab sphere. Arab attention was now focussed once again on the Palestinian–Israeli conflict. Arab support for Palestinian national rights and the PLO had been reaffirmed. Above all, the PLO's only serious competitor had relinquished any claims it may have had to the future of the occupied territories. With this breakthrough, the PLO could now insist that there was no legitimate alternative to the Palestinian option.

With its position in the Arab sphere significantly improved, the focus of PLO foreign policy activity shifted to the major power sphere. The PLO leadership sought to capitalize on the momentum generated by the *intifada* by undertaking a diplomatic initiative at the global level. The main target of this initiative was the US and Western powers. 'Arafat calculated that the US was the key to progress because its extensive and virtually unqualified support for Israel gave the latter little incentive to rethink its inflexible stand on the Palestinian question. If only the US could be encouraged to adopt a more evenhanded policy, Israel's position would be weakened and it would be obliged to reassess its policies.

The PLO initiative began shortly after the Algiers summit with the publication of a document prepared by 'Arafat's advisor and spokesman, Bassam Abu Sharif.[42] In this document, Abu Sharif set about to reassure the international community and Israelis about the PLO's intentions. He underlined the need for Israeli–Palestinian coexistence and affirmed that the PLO was prepared to accept resolutions 242 and 338, provided Palestinian national rights were also recognized. He further stressed the importance of direct negotiations between Israel and the Palestinians, through their chosen representatives, and stated that the PLO was prepared to accept the results of any UN supervised plebiscite in the West Bank and Gaza.

The initiative received further impetus after Jordan's disengagement from the West Bank. Stepping into the vacuum created by the Jordanian move, the PLO leadership now set about to entrench the Palestinian option. At its 19th session in Algiers (November 1988), the Palestine National Council adopted a declaration of independence proclaiming the establishment of a Palestinian state. This dramatic step, based on the UN General Assembly partition resolution (181) of 1947, was accompanied by a political statement outlining the PLO's new, more pragmatic program, including acceptance of UN Security Council resolution 242 and of the existence of Israel.[43] While this statement differed little from what 'Arafat had been saying for a number of years, it was expressed more clearly and in less conditional form. Its adoption by the PNC was intended to dispel suspicions about PLO aims and make the Palestinian option more acceptable to the US and the international community.

Benefiting from the increased flexibility provided by the PNC declarations, 'Arafat set about to articulate the new PLO policy in a way that would meet US conditions for initiating a dialogue. In his speech to a hastily convened UN General Assembly session in Geneva (December 1988), and especially in a press conference the following day, 'Arafat provided the clearest formulation to date of the PLO's peace initiative.[44] This led to the hoped–for opening as the US agreed to begin official discussions. In PLO eyes, this amounted to a significant breakthrough and tacit US acknowledgement that the Palestinian people constituted a distinct entity with the PLO as their principal representative.

After this initial progress, the initiative remained in limbo for several months as the PLO waited for the new governments in the US and Israel to define their policies. While waiting for further evolution in the US position, the PLO pursued its diplomatic initiative in Europe. This produced additional gains, as several countries upgraded the level of their contacts with the PLO and/or the status of PLO missions. The main breakthrough came in the form of an official visit to France by 'Arafat in May 1989, during which he was received by President Mitterand. During this visit, 'Arafat pressed his peace initiative further by declaring that those sections of the Palestine National Charter which rejected the existence of Israel had been rendered obsolete ("caduc") by the resolutions of the 19th PNC.[45] A little later, the European Community, in its Madrid declaration (June 1989), called for negotiations based on UN Security Council resolutions 242 and 338 as well as the principle of land for peace, and stated that no solution should be ruled out. It also insisted that the PLO must participate in, and not merely be associated with, the settlement process.[46]

While the success of the *intifada* and the political results which it produced at the global level made the PLO feel more self–reliant and confident in its ability to achieve a breakthrough, it still sought to reinforce its position in the Arab sphere. During this phase, the PLO gravitated increasingly toward Egypt for support of its peace initiative, believing that its diplomatic weight and links with the principal parties to the conflict could be very helpful. Egypt needed little encouragement in this regard. As noted earlier, it believed that helping to advance the Palestinian cause would not only legitimize its own peace settlement with Israel but also provide an opportunity to assume a leading role in the Arab system once again.

With Jordan's reduced involvement in the conflict, Egypt's role became more central than ever. As the PLO embarked on its initiative, Egypt had been active behind the scenes seeking to promote an opening to the US and, more generally, to generate some movement toward a settlement. The relationship between Egypt and the PLO was a complex one, however. Egypt certainly urged the US (and Israel) to be responsive to PLO overtures and demonstrate greater flexibility. It did not act as an unconditional supporter of the PLO, however, but rather sought to coax it too in the direction of flexibility and compromise. Its role, therefore, was that of a supportive intermediary—part advocate of the Palestinian cause, and part go-between trying to create favorable conditions for dialogue.

This dual role was clearly reflected in Egyptian diplomacy throughout this phase. During the summer of 1988 it had tried again to arrange a meeting between a US official and a group of Palestinians from both inside and outside the occupied territories, including persons with official links to the PLO. This attempt proved unsuccessful as the US sought to limit the meeting to Palestinians from the territories. At the same time, in the months leading up to the 19th PNC session, Egypt urged the PLO leadership to formulate a political program which would permit an opening. In addition, it consistently encouraged renewed PLO coordination with Jordan to facilitate the initiation of negotiations and the eventual achievement of a settlement.[47]

Egypt's advice had some impact since, in addition to the proclamation of a Palestinian state, the PNC approved a political statement that appeared to meet most, if not all, US conditions for PLO participation in the settlement process. The statement also supported the establishment of a confederation between the proposed Palestinian state and Jordan. While declaring its "support" for the establishment of a Palestinian state, Egypt hesitated for a few days before officially recognizing it. This hesitation apparently stemmed from concern about possible Israeli and US reactions, and worry that recognition might harm Egypt's standing as an intermediary and affect the level of US economic assistance.[48] Eventually, Egypt took the risk of recognition, believing that it stood to gain more in the Arab world.

Despite this passing cloud, the PLO continued to coordinate moves with Egypt and to benefit from Egyptian support. At the special UN session in Geneva, 'Arafat attempted to translate the PNC's new political declaration into a statement that would satisfy US conditions for the initiation of a dialogue. When the US judged his statement insufficently clear, President Mubarak personally telephoned US Secretary of State Shultz to argue that this was an opportunity for a breakthrough which should not be missed or the position of PLO and Arab moderates would be damaged. He then urged Shultz to listen carefully to 'Arafat's subsequent clarification.[49] These efforts, together with those of other states (notably Sweden) played a role in breaking the stalemate and opening official channels of communication between the US and PLO. While the US–PLO dialogue marked time in early 1989 as the new administration formulated its Middle East policy, Egypt remained active behind the scenes. In particular, it helped to arrange 'Arafat's visit to France.[50] Later in the summer, when the peace initiative became bogged down, Egypt would prove helpful in countering Israel's revived autonomy plan and proposing more satisfactory interim measures. Egypt thus emerged as the PLO's most effective Arab ally.

Elsewhere on the frontline, relations with Jordan continued to be strained. With its disengagement from the West Bank, Jordan's potential role in the settlement process declined substantially. At this point, it quietly nursed its wounds. The PLO, for its part, had seen its position and that of the Palestinian option enhanced considerably by the Jordanian move. Nevertheless, there was considerable resentment at the abrupt manner in which Jordan had withdrawn its assistance and reduced its economic links with the territories as well as at related "Jordanization" measures in the Kingdom itself. Many Palestinians believed that Jordan was deliberately trying to make life difficult so that the inhabitants of the West Bank and the PLO would be obliged to turn to it once again.

As PLO planning for its diplomatic initiative progressed and coordination with Egypt intensified during the fall of 1988, President Mubarak strongly urged Yasir 'Arafat to renew contacts and undertake a rapprochement with Jordan. 'Arafat was receptive to this suggestion, in part to consolidate the PLO's position and in part to improve the chances of the peace initiative. President Mubarak proceeded to arrange a tripartite summit in Jordan immediately prior to the forthcoming Israeli election (late October 1988). At this meeting, 'Arafat joined with Mubarak and Husayn in signaling to Israeli voters that they were seriously interested in peace. He also indicated that the PLO was prepared to accept a confederation between a Palestinian state and Jordan, hopefully making the Palestinian option more acceptable to Israel and the US.[51] This summit was followed by the PNC meeting, which reiterated 'Arafat's commitment to a Palestinian–Jordanian confederation. Jordan, in turn, quickly recognized the Palestinian state and approved the establishment of a Palestinian embassy in Amman.[52]

From this point on, relations improved gradually between the PLO and Jordan. This was helped by a considerable easing of the climate of mutual suspicion that had prevailed previously. Given this new climate and its own increased sense of self–confidence, the PLO leadership was able to deal with Jordan on a more equal footing and in a more positive manner. In spite of the rapprochement, however, there was by no means full coordination between the two during this phase. The PLO leadership was prepared to accept a Palestinian–Jordanian confederation but only after a Palestinian state had been established. Moreover, it resisted any notion of a joint Palestinian–Jordanian delegation to the proposed international conference, insisting instead on either an independent Palestinian delegation or a joint Arab delegation in which the PLO would participate on an equal footing. Jordan, for its part, regularly reaffirmed its support for Palestinian national rights and for the PLO as the representative of the Palestinian community. Its backing was largely confined to verbal support, however, as it engaged in only limited diplomatic activity in support of the Palestinian cause.

While foreign policy calculations played an important role in the gradual PLO–Jordanian rapprochement, domestic developments in Jordan also contributed. During this period, Jordan began to experience serious economic difficulties. A sharp drop in the value of the Jordanian dinar began in the spring of 1988. A further decline occurred following the disengagement decision, due in part to a transfer of dinar holdings to other currencies by the PLO as well as Palestinians in the Gulf and occupied territories.[54] Jordan experienced even more serious currency difficulties in the summer of 1989. These were eased largely through the assistance of Saudi Arabia and other Gulf states. The PLO also began to play some role in supporting Jordanian currency at this point, urging Palestinians to help sustain the value of the dinar by not transferring funds to other currencies.[55] This was needed, it was argued, to protect the financial position and living standards of Palestinians in the occupied territories whose savings were in dinars. Jordan also experienced serious political troubles. In April 1989 rioting broke out in various towns as East Bankers protested economic conditions and corruption and called for political liberalization. The PLO urged Palestinians in Jordan not to become involved in these troubles so that they would not be turned into a Palestinian–Jordanian conflict. This intervention was helpful in preventing the spread of the rioting to Amman and other cities of northern Jordan. Palestinians were apparently also urged not to figure too prominently among opposition forces in Jordan's subsequent parliamentary elections in November.[56] Thus the PLO sought not only to avoid provoking the Jordanian regime, but even assisted it in an effort to consolidate Jordan's diplomatic support.

While the PLO was able to gain the backing first of Egypt and then of Jordan for its initiative, Syria maintained its hostility toward the organization. The fundamental problem in Syrian eyes was the PLO's refusal to accept Syrian direction both in the Arab arena and in regard to the Arab–Israeli conflict. The problem was compounded by the PLO's cooperation with Syria's rival, Egypt, and even with its bitter enemy, Iraq. Syria was especially critical of the PLO's peace initiative both for its unilateral character and for its allegedly harmful impact on Palestinian and Arab interests.[57] It constantly emphasized that the existing balance of forces was unfavorable to the Arab world. In such circumstances, peace initiatives and concessions by individual actors would weaken Arab bargaining power and invite pressures for more concessions without achieving progress toward an honorable settlement. The best way to achieve Palestinian and Arab rights was to develop an overall balance of forces ("strategic parity") between Israel and the Arab states and to establish close coordination among frontline actors. Only then would Israel be prepared to negotiate seriously.

These views led to sharp disagreement with the PLO leadership on how best to deal with the conflict. Syria strongly condemned the Abu Sharif document.[58] While "supporting" the proclamation of a Palestinian state at the 19th PNC session, it registered its opposition to the accompanying political declaration. Moreover, Syria took no steps to recognize the Palestinian state or to receive a Palestinian embassy in Damascus.[59] It was also sharply critical of Yasir 'Arafat over the "concessions" made in his speech to the UN session in Geneva and the subsequent elaborations in his press conference the following day. Several months later, strong opposition was voiced to 'Arafat's declaration in France that the PLO Charter had been rendered obsolete by the PNC's new political program.[60]

Syrian–backed Palestinian groups voiced even more strident criticism of the PLO's peace initiative, presumably with Syrian encouragement.[61] These political attacks on the PLO's new course were accompanied by further pressure in Lebanon. Mainstream PLO forces were driven out of the Beirut area in the summer of 1988 and obliged to move south to Sidon. Opposition deepened when the PLO established contacts with General Michel 'Awn's regime following the establishment of two rival governments in the fall of 1988.[62] The Fateh presence in the south was then subjected to further pressure from Syrian proxies.

While very much opposed to the PLO leadership, its policies, and above all its independent course of action, Syria found itself in a weakened position during this phase. In addition to serious economic problems, Syria was experiencing difficulty on several fronts. The Soviet Union, Syria's superpower ally, was eagerly seeking detente with the US and consequently had a strong interest in defusing regional conflicts. It was unlikely, therefore, to provide as much support as in the past and was urging Syria to soften some of its stands on regional issues. Developments at the regional level also created difficulties for Syria. The defeat of its ally, Iran, and the ending of the Iran–Iraq war (August 1988) reduced Syria's leverage in the system. Saudi Arabia and other Gulf states no longer felt the same need to entice Syria away from Iran nor were they as intimidated by the possibility of terrorist measures. Moreover, the end of the war strengthened the position of Iraq, Syria's bitter rival. Finally, Syria was experiencing increasing difficulties in Lebanon, an area of crucial interest. Here it found its influence slipping as it proved unable to arrange for the election of a new President. Syria's position was increasingly challenged by the largely Christian–supported administration of General 'Awn, a challenge which led to intense fighting between March and August 1989. The situation was exacerbated by substantial Iraqi military assistance to General 'Awn's forces. Syria was thus obliged to concentrate its attention on Lebanon where it now found itself on the defensive. As a result of such difficulties, Syria—although strongly criticizing the PLO's direction and policies—was unable to mount a sustained campaign against them.

Although the PLO had made considerable headway among frontline states, it was still seeking broadly based support for its peace initiative in the Arab world. Several developments in the regional system strengthened its hand during this phase. Iraq's semi–victory and the end of the Iran–Iraq war greatly eased the pressure on Iraq, Saudi Arabia and the other Gulf states. Consequently they were now in a position to devote more attention and resources to the Arab–Israeli front. The changing balance of forces in the eastern Arab world was also more favorable to the PLO. On the one hand, the PLO's principal opponent, Syria, was now in a much weaker position. This was accentuated by the gradual drifting apart of Syria's own loose coalition, encompassing Algeria, Libya and South Yemen in addition to Iran. On the other hand, Syria's rivals (namely Iraq and Egypt) had improved their position considerably. Iraq's victory now enabled it to assume a much greater role in the Arab system and, indeed, challenge Syria in its own Lebanese backyard. Egypt, for its part, was gaining increasing acceptance in the system and was poised to play a much more active role. These developments were reinforced by the establishment, in February 1989, of the Arab Cooperation Council, encompassing Iraq and Egypt along with Jordan and the Yemen Arab Republic. While this organization was on the surface primarily economic in character, it also provided a framework for the development of a common front on various regional issues. The fact that the PLO was aligned with, and enjoyed the support of, key members of this emerging new force certainly enhanced its position.

This shifting balance of forces was reflected at the Casablanca summit of Arab leaders in May 1989. Egypt was officially re–admitted to the Arab system and immediately began to play an active role in the summit's deliberations. Syria found itself in a relatively isolated position and was on the defensive regarding Lebanon. These developments worked to the benefit of the PLO during deliberations on the Palestine question, one of two key items on the conference agenda. Here the PLO's major objective was to secure general Arab backing for its peace initiative. This was sought not only to enhance its chances of success at the global level but also to share responsibility for the initiative with the Arab states. By so doing, 'Arafat hoped to neutralize any opposition either from Arab sources (i.e. Syria, Libya) or within the PLO itself.[63] The PLO proposals were initially challenged by Syria, which submitted its own document questioning the PLO's approach and downplaying the PLO's role. However, it was not prepared to push this to a confrontation, partly because of general support among Arab leaders for the PLO initiative but mainly because Syria had other priorities at this point. To concentrate on protecting its interests in Lebanon and avoid antagonizing key states, Syria dropped its veto on Egypt's admission to the Arab League and decided not to press its opposition to the PLO's initiative too forcefully. It therefore accepted an Egyptian compromise formula which endorsed the new political program adopted by the PNC and reaffirmed earlier resolutions of the Fez (1982) and Algiers (1988) summits.[64]

The PLO also sought summit endorsement for the establishment of a group of frontline states (PLO, Jordan, Egypt, Syria, Lebanon) to coordinate policies in preparation for the convening of an international conference. This would have created an embryonic joint Arab delegation (thereby avoiding the issue of a joint Jordanian–Palestinian delegation) and generated pressures on Syria to join the search for a settlement (thus neutralizing its opposition). Syria rejected such a move as premature. The PLO also continued to seek financial backing from the Arab states, many of whom had apparently not fulfilled commitments made at the Algiers summit. This was left to be worked out on a bilateral basis, however.

The Stalled Initiative

While the PLO peace initiative produced some initial results at the international level (such as the US-PLO dialogue), these were basically symbolic in character; there had been little substantive change in US policy. Moreover, by the summer of 1989, the Palestinian initiative itself began to experience significant difficulties.

These were attributable to three main factors. The fundamental problem was Israeli policy. This continued to be characterized by considerable rigidity: rejection of self–determination or national existence for the Palestinian community; refusal to deal with its chosen representatives, the PLO; and unwillingness to return any of the remaining occupied territories to Arab control. In spite of the presence of some more flexible elements within the Israeli government, the existence of a coalition enabled the hardliners to block any movement. As a result, the sole modification to the status quo which Israel's national unity government was prepared to propose was a revised version of the Camp David agreement, involving elections in the occupied territories and an interim autonomy scheme under very restrictive conditions.[65]

US policy was a second source of difficulty. By the spring of 1989, the outlines of the new US administration's approach to the conflict had become clearer. Parts were encouraging to the PLO. The Bush administration called on the Israeli government to abandon any idea of a "Greater Israel" and accept the principle of land for peace. It also mentioned the legitimate political rights of the Palestinian people as one of the principles on which a settlement should be based. However, it was not prepared to endorse Palestinian self–determination or the establishment of an independent Palestinian state. Moreover, the US government regarded the Palestinian–Israeli conflict as both relatively intractable and not particularly acute at this stage. Hence it did not feel much sense of urgency about finding a solution. Instead, it decided to concentrate on limited step-by-step arrangements, believing that this was the only approach that offered any possibilities for progress. This cautious, lowest common denominator approach led it to endorse the general outlines of a May 1989 Israeli proposal for elections and limited autonomy in the occupied territories. Thereafter, Washington tried to pressure the PLO to accept this plan, with some modifications, since it appeared to be the party that was most eager for some movement.[66] It soon became clear, however, that as long as the Likud figured prominently in the government, Israel was unlikely to agree to any modifications that would meet even the most minimum PLO conditions. The question then became whether the new US administration would be sufficiently strong to support even a minimally balanced proposal and exert pressure on Israel to accept it.

The evolving pattern of superpower relations constituted a further obstacle. The development of a new and far–reaching superpower detente may have created a better climate for regional conflict resolution. At the outset, however, apart from important bilateral issues such as arms control, it was only the most acute or least intractable conflicts which became the focus of superpower efforts. In the Middle East this had meant the Iran–Iraq war and the Afghanistan conflict. When these seemed to have been defused, attention turned to major developments elsewhere, notably in China and in Eastern Europe. Furthermore, the significantly weakened condition of the Soviet Union and the far–reaching domestic change on which it had embarked led to a sharp retrenchment in its involvement in the third world. As a result, it was anxious to avoid any conflict with the US in these areas, and had little leverage over US policy. If the Soviet Union was not a serious competitor in a given area, the US lost some of its incentive to move.

As the obstacles to a settlement became more and more apparent in the latter half of 1989, the PLO leadership grew increasingly concerned about the future of its peace initiative. Faced with mounting uncertainty, the Arab sphere assumed renewed importance. The most immediate concern was to secure a sustained Arab diplomatic effort to press the US to intensify its diplomatic activity. Given the likelihood of a protracted conflict, the PLO was also anxious to obtain better access to the occupied territories and assured channels of assistance to the local population. Finally, it remained concerned about possible challenges to Palestinian autonomy and national aspirations in the event of a prolonged blockage in the settlement process.

Egypt continued to occupy a key place in the PLO's frontline strategy due to its close connections with both the US and Israel. This was reinforced by its renewed prominence in the Arab system. In view of the disappointing Israeli and US response to the PLO initiative, 'Arafat sought to encourage increased Egyptian diplomatic activity on the PLO's behalf. Coordination between the two further intensified after Israel's election plan was endorsed by the US. Egypt was to play an important intermediary role in this pre–negotiation stage. In particular, it was able to test ideas and suggest compromises which the PLO leadership had difficulty proposing officially. Egypt's intermediary role allowed the PLO to display flexibility without committing itself or accepting the original Israeli plan. By so doing, it attempted to encourage continuing US mediation efforts and, hopefully, the adoption of a more even–handed US position. At the same time, the

PLO and Egypt hoped to shift responsibility for possible failure of the negotiations to Israel.

Egypt proved very helpful in countering the Israeli plan, raising questions not only about the proposed initial step (elections) but also about the linkage of any interim arrangements to the overall settlement process and the basic principles on which such a settlement would be based.[67] In particular, Egypt was able to shift the focus of the first step from Israeli–organized elections to negotiations between Israel and the Palestinian community, and from negotiations involving one segment of the community to those with representatives of the Palestinian community as a whole (both inside and outside the occupied territories). In the process, it attempted to provide some *de facto* recognition for the Palestinian community as a distinct entity and for the PLO as the effective representative of that community. This helped to revive the faltering settlement process during the fall of 1989. Egypt was also successful in persuading the US and an important segment of the Israeli government to agree to procedural arrangements which were at least minimally acceptable to the PLO leadership.[68] Some concerns were expressed at this stage that Egypt might be inclined to press the PLO for too many concessions, thereby compromising Palestinian interests, but this apparently did not occur.[69] At any rate, by the spring of 1990 prospects for a procedural breakthrough seemed favorable. Hopes were soon dashed, however, by the collapse of Israel's coalition government.

In a further move to reinforce the PLO's frontline position, the PLO sought also to strengthen ties with Jordan. Two considerations figured prominently in this decision. On the one hand there was the practical issue of providing material support to the population of the occupied territories. To accomplish this it was essential to secure Jordanian cooperation. Specifically, a Jordanian link would facilitate access to the territories, assist the channeling of financial aid, and improve economic conditions by reestablishing markets for Palestinian agricultural produce in Jordan. The second consideration concerned the settlement process. Here 'Arafat believed that cooperation with Jordan and a willingness to establish confederal links with it in an eventual settlement might help ease the fears of US and Israeli policy–makers and thus reduce opposition to Palestinian self–determination. This in turn could improve the prospects for the initiation of a peace process in the near future.

Whatever the precise mix of motivations, 'Arafat sought to strengthen cooperation with Jordan in the course of an official visit in August 1989. To symbolize the improvement in relations, the PLO transferred the headquarters of the Palestinian National Fund to Amman and publicly encouraged Palestinians in the occupied territories, Jordan, and elsewhere to support the Jordanian currency in this period of financial crisis.[70] Jordan reportedly eased controls on the marketing of West Bank produce. As always, there were potential risks that, should Israeli and US opposition to Palestinian self-determination persist, Jordan might be tempted to reassert its interest in the West Bank and Gaza. The PLO leadership, however, was less concerned than before about possible Jordanian challenges. By this stage the previous climate of rivalry and mutual suspicion had eased considerably. Furthermore, the PLO was now able to deal with Jordan on a much more equal footing, due to its extensive popular support in the occupied territories and the emergence of a relationship of mutual rather than one-sided dependence. Jordan was now very much aware of the importance of Palestinian cooperation for maintaining political stability at a time of serious financial difficulties and increased opposition activity.

With the cooperation of two key frontline states seemingly assured, the PLO now felt less vulnerable in the event of a breakdown in settlement efforts. Still, as the peace initiative began to stall, the PLO leadership had some concerns on the Syrian front. Syria, as previously noted, was strongly opposed both to the PLO's approach to the conflict and its independent course of action. However, the momentum generated by the *intifada* as well as the support for the PLO within the Palestinian community and among Arab states generally made it difficult for Syria to obstruct this initiative. Given its weakened condition, relative isolation, and preoccupation with Lebanon, Damascus was in no position to mount a sustained attack against the PLO. Rather, it contented itself with continuing its political war of attrition, engaging in regular criticism of the PLO's policies and moves and encouraging even stronger attacks by its Palestinian allies. It may also have had some role in occasional attempts by dissident Palestinian elements to launch operations against Israel from Lebanon, Jordan and Egypt.[71] These were seemingly designed to embarrass the PLO as well as the host states and cause difficulties for its peace initiative. In any case, Syria was basically prepared to let the PLO's initiative take its course and position itself to benefit when the inevitable blockage occurred due to the expected inflexibility of Israeli and US policy.[72] When this happened, Syria believed that the PLO would be forced to reassess its strategy, the balance of forces would shift within the Palestinian movement, and the PLO would move closer to Syria for support.

While the possibility of such developments generated some concern within the PLO leadership, this was offset to a considerable extent by other calculations. Specifically, Syria's reduced influence in the area limited its potential leverage over the PLO. The anticipated support from other frontline states also lessened the PLO's vulnerability. The PLO, therefore, seemingly had less to fear from, and less to attract it to, Syria. Beyond this, 'Arafat had developed an Iraqi option which fulfilled several purposes.[73] One was to secure the backing of a rising power which appeared willing to serve as a defender of the Arab cause vis-à-vis Israel. In the event that Israel or the US obstructed the settlement process, the PLO could move to strengthen its links with Iraq as an alternative to alignment with Syria. This would enable 'Arafat to be perceived within the Palestinian community as making a strong response to such obstruction without becoming dependent on Syria. Furthermore, an Iraqi connection would help to keep Syria pinned down and neutralized, reducing its ability to exert pressure on the PLO. In effect, 'Arafat could try to use the Iraqi connection to trump the Syrian card and force Syria to accommodate itself to the PLO rather than vice–versa.

Conclusion

As the preceding analysis has shown, the Arab sphere in general and the frontline states in particular have consistently occupied an important place in PLO foreign policy. The PLO leadership has long recognized the need for a supportive environment in which the Palestinian movement can build a political community, develop its capabilities and pursue its national aspirations with relative autonomy. They have also realized the importance of strong and unambiguous support from the Arab world if these aspirations are to be taken seriously by Israel and the US. At the same time, the PLO has been all too aware of the potential for challenges to Palestinian autonomy and national objectives, particularly from the frontline states, and has been constantly on the alert to head off or overcome these. These concerns have grown whenever blockages have deepened or pressures intensified on the Israeli or US fronts, as was the case in the decade after Camp David. Ironically, its concerns have also been strong whenever an opening seems to develop, for fear of attempts (with the possible collusion of one or more frontline states) to bypass the Palestinian option.

During the 1980s—a time when the PLO was in most need of a supportive environment—conditions worsened in the Arab sphere. Most states in the eastern Arab world were preoccupied with the conflict in the Gulf and the challenge posed by the new Iranian regime. Consequently, they were unable to devote much attention to the Arab–Israeli conflict, let alone exert any pressure on the US and Western powers. Worse still, on the frontline itself the PLO's position became increasingly precarious. Here it was faced not only with the defection of the most important member of the Arab coalition (Egypt) but also serious pressures and challenges from the remaining states (Syria, Jordan and in Lebanon). To cope with these pressures, 'Arafat opted during this period for a diplomacy of mobility, seeking to diversify PLO ties and avoid dependence on any one frontline state. Despite this, by 1987 the PLO found itself in virtual isolation on the frontline, estranged from all the neighboring Arab states and confronting a Jordanian–Syrian axis aimed at marginalizing it. 'Arafat was now obliged to secure the support of other Arab states to counterbalance efforts to bypass the PLO.

On the eve of the *intifada*, therefore, the PLO found itself in difficult circumstances. The uprising would soon transform its regional position, however. The initial impact was greatest in the Arab sphere. Here, the uprising seriously undermined any claims neighboring Arab states may have had to the territories themselves or to tutelage over the Palestinian people. The accompanying intensification of Palestinian solidarity also tended to limit the ability of these states to penetrate the Palestinian political system and thus reduced their leverage within the movement. The *intifada* thus effectively undercut challenges from both Jordan and Syria. In particular, King Husayn was obliged to renounce the Jordanian option and step aside, leaving the road clear for the PLO. The momentum generated by the *intifada* also led Egypt to become more active in promoting the Palestinian cause. In the larger Arab system, the uprising served to refocus attention on the Palestinian–Israeli conflict and generate renewed political support from Arab governments generally.

The *intifada* not only strengthened the PLO's position vis–à–vis the frontline states, but also diminished its dependence on them. With the opening of its own front, the Palestinian community was now in a much better position to advance its cause through its own efforts. This growing sense of self–reliance was enhanced by the Palestinians' demonstrated ability to mount a forceful challenge to the status quo, obliging Israel and the US to take Palestinian nationalism more seriously. With its increased leverage and prospects of some progress, at least in the major power sphere, the PLO felt less need for Arab intermediaries. Consequently, the focus of PLO attention now shifted to the major power and Israeli spheres with the Palestinian declaration of statehood in November 1988, 'Arafat's appearance before the UN General Assembly, and the subsequent opening of a US-PLO dialogue.

A year after the launching of the PLO peace initiative, however, the obstacles to movement on the Palestinian–Israeli front appeared as serious as ever. Whatever their initial expectations, 'Arafat and the PLO leadership were obliged to conclude that the process would be slow and exceedingly difficult, with a satisfactory settlement by no means assured. As the prospects for an early breakthrough faded, the Arab sphere assumed renewed importance. The PLO had three basic needs in this area: active Arab diplomacy to convince the US of the necessity for stronger initiatives, including pressure on Israel; improved access and channels of assistance to sustain the population of the occupied territories in their resistance; and sufficient backing to overcome possible renewed challenges to Palestinian autonomy and national aspirations. The PLO's strategy was based largely on close cooperation with Egypt and Jordan, together with a developing Iraqi connection. Thus the attempt to diversify ties continued, but with less mobility and more continuity in alignment patterns. This strategy served to link the PLO to an influential new axis in regional politics.

Later in the year, the PLO would experience a series of major shockwaves which significantly weakened its position and forced it to reassess its strategy. The first occurred on the Israeli front. Here the PLO peace initiative collapsed in the spring of 1990 as the Israeli government rejected US Secretary of State James Baker's proposal that it enter into direct talks with representatives of the overall Palestinian community (even though these centered primarily on interim arrangements). Immediate prospects for movement toward a negotiated settlement were further reduced with the resumption of power in Israel of an ultra-nationalist government under Yitzhak Shamir. Finally, the strengthening of Israel's demographic capacity through greatly expanded Soviet Jewish immigration raised the specter of intensified Jewish settlement and an even more intransigent Israeli position regarding the occupied Palestinian territories.

The PLO's problems were further confounded by developments on the major power front. Here it faced the prospect of declining Soviet and East European support as the USSR limited its involvement and softened its regional policies in order to concentrate on domestic problems and the improvement of relations with the US. This left the US in a preeminent position in the area, without any real competition or counterbalancing force, at a time when its policy toward the Palestinian-Israeli conflict remained far from even-handed. US unwillingness to pressure Israel (despite the latter's effective rejection of the Baker proposals) only served to reinforce Palestinian concerns, as did a US veto of a UN Security Council resolution calling for an observer mission to be sent to the occupied territories in May. The following month, the US suspended its dialogue with the PLO over the latter's unwillingness to discipline a dissident guerrilla faction for an attempted raid on Tel Aviv.

With prospects for movement on the Israeli and major power fronts becoming increasingly bleak, the Palestinian community's confidence in its ability to achieve progress largely through its own efforts began to decline. With Palestinian frustrations building, the emphasis turned to the need for Arab backing and cover. What was now sought was not so much intermediaries and diplomacy as leverage and pressure to force the US and Israel to move towards a negotiated settlement. Deterrence of Israeli escalation was also a concern. In this climate—and given Iraq's military strength, potential economic leverage, and above all its proclaimed willingness to act on behalf of Arab interests—the Iraqi connection proved increasingly attractive to the Palestinian leadership and community alike.

In August 1990 the PLO experienced a further severe jolt—this time on the Arab front—as a result of Iraq's invasion of Kuwait. This move, which profoundly split the Arab world, also sharply divided the PLO's principal allies. Egypt and Saudi Arabia (supported by the Gulf states and Syria) strongly opposed Iraq. Jordan tilted towards Baghdad. Sentiment within most sectors of the Palestinian community, meanwhile, strongly favored Saddam Husayn. In the accompanying crisis atmosphere, the PLO found itself under intense pressure to choose sides. The weight of Palestinian attitudes soon led to a pro-Iraqi tilt in PLO policy. At the same time, however, 'Arafat's inclination was to play a mediatory role in order to preserve the PLO's diversified base of support.

Within the limits set by Palestinian opinion, then, the PLO's main task during the crisis was to engage in political damage control, seeking to defuse (and survive) the crisis while alienating none. Yet when this policy manifested itself in a refusal to support any condemnation or action against Iraq (notably at an Arab League summit meeting in Cairo in mid-August), the PLO soon came to be seen as an Iraqi ally.

This policy may have consolidated—even improved—'Arafat's position within the Palestinian community. It also strengthened ties with Jordan (where the government had come to depend, to some extent, on PLO restraint and support), and earned Iraqi gratitude. However it was uncertain what Iraqi backing would amount to in tangible terms, let alone achieve in the way of results. There was also a danger that Iraq (like Syria before it) would attempt to exercise tutelage over the PLO and reshape the balance of forces within the movement, thereby limiting Palestinian autonomy and perhaps eventually endangering 'Arafat's leadership. These dangers seemed likely to increase if the PLO's dependence on Baghdad grew and its base of Arab support narrowed.

In fact, the PLO's equivocation soon angered several major Arab allies. Chief among these were Saudi Arabia and the Gulf states, whose financial support was crucial to the PLO. Clearly, the PLO—and more particularly *Fateh*—would suffer significantly in financial terms both in the short- and longer-term. Furthermore, direct Arab aid and workers' remittances to the occupied territories would decline, weakening the local economy and hence the *intifada*. The position and economic future of Palestinians in the Gulf was also put in question, as those regimes now threatened by Iraq increasingly looked upon resident Palestinians as a potential fifth column.

The Iraqi invasion of Kuwait also did serious damage to the PLO's relationship with Cairo (whose political weight and diplomatic connections had proved useful in bringing Israeli-Palestinian talks close to realization in 1989-90), while confirming the organization's poor relations with Damascus. The PLO could not but be concerned by the rapprochement that was taking place between Egypt and Syria, and the increasing cooperation between these two countries (together with the Saudi Arabia) over the Gulf crisis. Given their antagonism toward the PLO, it was questionable how much effort they would make once the crisis was over to press for movement on the Palestinian issue or for a significant PLO role in any negotiations. Indeed, they might even seek to promote an alternative opening (such as Syrian-Israeli negotiations) or alternative representation of the Palestinian community. However, the PLO could probably count on the need for Egypt, Syria, and Saudi Arabia to reassert their legitimacy in the

Arab world by demonstrating continued devotion to Arab causes in the wake of the crisis. This would require pressing for some progress on the Palestinian issue. Besides, whatever opening might be attempted on the Syrian-Israeli front, it would still be very difficult for Syria and Egypt to pursue a settlement without the Palestinians—although they might shift positions on the timing of certain segments of any negotiating process, to the PLO's detriment.

In short, at a time when the PLO was increasingly in need of Arab backing, its base of diplomatic support was narrowing substantially, jeopardizing its diplomacy of diversification and seriously weakening the organization vis-à-vis its opponents. In spite of the important achievements of the *intifada*, therefore, the position of the PLO and the Palestinian community remained precarious.

Notes

The author wishes to thank the Social Sciences and Humanities Research Council of Canada for its financial assistance in carrying out the research on which this chapter is based.

1. For a discussion of the role of these different spheres in PLO policy-making, see Aaron David Miller, *The PLO and the Politics of Survival* (New York: Praeger, 1983); Helena Cobban, *The Palestinian Liberation Organization* (Cambridge: Cambridge University Press, 1984); Mohammed Selim, "The Survival of a Nonstate Actor: The Foreign Policy of the Palestine Liberation Organization," in Bahgat Korany and Ali Dessouki et al, *The Foreign Policies of Arab States* (Boulder: Westview Press, 1984).

2. Miller, *The PLO and the Politics of Survival*, p. 7.

3. For the text of President Reagan's speech and the subsequent talking points, see William B. Quandt, ed., *The Middle East: Ten Years After Camp David* (Washington, D.C.: The Brookings Institution, 1988), appendix D; *New York Times*, 2, 9 September 1982.

4. Donald Neff, "The Washington Summit: One Dark Cloud," and Lamis Andoni, "No Compromise," *Middle East International*, 19 December 1987.

5. Raymond Hinnebusch, "Revisionist Dreams, Realist Strategies: The Foreign Policy of Syria," in Korany and Dessouki, *The Foreign Policies of Arab States*, pp. 289-291, 295-297, 312-313; Patrick Seale, *Asad* (London: I. B. Tauris, 1988).

6. Emile Sahliyeh, *The PLO After the Lebanon War* (Boulder: Westview Press, 1986), chapter 6.

7. On PLO-Jordanian relations during this period, see Aaron David Miller, "Jordanian Policy: The Politics of Limitation and Constraint," and Rashid Khalidi, "Palestinian Politics after the Exodus from Beirut," in Robert O. Freedman, ed., *The Middle East After the Israeli Invasion of Lebanon* (Syracuse: Syracuse University Press, 1986); Emile Sahliyeh, "Jordan and the Palestinians," and Rashid Khalidi, "The Palestine Liberation Organization," in Quandt, ed., *The Middle East: Ten Years After Camp David*; Sahliyeh, *The PLO After the Lebanon War*, chapters 4-5.

8. For the text of the accord, see Quandt, ed., *The Middle East: Ten Years After Camp David*, appendix F.

9. This was evident in interviews about the relationship conducted by the author with high-ranking Jordanian and PLO officials during this period.

10. The suspension of political cooperation (and the reasons for this) was announced

by the King in a speech on February 19; *Amman Domestic Service*, 19 February 1986 (in *Foreign Broadcast Information Service—Middle East and South Asia*, hereafter *FBIS*). The suggestion for an alternate leadership was made in meetings with West Bank Palestinians and in interviews; *New York Times*, 23 February, 5 March 1986. Other measures included encouraging a former PLO official to assume the leadership of the Palestinian movement in Jordan, and the closing of Fateh offices in Jordan; *New York Times*, 9 April, 8, 9, 14 July 1986; *Le Monde* (Paris) 23 May 1986. On tacit Jordanian-Israeli cooperation, see *New York Times*, 23 October 1986, 9 August 1987; *Ma'ariv*, 13 December 1987 (*FBIS*).

11. Interviews with senior Jordanian and PLO officials; *Middle East Reporter*, 21 September, 26 October, 16 November, 14 December 1985. King Husayn also alluded briefly to cooperation with Syria in his speech to the 1987 Arab summit in Amman; *al-Ra'i* (Amman), 10 November 1987 (*FBIS*).

12. Text of the Husayn-Peres agreement in Quandt, ed., *The Middle East: Ten Years After Camp David*, appendix G; see also *New York Times*, 8, 12 May 1987.

13. Interviews with senior PLO officials; this was also hinted at in an interview by Fateh's Hani al-Hasan with *al-Anba'* (Kuwait) 28 August 1988. On PLO-Egyptian relations see also Sahliyeh, *The PLO After the Lebanon War*, pp 177-184; Louis Cantori, "Egyptian Policy Under Mubarak," in Freedman, ed., *The Middle East After the Israeli Invasion of Lebanon*, pp. 331-332, 336-340.

14. The PLO discovered this during the Israeli invasion of Lebanon when the Gulf states tended to concentrate less on exerting pressure on the US on behalf of the PLO than on influencing the PLO to withdraw from Lebanon in accordance with US wishes. See Rashid Khalidi, *Under Siege: PLO Decision-making During the 1982 War* (New York: Columbia University Press, 1986), pp. 147-165.

15. Lamis Andoni, "The Gains and Losses for the PLO," *Middle East International*, 21 November 1987. See also the statement delivered by Israeli Defense Minister Yitzhak Rabin to the Knesset, *IDF Radio*, 23 December 1987 (*FBIS*).

16. Interviews with senior PLO and Jordanian officials; Andoni, "The Gains and Losses for the PLO." See also 'Arafat's interview with *Radio Monte Carlo*, 5 February 1988, and his speech to the Libyan General People's Congress, *Tripoli Television Service*, 11 June 1988 (*FBIS*). The English-language text of the summit final statement printed in the *Jordan Times*, 12-13 November 1987 omitted reference to the PLO as the "sole, legitimate representative of the Palestinian people" (*FBIS*, 17 November 1987). For an indication of PLO dissatisfaction with its treatment at the summit, see *Voice of Palestine* (Sana'a) 10 November 1987, *Radio Monte Carlo*, 9, 10 November 1987 (*FBIS*).

17. For an overview of the relationship between Palestinians in the occupied territories and the PLO, see Helena Cobban, "The PLO and the Intifada," *Middle East Journal* 44, 2 (Spring 1990).

18. T. Porteous, "Egypt and the PLO: Healing the Rupture," *Middle East International*, 5 December 1987.

19. Fred Axelgard, "Reagan Pushed into Action," C. Berger, "Rebuff for Mubarak," Lamis Andoni, "Solid Arab Backing," *Middle East International*, 6 February 1988. For an outline of the Shultz proposals, see *Middle East International*, 19 March 1988. See also Jim Muir, "Why the US Peace Plan Can't Succeed as it is," *Middle East International*, 20 February 1988.

20. *New York Times*, 5 June 1988; *Jerusalem Post*, 4 July 1988 (*FBIS*).

21. Lamis Andoni, "Jordan and the PLO: Changing Tactics," *Middle East International*, 6 February 1988; *al-Qabas* (Kuwait), 1 February 1988, *Jordan Times*, 9 January 1988 (*FBIS*).

22. Lamis Andoni, "Leaflet(s) No. 10," *Middle East International*, 19 March 1988.

23. This restraint could be seen in the effort PLO Executive Committee member 'Abd al-Razzak al-Yahya to reassure the Jordanian government after the United National Leadership of the uprising had called upon Palestinian members of the Jordanian parliament to resign; Andoni, "Leaflet(s) No. 10." As noted later, it could also be seen in 'Arafat's dealings with King Husayn at the Algiers summit.

24. Lamis Andoni, "A Bitter Taste," *Middle East International*, 5 March 1988.

25. Lamis Andoni, "West Bank Ties," *Middle East International*, 14 May 1988. For the King's "Ramadan" speeches see *Jordan Times*, 28-29 April, 5-6 , 9, 12-13 May 1988; see also *Jordan Times* 9 April 1988 for the official statement outlining Jordan's position and Prime Minister Zayd Rifa'i's elaboration on these.

26. Lamis Andoni, "PLO and Syria Alter the Political Map," *Middle East International*, 30 April 1988; *al-Siyasa* (Kuwait), 27 April 1988 (*FBIS*).

27. See the letter of a member of the guerrilla group to President Asad and the prominence given it by the Syrian media, *Radio Damascus Domestic Service*, 28, 29 November 1987 (*FBIS*). See also the interview given by PFLP-GC leader Ahmad Jibril to *al-Quds Palestinian Arab Radio*, 22 August 1988 (*FBIS*).

28. Statement of the Ba'th Party National Command, *Radio Damascus Domestic Service*, 22 December 1987 (*FBIS*).

29. It is unclear whether the conflict was started by pro-Syrian forces to emphasize that they would not be swept aside in any PLO-Syrian rapprochement, or by Fateh to take advantage of detente with Syria to weaken its Palestinian opponents. See also Jim Muir, "The Torment Continues in Beirut's Camps," *Middle East International* 8 July 1988. For an analysis of the conflict by one of the leaders of the PLO dissidents, see *al-Mustaqbal*, 9 July 1988 (*FBIS*).

30. For a sample of the Syrian attacks on 'Arafat and Fateh, see *Radio Damascus Domestic Service*, 9, 11 July 1988 (*FBIS*), and Syrian Chief-of-Staff Hikmat al-Shihabi's interview in *al-Ba'th*, 31 July 1988 (*FBIS*). For a Fateh counter-attack see the statement by the Fateh Revolutionary Council, *Voice of Palestine* (Algiers) 20 July 1988 (*FBIS*) and 'Arafat's denunciation of the Syrian regime as "Zionists who speak Arabic," *Iraqi News Agency*, 14 July 1988 (*FBIS*).

31. Lamis Andoni, "Solid Arab Backing," MEI 6 February 1988.

32. 'Arafat to *Radio Monte Carlo*, 3 June 1988; 'Arafat speech to the summit, *Voice of Palestine* (Sana'a) 9 June 1988; 'Arafat press conference, *Algiers Television Service*, 10 June 1988 (*FBIS*). See also the PLO working paper submitted to the summit and the text of two resolutions on the Palestine question approved by Arab leaders, *Algiers APS*, 8 June 1988, *Voice of Palestine* (San'a), 10 June 1988 (*FBIS*).

33. Although the *New York Times*, 9 June 1988, reported that the summit rebuffed the PLO on the funding issue, most other reports told a different story; see *Radio Monte Carlo*, 10, 17 June 1988 (*FBIS*) and Michael Jansen, "The Funds Which Help the Intifada," *Middle East International*, 24 June 1988. The amounts provided by each state and the timing of payments were apparently left to later negotiations. Ensuring implementation of these commitments proved more difficult than expected, as the PLO's Salah Khalaf ("Abu Iyad") complained in *al-Qabas*, 30 November 1988 (*FBIS*).

34. Text of King Husayn's speech to the Algiers summit, *Amman Domestic Service*, 8 June 1988; *al-Qabas*, 16 June 1988 (*FBIS*). See also Lamis Andoni, "Implications for Jordan," *Middle East International*, 24 June 1988.

35. Reports to this effect were published in Israeli and East Jerusalem-based Palestinian newspapers; see *Al-Hamishmar* 16 May 1988, *Ha'Aretez*, 3 June 1988, *al-Quds*, 4, 6 June 1988 (*FBIS*). The latter report indicated that Jordan had decided against such action, at least at this time. A "ranking Jordanian official" also hinted at such measures, but said they would be carried out only if negative effects on the population could be avoided; *al-Ittihad* (Abu Dhabi), 7 June 1988 (FBIS). At a press conference after

the summit, Salah Khalaf acknowledged PLO awareness of such rumors; *al-Qabas*, 15 June 1988 (*FBIS*).

36. Information on these meetings was provided by a "senior Jordanian official" to *al-Qabas*, 16, 23 June 1988. The proposals in question asserted that the PLO or international channels (e.g. UNRWA) should be the only designated channels for financial assistance to the occupied territories. Jordan pointed out that it too was providing assistance in the form of salaries, etc. The proposal was then amended to make reference to international and "regular" (i.e. Jordanian) channels. Another proposal involved an assertion by the PLO of the right to represent all Palestinians no matter where they lived. This was qualified when it was pointed out that Palestinians living in Jordan proper were Jordanian citizens and could not be represented by anyone else.

37. Interview with a Western ambassador to Jordan. On the King's attitude, see *Ha'Aretz*, 3 June 1988; Crown Prince Hasan, *Jordan Times*, 15 June 1988; Information Minister Hani al-Khawasina, *al-Shira'* (Beirut), 8 August 1988; Interior Minister Raja'i al-Dajani, *Sawt al-Sha'b* (Amman), 30 August 1988 (*FBIS*).

38. Speech by King Husayn, *Amman Domestic Service*, 31 July 1988; press conference, *Amman Television Service*, 7 August 1988 (*FBIS*). On the calculus of the disengagement decision, see Lamis Andoni's chapter elsewhere in this volume.

39. Such views were expressed by PFLP leader George Habash and Fateh's Salah Khalaf, among others; *Voice of the People* (clandestine), 9 August 1988, *Der Spiegel*, 29 August 1988 (*FBIS*). The King denied this; *Amman Television Service*, 7 August 1988 (*FBIS*).

40. The PLO was apparently surprised by the move, and sought to have Jordan freeze several of the measures to allow it time to adjust. *Middle East News Agency* (Cairo), 15 August 1988; *al-Siyasa*, 16 August 1988; *Rose al-Yusuf* (Cairo) 22 August 1988 (*FBIS*).

41. Lamis Andoni, "The PLO's Thinking," *Middle East International*, 26 August 1988; Hani al-Hasan in *al-Anba'*, 28 August 1988 (*FBIS*).

42. An abridged version of this document was published in the *New York Times*, 22 June 1988. For US reactions, see Fred Axelgard, "PLO Peace Signals Ignored by Washington," *Middle East International*, 24 June 1988; for Palestinian reactions, see Lamis Andoni, "Controversy Follows the Trial Balloon," *Middle East International* 8 July 1988.

43. Text of the declaration of independence and political statement in *Journal of Palestine Studies*, 18, 2 (Winter 1989): 213-223.

44. Text of UN speech and press conference statement in *Journal of Palestine Studies*, 18, 3 (Spring 1989): 161-171, 180-181.

45. *Le Monde*, 3, 4, 5 May 1989.

46. Text of Madrid declaration in *Journal of Palestine Studies*, 19, 1 (Autumn 1989): 121-122.

47. *al-Sha'b* (Cairo) 9 August 1988; interview with Nabil Sha'th (Fateh), *al-Hawadith*, 26 August 1988; interview with Foreign Minister Ismat 'Abd al-Majid, *Uktubar* (Cairo), 11 September 1988; interview with 'Abdullah Hurani (PLO Executive Committee), *al-Ittihad* (Abu Dhabi), 26 September 1988; interview with President Mubarak, *al-Ahram*, 20 October 1988 (*FBIS*).

48. *New York Times*, 19, 21 November 1988; *Le Monde*, 22 November 1988; interview with Minister of State for Foreign Affairs Butrus Butrus Ghali, *Davar* (Tel Aviv), 21 November 1988 (*FBIS*).

49. Interview with President Mubarak, *al-Sharq al-Awsat*, 21 December 1988; *al-Anba'*, 24 December 1988 (*FBIS*).

50. Interview with Salah Khalaf, *al-Musawwar*, 11 May 1989 (*FBIS*). For an illustration of Egypt's previous activity as an intermediary with Western Europe, see R. Swann, "Egyptian Go-Between," *Middle East International*, 7 October 1988.

51. Interview with President Mubarak, *al-Anba'*, 24 December 1988 (*FBIS*); Max Rodenbeck, "Now Ready to Negotiate," and Michael Jansen, "A Foursome Agrees," *Middle East International*, 4 November 1988. At the summit, 'Arafat expressed strong interest in a confederation, while Husayn apparently said the question was premature. Statement by Prime Minister Rifa'i, *Amman Television Service*, 1 November 1988; Bassam Abu Sharif in *al-Qabas*, 25 October 1988 (*FBIS*).

52. Statement by Prime Minister Rifa'i, *Amman Television Service*, 15 November 1988 (*FBIS*).

53. Interview with King Husayn, *Amman Television Service*, 16 December 1988; interview with Salah Khalaf, *al-Bayan* (Dubai), 19 December 1988 (*FBIS*)

54. *London Sunday Mail*, 23 October 1988 (*FBIS*). This was denied rather weakly by the Jordanian Information Minister, *al-Dustur* (Amman), 25 October 1988 (*FBIS*). See also the statements by King Husayn and Prince Hasan in *al-Siyasa*, 8 December 1988 and the *Jordan Times*, 11 December 1988 (*FBIS*).

55. *Radio Monte Carlo*, 14 August 1989; *al-Sha'b* (East Jerusalem), 16 August 1989 (*FBIS*).

56. For further details, see Lamis Andoni's chapter elsewhere in this volume.

57. See, for example, the editorial in *al-Ba'th*, 1 December 1988 (*FBIS*).

58. *Tishrin* (Damascus), 27 June 1988 (*FBIS*).

59. *Damascus Television Service*, 16 November 1988; *Radio Monte Carlo*, 28 November 1988 (*FBIS*). See also Jim Muir, "The Divide with Syria Widens," *Middle East International*, 18 November 1988.

60. Press conference of Vice-President 'Abd al-Halim Khaddam, *Republica* (Rome), 20 May 1989 (*FBIS*).

61. See, for example, the statements made by various Palestinian dissident groups on *al-Quds Palestinian Arab Radio*, 20 June, 22 August, 12 November, 15 December 1988, 23, 24 May 1989 (*FBIS*).

62. Jim Muir, "Attempts to Break the Vicious Circle," *Middle East International*, 17 February 1989; statement by Bassam Abu Sharif, *Voice of Lebanon* (Beirut), 28 May 1989; *al-Anba'*, 21 August 1989 (*FBIS*).

63. Text of Palestinian working paper, *Voice of Palestine* (Algiers), 24 May 1989; 'Arafat's speech to the Casablanca summit, *Voice of the PLO* (Baghdad), 25 May 1989 (*FBIS*)

64. Syrian working paper, *Damascus Domestic Service*, 22 May 1989 (*FBIS*). Outline of differences in the PLO and Syrian papers, *Agence France Press* (Paris), 22 May 1989; Egyptian efforts to reconcile the two papers, *MENA*, 24 May 1989 (*FBIS*), *Le Monde*, 24 May 1989; text of summit resolution on the Palestine issue in *Journal of Palestine Studies* 19, 1 (Autumn 1989): 132-134.

65. For the text of the Israeli proposal, see *Journal of Palestine Studies*, 19, 1 (Autumn 1989): 145-148.

66. For a detailed account of US policy during this period, see Fred Khouri's chapter elsewhere in this volume.

67. For the Egyptian proposals see *Rose al-Yusuf*, 18 September 1989; President Mubarak's interview on *Jerusalem Television Service*, 20 September 1989 (*FBIS*); see also *New York Times*, 18 September 1989. For an outline of the PLO leadership's position on the proposals, see *al-Qabas*, 22 September 1989 (*FBIS*).

68. *New York Times*, 5, 15 November, 6 December 1989.

69. See Muhammad Hasanayn Haykal's article in *al-Ahram* (Cairo), 24 September 1989 (*FBIS*).

70. *Radio Monte Carlo*, 7 August 1989; *al-Watan* (Kuwait), 18 August 1989 (*FBIS*). For Jordan's decision to facilitate West Bank exports and PLO-Jordanian relations more generally, see comments by two PLO Executive Committee members in *MENA*, 10

September 1989, and *al-Anba'*, 19 September 1989 (*FBIS*).

71. *Jerusalem Domestic Service*, 8 September 1989; *Hadashot* (Tel Aviv), 7 September 1989 (*FBIS*).

72. Fida Nasrallah, "Syria Pays the Price of Isolation," *Middle East International*, 31 March 1989.

73. *Middle East Reporter*, 12 May 1990.

6

Jordan

Lamis Andoni

Less than one year after it began in December 1987, the Palestinian uprising resulted in a dramatic transformation of Jordan's political role and involvement in the Palestinian problem. On 31 July 1988 King Husayn reversed four decades of Hashemite policy with a historic speech relinquishing Jordan's responsibility for the West Bank. In doing so, the King conceded the new realities created by the *intifada*. The uprising's firm assertion of the Palestinian political identity of the West Bank had make it impossible for Jordan to continue any claim to represent the Israeli occupied territories.

For Husayn it was a painful decision that profoundly changed the dynamics of the Middle East conflict. Jordan's withdrawal from its previous role as self-proclaimed guardian of Palestinian interests to a secondary role in the peace process challenged the Palestine Liberation Organization to demonstrate its ability to fulfill its status as "sole legitimate representative of the Palestinian people" in practical terms. This in turn spurred an equally historic (and perhaps as painful) Palestinian shift four months later, when in November 1988 the PLO's Palestine National Council endorsed a moderate peace strategy based on a "land for peace formula" and the declaration of an independent Palestinian state.

Yet although disengagement was intended in part to reduce the domestic tensions stemming from the *intifada*, the manner in which it was implemented had the reverse effect, adding to already widespread discontent engendered by an increasingly serious economic crisis. When the government tried to impose an austerity program required by the International Monetary Fund, accumulated frustrations exploded into riots —the *haba* ["eruption"] of April 1989. These originated from where it hit hardest—the Jordanian south, the historical bedrock of Hashemite support. Moreover, what started as protests against government-imposed price increases soon turned into a nation-wide struggle for democracy and social equality that heralded one of the most serious internal crises in Jordan's history.

In retrospect, as this chapter shows, the *intifada* across the river, the profound political change it brought to Jordan's regional role, and the manner in which the government dealt with the process of disengagement all deepened the country's existing internal political, social and economic contradictions. In so doing, they propelled Jordan to a turning point. With the old ways of governing clearly unacceptable in the eyes of much of the population, it was inevitable that the regime would have to reassess its relationship with its Palestinian citizens and accept new rules for its social contract with the Jordanian people. This process—manifested in full parliamentary elections in November 1989, the first since 1967—promises to have a fundamental impact on the future development of both Jordan and Jordanian-Palestinian relations.

Jordanian-Palestinian Relations on the Eve of the *Intifada*

The state of PLO-Jordanian and Jordanian-West Bank relations on the eve of the *intifada* was an important factor in influencing Amman's official reaction and in determining the impact of the uprising on the country. The period preceding the uprising, especially the last two years, had been characterized by strained relations between Jordan and the PLO, and a renewed Jordanian claim of responsibility for the West Bank.

On February 19, 1986, King Husayn suspended political coordination with the PLO after failing to get Yasir 'Arafat to fully accept American preconditions for including the organization in the US-sponsored peace process, namely acceptance of United Nations Security Council resolutions 242 and 338, establishment of a joint Jordanian-Palestinian negotiating team, and recognition of the state of Israel. In a lengthy televised speech, Husayn challenged the PLO leadership by appealing to Palestinians to reconsider who should lead them.[1] With Husayn's speech Jordan began its most intense drive to reassert its claim to represent the West Bank since the 1974 Rabat Arab summit, which had recognized the PLO as the sole legitimate representative of the Palestinian people. Squeezed between American and Israeli insistence that he should represent the Palestinians, and the PLO's unwillingness to give him any form of mandate or to accept the US conditions, Husayn had decided to address himself directly to the Palestinians. It was a strategy motivated by a fear that the stalemate in peace efforts would encourage Israeli extremists (whom Husayn viewed as gaining ground) to force a mass expulsion of Palestinians from the West Bank to the East Bank as a prelude to transforming "Jordan into Palestine." But the Jordanian strategy was also aimed at strengthening direct ties with the Palestinian people and broadening the social and economic basis of support for Jordanian policies, in the hope of either pressuring the PLO to become more malleable or fostering the emergence of a strong local leadership in the territories.[2]

The main vehicle of this strategy was an ambitious $1.4 billion program to develop the West Bank and Gaza Strip. The controversial plan, never able to get off the ground due to a lack of sufficient funding,[3] proved self-defeating in more than one respect. While it failed to secure wider support for Jordan's policies in the West Bank,[4] it also further eroded the credibility of the Jordanian strategy among Palestinians in the West Bank and even among Jordanians themselves.[5] The measures undertaken by the government—the deportation of the late deputy commander of PLO forces Khalil al-Wazir ("Abu Jihad"), the closure of a number of PLO offices, tacit encouragement of the anti-'Arafat activities of Fateh renegade 'Atallah 'Atallah ("Abu al-Za'im")—reinforced long-held Palestinian suspicions that Jordan was seeking to replace the PLO.[6] Similarly, the cool reception given 'Arafat during the extraordinary Arab summit in Amman in November 1987, and the government's public and private characterizations of the PLO's role as "marginalized," provoked resentment among Palestinians and concern among many Jordanians about internal cohesion in the country.[7]

The Impact of the *Intifada* on Jordan's Political Role

The Jordanian government's attitude towards the PLO emanated both from its dismay at the collapse of the 1985 Amman joint peace strategy, and from the apparent weakening of the PLO's status on both the Arab and international levels. The *intifada*'s clear support for the PLO, however, quickly turned the government's policy calculations upside down. From the very beginning the uprising signaled the end of Jordan's representation of the West Bank. Soon thereafter the government (and later the regime itself) was forced to adapt by making the most drastic policy shift in its history.

Jordan's disengagement, however, did not become imperative (at least in the official view) until it became clear that other alternatives could constitute a serious threat to the regime and to the existence of the state. In fact, examination of the shift in Jordan's position shows that the interaction of the regional and international repercussions of the uprising left Husayn with few realistic and secure options other than to end Jordan's political responsibility for the West Bank.

In Palestinian terms, the *intifada*'s assertion of the Palestinian identity of the occupied territories made it unrealistic, even risky, for Jordan to continue its claim to represent the West Bank. The emergence of the Unified National Leadership of the uprising one month after its eruption left few doubts that the PLO's influence far outweighed that of any other party, including Jordan.[8]

On the Arab level, the *intifada* did not immediately translate into official and practical Arab recognition of the PLO's newly-strengthened position or of the political demands articulated by Palestinians in the occupied territories. The first sign of official Arab acknowledgement of an emerging new reality came with an emergency meeting of Arab foreign ministers in

Tunis in January 1988, which recognized the Palestinian identity of the occupied territories and the PLO's responsibility towards them. The Tunis meeting was significant in that it partially reversed the status of the PLO from that of a weak and apparently marginalized party at the Amman summit just three months earlier to that of the central Arab actor in the Arab-Israeli conflict. This transformation received full Arab recognition five months later at an Arab League summit in Algiers, which was specially convened in response to the demands of the PLO and of Palestinians in the Israeli-occupied territories.

Within Israel, the immediate impact of the *intifada* was to provoke a more militant mood. This strengthened the already dominant Likud partner in Israel's coalition government, which rejected territorial compromise. Indeed, within Likud some party figures called for the establishment of a Palestinian state in Jordan as a solution to the Arab-Israeli conflict.[9]

On the international level, the *intifada* propelled the Palestinian question to the forefront of regional conflict and refocused attention on the Israeli-Arab conflict. But this attention was not translated into practical moves towards a peaceful settlement in the region. Indeed, when the American administration finally revived its peace efforts, its main concern seemed to be to contain the *intifada* and limit its negative effects on US regional allies, rather than to seek a comprehensive settlement of the conflict.

The Disengagement Decision

Taken together, how did these factors compel the King to make his historic decision ?

The *intifada* had initially taken Jordan, like other actors, by surprise. For the first two weeks there was no official reaction and relatively limited coverage of the dramatic events across the Jordan River by the state-run media. Only on December 20 was the official silence broken with statements made by King Husayn during his visit to Moscow and by other Jordanian officials.[10] These indicated that Jordan hoped the *intifada* would revive the peace process, but did not express any recognition of the PLO's influence on the uprising. Instead, such statements stressed the "spontaneity" of the continuing protests in the West Bank and Gaza Strip. In an interview with the British Broadcasting Corporation and the *Washington Post*, Prime Minister Zaid Rifa'i went still further, implying that the uprising was an act of despair that necessitated the revival of the peace process: "What has taken place is a spontaneous reaction by people who reject the continuation of the occupation... [and who] have lost hope that peace can be realized. We believe what happened is one piece of evidence, among many, of the urgency of maintaining the peace process alive."[11]

Soon afterwards, however, the Jordanian government began to recognize both the PLO's influence over events and the hostility manifested by the UNLI towards Jordanian policies (and, in some cases, the regime itself). In mid-January the government extended an invitation to Yasir 'Arafat to visit Amman for his first bilateral visit since 1985. It did not, however, alter its previous preconditions for resuming political co-ordination with the PLO.[12] This move reflected a hope that the PLO would cooperate on Jordan's terms. It was aimed at advancing the peace process and, at the same time, possibly neutralizing the *intifada*'s hostility. But 'Arafat, strengthened by the uprising and still stung by his "humiliation" by Jordan at the Arab summit a few months earlier, shunned the gesture. The PLO leader seems to have calculated that the uprising would provide for new and better circumstances for the PLO in the peace process.[13]

Thus on the eve of US Secretary George Shultz's 1988 diplomatic shuttle mission to the Middle East, King Husayn found himself in a difficult position. He had no mandate from the PLO to convey any Palestinian position. The *intifada* reduced his ability to claim representation of the West Bank. His position was further weakened by American ideas, later articulated in the Shultz plan, that envisaged a ceremonial powerless international peace conference followed by bilateral negotiations between a Jordanian-Palestinian delegation and Israel. In both style and content these proposals differed little from those in the Camp David Accords between Egypt and Israel, which Husayn had already rejected.[14]

Jordanian suspicions were confirmed by the end of Shultz's third tour in the area in April.[15] American officials did not conceal the priority they gave to preserving the Camp David Accords, which they continued to view as a cornerstone of both the peace process and US regional influence. It was also clear that Washington expected Husayn to make a conciliatory gesture that would shift the balance in favor of the Israeli Labor party.[16] Privately some Jordanian officials expressed fears that some in Washington would be ready to sacrifice the regime and accommodate the Israeli claim that "Jordan is Palestine" if this appeared the only way out for Israel.[17]

Husayn, however, skillfully maneuvered himself out of this dilemma by handing the Americans a six-point diplomatic response that reconciled Jordan's necessary adherence to the Arab consensus with the need to keep the peace process alive. The response rejected unilateral and separate deals with Israel, reiterated Jordan's commitment to the convening of an international conference and stressed the importance of Palestinian self-determination and PLO participation. But by failing to endorse an independent Palestinian state or separate Palestinian representation, the response kept open Jordan's future options in the peace process.[18] Indeed, in a briefing to the editors of the local press Prime Minister Rifa'i argued that the PLO's insistence on leading an independent Palestinian state contravened the very principle of self-determination.[19]

By now, however, Husayn was already reconsidering Jordan's relationship with the West Bank. The first signal came three days after

Shultz's departure, when "an authoritative Jordanian source" leaked to *Radio Monte Carlo* that Jordan would not negotiate the future of the West Bank. Instead, it would only discuss "Jordanian problems" such as Israel's withdrawal from 15 square kilometers in the southern Araba Valley (occupied by Israel in 1968), its dispute with Israel over water rights, and other security concerns.[20] The leak was dismissed at the time by observers and even officials as a maneuver to pressure the PLO. A series of speeches given by Husayn during the Islamic month of Ramadan (in May), however, indicated that the monarch was seriously pondering a reorientation of Jordanian policy. The speeches given at Iftar feasts in different parts of the country contained clear and emotional appeals for the support of East Bankers. Although Husayn did not attack either the PLO or the Palestinians, his melancholic mood and apologies to "mainstream Jordanians" for his "continuous engagements away from them" revealed his disappointment and pain at Palestinian reactions to his policies.[21]

Still, the King did not make his final decision until after the emergency Arab summit meeting in Algiers in June 1988. Appealing directly for Arab financial aid to the frontline states (i.e. Jordan and Syria), Husayn's lengthy summit speech contained a strong political message: Jordan was ready to wash its hands of the West Bank if the Arabs and the PLO wished it to do so, but this did not absolve the Arab world from morally and practically recognizing Jordan's responsibilities and burdens as it stood astride the longest border with Israel.[22] Husayn's message, or perhaps deliberate warning, was evidently missed. The summit decided to channel funds to the occupied territories without allocating any for Jordan.[23] Jordanian officials, who did not hide their bitterness at the Arab "apathy" to Jordan's concerns, later described the Algiers Summit resolutions as having "finalized the separation which started in the 1974 Rabat Arab summit between Jordan and the West Bank into a permanent divorce."[24]

King Husayn pondered for little more than a month. When he did not see an Arab and Palestinian response, he went on Jordanian television and announced he was conceding to the Arab consensus: "In view of this line of [Arab] thought... it becomes our duty to be part of this direction since there is a general conviction that the struggle to liberate the occupied Palestinian land could be enhanced by dismantling the legal and administrative links between the two banks...."[25]

Jordan's failure to coordinate its step with the PLO beforehand, together with the cynicism and pain evident in the King's speech, provoked suspicions that Husayn meant to catch the PLO off balance so as to prove its inability to handle the responsibility it had always sought. Certainly, Husayn had presented the PLO with its toughest challenge ever. Yet he was also providing the PLO with its first, and probably last, historical opportunity to assert its exclusive representation of the Palestinian people and demand for Palestinian statehood.

The text of Husayn's speech underscored the changes in the Jordanian position towards, and role in, the Palestinian issue.[26] Husayn also hoped to strip the so-called "Jordanian option" from Israel by firmly declaring that "Jordan is not Palestine." Now that he had withdrawn from the role of an intermediary or potential substitute, he was also challenging both Israel and Washington to confront the PLO, thus hopefully lessening political cross-pressures on Jordan. Husayn sought to draw a permanent line between Jordan's sovereignty and that of the PLO by depriving the PLO of any right to influence Jordan's Palestinians, whom he described as Jordanians. But being the wily survivor of the Middle East quagmire that he is, Husayn did leave the door open to reverse his decision. He dissolved the parliament a day before his announcement, and without enacting the required constitutional amendment to legalize a separation between the two banks. In his speech he also left the final word on the issue to the Palestinian people by stressing that in 1950 Jordan "responded" to their "wish" to unite ,while "today" Jordan was responding to the wish of the PLO "to secede."[27]

Although King Husayn deliberately kept his options open, he was evidently aware that his historic step could turn into an irreversible strategy. In fact, it did—in November 1988, when the PLO finally seized the initiative and launched its new peace strategy based on the establishment of an independent Palestinian state alongside Israel. With this, Jordan's role receded to that of a backer of the PLO initiative.

Jordan's withdrawal to the backbenches of the peace process had a two-fold impact on Jordan's political status, regionally and internationally. On the one hand it relieved it from heavy pressures to substitute for the PLO and the Palestinian people. This the King now viewed as an act of political suicide. On the other hand, it reduced Jordan's importance in the peace process, at least as far as the West was concerned. Insofar as Jordan's involvement in the Palestinian question (and American expectations that Jordan would speak for the Palestinians) have been important in determining the amounts of Arab and foreign aid to the country, the move had important economic implications. With its role now diminished, and with the aid commitments to Jordan proclaimed at the 1978 Baghdad Arab summit having expired, the resource-poor country faced the threat of declining aid levels even as it faced mounting economic problems.

To compensate for this, King Husayn immediately moved to assert Jordan's status on two axes, both based on Jordan's role as moderating force in the region. The first axis remained the Palestinian problem. In the immediate aftermath of his political disengagement from the West Bank, Husayn continued to assert Jordan's major role in any future peace process, stressing both its historic association with the Palestinians and its long border with Israel. Husayn also used his good relations with the US, the West and the Soviet Union to assert a revised role for Jordan in the peace process, especially in setting the stage for peace negotiations during any preparatory phase. The insistence of the US and the Israeli Labor Party that any future Palestinian entity should be associated with Jordan, together with the PLO's own vision for a future confederation between Jordan and the state of Palestine, strengthened Jordan's position in this regard. Yet, despite disengagement, the King's position remained problematic in some respects. In May 1989 the US endorsed Israeli Prime Minister Yitzhak Shamir's proposals for local elections to choose Palestinian interlocutors in the occupied territories, to be followed by direct negotiations with a joint Palestinian-Jordanian delegation leading up to Palestinian "autonomy." This resurrected suspicions among Palestinians that the American administration might still pressure Jordan to act as the senior representative of Palestinians. If so, Husayn (in dire need of economic aid) would find himself under tremendous pressure to comply. In a televised speech to the nation following the April 1989 economic riots, Husayn alluded to such pressures but pledged not "to submit."[28]

The second axis of Jordan's post-disengagement political direction was to assert Jordan's status as a regional catalyst. This objective was partly achieved with the formation in February 1989 of the Arab Cooperation Council (ACC), comprising Jordan, Iraq, Egypt and North Yemen. Although Husayn had been promoting the idea of regional coordination or a common economic market among the states of the Mashreq since at least 1986, the idea gained greater importance for Jordan in 1989 for several reasons. First, Jordan's disengagement from the West Bank necessitated the assertion of a compensatory regional role. Second, by joining a larger political coalition (representing 80 million Arabs) Jordan strengthened its position in the face of any future Israeli or American pressures. It also strengthened Husayn's position against any possible repercussions from the establishment of any future independent Palestinian state, although the King has repeatedly declared that this would not constitute a threat. Finally, the Council brought Iraq (just emerging from its exhausting war with Iran) back to the dynamics of inter-Arab power politics and paved the way for Egypt's full return to the Arab League, thereby counter-weighing the influence of Syria by further undercutting its regional role.

The *Intifada* and the Internal Situation in Jordan

When the *intifada* first erupted, there was speculation that political disorder would spread to Jordan. Such scenarios were based on the assumption that Jordanians of Palestinian descent would turn against the Hashemite regime. Yet despite such predictions (based in part on a simplistic view of Jordanian society), the first serious outburst of disorder to challenge the regime's stability came from "mainstream Jordanians," and was directed not against foreign policy but rather social inequality and restrictions on political freedoms.

It would be inaccurate, however, to conclude that neither the *intifada* nor Jordan's disengagement from the West Bank had any connection to events in April 1989. The factors that led to the April political crisis were far more complex than this. Jordanians, regardless of origin, hoped for greater political freedom in the wake of the King's announcement. Instead, the measures undertaken by the government of Prime Minister Zaid Rifa'i to "Jordanize" the country and its institutions made Palestinians feel that they were "suspect." They also alienated East Bankers, who felt increasingly isolated from the decision-making process in the country. Meanwhile, all Jordanians (except for the very affluent) were hit by the economic crisis.

There is no doubt that the Jordanian decision to relinquish the responsibility of the West Bank, despite its challenging tone, succeeded in defusing some of the endemic tensions in Palestinian-Jordanian relations. It was, after all, the first real breakthrough in resolving the historical competition between Jordan and the PLO. According to official figures, between December 1987 and August 1988 the security and police departments dealt with 117 demonstrations of anywhere between 100 and 2,500 people organized in Jordan in support of the *intifada*.[29] After disengagement, attempts to organize similar demonstrations declined.[30] In part this was because the government sought to curb the number of these activities following disengagement by denying the required interior ministry approval to organizers,[31] while a semi-official campaign against "dual loyalty" was partly successful in planting fear among the Palestinians of a possible official crackdown on Palestinians in general.[32] But this was far from the sole reason. One of the major issues that concerned Palestinian organizers of demonstrations in Jordan (Palestinian suspicions that Jordan wanted, or was being pressured by the US, to substitute for the PLO) had been partly eliminated as Palestinians realized the opportunity Jordan's disengagement from the West Bank now provided the PLO. Furthermore, tensions shifted from the sensitivities and mutual suspicions between Jordan and the PLO (and to a certain extent the Palestinians in general) to internal political and social conflicts as Jordan's economic crisis deepened.

In retrospect, it seems that the government and the security department were so concerned with containing the effects of the *intifada* among Palestinians that they ignored the increasing alienation of wider sectors of the population, including members of the political elite, who felt excluded from political decision-making.[33] This overemphasis by the government on the Palestinian factor as a potential source of instability—and consequent negligence of the internal socio-economic dimension of the crisis—was reflected in a series of restrictive measures taken prior to and after disengagement.

The major practical measure concerned West Bank Palestinians: a day after the King's announcement, the government stripped West Bankers of their Jordanian citizenship and reduced the term of their passports, which became strictly travel documents, to two years. Then the government stopped paying the salaries of most of 24,000 government employees on the West Bank and Gaza Strip, excepting only the Department of Awqaf (religious endowments). In his July 31 speech King Husayn stated that disengagement would not affect the status of Jordanians of Palestinian origin, who retained the same rights and obligations as "any other [citizen] irrespective of his origin."[34] Later, however, officials offered interpretations of this that reflected resentment at Palestinian support for the PLO and cast doubts on the "loyalty" of Jordanians of Palestinian descent.[35]

A clampdown on the local press and Jordanian journalists also followed the disengagement announcement. Severe government restrictions started in May 1988 when American NBC television correspondent Rick Davis was expelled and the credentials of (Jordanian) assistant producer Samira Kawar were withdrawn. The government, citing an eight-minute NBC documentary about the repression of Palestinians in Jordan, accused Kawar of bias and made clear reference to her Palestinian origin. Measures were also taken against other journalists.*

In the same period, official criticism mounted against local press editorial policies. After disengagement the government invoked the emergency powers of the Economic Security Committee to change the board of directors and responsible editors of the local newspapers, citing financial reasons.[36] The Jordan Press Foundation, which publishes *al-Ra'i* (the country's leading daily) and the English-language *Jordan Times*, was the main victim of the government's coup. Those removed included the chairman of its board of directors and editor-in chief, Mahmud al-Kayid. An East Banker and supporter of the regime, Kayid had allowed greater freedom of expression in the two newspapers and had refused to launch attacks against the PLO, even at the times of strained relations between Jordan and the organization. Mahmud Sharif, one of the founders of *al-Dustur* daily and a staunch defender of the regime, was also removed from his position. Sharif (who is of Palestinian origin) had always been careful that his newspaper asserted loyalty to the regime, but had also tried to avoid provoking Palestinian sentiments. But, as the drastic change in the information policies of the newspapers showed, the previous cautious and balanced equation was no longer tolerated as the government pushed ahead with its own concept of "Jordanization." Soon *al-Ra'i* began a provocative campaign against the PLO. In the following months at least three journalists

***Editor's note*: The Jordanian government (pointing to an article on the repercussions of the *intifada* in Jordan) took similar measures against Lamis Andoni herself, who had her press credentials and passport withdrawn, and was banned from working for the local media. She was also repeatedly questioned by Jordan security services, and publicly accused by then Information Minister Hani Khasawna of being a "liar and a traitor." Andoni's status and passport were reinstated in the summer of 1989 by the new government of Sharif Zaid bin Shakir.

were fired for publicly opposing the new information policies as the margin of free expression in the local press was almost eliminated.

These government-imposed changes in the local press proved to be the key to other official steps aimed at "Jordanization." *Al-Ra'i* spearheaded an unprecedented campaign against the political activities of Jordan's professional associations, which were seen by officials as influenced by Palestinian factions. Ironically, the new editor-in-chief of *al-Ra'i* appointed by the Economic Security Committee, Rakan al-Majali, was himself the elected president of Jordan's Press Association. In a series of scathing articles Majali accused the associations of "hypocrisy" and implied that they were manipulated by competing political groups at the expense of their dedication to the protection of professional ethics. He also argued that disengagement from the West Bank should also apply to the professional associations.[37] This latter campaign came against a backdrop of official criticism, mainly in private talks or meetings with journalists, of the role that the associations had played in organizing activities in solidarity with the *intifada*. But official resentment of the professional associations was also rooted in the influence that banned political groups, including Palestinian factions, have had in determining the outcome of the elections and orienting the activities of these important popular organizations. Indeed, there was widespread speculation that the government was preparing the ground for dissolving the elected councils of the country's eleven professional associations, both to put an end to the influence of PLO groups and to stop the associations' political activities.

The campaign soon backfired, provoking considerable popular resentment. But the government continued on other fronts, imposing restraints on virtually all forms of political activity. It even allowed the followers of the renegade Fateh leader Abu al-Za'im to disrupt a solidarity meeting held on the anniversary of the *intifada* as the Jordanian security forces simply looked on.[38] The government was apparently alarmed by the fact that solidarity meetings with the *intifada* held at the professional associations' headquarters had also turned into occasions for Palestinians and Jordanians alike to call for greater political freedom.[39]

Meanwhile, an atmosphere of intimidation against Jordanians of Palestinian origin was evident at other levels, especially in government offices.[40] Although there is no evidence that the maltreatment or humiliation of Palestinians, including West Bankers, was part of an official policy, there are indications that the hostility expressed by some officials and the press campaign against the PLO and "dual loyalty" of the Palestinians generated a similar atmosphere among some East Bank government employees. There is also no doubt that some East Bankers, especially among the less politicized, were reacting to the *intifada*'s opposition to Jordan's policies prior to disengagement, which they viewed as hostile to Jordanians in general.[41] Similarly, special security measures were instituted in some (particularly public) schools. These banned students from wearing the black-and-white checkered Palestinian *kuffiyya*, on the grounds that it would provoke hostilities between Jordanians and Palestinians.[42]

In another area, statements by officials in the Rifa'i government indicated that a policy of absorbing Palestinian refugee camps was being contemplated for the future. In April 1989, a day prior to the eruption of rioting in the south, the then-Interior Minister Raja'i Dajani announced that the 1986 electoral law would be amended to exclude the West Bank and to eliminate the status of eleven Palestinian refugee camps as separate Palestinian electoral districts. Since the earlier 1986 law had been criticized as undermining the PLO's representation of West Bank Palestinians, the reinclusion of the camps into Jordanian governates was not necessarily rejected by the Palestinians. But what did provoke resentment and fear was the tone Dajani (himself a Palestinian) had used to describe the camps as settlements and "so-called refugee camps." The clear implication was that the camps residents were no longer expected to express their Palestinian political identity, and their right to vote might come at the cost of their right to return to their homeland and to Palestinian self-determination.[43]

Despite the fact that these measures were aimed at drawing a permanent line between the domain of Jordan and that of the PLO, they in fact had far-reaching consequences for the internal situation in Jordan, affecting the lives of virtually all Jordanians regardless of origin. The restrictions on the press and the professional associations had narrowed (if not closed) one of the few channels of communications between the people and the government, and between the people and the regime itself. Both the local press (although it has never been "free") and the professional associations (with a membership of 50,000 Jordanians in 1989) had, in the absence of political parties and the continuation of strict emergency and martial laws, provided two of the few "legitimate" forums for political expression.

Another such forum was the Jordanian parliament. Although most of its members were elected 21 years earlier in a completely different situation and its efficiency was curtailed by martial law, the 1984 resurrection of parliament had opened an important channel for popular expression and demands.[44] Consequently, its dismissal in July 1988 as a prelude to Jordan's disengagement from the West Bank effectively closed another significant channel of communication and participation. At that time the government promised new general elections. But in practice it took more than nine months to amend the electoral law in order to allow exclusive balloting in the East Bank. Until the outbreak of the April protests against government-imposed price increases, there was no official announcement about the date of the elections. This increased an existing feeling of exclusion among large sectors of Jordanian society—including the traditional political elite, which repeatedly complained that it was being increasingly denied access to the King.

This growing sense of isolation was a dangerous signal, and one that the government and palace failed to correctly assess at the time when Jordan's socio-economic hardships were reaching a critical point. By the end of 1988, it became evident that the oil-rich Arab states had no intention of renewing their financial commitments to Jordan, or even paying the remaining 55 percent of the $1.25 billion aid they had pledged in 1987. Economic problems were further aggravated by heavy foreign debts, the result of dependent development policies based on unsustainable sources of external funding, and the foundering of some costly projects due to mismanagement or corruption (or both). Jordan's decision to relinquish responsibility for the West Bank, or more accurately the measures that accompanied it, led to the decline of remittances and investment by 330,000 Jordanian expatriates, the majority of whom are of Palestinian origin. An estimated $2 billion in Jordanian dinars were believed to have been exchanged to dollars between July and August 1988 by Palestinians in the Gulf and the West Bank who were worried that Jordan was no longer safe for their money.[45] In an attempt to stop the capital flight, the Rifa'i government (already lacking in political credibility) took a series of austerity measures, including a 37.5 percent cut in the value of the Jordanian dinar and the imposition of restrictions on foreign currency transactions. It later agreed to endorse an International Monetary Fund (IMF) "readjustment program" in return for $250 million in stand-by credits needed to enable Jordan to ask for a rescheduling of its foreign debts.

The April 1989 Riots

The IMF agreement, which involved sharp cuts in public expenditure and steep increases in prices of basic commodities (except for bread, sugar and rice), was the immediate trigger for the violent riots of April 1989 that led to the fall of the Rifa'i government. At least ten people were killed in the protests, which started in Ma'an in south Jordan and later spread to Karak, Tafilah, and Salt (just 24 kilometers west of the capital) before being brought to a halt by the security services and Jordanian army through armed force, strict curfews, and the detention of hundreds of Jordanian political activists. The disturbances might have spread to other areas and the capital had the King not responded to popular demands by accepting the resignation of Prime Minister Rifa'i. Shortly thereafter, Field Marshal Sharif Zaid bin Shakir was asked to head a new government.

But the riots had already sparked one of the most serious political crises in Jordan's history. In the wake of the rioting in Ma'an, protests against price rises grew into nation-wide opposition to the economic policies and curbs on political freedoms imposed by the Rifa'i government. During and after the riots, the popular message of the protests broadened from a demand for the resignation of the Rifa'i government to a more serious warning to King Husayn that the Jordanian people would no longer tolerate authoritarian government and exclusion from the decision-making process.

These popular demands were articulated in a number of leaflets and petitions addressed to King Husayn and Crown Prince Hasan.[46] The main points of these included the holding of general parliamentary elections to allow popular representations through the parliament; the lifting of emergency and martial laws, and removal of restrictions on the freedoms of expression and the press; popular participation in the decision-making process, especially on issues of crucial political and economic importance; a return to the 1953 constitution (which guaranteed the freedom of expression and allowed the formation of political parties); and the introduction of economic reforms to wipe out corruption, mismanagement and inefficiency, so as to enable the country to pursue policies aimed at lessening its dependency and increasing its self-reliance. Such demands, although amounting to radical changes in the system of government, fell short of calling for an end to the monarchy. But all the leaflets also contained unprecedented warnings to King Husayn that his leadership was not tied to the absolute and unquestioning loyalty of the population, but rather to his ability to respond and accommodate popular aspirations in a more democratic system.[47]

Palestinians and the Protests

As the preceding analysis suggests, it would be misleading to claim that the April protests were a direct consequence of the *intifada*. There were, however, many indications that Jordanian protesters were influenced by the daring manner in which young Palestinians confronted armed Israeli soldiers across the river.

At one level, the protests showed that the barrier of fear constructed by Jordan's security and intelligence departments (which had grown tremendously in influence and size since 1979) had started to break down. Many political activists suggested that television scenes of the *intifada* played an important role in the process. These scenes were almost duplicated in Jordanian cities where youths wearing red-and-white checkered Jordanian *kuffiyya*s hurled stones at security forces and blockaded streets with burning tires and barrels.

Still more significant were the indirect effects of the *intifada*, including official reaction to the perceived "Palestinian threat." These intensified internal contradictions at a time when Jordan's disengagement from the West Bank shifted the focus of attention to socio-economic concerns and raised expectations for wider political participation. Such expectations were based on the argument that by relinquishing its responsibility for the West Bank, Jordan had been relieved of a major burden—one that had repeatedly cited by officials to justify curbs on political freedoms and the continuation of martial law since the 1967 Arab-Israeli war. Moreover, King Husayn's success in recent years in maintaining good relations with all (or nearly all) his powerful Arab neighbors—Egypt, Syria, Iraq and Saudi Arabia—had reduced the danger of Arab attempts to destabilize Jordan.[48] Taken together, these two factors were seen by many as providing Jordan with a rare opportunity to relax restrictions on political freedoms in the country.

In theory, the resolution of the historical competition between Jordan and the PLO should have also reduced internal tensions. In practice, however, the government's attempts to put an end to PLO influence among Palestinians in Jordan backfired. The *intifada* itself had a tremendous effect on Palestinians (especially the younger generation, the vast majority of whom were born in Jordan), reinforcing their Palestinian identity. Because of this, the government's unsuccessful drive to win them over provoked resentment. Indeed, the government's campaign had the unwitting effect of increasing the PLO's influence on Palestinians in Jordan by alienating many of the latter from the regime.[49]

Yet when the rioting did erupt in April, the role of the mainstream PLO proved to be a moderating one. King Husayn himself admitted the PLO's influence a few days after the riots when he indicated, with gratitude, that the PLO had helped to restrain Palestinians and PLO factions from engaging in the April price protests.[50] PLO officials in Amman, especially of the mainstream Fateh faction, say that the organisation did give instructions to its affiliated members and supporters to restrain Palestinian reactions, particularly in the refugee camps. Palestinians in Jordan were responsive to this mainly because they shared the PLO's fear that their involvement might be used against them, or that it would be deliberately misinterpreted as part of a Palestinian attempt to turn Jordan into a Palestinian state.

It would be untruthful, however, to state that the Palestinians played no part in the protests. They did, whether through the professional associations, banned political parties, or the demonstrations themselves.[51] Palestinian and Jordanian activists expected that Palestinians would have played a bigger part had the riots spread to Amman, Zarqa and Irbid, where most are concentrated. Furthermore, the Jordanian wings of the Marxist Palestinian groups, namely the Democratic Front for the Liberation of Palestine (DFLP) and the Popular Front for the Liberation of Palestine (PFLP), issued leaflets supporting the popular demands and called for an end to the economic austerity measures.[52]

The activities of Palestinian groups and their Jordanian extensions have always been a major concern for consecutive Jordanian governments and security officials. According to former Prime Minister Ahmad 'Ubaydat (who was also the head of the Directorate of General Intelligence between 1974 and 1982) the presence of the Palestinian factions and popular organizations, in the absence of parallel Jordanian institutions, has always raised serious security concerns for the intelligence department.[53] In the view of Jordanian officials, this problem used to intensify during periods of strained relations between Jordan and the PLO. Thus the improvement of relations between Jordan and the PLO, particularly following Jordan's recognition of the independent Palestinian state, was a pacifying factor. On the other hand, the continuation of Jordanization policies, coupled with an economic crisis that had increasingly direct effects on the daily life of Jordanians of Palestinian origin, remained provocative. Moreover, there are limits on the PLO's ability to restrain the Palestinians in times of economic hardship: while the PLO can always play a role in preventing a Palestinian outburst against the regime, it cannot control grassroots Palestinian reactions to conditions of social and economic inequality or suppression of freedom of expression.

Several structural reasons also explain the eruption of the riots in the predominantly Transjordanian (non-Palestinian) areas. While the majority of government employees are East Bankers, Palestinians have always depended more on professional and labor skills. This, coupled with the usual impact of austerity measures on state employees, explains why the population of the south (most of whom are employed by the state and the army) was the first to erupt. Another more complex factor is that despite the strained periods between the regime and the Palestinians, there has always been a feeling among "mainstream Jordanians" (especially outside the capital) that the regime takes their loyalty for granted and that they are "neglected and even forgotten."[54] Some East Bankers even feel that the regime takes the "Palestinians more seriously, out of either fear, or respect, or both."[55]

In this context, Jordanians of Palestinian origin were caught in a difficult position. If they failed to join the growing popular consensus which emerged after the April events, they would be seen by Transjordanians as apathetic and insensitive in the struggle for reforms. It would also feed allegations that Palestinians were not affected by the economic crisis, and even responsible for it by smuggling their money abroad.[56] If Palestinians did take an active part in the social and political struggle for reforms, they would have to do so within a Jordanian context. Otherwise, their activities would only worsen their relationship with both Transjordanians and the regime.

After the *Haba*: New Beginnings?

Given the complex situation outlined above, in the aftermath of the April riots Palestinians in Jordan were acutely sensitive to indicators of the new government's approach to the "Jordanization" issue and to questions of economic and political reform.

In the first of these areas, the government of Field Marshal Sharif Zaid bin Shakir appeared to adopt a new and more positive attitude. Officially, at least, Palestinians were no longer suspected of dual loyalties: instead government officials now characterized the Palestinian origin of some citizens as an "asset." Indeed, by the first anniversary of the disengagement decision it was apparent to most that the abrupt manner in which disengagement had been implemented (although not disengagement itself), and the policies that had accompanied it, had proven self-defeating. Calls for a reassessment or reversal or these policies were increasingly voiced by prominent Jordanian politicians of both East Bank and Palestinian origin, including members of the political establishment both inside and outside government.[57] In August, PLO chairman Yasir 'Arafat visited Jordan and the government allowed the reopening of the Palestine National Fund (PNF) headquarters in Amman (closed in 1986). The move (which helped the PLO in its efforts to channel funds to the *intifada*) signaled a marked improvement in PLO-Jordanian ties. It was also widely interpreted as a gesture of PLO support for the ailing Jordanian economy.[58] Such PLO-Jordanian rapprochement served to significantly ease tensions among Palestinians in Jordan.

In the area of political reform, initial signals were more mixed. In his royal designation letter to the new prime minister, King Husayn charged the interim government with "the re-professionalization" of professional associations and halting of the politicization of religion. The first of these instructions appeared to challenge an important channel of expression and popular participation, while the second part of the King's directive was clearly aimed at undercutting the influence of the Muslim Brotherhood and other Islamic groupings. Moreover, liberalization itself posed clear potential risks to the regime. Among these was the fear that political liberalization would imply greater freedom for organized Palestinian activities and public manifestations of Palestinian nationalism in Jordan. This in turn might further aggravate Jordan's existing identity crisis and strengthen Israeli claims that Jordan was a substitute Palestinian homeland. Finally, there were important sources of resistance to reform within the regime, both from the segments of the traditional political elite and from the security services.

Yet not to allow greater political freedom would also worsen domestic political tensions, angering both East Bankers and Palestinians. Increasingly, therefore, liberalization emerged as the only viable option. The caretaker government, aware of the danger inherent in continued restrictions on popular expression, eventually reversed many of the punitive measures against journalists endorsed by its predecessor and pledged to guarantee a freer press. Most of the political detainees arrested during the April riots were released. A "national charter" was promised, which would spell out the rights and obligations of individuals and groups within the Jordanian political system. A drive against corruption was initiated. Most important of all, the regime announced that full parliamentary elections would be held on 8 November 1989.

The PLO and the Elections

All of this only served to increase the importance of the debate regarding the appropriate role of Palestinians in the reform process in Jordan. As a result of the *intifada* on the one hand, and the liberalization process on the other, clear differences in political priorities emerged among many Palestinian and Jordanian activists. While all agreed that the two issues were complementary, the former tended to stress the need to lend greater support to the Palestinian national struggle, while the latter tended to emphasize the importance of the struggle for democratic freedoms in Jordan. With the promise of elections, further differences emerged as to the appropriate role Palestinians should play. Many Palestinian members of the political establishment argued for full Palestinian participation, a view that was also put forward by some Palestinian radicals who still feared under-representation. A second grouping (including most of the Palestinian nationalist groups and the Jordanian left and opposition) advocated full Palestinian participation in the ballot, but argued that East Bankers should be given preference as candidates in order to underline the Jordanian identity of parliament. Finally, an emerging "nationalist" East Bank trend called for the exclusion of Palestinians from the vote, citing the Palestinians' voting power, superior political organization, and the PLO's influence over Jordanians of Palestinian origin.

During this period, Jordanian officials were also concerned to realize what had been one of the major positive objectives of disengagement, namely the demarcation of the PLO's authority from that of the Jordanian state. The regime certainly had a variety of tools available to it whereby it might reduce the direct influence of the PLO and Palestinian activists on the elections, including security regulations and the provisions of the 1986 electoral law, which barred candidates affiliated with political groups from running for parliament.[59] Yet the regime was reluctant to enforce this ban, rightly fearing that the use of such restrictive measures would seriously compromise the credibility of the elections. Instead, Jordan used Egyptian and Iraqi channels to request PLO non-interference in the electoral process.

The issue of the Palestinian and PLO role in the elections was also shaped by the Arab-Israeli conflict itself. As prospects for a negotiated Palestinian-Israeli settlement remained remote, Israeli assertions that "Jordan is Palestine" seemed to increase.[60] This trend alarmed both Jordanian and PLO officials, who feared that a strong showing of Palestinian influence and representation in the November elections would be seized upon by Israel to further its claims. As a result, a tacit agreement emerged between Jordan and the PLO (including even its leftist groups) that the elections should serve as a vehicle to reassert Jordan's Jordanian identity. Although not officially prevented from doing so, Palestinian activists affiliated with the PLO refrained from running for office. This "understanding" automatically reduced the number of potential Palestinian candidates, since most activists were already associated with the PLO or one of its constituent organizations.

Palestinian groups were less united on other issues concerning the election. The DFLP had already responded to the altered political environment in Jordan by announcing the "disengagement" of its Jordanian wing to form a new, independent political party, the Jordanian People's Democratic Party. The PFLP refused to follow suit, arguing that the liberation of Palestine and the struggle for democracy were inseparable. The Jordanian Communist Party remained divided over this same issue until the eve of the election.[61] Meanwhile, a policy of "non-interference" was pursued by the main Palestinian group, Fateh. Although individual Fateh activists were active in the campaign, Fateh as a whole refused to nominate candidates or even grant them public backing.[62] This policy of non-intervention had the practical effect of discouraging many Palestinians from voting—contributing to the low turnout (not exceeding 40 percent) in many refugee camps and other predominately Palestinian areas—and clearly harmed the electoral chances of many sympathetic candidates.

In addition to its desire not to strengthen Israel's assertion of Jordan as a Palestinian homeland, the Fateh leadership (and 'Arafat in particular) had other objectives at stake in the Jordanian elections. If PLO discouragement had the effect of reducing Palestinian participation, it would demonstrate the PLO's influence over the the Palestinian community as a whole and hence further the PLO's long-term strategy of asserting the central role of the PLO in the peace process. It would signal, for example, to the US and Israel that the sort of election they proposed for the occupied territories could not be conducted without the PLO's cooperation: if the organization was able to curb balloting in Jordan, it could certainly disrupt it completely on the West Bank and Gaza. It would also undermine any possible future attempts to resurrect the "Jordanian option," and would strengthen the PLO's position vis-à-vis King Husayn in any negotiating process regarding confederation between Jordan and a future Palestinian state. Finally, many Fateh leaders felt that King Husayn remained the best guarantor of future Jordanian stability. As a result, they did not favour the growth of a Jordanian "opposition," believing that neither the Islamists nor the left would be capable of pulling the country together should the regime collapse.[63]

The Muslim Brotherhood and Hamas

One of the most important developments in Jordan following the government's August announcement of a date for the elections was the unfolding strength of the Muslim Brotherhood (*Ikhwan*). The Ikhwan platform contained a number of elements, including the expansion of political freedoms, resolution of the economic crisis, an end to corruption, and the application in Jordan of *shari'a* (Islamic law). It also called for greater support for the *intifada*—and for the radical Islamic movement in the occupied territories. In so doing, it revealed a significant rejectionist trend in the country that opposed a peaceful negotiated settlement of the Israeli-Palestinian conflict.

The Ikhwan was bound to emerge as a powerful political force in Jordan, if only because it had been the sole legal political group (officially registered as a "charity") in the country at a time when all other political parties were banned. Through the 1950s the Ikhwan found a common interest with King Husayn in battling the radical influences of Nasirism. In 1957 it stood by the King during his showdown with the leftist-nationalist government of Sulayman Nabulsi. Since then, the movement had been tolerated (and sometimes encouraged) as a counter-weight to the left and Palestinian radicals.

Although they fielded candidates throughout the country, the Ikhwan concentrated much of its efforts on Palestinian refugee camps and other predominately Palestinian areas. There, the *intifada*, the emergence of *Hamas* (the "Islamic Resistance Movement") in the occupied territories, and the continuing lack of major progress towards a peace settlement gave the Muslim Brotherhood a significant boost. Hamas (which had come into being as the resistance wing of the Muslim Brotherhood in Gaza in February 1988) called for the liberation of all Palestine, declaring that "Palestine is an odd number that does not divide in two." In their rallies and speeches in Jordan, Ikhwan leaders echoed this, rejecting the PLO's endorsement of a two-state solution and negotiations with Israel, and expressing instead full-fledged support for Hamas. Ikhwan candidates refrained from directly attacking the PLO, so as to avoid antagonizing the large sector of Palestinians in Jordan who opposed the PLO's political positions but not the organization itself. Through slogans like "Palestine is an Islamic endowment," however, they did seek to gain the support of Palestinians opposed to a two-state solution, especially Palestinians who originated from within Israel's 1948 borders and who felt that the PLO's declaration of an independent state within the West Bank and Gaza Strip ignored their interests.[64] Some radical candidates also called for the opening of Jordan's borders to allow armed struggle against Israel, a demand that Ikhwan's leadership was not expected to pursue upon election but which embarrassed the authorities nonetheless.

The emergence of Hamas and the failure of peace efforts, coupled with the deterioration of economic conditions in the camps, the strict grip of the security services and the historic repression of the left, led thousands of refugees to turn to the Muslim Brotherhood. The degree of electoral support garnered by the Muslim Brotherhood in the refugee camps did not, however, necessarily reflect the political orientation of the bulk of Palestinians in Jordan, most of whom in fact refrained from voting at all. In other cases, populists such as Shaykh 'Abd al-Munim Abu Zant (who was deported by Israel in 1968, and who won broad support for his past denunciations of the suppression of political freedoms in Jordan) served to boost the electoral chances of other, less prominent, Ikhwan candidates.

The size of grassroots support for the Brotherhood, along with its radical slogans (including calls for the domestic application of Islamic law) alarmed the authorities, who had long viewed the movement as an ally of the establishment. Husayn first tried to neutralize the Ikhwan after the April riots by promising to reinstate members of the Brotherhood who had been expelled from their civil service positions during the Rifa'i era, and pledging not to bar their most outspoken candidates from seeking election on security grounds. Later, the emerging strength of the Brotherhood was believed to be instrumental in convincing the regime to set aside regulations which barred other political activists from seeking election. In September, 62 leftist activists detained during the April riots were released. The repression of the JCP was relaxed, allowing its leaders to emerge from hiding. In October the Interior Minister announced that activists would be able to stand for election, thus allowing the left and supporters of Palestinian groups to compete on a more equal footing with the Brotherhood.

Within the PLO, there were some initial fears that Jordan might use the growing strength of the Muslim Brotherhood to undermine the PLO's position in Jordan and the occupied territories. In practice, however, this strategy was far too risky for Jordanian decision-makers to entertain. Indeed, the rise of the Ikhwan had the effect of reducing the comparative threat of Palestinian activism earlier perceived by the government.[65]

The Intifada *and the Election Campaign*

As already noted, the issue of the *intifada* and other Palestinian concerns figured prominently in the election campaign. This reflected not only efforts to attract Palestinian votes, but also the broad impact of the *intifada* throughout Jordan. Election rallies commonly began with a minute of silence in memory of the martyrs of the uprising. Most candidates (in contrast to the Muslim Brotherhood) expressed support for the PLO. Another common theme was the link between the *intifada* in the territories and the struggle for political freedom in Jordan. In many meetings, comparisons were drawn between the Palestinian resistance to Israeli occupation and repression in the Arab world; political liberty was commonly cited as an essential element for the effective mobilization of popular support for the uprising. In the refugee camps, election meetings provided a forum for the expression of Palestinian resentment of government security measures, especially those restricting rallies and other demonstrations of solidarity with the *intifada*. Demands were also voiced for a reversal of those administrative measures that had accompanied disengagement.

Many candidates, regardless of affiliation, called for the opening of

Jordan's borders to armed struggle. The salience of this issue was underscored by continuing attempts by Palestinian guerrillas to infiltrate into Palestine across Jordan's borders: as of September 1989, seven such attempts had been reported in the past year, including two carried out by lone Jordanian soldiers. On September 7, a rocket attack was launched across the border from a hill in the north of Jordan. When this latter attack was claimed in Damascus by the PFLP, the Jordanian security services immediately rounded up the PFLP's leadership in Amman (who insisted that they had not been involved). Privately, Jordanian officials blamed Syria, suggesting that the attack was intended to embarrass Jordan and disrupt political liberalization.[66]

The incident highlighted the potential contradiction between Jordan's security needs and Palestinian national struggle. It also highlighted the potential tensions between the reform process and the Palestinian struggle: many parliamentary candidates were critical of the timing and nature of the attack, expressing the fear that it could undermine the democratic process in Jordan by providing a pretext for tighter security restrictions. At the same time, however, Israel's repression of the *intifada* contributed to widespread support for armed struggle; the arrest of the PFLP officials brought numerous demands during the campaign for an end to the interrogation and detention of Palestinians and Jordanians involved in armed attacks on Israel.

A Point of No Return?

The results of the November elections were a major victory for the Muslim Brotherhood. With twenty-two seats (and a further ten independent Islamists elected), it emerged as the single largest group in the new eighty-seat parliament. The left scored quite low in the poll, but the Jordanian Communist Party, the Jordanian People's Democratic Party and the Jordanian wing of the PFLP did succeed in winning one seat apiece. All told, some fifteen leftist and nationalist candidates won election.[67] The remainder of those elected comprised a mixed group of tribal candidates, former government ministers, and independents. About eight percent of the 650 candidates running for election were of Palestinian origin; nine Palestinians were elected, most of them associated with the Islamist bloc.

The election propelled the liberalization process to new heights. Given the popular dissatisfaction and tensions that had long lain beneath the deceptively tranquil surface of Jordanian politics—only to burst forth in April—King Husayn quickly recognized that he needed to respond to demands for greater political participation if he was to avert a full-scale explosion. Immediately after the elections, he declared the process "irreversible". The King also noted that the past was "buried," meaning "the past which allowed some the freedom of [political] activities and denied others the same freedom." His remarks suggested that he believed it urgent to increase political pluralism so as to undercut the popular strength of the religious movement.[68] Yet elsewhere there was also evidence of a residual belief among many in the regime that political pluralism needed to be contained and controlled—insulated from the influence of the PLO and radical Arab states. This was reflected in the continuing prominence given the idea of a "national charter" which would define the relationship of political forces to the state and regime as a whole.

In practice, however, the idea of "regulating" pluralism soon encountered strong resistance from both the public and from the new parliament, which between December 30 and 1 January 1990 subjected the newly-appointed government of Mudar Badran to a grueling 22-hour debate over its proposed program before granting it a vote of confidence. Faced with such pressures, the Badran government made a series of unprecedented political concessions. In the span of one month, most of the restrictive press measures instituted during the Rifa'i era were reversed. The government pledged to lift martial law (in force since 1967), revise the 1939 Defense Law, and dramatically limit the authority of Jordan's security services. Thousands of impounded passports were to be returned, and travel and work restrictions were lifted on political activists. The government promised to reconsider restrictive press legislation; to repeal the notorious 1953 law against communism; to reinstate civil servants fired in the past for security reasons; and to no longer require security clearance for government jobs and scholarships. It also promised to reconsider the administrative measures that had accompanied disengagement so as to facilitate the the movement of people and products across the bridges pending the establishment of an independent Palestinian state.

Conclusion

The Palestinian uprising in the occupied territories affected Jordan more deeply than any other Arab country. The *intifada*, by asserting the Palestinian identity of the West Bank, undermined an important foundation of the Jordanian regime: Jordan's claim of responsibility for the Palestinians. Since 1950 this had been critical to the regime's prestige at home and abroad, and had helped to ensure a steady lifeline of Arab and other foreign aid to the country. Despite formal recognition of the PLO as sole legitimate representative of the Palestinian people in 1974, Jordan had continued to seek a senior political role in the West Bank—a desire evident in the Amman Accord of 1985, and Jordanian policy in the wake of the Accord's subsequent collapse. Faced with the start of the *intifada* in December 1987 and the uprising's unequivocal affirmation of the PLO's leadership of Palestinians in the occupied territories, however, it was clear this position could no longer be maintained. Indeed, Jordanian disengagement eventually became the only route whereby Jordan could avoid possible collision with the uprising and the PLO—a collision that was bound to have serious domestic repercussions.

Yet, although fear of domestic unrest was a major reason for the regime's decision to disengage, its adaptation to this new reality was poorly conceived and implemented. The narrow-minded "Jordanization" policy pursued by the government of Zaid Rifa'i alienated not only the Palestinians against whom it was directed, but also East Bankers dismayed at the progressive erosion of their already limited political freedoms. Combined with economic crisis and charges of government corruption, this generated an increasingly tense atmosphere, culminating in the April 1989 riots. Faced with a rapid erosion of the regime's standing among Palestinians and East Bankers alike, King Husayn had essentially two choices: to repress popular demands, at further cost to his legitimacy; or move in the direction of political liberalization. As the November 1989 elections clearly demonstrated, it was upon the latter path that the regime embarked.

Future political developments in Jordan will continue to be shaped both by domestic political dynamics and by events further afield—including not only the *intifada*, but also the regional crisis that erupted with Iraq's August 1990 invasion of Kuwait. With regard to the former, Jordan looked on with dismay at the evolution of the "peace process" in the wake of disengagement. Under the proposals advanced by US Secretary State James Baker in 1989-90, Cairo emerged to increasingly assume Jordan's traditional role as potential broker-cum-proxy for the Palestinians.[69] By the same token, however, Jordan could take little comfort in the collapse of the Baker initiative, the accession of a hardline Likud government in Israel, and the suspension of the US-PLO dialogue, all of which raised several equally dangerous possibilities. First, Israel might resort to greater violence and force Palestinians from the occupied territories to the East Bank in an attempt to end the *intifada*.[70] Second, Jordan might find itself under renewed pressure to reverse its disengagement decision. Although Husayn continues to view such a step at the PLO's expense as "political suicide," many Palestinians remain suspicious. Finally, any forced exclusion of the PLO from any future negotiating process would provoke waves of Palestinian anger not only within the occupied territories but also in Jordan.

Moreover, new and intense pressures were placed on Jordan following the eruption of the Gulf crisis. On one side, the US and the conservative Arab Gulf states pressed Jordan to break its long-standing ties with Iraq. Within Jordan, however, virtually all sectors of public opinion expressed strong opposition to US policy and support for Iraq. In the short term, King Husayn's refusal to bow to Western pressures strengthened his domestic standing.[71] But the economic costs of this policy are likely to be severe.[72] Meanwhile, the crisis effectively destroyed what was to have been a centerpiece of Jordan's post-disengagement foreign policy: the Arab Cooperation Council.

Regional events thus continue to spill over into the arena of Jordanian domestic politics. All of these developments, coupled with Israeli intransigence, continuation of the *intifada*, a stalemated peace process, and deteriorating economic conditions in Jordan, will likely radicalize the political atmosphere and strengthen the position of religious extremists. Already there is evidence that, in the wake of the November elections, the radical supporters of Hamas are gaining greater strength within the Muslim Brotherhood. In a different area, there are signs that the greater political freedoms now exercised by Palestinians are being exploited by some to mobilize Transjordanian nationalist sentiments against further political liberalization.[73] Finally, the whole process of democratization is beset by a host of questions that have as yet remained unanswered, ranging from the changing role of tribalism in the Jordanian political system to the fundamental issue of how far the King is willing to go in surrendering his present legal and political powers.

Thus, as they have been since December 1987, the regional and domestic pressures buffeting Jordan and the Hashemite monarchy are intense. By July 1988, disengagement had become an essential gesture if the King was to maintain his balance: the *intifada* forced Husayn to surrender his historic claim to the West Bank in the hope of stabilizing conditions at home. After April 1989, democratization became no less important: the November elections became part of a process of democratization designed to rebuild the regime's shaken legitimacy. Three years after the start of the *intifada*, King Husayn continues to walk an increasingly unsteady political tightrope.

Notes

1. *Jordan Times*, 20 February 1986. See also Judith Miller, "Hussein challenges the PLO," *New York Times*, 25 February 1986.

2. Although these objectives were denied by senior Jordanian officials, the Ministry of Occupied Territories' Affairs was engaged in the promotion of pro-Jordanian elements and leaders in the West Bank.

3. Oil-rich Arab countries refused to finance the program, while the U.S. offered only $14.5 million for the plan.

4. A poll concluded jointly by the Palestinian *al-Fajr* daily, the New York-based *Newsday* and Australian Television in August 1986 showed that more than 93% of the Palestinians in the occupied territories supported the Palestine Liberation Organization, while 3% backed King Husayn. See *Journal of Palestine Studies* 16, 2 (Winter 1987).

5. In interviews conducted by the writer with prominent Jordanians in early 1987, many expressed resentment of the government policies which alienated Palestinians and the PLO, and "put Jordan's supporters in the West Bank in the same basket with collaborators with Israel" (in the words of one former senior Jordanian official). He was referring to the government's dependence on suspect figures like Mustafa Dudin, who headed the pro-Israeli Village Leagues, to promote Jordanian policies.

6. Abu al-Za'im, a former head of PLO military intelligence, broke away two weeks after Jordan's suspension of coordination with the PLO in February 1986. Although the

government never officially recognized him, he was allowed to carry out public activities and "rallies" against the PLO leadership. He was allowed to have armed guards, and to organize activities in the refugee camps. In May 1986, his men attacked officials in PLO Chairman Yasir 'Arafat's office in Amman.

7. The offhand reception given by Prime Minister Rifa'i to Yasir 'Arafat at the airport when the latter arrived to attend the Amman summit was televised and seen in the West Bank. During the summit, 'Arafat deliberately boycotted the official dinner in protest of his treatment.

8. The first leaflet from the Unified Leadership was signed by the Palestinian national forces on January 8, 1988. A second leaflet two days later was signed by the "Unified Leadership of the *intifada*." The third added "Unified National Leadership of the Uprising—the Palestine Liberation Organization" and this has continued. Communique number 7 on 2 February 1988 warned members of Israeli-appointed municipalities to resign. This was an implicit criticism of Jordan, since it backed Israeli appointment of these councils in 1987. Communique 8, a week later, attacked pro-Jordanian figures in the West Bank and Gaza, describing them as subservient to Amman and to Arab reactionary circles. Communique number 10 was the most hostile. It also reflected a controversy inside the UNL, because two communiques were issued at the same time: one called on West Bank deputies to quit the Jordanian parliament, while the other did not. Still, the message was not missed by Amman.

9. The "Jordan is Palestine" theme was also put forward by the Israeli Foreign Ministry, which has distributed publicity materials stressing the Palestinian character of Jordan. See, for example, Moshe Aumann, "The Palestinian Labyrinth: A Way Out," (Jerusalem: Israel Academic Committee on the Middle East, 1985) distributed by Israeli embassies and consulates in Canada.

10. During a dinner hosted by then Soviet President Andrei Gromyko, King Husayn made the first official reference to the *intifada*; see the full transcript of the King's speech in the *Jordan Times*, 22 December 1987.

11. Full transcript of the interview made by Samira Qawar, published in *al-Ra'i* (Amman), 4 January 1988.

12. Personal interviews with senior PLO leaders in Amman, March 1988.

13. 'Arafat instead sent Palestinian delegations in January and March to hold talks with the government.

14. The *Jordan Times*, 7 March 1988, carried an English translation of Shultz's proposals as published originally in the Israeli press.

15. Lamis Andoni, "Balancing act," *Middle East International*, 16 April 1988.

16. Personal interviews with American officials accompanying US Secretary of State George Shultz during his three short visits to Amman in the first week of April 1987; see Andoni, "Balancing act."

17. According to one former advisor to Husayn in the 1970s, the King started taking this possibility seriously after the 1970 civil war, when American officials told him that they were ready to sacrifice the regime if the "Palestinians" were to take over. Personal interview, September 1988.

18. Full text of Jordanian reply in *Jordan Times*, 9 April 1988.

19. Nemat Salameh, "Jordan outlines stand on American peace initiative," *Jordan Times*, 9 April 1988.

20. *Radio Monte Carlo*, 11 April 1988. The report was from Amman-based correspondent Randa Habib.

21. See the Jordanian press on 8 May 1988, which carried the official news agency *Petra* report on the King's meeting with community leaders in Karak.

22. *Jordan Times*, 9-10 June 1988. See also *Middle East International*, 24 June 1988.

23. The Algiers extraordinary summit resolutions did not allocate funds for the East

Bank, or through Jordan for the West Bank. In his speech to the summit (published in the *Jordan Times*, 9-10 June 1988) Husayn reminded the Arab states that his country still paid the salaries of 18,000 government and religious employees in the West Bank, in addition to 6,000 employees in the Gaza Strip.

24. *Middle East International*, 24 June 1988.

25. The official translation of King Husayn's speech on 31 July 1988 as distributed by the Palace; *Jordan Times*, 1 August 1988.

26. *Jordan Times*, 1 August 1988.

27. *Jordan Times*, 1 August 1988.

28. Text of King's speech in *al-Dustur* (Amman), 27 April 1989.

29. *Jordan Times*, 30 August 1988, quoting assistant public security director Major General Yusif Gharayba.

30. According to personal interviews with Palestinian activists in April-May, 1988.

31. Jordanian and Palestinian activists reported that the Interior Ministry refusaed to allow a solidarity rally in January 1988, while the chairman of the Professional Associations Council sent a letter on February 8 to the prime minister and the mayor of Amman to protest "the banning of activities of the associations and implied threats from the concerned department [i.e. the security forces] that in case the associations did not comply with the ban, unpleasant physical or moral harm might be done [to the organizers]". Copies of the letters were obtained by this writer. Professional organizations, which include members from the West Bank, suspended meetings immediately following the disengagement to avoid the question of who was a member. The government, however, did not press the issue further.

32. The press campaign to end the duality of identity started in May 1988 (during the same period of the King's Ramadan speeches) by the government-controlled newspaper *Sawt al-Sha'ab*. The articles were signed by the political editor, who, according to editorial sources, was actually former information minister Hani Khasawna.

33. See Tony Walker and Lamis Andoni, *Financial Times*, 10 October 1988.

34. Full text of King's speech in *Jordan Times*, 1 August 1988.

35. Such remarks were mostly made in private meetings with journalists and writers, including foreign correspondents.

36. *al-Ra'i* newspaper, the biggest among Jordan's three Arabic dailies, had actually made a profit of JD23 million in 1987—thus defying government allegations that financial reasons prompted the change.

37. Rakan Majali, "The unprofessional professional associations," *al-Ra'i*, 6 October 1988.

38. Eyewitness accounts of the disruption of the solidarity meeting on the occasion of the first anniversary of the *intifada* on 8 December 1988. A letter by Deputy Layth al-Shubaylat to the prime minister on 8 February 1989 referred to the incident and said that Abu al-Za'im's group "enjoyed official sponsorship."

39. Eyewitness accounts. This writer covered a number of these meetings and demonstrations, during which slogans of "No to Arab repression...No to Arab silence [on Israeli suppression]" repeatedly rang out.

40. Palestinians reported ill-treatment by junior officials in government departments, such as passport and other offices. A repeated example was that officials would tell Palestinian applicants for civil papers to "go to 'Arafat..." There was no evidence that this attitude reflected a systematic campaign or clear instructions, but such incidents increased immediately after the disengagement and declined a few months later.

41. Personal interviews. Although this trend was not prominent, it emerged among apolitical young people and in some rural areas.

42. Personal interviews with pupils in public and private schools. Most reported that school principals and teachers confiscated the Palestinian *kuffiyya*, although some in

public schools reported that the security forces intervened to do the job without harming them. Activities like Palestinian plays, songs and poetry did not cease, nor were they banned in private schools, where there is less government supervision and probably less threat from a security point of view.

43. *al-Ra'i*, 17 April 1989. The relationship between the refugee camp residents' right to vote and their right as Palestinians to return and to self-determination depends on how the government's concept of Jordanization will evolve in the future.

44. Parliament's role was enhanced by by-elections to fill the vacant seats of eight deputies who had died in the East Bank. The new deputies were very outspoken, especially Riyadh Nawaysa (Karak) and Layth al-Shubaylat (Amman) who were the only ones to vote against the 1986 electoral law and the 1988 budget.

45. According to issue number 28 of *Jordan's Economic Monitor*, remittances decreased from JD 25 million to JD 12 million in the two months following disengagement. One issue earlier the *Monitor* noted that "expatriates left the banks and returned to money changers in order to get more for their dollar.... after the dollar price hit 400 fils in the parallel market against 377 fils in the banking system... in the third week of August 1988, exactly three weeks after the disengagement." With the closure of the money changers in February remittances continued to be absorbed in the black market in the Gulf and Jordan, and bankers complained that the "leakage was gaining momentum." See Lamis Andoni, "Jordan rules out further devaluation," *Financial Times* 3 April 1989; Tony Walker, "Jordan's consumer spree comes to an end," *Financial Times* 10 November 1988; K. Said Abu Reish, "Hussein, Arafat fighting all the way to the Bank," *The Washington Report*, December 1988, reprinted from the *Washington Post*, 30 October 1988. The latter, however, implied that Palestinian reluctance to keep their savings in dinars was partly incited by the PLO.

46. The most important of these were the Karak appeal of April 19, the cable to Prince Hasan by the professional associations in April, and the Salt document sent to King Husayn on May 8. Copies of these and other leaflets were obtained by the author.

47. In the cable to Prince Hasan, the presidents of Jordan's eleven associations stated: "this small country, whose very existence is threatened, is looking forward to the necessity of a change in the leadership's attitude to issues, for instead of [the monarchy] being a last resort for all [the citizens], recent consecutive governments were able to convince it that every criticism that is directed at the government is actually directed at the leadership, something which enabled the governments to claim the [monarchy's full endorsement of their behavior] ...consequently the governments have shrunken in role and influence and yet at the same time have grown in tyranny, thereby no longer depending on their efficiency to prove their presence. Instead [the governments] were hiding under the umbrella of his Majesty, capitalizing on the king's popular credibility... while they exploit this without adding any assets to it... if the situation remains the way it is, this credibility, which constitutes the basis of national unity, will be eroded."

48. Unlike the 1950s, 1960s, and 1970s, both the Ba'athist ruling parties in Iraq and Syria have in general reduced their support to their affiliated organizations in other Arab countries. The danger to the Jordanian regime was further reduced after the eruption of the 1980 Iraq-Iran War by rapprochement between Baghdad and Amman. Syrian-Jordanian reconciliation at the end of 1985 also decreased the fears from Syrian-inspired groups. But Jordan retains the right to detain and try members of Ba'athist parties or Syrian-backed Palestinian groups. Egypt's radical influence virtually disappeared after the death of president 'Abd al-Nasir in 1970.

49. For example, some Palestinians interviewed in April and May 1989 by this writer said that their decision to run for parliamentary elections or even vote would depend on the PLO's position on the issue.

50. See full text of the interview in *al-Siyasa* (Kuwait), in *al-Ra'i*, 23 April 1989.

51. Personal interviews with Palestinian activists, businessmen and women in April-May 1989. Two of the presidents of Jordan's professional associations are of Palestinian origin. Many of the activists detained by the authorities (especially among university students, and including the only female, Tahani Shakshir) were of Palestinian origin.

52. The Jordanian wing of the DFLP was founded in 1974, while the PFLP's Jordanian wing was formed in 1976. Both wings recruited Jordanians and Palestinians, and both endorsed programs separate from those adopted by their parent organizations.

53. Personal interview with Ahmad 'Ubaydat, March 1988.

54. See a series of features on "the opinion of the people" in the south in *al-Ra'i*, 17 through 21 May 1989.

55. Personal interview with prominent Jordanian personalities, including a former minister, May 1989.

56. Jordanian economists refute such claims, noting that wealthy Palestinians and Transjordanians alike tended to protect their capital in times of political and financial uncertainty. Furthermore economists predict that the Palestinian element of the Jordanian population would soon be hit hard by the crisis, as unemployment (estimated at 17% in May 1989) would increase in both the private and public sectors. Personal interview with economist and columnist Fahed Fanek, 17 May 1989.

57. Prominent among these were two former deputy prime ministers, Tahir Masri (who served in the new cabinet until August) and Sulayman Arar.

58. Although the amount of funds involved was relatively small, the move itself helped to restore the confidence of Palestinian expatriates in Jordan. Indeed, one senior Jordanian official interviewed by the writer in June 1989 suggested that "the confidence of the Palestinians, especially expatriates, was far more important than the agreements with the International Monetary Fund."

59. The 1986 electoral law significantly underrepresented urban and predominately Palestinian areas, including Amman. For the law and an assessment of its political implications, see: *al-Ra'i*, 10 October 1989; "Mashru' qanun al-intikhabat al-jadid li-majlis al-niyabi," *al-Urdun al-Jadid* (Spring 1986).

60. This view was put forward by both Israeli Prime Minister Yizhak Shamir and Foreign Minister Moshe Arens. In an interview with Israeli television on 21 December 1989, Arens said that he resented "claims that Palestinians were a stateless people, because they have a Palestinian state in the East Bank." For a discussion of the growth of the "Jordan is Palestine" idea within Israeli politics, see *Jerusalem Post* (international edition), 30 December 1989, p. 17.

61. Although the Palestine Communist Party (based in the occupied territories) split from the JCP in 1982, much of the latter's membership and leadership is of Palestinian origin. During the summer of 1989, the party's East Bank leaders suggested that priority be given to the democratic struggle in Jordan. Its Palestinian leaders (affiliated with PLO institutions) argued that although Palestinians should contribute to the struggle for democracy, their special circumstances should also be taken into account.

62. 'Arafat responded favourably to Jordan's request for non-interference (made through Iraq and Egypt) and authorized two statements published in the Jordanian press by (PLO Ambassador to Jordan) 'Umar Khatib and (PLO Executive Committee member) Muhammad Milhelm during the election campaign that denied support for particular candidates; *al-Ra'i*, 3 November 1989; interview with senior PLO official, Tunis, 23 November 1989. Some Fateh leaders (notably Faruq Qaddumi and Salah Khalaf) would have preferred that it play a more assertive role in supporting friendly candidates. But overall, the interest Jordan and the PLO shared in avoiding a strong showing of Palestinian identity during the elections won out.

63. Interviews with several senior Fateh officials, Tunis, November 1989.

64. Interviews with Dr. Ali Hawamda, September 1989; Ziad Abu Ghanayma, 7

October 1989—both members of the Muslim Brotherhood leadership. During a mass rally of more than 8,000 people on 3 November 1989, Ikhwan candidates condemned "those who were ready to compromise Palestinian land." One of them ('Abd al-Munim Abu Zant), however, paid tribute to the soul of Khalil al-Wazir, the Fateh leader and deputy commander of PLO forces assassinated by Israel in Tunis in April 1988.

65. For its part, however, Fateh did not seek to counter the *Ikhwan*'s influence as the latter stepped up its campaign against the PLO program, both because of its pledges of noninterference and because it was far from enthusiastic about helping the left to gain ground at the Brotherhood's expense in Jordan.

66. PFLP second-in-command Abu 'Ali Mustafa denied such accusations, arguing that the PFLP's sole motive was to escalate armed struggle against Israel and reduce Israeli military pressure on the *intifada*. Interview, Baghdad, 17 October 1989.

67. In an effort to promote democratization and undercut the influence of the Islamic movement, leftist and nationalist groups undertook to coordinate their activities within the framework of the "Arab Jordanian Nationalist Democratic Bloc" in July 1990. As the long title of the Bloc suggested, however, the ideological and other differences between them had yet to be fully resolved.

68. Personal interview with King Husayn, in *al-Hayat* (London), 17 November 1989. In an earlier interview with *al-Hayat*, 10 November 1989, King Husayn conceded he had been taken by surprise by the strength of the Muslim Brotherhood. According to his aides, Yasir 'Arafat was equally astounded (and dismayed) by the result.

69. In the view of many Jordanian official the proposal for elections in the occupied territories made by Shamir and taken up by Baker would have reduced the likelihood of an international conference (in which Jordan would participate) and marginalized the role of the PLO. The result would thus be a repetition of the Camp David Accords (and its Palestinian autonomy provisions), which Jordan believes would be no more successful in achieving any meaningful and stable resolution of the Palestinian-Israeli and Arab-Israeli conflict. Egypt's role in all this provoked significant resentment in Jordan: during five days of demonstrations in December 1989, Palestinian and Jordanian protesters shouted slogans likening Egyptian president Husni Mubarak to the late Anwar al-Sadat.

70. Some Jordanian officials believe that the US might support mass expulsions.

71. Popular opposition to American policy in the Gulf has, of course, been further intensified by Washington's continued support for Israel: most Jordanians and Palestinians viewed US support for Kuwaiti sovereignty as hypocritical given its rejection of the very principle of Palestinian self-determination. For an overview of initial Jordanian reactions, see this author's articles in the *Christian Science Monitor*, 7, 16, 20, 22 August 1990.

72. Excluding cement and phosphates, 40 percent of Jordan's exports go to Iraq; Jordan imports 90 percent of its oil from Baghdad. A full embargo on this trade might cost Jordan anywhere from $500 million to $3 billion, increasing unemployment to more than 30 percent. Interviews with economist Fahd Fanek and with a former senior Jordanian trade official, August 1990.

73. Resentment of Palestinian political activity led to an incident on 13 December 1989 in which a group of East Bank students at Yarmuk University destroyed a Palestinian folklore exhibit on the grounds that it was a threat to their national identity. According to a parliamentary committee subsequently entrusted to investigate the incident, members of the local security and intelligence services opposed to liberalization had incited the students.

7

Egypt

Bahgat Korany

As the *intifada* entered its fourth year in December 1990, the continuing Palestinian uprising had already cost Palestinians hundreds of dead, thousands of wounded, and tens of thousands detained in Israeli prisons.[1] Not surprisingly, the *intifada* has had an enormous consequent impact on the Arab consciousness, as well as on the relations between different Arab governments and their respective civil societies.

Among Arab states, Egypt's response to the uprising is both instructive and unique: instructive because Egypt, the most populous country in the Arab world, had traditionally exercised a special weight in inter-Arab politics since the Second World War; unique, because Egypt is the only Arab country to have broken Arab ranks and established formal diplomatic relations with Israel. Anwar al-Sadat's 1977 trip to Jerusalem and the subsequent 1978 Camp David accords led to the conclusion in 1979 of a formal peace treaty between Egypt and Israel. This treaty included specific legal obligations, guaranteed by the tenets of international law and enforced by the international community (especially the United States, Egypt's most crucial source of economic aid). By the end of the 1970s—with diplomatic relations broken off with almost all Arab countries, with the Arab League headquarters removed from Egypt to Tunis, and with an Israeli ambassador resident in Cairo—it therefore seemed as if Egypt had switched roles, replacing Arab ties with Israeli-American ones. Indeed, within Egypt itself, some influential Egyptian writers reopened the eternal question of the significance of Egypt's Arab identity.[2]

The 1980s, however, would tell a different story. In October 1981—six months before the final evacuation of Israeli troops from the Sinai—Egypt's President Sadat was murdered, and replaced by his Vice-President, Husni Mubarak. This succession seemed to be the expected constitutional change, and Egypt's political ties (and treaty relationship) with Israel and the US remained intact. Yet Mubarak's subsequent attempts to reintegrate Egypt into the Arab system showed that the new president had second thoughts about Egypt's foreign policy restructuring of the 1970s. This reintegration started with Egypt's readmission to the Islamic Conference Organization in 1984.

During the November 1987 Arab summit in Amman, only Syria and Libya were adamantly opposed to Egypt's formal readmission to the political council of the Arab League without abrogation of the Egyptian-Israeli peace treaty. Moreover, even they chose not to obstruct the reestablishment of bilateral diplomatic relations between Cairo and other Arab states. Within a week of the summit, eight countries had done so. Egypt was allowed to formally participate in the Arab League summit at Casablanca in May 1989, and by early 1990 all Arab countries except Libya (but including Syria) had sent their ambassadors back to Cairo. Moreover, by the spring of 1990 Arab League members had accepted Egypt's insistence on a return of the League's headquarters back to Cairo—alongside the Israeli embassy and its various commercial and cultural offices.

It is here one arrives at the crux of the contradiction that now shapes contemporary Egyptian policy toward the Palestine issue: as long as the Palestine issue has remained unresolved, Egypt has been caught in the midst of cross-pressures between the traditional demands of the Arab system and those of its new partner, Israel. Moreover, whenever the Palestinian situation deteriorates (manifested, for example, by the rise in Israeli repressive measures or the escalation of the *intifada*), Egypt's position becomes increasingly less tenable. Cross-pressures intensify, pulling Egyptian foreign policy in different directions. The result is what might be termed foreign policy *role-conflict*.[3]

The *intifada* is the second major manifestation of role-conflict in Egyptian foreign policy at this level, the first being Israel's 1982 invasion of Lebanon. The *intifada* is, however, the most important, having taken place at a time when Egypt's reintegration into the Arab world is almost complete. Like Israel's 1982 invasion of Lebanon before it, the *intifada* has served to highlight the contradictions of Egypt's position and aggravate potential role-conflict in its foreign policy. This chapter will examine how Egypt has sought to reconcile its traditional role as an Arab regional leader with its new role as Israel's partner in the "peace process". It will show how Egyptian policy-makers have been bound to face hard choices between incompatibles in the 1980s. A systematic survey of the Egyptian press will be used to show in concrete terms these hard choices, their effect on relations between state and civil society in Egypt, and how policy-makers faced up to them. Examination will also be made of Egyptian foreign policy behavior towards two key development spurred by the *intifada*: the declaration of an independent Palestinian state by the Palestine National Council in November 1988, and the evolution of Israel's election proposal for the occupied territories in 1989-90. Finally, analysis of these areas will be used to shed light on the continuing dilemmas faced by Egyptian decision-makers as a consequence of the *intifada*: following Egypt's formal reintegration into the Arab system in the late 1980s, what are the chances of role-conflict for the 1990s and how might Egyptian policy cope with them?

Egypt's Foreign Policy Roles

Before proceeding to such questions, it is important to outline the evolution of Egyptian foreign policy, and in particular how Egypt's traditional active role as an Arab leader in the 1950s and 1960s was changed—in fact, restructured—in the 1970s by the signing of the 1978 Camp David accords and later the 1979 peace treaty. This in turn will serve to highlight the tension created between Egypt's political and treaty relationship to Israel (and the US) on the one hand, and Arab obligations and imperatives rooted in its regional environment and political culture.

Arab Leader: The 1950s and 1960s

In the post-war period (and especially after 1952) Egypt prided itself on being at the forefront of Arab nationalism based on "anti-colonialism and anti-Zionism." Since for many Arabs the Palestinian question has had a great symbolic significance, positions toward Palestinian-Israeli confrontation have been at the center of foreign policy and even legitimacy-building for many Arab regimes. Even pre-revolutionary Egypt had to rush into the first Arab-Israeli war in 1948; its subsequent defeat weakened the monarchical regime and set the stage for the 1952 Free Officers coup.

Because of these young officers' experience in their first direct confrontation with Israeli forces on the battlefield and, of course, of Gamal 'Abd al-Nasir's revolutionary ethos, Nasirism was associated with the "restoration of Arab rights" in Egypt's international and regional foreign policy role-set. It was principally this association that shaped Egypt's policy in the 1950's and 1960s, as evidenced by the 1955 Czech arms deal, the 1956 Suez invasion and the June 1967 Arab-Israeli War.

In retrospect, this last war initiated a decline in the charisma of Nasirism and a reconsideration of many aspects of its belief system, nationally and internationally. Even though masses poured into the streets on 9-10 June 1967 to prevent Nasir from resigning, Egyptian and Arab public opinion became increasingly vocal in questioning his leadership and his regime. Street demonstrations took place for the first time in February 1968 to ask for heavy punishment for those responsible for the defeat. Nasirist charisma was no longer unconstrained, was constantly scrutinized, evaluated and questioned— with damaging effects among the highest ranks of the polity itself. Public debates raged between, on the one hand, Nasir's confidant, Muhammad Haykal and his *al-Ahram* fiefdom, and on the other, the only political organization allowed, the "people's" Arab Socialist Union.[4] These divisions were not limited to temporary bickering or tactical infighting, but went so far as to question the regime's *raison d'être* of a "new society."

After the debacle, different social groups who were hurt by the regime's statist policies reemerged to put the regime on the defensive. While the conflict between the state and civil society intensified, group pressures increased for economic privatization. Moreover, "measures of destruction, the diversion of public funds to war costs, the ability of the government to extract resources more easily from the public sector than the private sector, all placed the public sector under severe resource pressures and gave it the air of a sinking ship."[5] In this context, the *ancien regime* elements asked for more and more concessions, slowing the pace of social reform.[6]

From the perspective of Egyptian foreign policy, one of the most important characteristics of the late 1960s was the change in Egypt's regional status. Egypt's multifaceted preeminence in the region was reflected in the Arab League. It was in Alexandria in 1945 that the meeting was convened to establish the League. The minutes of this meeting are full of speeches affirming Egypt's accepted preeminence. It was in Cairo that the headquarters of the new regional organization were located. Until the late 1950s, Egypt's share in the League's budgets was between 40 and 50 percent, and in 1974 of the 253 permanent and non-permanent staff members of the League, 166 were Egyptians. Until the League was forced to move to Tunis after Egypt's separate peace with Israel, all three Secretary-Generals had been Egyptian. Various quantitative indicators indicated Egypt's centrality. One study of official visits for the period 1946-1975 confirmed Egypt's preeminence among Arab and other Third World countries. Another, using as an indicator meetings between Arab leaders for the period 1966-1978, concluded that "Egypt is situated at the heart of the center."[7] It was partly because of this Egyptian hegemony and preeminence that Cairo supported, by word and deed, revolutionary movements all over the Arab world. Indeed, at the time of the 1967 war, 70,000 Egyptian troops were engaged in Yemen to support the Republican government against the deposed monarch, financed by Saudi Arabia.

With the 1967 debacle, however, the Arabs—both conservatives and radicals—had to close ranks and meet at the highest level (the Khartoum summit of August 1967). The summit ended by approving two important decisions: it put an end to the Yemeni civil war and sanctioned the withdrawal of Egyptian troops; and it decreed financial support by oil-producing countries to front-line states suffering from the effects of the defeat. This decline in Egyptian hegemony became Egyptian financial subservience to what would emerge in the 1970s as political petrolism.[8]

It is in this context of Egyptian national disarray and Arab regional flux that Nasir himself died on 28 September 1970. Consequently, whoever Nasir's successor was, he would have to come to grips with all these political and societal, national and regional, problems. Moreover, as an outsider to the inner group, Anwar al-Sadat had also to first build his own bases of power. This is a difficult task even in a normal situation, but it was compounded for Sadat by his succeeding an erstwhile charismatic leader whose death had left a huge leadership vacuum.

Egypt's Foreign Policy Restructuring in the 1970s

Compared to Nasirism as a belief system, Sadatism was associated with accommodation to the West, especially the US, and ended by accommodating Israel too. Only four months after assuming power, Sadat offered an interim agreement whereby Egypt would reopen the Suez Canal—a clear message to the West and Israel that the war option could be downgraded. In May 1971 (while busy liquidating self-avowed Nasirists and consolidating his political authority) Sadat received William Rogers, the first US Secretary of State to visit Egypt since 1953. Only when efforts to convince Washington to collaborate for a political solution to Israel's occupation of Egyptian territory failed was Cairo forced in October 1973 to resort to war as the only alternative.[9] But this war was not only limited to the liberation of Egyptian territory (and hence ignoring the Palestinian context) but actually based on much more limited objectives: occupying only eight to ten kilometers of the Israeli-occupied Sinai.[10]

The war was a limited victory, but one which enabled Sadatism to free itself from the legacy of its predecessor, Nasirism, to the extent that not even lip-service need be paid. In fact, the post-1973 era signaled a restructuring of Egypt's policies both nationally (the "open door" economic strategy or *infitah*) and internationally (close collaboration with the US). As early as November 1973, Henry Kissinger was invited to Cairo where a long-term relationship of coordination was established between him and Sadat. The first few hours of this initial meeting resulted in the restoration of diplomatic relations (severed in 1967) between Cairo and Washington.[11]

We already know the rest of the story, from Kissinger's shuttle diplomacy to the signing of the first and second disengagement agreements (1974 and 1975 respectively). What is important to reiterate is that the change in US administration from Nixon to Ford to Carter did not slow the emergence of relations between Cairo, Washington—and Jerusalem. Egypt's foreign policy role-restructuring was complete in the late 1970s with the signing of the 1978 Camp David accords and especially the 1979 peace treaty between Egypt and Israel.

As an international legal document, the treaty set forth specific rights and obligations for the contracting parties (i.e., an international regime)[12] supervised by an international community represented by the US. Consequently, it has formidable moral and effective enforcement credentials. As a bilateral agreement the treaty formalized the separation between Egyptian-Israeli relations and the Palestinian issue. In its legal consequences, in addition to its political implications, it imposed on Egypt the necessity of reconciling what seemed irreconcilable: Egypt's role conflict between her traditional Arab brothers and her new peace partner, while both still in a state of belligerency toward each other. In regard to this role-conflict, article VI of the treaty (characterized by Prime Minister Begin as the "spirit" of the agreement) is key. Three relevant items of this article deserve quotation:

> 2. The Parties undertake to fulfill in good faith their obligations under this Treaty, without regard to action or inaction of any other party and independently of any instrument external to this Treaty.
>
> ...
>
> 4. The Parties undertake not to enter into any obligation in conflict with this Treaty.
>
> 5. Subject to Article 103 of the United Nations Charter [which permits collective self-defense], in the event of a conflict between the obligations of the Parties under the Present Treaty and any of their other obligations, the obligations under this Treaty will be binding and implemented.[13]

In other words, Egypt's obligations toward Israel were to have absolute priority in its gamut of relations, and thus determine its foreign policy role-set. Much more bluntly, in case of military conflict between Israel and any of Egypt's Arab brothers, Egypt cannot invoke its previous defense agreements with any of these countries to take their side. Egypt is allowed to be either neutral or indifferent—a blatant case of role-conflict for an erstwhile regional leader.

As expected, even before it became a legally-binding reality, this potential role-conflict caused dissension between leadership and society. It even sparked dissension among the ranks of Sadat's own ministers as evidenced by the resignation of two Egyptian foreign ministers, Ismail Fahmy and Muhammad Ibrahim Kamel, in 1977 and 1978[14]—an unprecedented event in Egypt's recent history. Despite an authoritarian political system, opposition to the treaty—and hence demand for role-congruence—still expressed itself in varying forms, from refusal by different associations to receive Israelis to violent street demonstrations.

Intense government efforts were made to condition Egyptian public opinion. No less than 1,826 articles and comments dealing with the peace process with Israel appeared in the Egyptian press (that is, seven dailies, ten weeklies, and one quarterly) between November 1977 and 30 April 1979 when the plebiscite was organized to approve the treaty.[15] Notwithstanding this emphasis in the media on the issue of peace with Israel, public attitudes towards Begin's Israel did not change much during these years. One indication of this can be found in a 1980 survey of attitudes toward the treaty among Egyptian university students.[16] Among the respondents, 46 percent favored the treaty but displayed no euphoria about its conclusion. On the contrary, most showed a feeling of resignation: the treaty was already in place and there seemed to be no immediate alternative. Those who favored the treaty believed it should be implemented in good faith, but that Egypt should not move beyond fulfilling its strict legal terms. They were ready to wait and see if Israel's policy would evolve to reinforce the peace process. But 36 percent of the respondents simply did not favor the treaty, and another 18 percent were undecided. Slightly more than one-third (37 percent) believed the treaty could prevent another war between Egypt and

Israel, but a full 57 percent did not. Only one-fourth of the respondents expected any improvement in their individual lot as a result of the signing of the treaty, while 56 percent said they expected no such improvement. Even more revealing is the students' perception of Israel: 14 percent believed that it was serious about Palestinian autonomy talks, compared to 70 percent who did not think so. Given such mistrust of Israeli policy, as well as the fact that 79 percent of respondents said they identified with an Arab national identity (even though they were frustrated by the policies of the Arab regimes), it should not surprise us that there was little enthusiasm for the Egyptian-Israeli treaty.

It is clear, therefore, that Egyptian popular support for the normalization of relations with Israel did not advance as quickly as the Israelis had hoped, government policy notwithstanding. Tired of war and the threat of war and skeptical about the capability of most Arab regimes to face up to the next crisis, many Egyptians were ready to give their leader a chance to explore peace with Israel. There was the hope that his speedy decisions would prove to be the right ones, but little enthusiasm for the process. Consequently, the political system had to become more authoritarian to keep control, hence the mass arrests of September 1981, followed by the slaughtering of Sadat himself on 6 October 1981—an act of untypical violence in Egyptian history. But the disappearance of Sadat did not—and could not—put an end to Egypt's role-conflict. On the contrary, the 1980s were characterized by major regional events that brought this role-conflict to the fore in an inescapable and brutal way: first the 1982 Lebanese invasion, and later the 1987 *intifada*.

Role-Conflict in the 1980s: Egypt, Israel and the Palestinians

A new Egyptian leadership—under Husni Mubarak—came face to face with role-conflict only nine months after it came to power, when in June 1982 Israel invaded Lebanon. The incidence and effects of role-conflict are evident through a survey of the Egyptian press of the period, both governmental and opposition.[17] The six main newspapers surveyed (3 dailies and 3 weeklies) reflect the diverse political attitudes represented in the People's Assembly.

The three dailies—*al-Ahram*, *al-Akhbar* and *al-Gumhurriyya*—are called in official Egyptian parlance the "national press," and should be called more precisely the governmental press because they are not supposed to depart from the government's stated position. The three weeklies represent the different shades of the opposition, from the right (*al-Ahrar* of the Socialist Liberal Party), the socialists (*al-Sha'b* of the Socialist Labor Party) and the Marxist left (*al-Ahali* of the Progressive Unionists).

What is important to single out at the outset is that at the beginning of the invasion, the governmental press first ignored then attempted to downgrade the importance of Israel's action. The leftist opposition, on the contrary, emphasized the magnitude of the invasion as confirming Israel's "bad faith," and the "opportunism" of its leaders in trying to entrap Egypt and keep it away from the conflict so as to liquidate the Palestinian issue. For instance, what strikes the reader of *al-Ahali* during this period is the toning down of its basic Marxist viewpoint. Concepts such as the primacy of class conflict or the world socialist revolution and its impending victory over doomed capitalism hardly figured in its editorials or news coverage. Compared to the avowedly non-Marxist press, *al-Ahali* was militant in its criticism of Pax Americana, but the other opposition papers and even the "national press" were critical of what was perceived as US acquiescence in the policies of Begin and his defense minister, Ariel Sharon. On other issues such as criticism of the structure of inter-Arab politics, the Egyptian-Israeli peace process, and the demand for retaliatory measures against Israel, *al-Ahali*'s stand was even nearer to the nationalist ethos which increasingly dominated the other newspapers.

This narrowing of the ideological gap among the various threads in Egypt's political life explains the emergence of a national front against the continuation of the peace process with Begin's Israel, a national front regrouping the different political forces but certainly headed by the leftist opposition.[18] To attenuate mounting domestic pressure and the tension of role-conflict, Egyptian leadership tried to rally international (especially US) support for collective action in favor of a general peace process and settlement. There was rarely mention of reneging on Egypt's treaty obligations or resuming a belligerent relationship with Israel. The initially moderate tone of Egyptian statements increasingly harshened, however, as Israel's action provoked condemnation by the vast majority of the international community, including many of its traditional friends.[19]

Consequently, for the first time since the mid-1970s the Egyptian position on regional affairs was welcomed in Palestinian circles, but violently criticized by a sector of the Israeli press. To counteract the Palestinian-Egyptian rapprochement, Israel's foreign minister sent a message to Egypt's foreign minister to explain the invasion, but this message was ignored. For the first time since the conclusion of the Camp David accords, official Egyptian-Palestinian talks took precedence over those with Israel.

Egypt's Role-Conflict and the *Intifada*

The intensification of Palestinian-Israeli conflict represented by Israel's 1982 invasion of Lebanon illustrated the scope and nature of the potential role-conflict engendered by Sadat's restructuring of Egyptian foreign policy and Egypt's post-1979 treaty relationship with Israel. When this conflict escalated again with the eruption of the Palestinian uprising in the Israeli-occupied West Bank and Gaza Strip in December 1987, Egypt again was beset by conflicting cross-pressures.

What differentiates Egypt's reaction to the *intifada* from its response to the invasion of Lebanon, however, is the relative lack of conflict between the government and civil society with regard to Israeli behavior. As expected, it was civil society with its different associations that started the protest, mobilizing public opinion in favor of the *intifada* and marshaling demonstrations. In January 1988, four Egyptian opposition parties (the leftist National Progessive Unionists, the center-right Wafd, the Socialist Labor Party, and the conservative Socialist Liberals) announced the joint formation of an "Egyptian National Committee in Support of the Palestinian Uprising." Members of the Muslim Brotherhood, communists and Nassirites were also active in the committee. Trade unions and various professional associations undertook initiatives in support of the *intifada*.[20]

These manifestations, however, did not conflict sharply with official policy. Indeed, the ruling National Democratic Party also announced its intention to participate in the Egyptian National Committee

A review of the Egyptian press during the first sixteen months of the uprising underscores the point.[21] Only once during this sixteen month period did the police clash with demonstrators when pro-uprising demonstrations turned violent and ugly. Moreover, official reactions both at the level of the legislature and the executive did not lag behind as was the case during the 1982 Lebanese invasion. Thus a few days after the beginning of the *intifada*, on 17 December 1987, the Committee of Foreign Affairs of the People's Assembly denounced the illegal practices of Israeli occupation authorities. On December 21 Egypt's Foreign Ministry summoned Moshe Sasson, Israel's ambassador in Cairo, to hand him a protest against his government's practices. As if this was not explicit enough, Minister of State for Foreign Affairs—Butrus Butrus Ghali—reiterated to Israeli radio Egypt's denunciation of Jerusalem's arbitrary measures and demanded that they cease. This was followed by a second denunciation on December 23, and a third on December 27. On 1 January 1988, Dr. Usama al-Baz (Mubarak's special adviser) revealed that Egypt had refused to receive an Israeli minister who had offered to come to Cairo to explain Israel's policy in the occupied territories.

The perusal of the Egyptian press during this period shows two aspects of Egypt's reactions to this event. First, the choice of words by both governmental and non-governmental sources gives the impression that many of the popular organizations are supported in their protest by governmental action. Second, Egypt's frequency of official protest was accelerating and its tone was harshening. Thus, on 7 April 1988, Vice-Premier and Foreign Minister Ismat 'Abd al-Meguid declared in front of the People's Assembly that every Palestinian martyr killed by Israeli bullets is an Egyptian one. As for Usama al-Baz, the President's adviser, he repeated the by-now-expected protest, and also insisted that the Palestinians had the right to resist Israeli occupation as the peoples of Europe resisted Nazi occupation.[22]

In a presidential system like Egypt's, no political movement can take place without at least the implicit support of the presidential center. Still, for support to be complete, it has also to include behavior—both verbal and in deed—by the President himself. The analysis of news items shows that presidential support was gradual in its explicitness and started first through Suzanne Mubarak (the president's wife) who headed the wives of Arab ambassadors in a committee in support of the *intifada*.[23] When Mubarak himself intervened explicitly, it was in a very balanced tone. Protest yes, but not in the inflammatory tone of his different ministers or of his articulate adviser, Dr. al-Baz. It was, however, left to Egypt's Vice-Premier and Foreign Minister to declare that the Palestinian cause was at the top of the list of priorities of President Mubarak.[24] Indeed in his travels in Western Europe and the US at the time, Mubarak talked about the Palestinian issue, much less as a protester and much more as a mediator (an issue discussed below).

This distinction between the President and the other levels of government was—it should be reiterated—much less in content than in tone. As early as May 1988 (i.e., six months after the beginning of the uprising), all political parties affirmed that there was no difference between their position and that of the government, and hoped that this popular/official convergence existed similarly in all Arab countries. As if to concretize this convergence, Egypt's Postal Department decided to issue a stamp to commemorate the uprising.

It is interesting to note that amid such popular and official support, very few remembered that in fact the main Palestinian office in Cairo had been shut a few months previously by the Egyptian government in resonse to criticism by some Palestinian leaders of Egypt's continued respect of the Camp David accords. This anomaly was soon corrected and the office was declared reopened.[25] Significantly, this event went almost unnoticed because of the intense level of direct Egyptian-Palestinian meetings.

A month after the beginning of the *intifada* a high level meeting was held in Cairo between the Vice-Premier and Foreign Minister, 'Abd al-Meguid, and a visiting Palestinian delegation. A week later, Egypt's ambassador in Tunisia conferred with Yasir 'Arafat and informed him of Egypt's full support for the *intifada*. In a period of five months, Arafat himself visited Cairo publicly and met with Mubarak eight times.[26] Almost no Arab capital was visited as much by Arafat during such a short period. Obviously, Egyptian behavior toward the Palestinian issue was much less schizophrenic and the coordination between state and civil society seemed to be very smooth indeed compared with the role-conflict that dominated Egypt during the 1982 Lebanon invasion.

This lack of schizophrenia in Egypt's foreign policy was evident in the striking similaritiy with which both the governmental and opposition press treated the *intifada*. According to a team of Egyptian social scientists who content-analyzed eight Egyptian newspapers for a six month period from December 1987 to March 1988, *al-Ahram*—a government newspaper—was at the forefront in its coverage of *intifada*, its support of the Palestinian cause and its direct and explicit criticism of Israel, by word, photo and caricature.[27] Of a total of 2,648 news items published during this period, *al-Ahram* came first with 806 or 31 perecent of the total. Moreover, 92 perecent of this material was published on the first page (representing 43 percent of all the material that this newspaper published on the first page during this 6-month period). Thus not only was the coverage massive, but it was also given great prominence. Moreover, to catch the reader's attention, the press coverage included a substantial portion in photos: 405 photos of the 2,648 total news items, or 15 percent. *Al-Ahram* again occupied the first place, publishing 113 photos or 28 perecent of total photos. However, *al-Gumhurriyya*—another governmental newspaper —preceded *al-Ahram* by publishing more photos on its first page: 36 percent of all photos published on the first page for this period. As for articles and editorials, they were 440 or 17 percent of the total, with *al-Ahram* again occupying the first place with 44 percent of the total of articles published.

An End to Role Conflict?

The collection and analysis of data conducted for this chapter—confirmed by other researchers—indicates the scope of Egypt's support for the *intifada*, at both the governmental and popular levels and by both the "national" and opposition press. This instance of Egypt's foreign policy behavior is in contrast to its reaction during the earlier instance of role-conflict, on the occasion of Israel's Lebanon invasion in the summer of 1982. Then it was the opposition with its newspapers that took the lead, while the governmental newspapers lagged behind. Street politics was also used by the opposition, and clashes with the police were frequent. In 1987-1989, on the contrary, state and civil society were on the same wavelength. Moreover, governmental newspapers like *al-Ahram* and *al-Gumhurriyya* were leading the coverage of the *intifada*, both quantitatively and qualitatively (i.e. how much was published and where it was published). The main question, then, especially after Egypt's formal readmission into the different organs of the Arab system, is this: do the late 1980s signal the end of Egypt's role-conflict for the 1990s?

Logically the answer should be no. There will be periods of high and low tension among the different components of the role-set, Egypt's role-conflict will fluctuate but not disappear overnight. For as long as the Palestinian issue is unsettled and Egypt maintains its full treaty obligations with Israel, Egypt is of necessity in a different legal and political position from other Arab countries. Consequently, its policy-makers are bound to face occasional hard choices.

Recognition of the Palestinian State

Since the eruption of the *intifada*, the most difficult instance of role-conflict facing Egyptian policy-makers seemed to be on the eve of the declaration of an independent Palestinian state in November 1988. Egyptian policy-makers were in close contact with Palestinian officials before the declaration to counsel moderation and especially to guarantee explicit acceptance of the principle of the existence of the state of Israel. Thus almost three months before the declaration, President Mubarak affirmed that Egypt would be ready to accept what the PLO accepts regarding a Palestinian state as long as "this decision conforms to logic, wisdom and delicate calculations."[28] In other words, such a declaration needed to take into consideration the realities of the regional and international contexts, including of course Egypt's obligations in the Egyptian-Israeli peace treaty. It was then left to Vice-Premier and Foreign Minister 'Abd al-Meguid to explicit the framework within which the Palestinian state could be declared: UN resolutions. He went as far back in history as the UN partition resolution of 1947 "which stipulated the establishment of two states in Palestine: an Arab and a Jewish one."[29] In other words, a Palestinian state is part and parcel of the establishment of a Jewish state, and not in its place. Even such a relatively radical Egyptian policy-maker as al-Baz insisted that "the declaration of an independent Palestinian state helps to advance peace efforts for all concerned, and not to hurt any party."[30]

Despite all these clarification and provisos, and the intense previous coordination with the PLO, Egypt seemed to hesitate in giving its full recognition once the Palestinian National Council made public its declaration of an independent Palestinian state. At first, Egypt (through Mubarak himself) declared that Cairo supported the PNC decision which—and he thought important to clarify this—clearly recognized UN Security Council resolutions 242 and 338. As for Egypt's recognition, Mubarak insisted that support was stronger than recognition.[31] A day later, al-Baz repeated what Mubarak had said (but in different words) and concluded in the same way: that support was stronger than recognition.[32]

Palestinian officials were not happy with this, however, and started to press for explicit recognition. Shaykh al-Sayah (President of the Palestinian National Council) went to Cairo and asked for "an explicit recognition of the state instead of only support."[33] This recognition finally came on November 20, five days after the Palestinian declaration. With the exception of countries like Syria and Libya who found the PLO declaration too moderate ("capitulationist"), Egypt was one of the last Arab countries to give its recognition (which even came after that of such non-Arab countries as Pakistan and Turkey). The Egyptian declaration also thought it important to insist that the recognition was part of continuing efforts to advance the general peace process in the region.

Egyptian hesitation before recognizing the Palestinian state thus provided a clear manifestation of Egypt's role-conflict at the international level. Such role-conflict is usually associated with divisions within the foreign policy elite itself. These divisions also show that policy-making is not (if it ever is) the simple idiosyncratic expression of preferences by the man at the top.

In the Egyptian case, the three main pillars of current Egyptian foreign policy-making have been Dr. Ismat 'Abd al-Meguid (Egypt's Vice-Premier and Foreign Minister); Dr. Butrus Butrus Ghali (Minister of State for Foreign Affairs); and Dr. Usama al-Baz (Under-Secretary of the Ministry of Foreign Affairs and, more importantly, the head of President Mubarak's Political Office). Among the three, al-Baz is the least well known outside Egypt, probably because of his relatively subordinate position in the bureaucratic hierarchy (on paper, he is not of ministerial rank). Indeed, the formal line of foreign policy authority runs from Mubarak to 'Abd al-Meguid to Ghali. But al-Baz's proximity to the top decision-taker makes him Mubarak's closest civilian advisor, and an effective gate-keeper and influential participant in the decision-making process. Although ambitious and almost conspiratorial, al-Baz's political views fall closest to Nasirism and his affinity lies with Egypt's traditional role as an Arab leader. He has maintained close contacts with many Palestinian policy-makers, and Mubarak has usually entrusted him with delicate missions to the Gulf countries, Damascus, and even Tripoli. As for Butrus Ghali, he acquired his doctorate in the late 1940s in the most strict French legal tradition at the University of Paris, and is prone to "lecture" his colleagues on the international legal consequences of their actions. He could be surmised to counsel moderation in recognizing the Palestinian state, and probably to overemphasize the possible adverse consequences of such an act on relations with Israel and possibly the US. 'Abd al-Meguid—also of French legal background—could also be sensitive to these arguments.

'Abd al-Meguid formally denied the existence of any differences within the foreign policy elite regarding recognition of the Palestinian state. In an interview giving "his personal opinion and not Egypt's formal position," however, he insisted that it was of fundamental importance that prior to any declaration of the establishment of a state must come enunciation of its political program—implicitly suggesting therefore that Egypt could not offer formal recognition to a Palestinian state before having a clearer idea about the political program it would adopt.[34]

Even though one should not exaggerate the potential frictions and differences among Egypt's foreign policy elite, it is still true that in a situation of foreign policy role-conflict different positions and nuances will inevitably emerge among policy-makers. Consequently, it is no coincidence that the few days that separated the PNC's declaration of Palestinian statehood from Egypt's formal recognition of that state coincided with al-Baz's absence from the country.[35] His return seemed to tip the balance in favor of recognition, the decision was made, and formal recognition was announced.

Role Conflict and Mediation: Egypt in the Peace Process

If (as the previous case suggests) role-conflict continues to exist in Egyptian foreign policy, one would expect policy measures intended to avoid or attentuate such conflicting cross-pressures. To escape the tension of role-conflict, for example, policy-makers might procrastinate over difficult decisions or speak in general terms. Alternatively, they may try to bridge the gap between the conflicting parties (and hence the conflicting pressures on state policy) by playing a mediatory role.

In fact, a few indicators do show that Egypt, in supporting the Palestinians, took pains, both publicly and privately, to affirm that it did not intend to violate its legal obligations toward Israel, its treaty partner. Indeed, one of Egypt's first reactions to the *intifada* thought it important to mention this obligation explicitly, and to reiterate that Egypt would continue to respect these obligations. As mentioned before, when President Mubarak added his voice to those in the government and the opposition supporting the *intifada*, this support came later. The tone was much more moderate, and emphasized the importance of settling the Palestinian issue for the sake of peace of all states concerned, and foremost Israel. The objective was then to encourage Israeli policy-makers to come forward and become involved in finding a solution, rather than simply condemning Israeli actions. Consequently, Mubarak's first declaration on 21 January 1988 emphasized a mediatory role. On occasion, Mubarak suggested that he was even prepared to break his moratorium on visiting Israel, provided some progress could be achieved on the Palestinian issue.[36] Similarly, President Mubarak played an important role in encouraging the United States to open a direct dialogue with the PLO.[37] The emphasis was thus on mediation to reduce the gap in Egypt's obligations and harmonize different role-demands.

Egypt's attempts at mediation later came to the fore in much more active way following the elections initiative proposed by Israeli Prime Minister Yitzhak Shamir in April 1989. As subsequently adopted by Israel's coalition government on May 14, the initiative was clearly unacceptable to the PLO.[38] As a result, through the summer Egypt sought to narrow the differences, effectively lobbying the United States (and Israel) on the PLO's behalf. Later, in July 1989, Mubarak privately communicated his own ten-point initiative to Israel through US channels. This initiative (made public in

September) established a series of principles under which any elections in the occupied territories would take place, and was designed to facilitate the holding of direct Palestinian-Israeli discussions in Cairo on the elections issue.[39] President Mubarak subsequently traveled to Washington to discuss his proposals with US President George Bush in October.

The Mubarak proposals were partially successful insofar as they appeared more-or-less acceptable both to the PLO and to the Israeli Labor Party. They were opposed, however, by Israeli Prime Minister Yitzhak Shamir and his Likud Party, and were rejected by the Israeli cabinet on a tie vote.

Shortly thereafter, attention shifted to a five-point framework for Israeli-Palestinian dialogue in Cairo proposed by US Secretary of State James Baker on October 10. Reflecting both Egypt's role-conflict and the mediatory policy it had adopted, the second point of Baker's framework noted:

> The United States understands that Egypt cannot substitute for the Palestinians itself and Egypt will consult with Palestinians on all aspects of that dialogue. Egypt will also consult with Israel and the United States.[40]

These proposals were accepted by the Israeli Labor Party and, conditionally, by the Palestine Liberation Organization. Egypt itself formally accepted the Baker initiative on December 5, following a meeting between Foreign Minister Ismat 'Abd al-Meguid and US Assistant Secretary of State John Kelly. Cairo's acceptance was accompanied by five Egyptian "assumptions" which seemed designed to make the Baker plan more palatable to the PLO.[41] At the same time, Cairo continued to urge the PLO to show flexibility in key areas so as to facilitate Israeli willingness to participate in Israeli-Palestinian negotiations. In January the Egyptian foreign minister traveled to Washington to discuss the modalities of the proposed Palestinian-Israeli dialogue. During that same month, President Mubarak also held three major meetings in Cairo with PLO Chairman Yasir 'Arafat, and one with Israeli Labor Party leader Shimon Peres.

Despite Egyptian (and US) efforts, however, Prime Minister Shamir and the Likud Party refused to endorse the Baker plan. This in turn sparked the collapse of Israel's "national unity" government in March 1990 and its replacement by a hard-line Likud coalition. In June, the United States broke off its dialogue with the PLO, following an abortive Palestinian attack on a Tel Aviv beach. The Egyptian government had lobbied hard against this move, urging the US not to suspend contacts and pressing the PLO to codemn the attack in stronger terms. Later, Egypt worked behind the scenes in an effort to reactivate the dialogue, until the Gulf crisis became paramount in the summer of 1990.[42]

Conclusion

In the Arabs' continuing confrontation with Israel, the *intifada* has already had a regional and international impact similar too—if not greater than—the October 1973 Arab-Israeli war. At least at the declaratory level, all Arab countries have been firmly on the side of the *intifada*.

This analysis has attempted to go beyond this general declaratory level to systematically investigate an important and particular case: that of Egypt. Egypt's particularity stems from its own weighty geo-strategic position in the Arab world, a position that formed the basis of its leadership role through the 1950s and 1960s. Egypt's particularity also acquired an additional (and possibly more dubious) aspect in the 1970s when Egypt, through its go-it-alone diplomacy, reconciled itself to Israel and signed a formal peace treaty. Consequently, it was ostracized by almost all the Arab world. The 1980s, however, witnessed mounting domestic pressures and sustained foreign policy efforts to reintegrate Egypt into the Arab fold—but without surrendering, voluntarily or otherwise, its legal obligations toward Israel or its political relationship with the United States. Because of the incompatible demands between its traditional and new partners, Egypt found itself in the midst of sustained cross-pressures, a situation of role-conflict.

The *intifada* has been the most recent, most serious, and most conspicuous example of this. This study (through systematic survey of official statements, and of the government and non-government press) has found, however, that Egypt's role-conflict during the Palestinian uprising has been less than during the initial stage of Israel's 1982 invasion of Lebanon, most probably because Israel's actions in the occupied territories are more greatly condemned by the international community, including Israel's traditional allies. Other independent analyses have reported similar findings.

Given this, will Egypt witness an end to role-conflict in its foreign policy in the 1990s? The preceding analysis—notably the case study of Egypt's recognition of Palestinian statehood in November 1988—suggests that it will not. As long as the Palestinian conflict remains unsolved and Egypt intends to respect its treaty obligations with Israel (and the US), role-conflict will continue to haunt (and even divide) Egyptian policy-makers. They will face incompatible choices and have to evaluate costs of alternative behaviors. They will hesitate and procrastinate, and might find their salvation in promoting a mediatory role as bridge-builder and conflict-manager. President Mubarak's active role in the complex triangle of Israeli-US-PLO diplomacy represents perhaps the clearest recent example of this, as Egypt seeks to avoid the dilemmas of role-conflict by promoting dialogue between Cairo's incompatible role-partners.

Notes

This chapter is part of an ongoing research project on Egyptian foreign policy. The author is grateful to the Social Science and Humanities Research Council of Canada for financing this research.

1. For a detailed assessment of the impact of the *intifada* on Palestinian human rights, see Raja Shehadeh's chapter elsewhere in this volume.

2. These included Tawfik al-Hakim, Husayn Fawzi, Lewis Awad, Anis Mansour, Mustafa Amin, and Nobel prize-winner Naguib Mahfouz. As Abdel Monem Said Aly notes: "They varied in their analyses and points of departure, but they agreed on the following themes: Egypt has an older civilization than the Arab one. Its civilization is part of the Mediterranean culture, hence it is more attached to the Greco-Roman traditions than the Arab-Islamic values. In short, Egypt is part of European and Western civilization. The Arabs are still nomadic barbarians who cannot understand that peace with Israel is an expression of the civilized conduct of world politics on the one hand, and a meeting between two great, ancient civilizations on the other. Egypt, therefore, should conclude peace with Israel and be neutral, like Switzerland, in world politics in general and the Arab-Israeli conflict in particular." Abdel Monem Said Aly, "Egypt: A Decade After Camp David," in William B. Quandt, ed., *The Middle East: Ten Years After Camp David* (Washington, D.C.: The Brooking Institution, 1988), p. 71. For a convenient collection of the documents of this debate, see Saad Eddin Ibrahim, *Egypt's Arabism* (Cairo: al-Ahram Press, 1979) [in Arabic].

3. It is now accepted that one profitable way to conceptualize and explain a country's foreign policy is to conceive of it as a role on the international scene. Such a conceptualization has an organizational, descriptive and explanatory value.

The application of the role concept in foreign policy analysis is not new. Kautilya—in the ancient Hindu world—described six types of foreign policy (accommodation, hostility, indifference, attack, protection, and double policy). He correlated specific roles with their sources. Thus a king of inferior status is correlated with a role of accommodation, protection or double policy. Superior status, on the other hand, leads to a foreign policy of hostility (i.e. a type of cold war) or attack (imperialism). When an international system is dominated by conflict among kings of roughly equal status, the appropriate foreign policy of others is abstention from taking sides, or indifference (in modern terminology: non-alignment). Contemporary international relations theory has also used role conceptualization, if only implicitly. Thus whereas Morgenthau dealt with active and passive policies in his *Politics Among Nations*, his discussion of bloc leader, bloc member, satellite, aligned, non-aligned, and so forth indicates a conceptualization of foreign policy as a patterned behavior where an actor occupies a certain position (e.g. ally, bloc leader), and thus obeys certain rules and expectations linked to this position (i.e. role demands or requisites in the language of "role theory"). Thus in the balance of power analysis, the balancer is expected to perform a specific (e.g. integrative) role.

Given the complexity of international relations, however, any international actor is called upon to play different roles, and thus adapts to the demands of specific contexts and the specific groups by compartmentalizing its role. Thus in one context, an actor assumes the revolutionary role, or the protector, or the leader, or the mediator. In this case, foreign policy is more precisely a role-set. Indeed, we hardly know a country—even the most passive—which plays only one role on the international scene. Thus a country can be both an aid-receiver and a regional leader, both a mediator at a certain level and a warlike bloc-builder at another level. But what if a country is asked simultaneously by two different audiences to stand up and be counted, to choose among what seem to be mutually exclusive roles? In this case, its policy-makers face hard choices: whatever the choice is made, costs seem high and tension among the different parts of the role-set divide the policy-makers. In other words, the country faces *role-conflict* in its foreign policy. For further details, see: Kal Holsti, "National Role Conceptions in the Study of Foreign Policy," *International Studies Quarterly* 14, 3 (1970): 233-309; Bahgat Korany, "Foreign Policy Models and their Relevance to Third World Actors: A Critique and Alternative," *International Social Science Journal*, 26, 1 (1974): 76-103; Bahgat Korany, *Social Change, Charisma and International Behavior: Toward a Theory of Foreign Policy in the Third World* (Leiden and Geneva: Sijthoff, 1976); Bahgat Korany, Ali E. H. Dessouki et al., *The Foreign Policies of Arab States*, (Boulder: Westview, 1984); Stephen Walker, ed., *Role Theory and Foreign Policy Analysis* (Durham: Duke University Press, 1987).

4. As Mark Cooper has noted, "Division at the top made it difficult either to effectively suppress or satisfy the demands coming from the bottom. Demands in the middle drove the segments at the top farther apart. In the process the arenas of politics (the institutions) expanded as groups sought a forum to state and press their demands. The combination of escalating elite divisions and escalating mass inputs made the balancing act which [Nasir] had performed before the war increasingly difficult. The margin for error was dramatically reduced. Elites could not tolerate minor defeats and masses could not be as easily rendered quiescent." Cooper, *The Transformation of Egypt* (Baltimore: The John Hopkins University Press, 1982), p. 43.

5. Cooper, *The Transformation of Egypt*, p. 40.

6. Thus it was in this period that old sequestration measures were relaxed and the majority were even abolished: 1643 out of a total of 1771. Thus when Sadat arrived in power, only 128 sequestration cases (touching only 577 individuals of the previous total of 8779) were pending.

7. William Thompson, "Center-Periphery Interaction Patterns: The Case of Arab Visits 1946-75," *International Organization* 35, 3 (Summer 1981): 355-373; A. Diskin and S. Mishal, "Spatial Models and Centrality of International Communities," *Journal of Conflict Resolution* 25, 4 (December 1981): 655-676.

8. Bahgat Korany, *How Foreign Policy Decisions Are Made in the Third World: A Comparative Analysis* (Boulder: Westview Press, 1986), pp. 93-94.

9. Korany, *How Foreign Policy Decisions Are Made in the Third World*, pp. 87-112.

10. Lieutenant General Saad El-Shazly, *The Crossing of the Suez* (San Francisco: American Mideast Research, 1980), pp. 36-38.

11. Henry Kissinger, *Years of Upheaval* (Boston: Little, Brown & Co., 1982), pp. 614-666.

12. Stephen Krasner, "Structural Causes and Regime Consequences," *International Organization* 36, 2 (Spring 1982): 185-206.

13. *The Official Text of the Egyptian-Israeli Treaty* (Cairo: Egyptian Foreign Ministry, 1981).

14. Ismail Fahmy, *Negotiating for Peace in the Middle East* (Baltimore: The Johns Hopkins University Press, 1983); Muhammad I. Kamil, *al-Salam al-Dai'* [The Lost Peace] (London: Saudi Publications, 1985).

15. For details see Bahgat Korany, "The Cold Peace, the Sixth Arab-Israeli War and Egypt's Public," *International Journal* 38, 4 (Autumn 1983): 652-673.

16. Edward Azar and Abdel-Monem Almashat, "Contradictions and Skepticism: How Egyptian Students View the Peace Process," *International Interactions* 8, 3 (1981): 379-397. In this case the "alert elite" consisted of 131 fourth-year students majoring in political science at Cairo University (34 per cent female and 66 per cent male). Despite the limitations inherent in survey research in developing polities, the crucial role of students in Egyptian politics makes the results noteworthy.

17. Korany, "The Cold Peace," pp. 652-673.

18. For details, see Mustapha K. El-Sayed, "Egyptian Popular Attitudes toward the Palestinians since 1977," *Journal of Palestine Studies* 18, 4 (Summer 1989): 39-42.

19. A sample of salient governmental actions would include the following:

2 July 1982: Egypt informed the Security Council of an imminent joint Egyptian-French initiative on the situation in the Middle East;

10 July: Egypt declared its rejection of a Palestinian homeland in Jordan;

15-18 July: President Mubarak appealed to Arab leaders to hold a summit meeting to study the situation in the region. Foreign Minister Ali said that Sudan and Jordan approved Egypt's plan to hold an Arab summit on Lebanon, and the Sudanese president flew to Riyadh to seek Saudi support for the plan;

24 July: Egypt affirmed that the withdrawal of Palestinian forces from Lebanon should be linked to a comprehensive solution of the Palestinian question;

25 July: In a speech marking the thirtieth anniversary of the 1952 revolution, Mubarak described Israel's invasion as "a violation of the spirit of peace";

28 July: President Mubarak asked President Reagan to re-evaluate American policy in the Middle East in order to achieve a just peace in the region;

31 July: Egypt reiterated the necessity of an immediate United States-Palestinian dialogue to resolve the Palestinian question;

3 August: Prime Minister Ali expressed his concern about the prospects for Egyptian-Israeli relations and affirmed that Israel's invasion of Lebanon would force the "indefinite postponement" of the autonomy talks;

22 August: Mubarak reiterated the necessity of a Palestinian entity in Gaza and the West Bank;

23 August: Egypt asked Israel to withdraw completely from Lebanon;

26 August: Ali declared that Israeli withdrawal from Lebanon was a prerequisite for the resumption of the peace efforts;

27 August: Egypt formally rejected the resumption of the autonomy talks until Israeli troops withdrew from Lebanon;

15 September: The Egyptian government assailed Israel's advance into west Beirut;

20 September: Egypt recalled its ambassador to Israel as an "expression of resentment" over Israel's complicity in the Beirut massacre.

Egypt also made repeated protests to Israel, and several messages were sent by President Mubarak to President Reagan and other heads of state (notably in Western Europe).

20. For details, El-Sayed, "Egyptian Popular Attitudes toward the Palestinians since 1977," pp. 43-48.

21. A total of 108 news items (events, declarations, opinion articles and editorials) were analyzed dealing with the *intifada*. These were published between December 1987 and March 1989 in the six Egyptian newspapers.

22. *al-Ahram* (Cairo), 17 April 1988.

23. *al-Ahram*, 6 March 1988.

24. *al-Ahram*, 4 May 1988.

25. *al-Ahram*, 2 September 1988.

26. During this period 'Arafat visited Cairo on 22 September, 24 October, 22 November, 4 December, 19 December 1988; and again on 12 and 27 February 1989.

27. *al-Ahram*, 12, 19, 26 October 1988.

28. *al-Ahram*, 31 August 1988.

29. *al-Ahram*, 17 October 1988.

30. *al-Akhbar* (Cairo), 24 November 1988.

31. *al-Gumhurriyya* (Cairo), 18 November 1988.

32. *al-Akhbar*, 19 November 1988.

33. *al-Qabas* (Kuwait), 20 November 1988.

34. *al-Mussawar*, 23 August 1988; Salwa Gom'a, "Who Makes Egypt's Foreign Policy?" paper presented to the annual conference of the Middle East Studies Association,

Toronto, November 1989.

35. Gom'a, "Who Makes Egypt's Foreign Policy?"

36. *al-Ahram*, 29 December 1988, 24 January 1989.

37. Yasir 'Arafat acknowledged the Egyptian role at a joint news conference with President Mubarak, *Middle East News Agency*, 18 December 1988 (in *Foreign Broadcast Information Service—Middle East and South Asia*, hereafter *FBIS*).

38. Text in *Journal of Palestine Studies* 19, 1 (Autumn 1989): 145-148.

39. The ten points called for: i) an Israeli commitment to accept the result of elections in the occupied territories; ii) international observers to monitor the voting; iii) full immunity for Palestinian elected representatives; iv) the withdrawal of Israeli troops from balloting areas during the election; v) an Israeli commitment to start talks on the final status of the territories by a certain date; vi) a freeze on all Israeli settlement activities; vii) complete freedom of speech for all candidates; viii) a ban on the entry of Israelis into the occupied territories on election day; ix) the participation in the voting of Palestinians in East Jerusalem; and x) Israeli acceptance of "the four principles of American policy in the Middle East," namely "the settlement should be based on Security Council Resolutions 242 and 338," "the principle of trading land for peace," "security guarantees for all states in the region," and "the recognition of the political rights of the Palestinians." Text in *Journal of Palestine Studies* 19, 1 (Autumn 1989): 144-145.

40. Text in *Journal of Palestine Studies* 19, 2 (Winter 1990): 169-170.

41. Egypt's "assumptions" (reportedly coordinated with the PLO) were that the Palestinian delegation to the talks would represent all Palestinians, inside and outside the occupied territories; that the Israeli-Palestinian agenda would be open; and that the elections dialogue was part of a broader process leading to an international peace conference. Text in *Journal of Palestine Studies* 19, 2 (Winter 1990): 159.

42. Husni Mubarak, *Middle East News Agency*, 22 July 1990; Usama al-Baz, *al-Watan* (Kuwait), 26 July 1990 (*FBIS*).

8

Syria

Fred Lawson

During the first year of the Palestinian uprising, Syrian policy went through four distinct phases. Damascus framed its initial reaction to the clashes that broke out between youths in the Gaza Strip and the West Bank and Israeli troops during December 1987 in terms of inter-Arab and US-Syrian relations. Specifically, the Syrian regime drew an explicit connection between the resort to violent protest by the Palestinian population and efforts on the part of Cairo and Washington to appease or conciliate Tel Aviv/Jerusalem, arguing that the latter directly precipitated the former. In mid-February 1988, Damascus took a different tack in its public pronouncements regarding the *intifada*. Syrian officials toned down their criticisms of both Egypt and the US, suggesting instead that international negotiations among representatives of the Soviet Union, Algeria, Jordan, the United States and Syria might help provide "a common denominator regarding all issues raised so that a radical solution to the Palestinian problem can be reached."[1] By the summer, however, Damascus dropped this more moderate orientation and began calling the uprising an example of armed nationalist struggle against foreign domination in the tradition of the Algerian war against French colonization and the Vietnamese war against American occupation. This orientation shifted to one of virtual silence concerning Palestinian affairs beginning in November 1988, leaving some observers to conclude that Syrian president Hafiz al-Asad had learned the value of moderation after a year of "banging his head against a brick wall" in attempting to wrest control of the Palestinian movement from the mainstream of the Palestine Liberation Organization (PLO) and its local activists in the occupied territories.[2]

These shifts in overt orientation toward the *intifada* appear puzzling in light of Syria's consistent championing of a relatively militant line with regard to the Arab-Israeli conflict. Since at least 1967, and perhaps as early as 1936, successive regimes in Damascus have rejected virtually every attempt to work out a negotiated settlement to the basic issues involved in the conflict. The present regime adopted a somewhat more pragmatic approach in its dealings with both Israel and the Palestinian national movement during the first months after it seized power in November 1970, going so far as to accept the terms of United Nations Security Council Resolution 242 at the end of 1971. Nevertheless, Damascus coordinated its military plans with Cairo in the period leading up to the October war of 1973 and agreed to a ceasefire only after protracted mediation on the part of US Secretary of State Henry Kissinger. Subsequent efforts to broaden the scope of Syrian-Israeli bargaining proved futile: by the time Egypt's President Anwar al-Sadat traveled to Jerusalem in 1977, Syria had assumed the leading role in the Steadfastness and Confrontation Front, a loose alliance of Arab states opposed to Cairo's peace initiative and the greater American presence in Middle Eastern affairs it entailed. Damascus even sponsored a mόve by dissident factions within the PLO to oust the organization's more moderate leadership and replace it with one more singlemindedly committed to armed struggle as a means of achieving Palestinian objectives in the wake of the Israeli invasion of Lebanon in the summer of 1982. One would thus have expected the Syrian government to have greeted the uprising with wholehearted enthusiasm and direct encouragement.

In an effort to explain why Damascus assumed instead a decidedly more ambiguous position *vis-à-vis* the uprising, this chapter will first spell out the four phases of early Syrian policy toward the *intifada*. It will then attempt to situate the regime's policies within the strategic context confronting Damascus during the months immediately following the eruption of the uprising in December 1987, particularly with regard to developments in Lebanon and trends in relations between Syria and the PLO. In broad terms, it will argue that whenever the strategic position of Syrian forces and that of their major allies in Lebanon deteriorated, especially in the presence of repeated Israeli military incursions into the country, the Syrian regime ignored or downplayed the significance of the uprising so as to prevent militant activity in the West Bank and Gaza Strip from providing either allies or a model of insurrection against outside occupation to those challenging Syrian predominance in central and eastern Lebanon. But at the same time, Damascus consistently attempted to undermine the supremacy of Fateh, the organization led by Yasir 'Arafat, over the Palestinian national movement and manipulated its policy so as to weaken mainstream forces in the PLO.

The interaction of these two dynamics provided the basis for Syrian policy throughout the first year of the *intifada*. It would continue to do so as the uprising in the occupied territories entered its second and third years.

Syrian Policy During the First Year of the Uprising

On 16 December 1987, the day Arab merchants in East Jerusalem began the first of the general strikes that became one of the primary components of the *intifada* in urban areas, Syrian domestic radio read an editorial from the party daily newspaper, *al-Ba'th*, charging the Egyptian government with attempting to improve relations between Cairo and Tel Aviv/Jerusalem "while our children's bodies were falling on Palestinian soil." Cairo's policies were accused of being a clear abandonment of "Arabism" at a time when "Sharon was celebrating the moving of his ministry to the holy city of Jerusalem, Rabin was signing a military agreement with Washington, and Zionist officers were coordinating with the Pentagon to carry out a new aggression." The uprising thus represented a call to all true Arab nationalist regimes to commit themselves to creating "a new Arab situation that would impose the Arab nation's will on its enemies." In this way, echoed the daily *Tishrin*, "the heroic stand of the masses in the occupied territory will inevitably foil all capitulatory plans in the Palestinian arena and all the Egyptian regime's attempts to force the Palestinian right wing to recognize Israel in advance" of any comprehensive peace talks.[3]

A week later, Syrian state radio broadcast a lengthy statement concerning the uprising in the name of the national command of the Ba'th party reiterating Damascus' view "that the Arab-Israeli conflict epitomizes the basic contradiction in the entire Arab region between the Arab nation, its aims and interests, on the one hand, and the imperialist and Zionist forces' ambitions to restore their domination over the entire Arab homeland on the other." The significance of violent protest in the occupied territories lay not only in its inseparability from popular resistance in the neighboring areas of the Golan and southern Lebanon, but also in its illustrating "that panting after US-Zionist settlement schemes, capitulating to them, and deviating from the sound course are only attempts to abort these Arab victories and persist in submitting to the will of the agents [of western imperialism]." The commentary therefore concluded that "the uprising is a resounding cry in the face of the capitulationists and defeatists in the Palestinian arena and the Arab arena in general."[4]

Drawing an analogy between popular resistance to Israeli occupation and popular discontent with the policies of the Mubarak regime in Cairo remained a dominant feature of Syrian pronouncements concerning the *intifada* as 1988 began. On 13 January, Syrian radio read an excerpt from *al-Thawra* claiming that "our people's uprising in the occupied homeland has not only embarrassed the Egyptian regime, but also placed it at a serious impasse. This impasse is the expansion of the occupied homeland's uprising into the Egyptian streets, a demonstration expressing solidarity with the uprising and calling for the expulsion of the Israeli ambassador from Cairo and the withdrawal of the Egyptian ambassador." By adopting new regulations severely limiting street demonstrations and rounding up Palestinian sympathizers, the Egyptian government was in effect "cooperat[ing] with the Zionist entity in repressing the popular uprising which spread from the occupied territory to Egypt." Only by repudiating the 1979 peace treaty with Israel could Egypt's rulers be relieved of this popular pressure and "restore Egypt to its pan-Arab role, away from the accords of humiliation and submission" reached at Camp David.[5]

Syrian-sponsored Palestinian organizations largely followed Damascus' lead during the first months of the uprising, arguing that violent resistance in the Gaza Strip and West Bank underlined the bankruptcy of the Camp David agreements. As Ahmad Jibril, the secretary-general of the Popular Front for the Liberation of Palestine-General Command (PFLP-GC) stated in early February, "During most of the demonstrations, if not all, there was not a single slogan advocating the type of settlement currently proposed by certain Arab, Palestinian, or international circles." The leaders of the collective actions in the occupied territories, Jibril asserted, "look upon the PLO as an achievement brought about by blood, sweat, and tears. They feel that for the time being the PLO is not in good hands." In fact, he claimed, "It would be illogical for them to die inside the occupied territory so they can 'carry' Yasir 'Arafat on their shoulders to an international conference, which would result in the recognition of the Israeli enemy and the normalization of relations with it, as was the case with Egypt in 'Camp David.' " The primary challenge to these grassroots leaders came not from the Israeli authorities or Palestinian collaborators, but from "the Arab reactionary camp, with Palestinian leaderships in collusion, and certain international circles [who] might try to thwart this uprising by suggesting bribes which might deceive our people in the occupied territory."[6]

Thus Syria's initial response to the uprising was couched primarily in terms of inter-Arab diplomacy: Damascus and its allies took advantage of the rebellion in the occupied territories to score points against those Arab regimes who advocated extending the Camp David framework into a general set of guidelines for Arab-Israeli negotiations. Cairo in particular was consistently portrayed as a lackey of both Washington and Tel Aviv/Jerusalem, whose own leadership could expect to face the same sort of resistance to its regional policies as had broken out in the West Bank and Gaza. This movement would take the form of a spontaneous uprising of the general population whose success would restore a properly pan-Arab orientation to Egyptian foreign policy and vindicate the rejectionist stance taken by the Syrian government in the years after 1979.

Syrian pronouncements regarding the *intifada* continued to emphasize international diplomacy as the winter came to a close. The foreign minister of Algeria, prime minister of Jordan and chief Middle East expert of the foreign ministry of the USSR passed through Damascus in quick succession on 15-16 February; each one of these diplomats conferred with Syrian officials concerning the implications of continued violence in Gaza and the West Bank. One report suggested that these discussions had the twin objectives of "unifying the Arab stand on current moves, especially regarding US activities aimed at containing the popular uprising and divisive solutions promoted by the US Middle East envoy Richard Murphy" and "crystallizing a clear Soviet position, in order to probe new stands and views on developments in the Middle East as well as ways of finding a solution to the Palestinian problem."[7] The visits of these diplomats coincided with meetings between the United Nations under-secretary general for political affairs and the Syrian foreign minister, Faruq al-Shar', and Vice President 'Abd al-Halim Khaddam; these talks, both of which were attended by the Syrian representative to the UN Truce Supervision Organization, underscored Damascus' interest in pursuing a negotiated settlement to a wide range of issues related to the Arab-Israeli conflict, but one fundamentally different from the bilateral negotiations US Secretary of State George Shultz was expected to press local governments to initiate during his visit to the eastern Mediterranean at the end of February.

Syrian policy toward the *intifada* began to focus more closely on the struggle between the Arab population of the West Bank and Gaza and the Israeli armed forces in the wake of Secretary of State Shultz's follow-up tour of the region in early April. On the 14th, Damascus radio broadcast the first of two interviews with prominent Palestinian activists who had been deported from the occupied territories three days before. One of the deportees, a teacher in the Islamic university of Gaza and khatib at the al-Qassam mosque in the Bayt Lahya district, began these interviews by saying: "The uprising is the journey of blood, the journey of bare chests facing the criminal Israeli military machine. The uprising is the revolution of a people who stand with their backs against the wall resisting the fiercest onslaught against our nation during this generation." His comrades emphasized the "internal" origins of the *intifada*, agreeing that "the principal cause of the uprising is [the] occupation" of Palestinian land by Israeli forces. Nevertheless, the initial set of interviews ended with a call for "unity and cohesion" between the Palestinian people and "the other Arab peoples" that "will manifest itself in practice along the path of liberating our land in advance of ridding our homeland of all vestiges of imperialism."[8]

By early July Syria's public position on the *intifada* began to give primary attention to the issues raised by the Palestinian deportees interviewed three months earlier. Damascus radio observed on 9 July that "The popular uprising in the occupied territories was a natural reply to occupation, the annexation plans, the means of fascist repression, religious and racial discrimination, the crimes of expulsion and mass punishment, genocide, war crimes, and the disavowal of the Palestinian people's national inalienable rights." Diplomatic or inter-Arab motivations for the rebellion were clearly accorded secondary status: "The uprising erupted for the objectives of liberation and not for reactivating the situation, just as the glorious October war of liberation was a war of liberation for the sincere, patriotic, and pan-Arab people and not a war to reactivate the situation."[9] Such phrasing was of course a veiled criticism of the Egyptian regime, whose former leaders had justified the 1973 war as a means of upsetting the regional status quo and refocusing the attention of the superpowers on the Arab-Israeli conflict. But criticizing Cairo now took a distinct back seat to highlighting the conditions within the West Bank and Gaza Strip that had precipitated the rebellion.

Internal aspects of the uprising continued to provide the basis for Damascus' commentary throughout the summer. Syrian state radio observed on 14 July that "We believe there is no need for more talk about the traitor al-Sadat's experience which the Arab masses know well, and they also know that the defeatist approach followed by al-Sadat leads neither to the Arab nation's long- nor short-term objectives." Instead, the commentator urged his listeners to predicate their actions upon another set of principles: "The other approach calls for adherence to rights and struggle in all fields as well as to all means for achieving pan-Arab objectives, and for not relinquishing or ceding any of them. No single event in history indicates that occupiers or colonizers have given up land through their own will or desire, or as a result of speeches, sermons, or honeyed talk." Like the Algerians and Vietnamese before them, "the Palestinian stone-throwers have developed a direct confrontation with the most ferocious weapons of the Israeli occupation and have decided with determination to shake the land under occupation."[10]

This markedly militant stance toward the *intifada* persisted until the fall of 1988, when Damascus adopted a studied silence concerning events in the occupied territories. As relations between Cairo and the mainstream PLO warmed during August and September, the Syrian regime revived comparisons between the twin "capitulationists," 'Arafat and Sadat. *al-Thawra*, for instance, editorialized that:

> The suspect movements of the Palestinian rightist clique at this particular time are almost similar to the movements of the murdered al-Sadat inasmuch as al-Sadat exploited the October victory, turning it into a bargaining counter and negotiating over the Arab cause. Whereas 'Arafat's movements today are motivated by an illusion that the brilliant victories being achieved by the uprising against the Zionist enemy and its repressive war machine can be exploited.[11]

But such comparisons aside, Damascus dramatically scaled down both the frequency and the intensity of its pronouncements regarding the *intifada* as the first year of the uprising drew to a close. When the mainstream PLO announced on 15 November its intention to establish an independent state alongside the State of Israel, Syria's state-run news media ignored the story completely, concentrating instead on the heightened security measures imposed on the occupied territories that day "but without so much as mentioning the declaration of independence which prompted the crackdown."[12]

Three clear shifts in Syrian policy toward the *intifada* are evident in all this. During the first two months of the uprising, Damascus paid scant attention to the popular aspects of the demonstrations and reprisals in the West Bank and Gaza Strip and concentrated instead on the *intifada*'s presumed implications for inter-Arab diplomacy. Collective violence in Palestine was portrayed as a renunciation of all attempts to conciliate Israel, and particularly of the Camp David accords. By the third month of the uprising, Damascus began hinting that a multinational solution to the basic conflict underlying the rebellion offered the best chance of ending the violence in such a way as to advance the interests of Arab nationalism. But beginning in the *intifada*'s fifth month, the Syrian regime adopted a much more militant orientation toward events in the occupied territories, affirming the duty of a population suffering foreign occupation to take up arms to achieve national independence. This posture was succeeded by a considerably more muted stance beginning in the ninth month of the uprising, as officials in Damascus were "left mumbling that they 'support' the idea of a Palestinian state, without announcing explicit recognition."[13]

Charitable observers have discerned a "trend toward moderation" in Syria's policy during the first year of the uprising. In this view, repeated defeats in regional diplomacy and growing support for Fateh put Damascus in an increasingly isolated position in the Arab world as 1988 went by. The "marginalization" of the al-Asad regime forced the Syrian leadership to change its tune on a variety of issues, the most salient of which was the Palestinian movement. Faced with a resurgent Fateh, Damascus elected to bide its time in a policy of "deliberate inaction,"[14] waiting for the inevitable failure of 'Arafat's attempt to further the Palestinian cause through negotiations with the US and Israel. But this perspective overlooks significant variations in Syrian policy in the twelve months following December 1987—the al-Asad regime adopted a substantially more militant orientation toward the uprising during the spring and summer of 1988 than it had before—and it fails to deal adequately with the timing of evident shifts in Syrian policy—why the "trend toward moderation" occurs only after September 1988.

These matters can be accommodated more effectively by linking trends in Syrian policy toward the *intifada* to developments in Lebanon during 1987-1988. The security of Damascus' position in Lebanese affairs varied widely over the first twelve months of the uprising, and changes in the vulnerability of Syrian forces and their primary allies had a direct impact on the al-Asad regime's position regarding events in the occupied territories in general and the role of the mainstream leadership of the PLO in Palestinian affairs in particular. Tracing out the connection between periods of instability in Lebanon and shifts in Syria's Palestine policy is therefore a crucial first step in explaining Damascus' policy toward the *intifada*.

Challenges to Syria's Position in Lebanon

Syria and its allies found themselves in a precarious strategic position in Lebanon during the last weeks of 1987. Syrian forces stationed in West Beirut became subjected to a series of bombings and machine gun attacks in late October, responsibility for which was claimed by a group calling itself the Liberation Battalion (LB). A spokesperson for this organization told a western news agency on 17 November that such strikes "will continue... until Syrian troops withdraw from Lebanon."[15] A month later, the LB was joined in its offensive by members of the Khalil 'Akkawi squad of the 9 February Organization, who carried out a wave of attacks against Syrian positions around Tripoli. In response to these operations, Syrian commanders redeployed their units in Lebanon, concentrating them in more secure locations, while at the same time stepping up reconnaissance and tactical air missions in the central Biqa' Valley to prevent these groups from linking up with Iranian-sponsored formations of Hizbullah militants and Revolutionary Guards based outside al-Masna'.[16]

Fighting between members of the LB and Syrian troops escalated sharply in late December, as LB guerrillas launched several rocket attacks on Syrian command posts in Beirut and Tripoli. These attacks coincided with a general strike by supporters of the predominantly Maronite Lebanese Forces to protest the stricter security measures implemented by Syrian personnel north of the capital. And on the 20th heightened tensions in the Shuf precipitated a clash between Syrian troops and a column of militiamen affiliated with the predominantly Druze Progressive Socialist Party.[17] Around 20 December, the military command of the predominantly Shi'i Amal movement, Syria's closest ally in Lebanon, put its forces on "a maximum state of alert" in response to movements by fighters associated with Hizbullah, the Syrian Social Nationalist Party and the Lebanese Communist Party in the districts around Tyre. According to diplomatic sources, the first of these organizations was beginning once again to raid Syrian positions after a lull of almost two years.[18]

On 25 December, the leader of LB, Ka'an Naji, signaled his organization's growing influence in Lebanese affairs by announcing that LB fighters intended to expand their operations into the Biqa' and the mountainous areas north of Beirut. Naji blamed Damascus for Lebanon's growing economic difficulties, observing that "Gasoline, bread, and even electricity are confiscated here and taken to Syria; this is in addition to the theft of cars, houses, shops, and even pharmacies... The value of our Lebanese currency has dropped to an unbearable limit. The Syrians are trying to impose their currency on us at a price which suits them...Therefore, I emphasize that the Syrian presence in Lebanon is an occupation, for it was established despite the will of the Lebanese." To end this occupation, he promised to continue waging "guerrilla warfare" against Syrian units in an effort to drain their resources and sap their morale.[19] In the wake of this announcement, attacks by LB and 9 February fighters on Syrian positions persisted throughout January and February 1988.[20]

At the same time Syrian units in Lebanon found themselves under increased pressure from local militias, Israeli commanders escalated their forces' military operations in the southern part of the country. An Israeli Defense Forces armored column moved into Marji'yun on 26 November 1987, setting up checkpoints and carrying out search and destroy missions in surrounding districts. The following day a second column entered the western Biqa' and deployed its tanks at a number of crossroads outside Maydun.[21] These troops were reinforced in mid-December; at the end of the month an additional tank company took up positions in the Jazzin area, while Israeli military helicopters stepped up their raids in the "security zone" along the border between the two countries.[22]

On 1 January 1988 these units advanced toward the town of Qabikha supported by units of the Israeli-sponsored South Lebanese Army. Members of Amal's militia attempted to prevent the IDF from capturing the town, but were beaten back with heavy losses. At the same time, Israeli helicopter gunships raided Hizbullah encampments around Maydun and fighter-bombers struck positions occupied by the PFLP-GC outside Sidon.[23] Israeli aircraft then carried out rocket and machine gun attacks on Amal strongpoints just outside the "security zone," while IDF gunboats shelled the Palestinian camp of al-Rashidiyya in Tyre. On the 3rd IDF air and naval units hit a string of Palestinian and Lebanese targets along the coast: alleged command posts of Fateh and the PFLP-GC outside Sidon were attacked from the air; Druze-controlled ports at Damur and Jiyya were shelled from the sea.[24]

Israel's coordinated air and sea raids in the area north of Sidon led the leadership of Amal to announce on 16 January that it intended "unilaterally and unconditionally" to lift the siege of the largest Palestinian camps around Beirut and Tyre that its militia had imposed in the summer of 1985. The announcement, billed as "a gift to our people in the occupied territories," accelerated the deployment of Syrian troops on the perimeters of the camps, stretching Syrian forces in Lebanon dangerously thin.[25] As Damascus' hold over Lebanese affairs weakened, Iranian-backed Hizbullah and Revolutionary Guards fighters stepped up their efforts to "Islamize" the country; representatives of the moribund World Organization of Islamic Liberation Movements visited Shi'i leaders in southern Lebanon in early February and discussed ways of "cleaning... South Lebanon of all elements hostile to helping [the] Islamic struggle in Palestine." The visit precipitated a string of armed clashes between pro-Iranian and pro-Syrian militias in the area, leading a delegation of high-ranking Lebanese officials to travel to Tehran at mid-month to discuss ways of relieving tension with the Ayatollah Husayn Ali Montazeri. But instead of offering to mediate the conflict, Montazeri is reported to have urged the Lebanese to set up an Islamic republic: "It is against all practices and international laws," he told his guests, "that a minority should rule over a majority of Shi'i and Sunni Muslims. The political and economic structures of Lebanon must be controlled by Muslims."[26] In response, Syrian troops arrested some 20 Hizbullahis and set up checkpoints around their base of operations in southern Beirut.

Events in Lebanon thus left Syrian forces in a precarious position throughout the first months of the *intifada*, leading Damascus to play down the legitimacy of challenges by indigenous populations to foreign occupation and emphasize instead the diplomatic aspects of the uprising in the occupied territories. Syria's forces in the country had become so overextended by the end of February that the al-Asad regime adopted a two-pronged strategy of relieving pressure on its western front: it welcomed Secretary of State Shultz with an announced willingness to take part in an international conference to discuss the disposition of the occupied territories, including of course the Golan Heights, and it responded favorably to communique number 9 issued by the Unified National Leadership of the *intifada* (UNLI), which called for a reconciliation between Yasir 'Arafat's Fateh and the Syrian Ba'th. Shultz rejected the idea of an international conference on Palestine out of hand; Syrian policy toward the uprising during March and April 1988 consequently turned to the tricky issue of rapprochement with the mainstream PLO.

Rapprochement with the PLO

Relations between Syria and the Fateh-led mainstream within the Palestine Liberation Organization reached a nadir in 1986, when the Syrian-backed Amal militia initiated a second round of the "war of the camps" in south-central Lebanon. PLO fighters held off this assault, as they had held off a similar one the previous year; and their success re-established the Palestinians as a significant force in Lebanese politics. In the words of one observer, by early 1987 the PLO was poised to extend its influence beyond the well-fortified camps and into surrounding areas:

> In Sidon, the regional capital of the south, this has already happened, with the Palestinians now effectively in control of the whole city as well as 'Ain al-Hilwa camp. With the capture of Maghdousheh, the Palestinians even seriously threaten Shi'ite communications between the south and Beirut. In Beirut, the Shi'ites' main concern is that the consolidation of Palestinian positions in the three camps of Bourj al-Barajneh, Sabra and Chatila will enable them eventually to 'recapture' the capital or at least to pose a serious challenge to Amal's domination, as well as encouraging Sunni resistance.[27]

The growing power of the PLO precipitated overtures from both the Druze and Sunni leaderships aimed at re-creating the pre-1982 National Movement of Progressive Forces and thereby undercutting the dominance of Amal in the capital and its southern hinterlands.

Damascus reacted to these developments by moving its armed forces back into West Beirut in early February, shutting down the headquarters of the local militias and setting up check points at key intersections throughout the city. Syrian troops took up positions around the perimeters of Burj al-Barajina and Shatila camps, facilitating the delivery of food and medicine to the inhabitants; but they kept 'Arafat loyalists bottled up inside, preventing them from consolidating their strength relative to Fateh dissidents led by Sa'id Musa Muragha ("Abu Musa") and other groups associated with the Syrian-sponsored Palestine National Salvation Front. A standoff between Syrian troops and their Amal allies on one side and Druze militia and Palestinian guerillas on the other was broken in mid-April with the Syrian army's entry into Burj al-Barajina and Shatila. This move prompted the leaders of the Palestinian national movement to put aside their many differences and use the occasion of the 18th meeting of the Palestine National Council in Algiers on 20-25 April to reaffirm the unity of the largest factions within the PLO and begin exploring the possibility of formal talks with both the Syrian regime and the main Lebanese parties.[28]

This initiative bogged down during the summer and fall of 1987 as Damascus turned its attention to events related to the Gulf war and Amal continued its siege of al-Rashidiyya and 'Ayn al-Hilwa camps. By early November, when Arab heads of state gathered in Amman for an extraordinary summit, Syrian-PLO relations had improved little from what they had been a year before. Nevertheless, in the immediate aftermath of the conference 'Arafat remarked that "the Amman summit contributed toward creating a positive atmosphere between the two sides, affirming that the dialogue between Damascus and the PLO had already begun before the summit."[29] On 3 December Damascus released some 150 'Arafat supporters detained since Fateh was driven out of Tripoli four years earlier; at the same time, it was reported that discussions were underway concerning the reopening of the PLO's offices in West Beirut, a move that *Voice of Lebanon* radio said "would signal a remarkable development and improvement in Syrian-Palestinian relations."[30] At the end of the month, the Abu Dhabi newspaper *al-Ittihad* reported that Syrian Vice President 'Abd al-Halim Khaddam had sent a message to the leaders of the PLO spelling out the differences that remained between the two sides and reviewing "security arrangements in the Palestinian camps in Lebanon." The paper quoted "an informed Palestinian source in Rabat" as saying that "dialogue between the two sides on a political level will resume at the beginning of 1988."[31]

It was only in the wake of the assassination of Khalil al-Wazir ("Abu Jihad") in Tunis on 16 April that Hafiz al-Asad and Yasir 'Arafat at last met to formalize the Syrian-Fateh rapprochement. On the 24th 'Arafat arrived in Damascus accompanied by Salah Khalaf ("Abu Iyad") for his first visit to the Syrian capital in five years; the following day they joined Faruq

Qaddumi and other members of the central committee of Fateh at the presidential palace, where they were formally received by President al-Asad and Foreign Minister al-Shar'.[32] At a series of meetings that week, Damascus reversed its opposition to an expanded PLO presence in Lebanon. According to one Palestinian official present at the talks, "the Syrian officials spoke positively about the Palestinian presence in Lebanon. It seems that Damascus does not believe any more that the PLO presence in Lebanon constitutes a point of contention."[33] Furthermore, the two parties agreed "to preserve and escalate the uprising in the occupied territories; to voice joint rejection of the Shultz initiative, as this initiative ignores the Palestinian people's legitimate rights; [and] to insist on the convening of an effective international conference to resolve the Arab-Israeli conflict."[34]

Immediately following the departure of 'Arafat from Damascus, the UNLI broadcast a call to the Syrian regime to form a military alliance with the PLO. And on 1 May the official Bahraini news agency reported that Syria had authorized "several" battalions of Fateh guerillas to return to Syrian territory and was considering allowing these units to resume operations in the Biqa' Valley.[35] These events represented the high point of the rapprochement between Syria and the mainstream PLO, a reconciliation that one observer called "perhaps the most important result (or perhaps achievement) of the Palestinian uprising in the occupied territories."[36] But despite the optimism it generated among Palestinians throughout the Arab world, this reconciliation soon fell apart. And the rapidity of its collapse indicates the tenuous connection between the Syrian-Fateh rapprochement and the *intifada*. Growing conflict among the most powerful Lebanese factions and an escalation in Israeli military activity in south-central Lebanon in the spring of 1988 demonstrated to Damascus the futility of pacifying Lebanon by co-operating with the mainstream PLO. On the contrary, the boost that the rapprochement had given to 'Arafat loyalists enabled them to reassert their control over the key camps of Shatila and Burj al-Barajina, providing a new potential basis of support for Syria's enemies in the districts south of Beirut.

Renewed Instability in Lebanon

On 2 May 1988, a force of some 2,000 Israeli soldiers crossed the border into southern Lebanon around al-'Arqub, while an additional company of IDF paratroopers landed west of al-Khalwa along the 'Ayn 'Ata road leading into the Biqa' valley. These troops, supported by tanks and armored cars, moved along the western slope of Mount Hermon over the course of the next two days systematically searching villages for Palestinian guerillas; they then attempted to advance on the towns of Maydun and Mashghara at the southwestern end of the Biqa'. Outside these two towns the IDF encountered stiff resistance from Amal units and small groups of

Hizbullahis, but on the morning of 4 May Beirut radio announced that Maydun had fallen to the Israelis and their allies in the South Lebanese Army. The IDF then opened fire on Syrian positions outside Mashghara, while patrolling the airspace over southern Lebanon with fighter-bombers and helicopter gunships. After a day of intense fighting in the hills north of Maydun, the Israeli units began withdrawing to the "security zone" along the Lebanese border, leaving small contingents at strategically located crossroads around Jazzin and Maydun.[37]

As the IDF retreated, Hizbullah militiamen took up positions on the northern side of Maydun. A spokesperson for the party held an impromptu news conference at Mashghara on 5 May in which he credited Hizbullah with driving the Israelis out and vowed to reassert the party's predominance in the area.[38] Amal reacted to the resurgence of Hizbullah influence in the south by challenging the party's hold over the suburbs surrounding Beirut: in two days of fighting, Amal succeeded in capturing a number of Hizbullah strongpoints, only to be driven back when Revolutionary Guards stationed around Ba'lbak reinforced the Hizbullahis and assisted them in recapturing the positions they had lost. Syrian troops provided logistical support for the Amal fighters but refused to intervene in the battle directly. Consequently, by mid-May Hizbullah and its allies were able to establish firm connections with the pro-Fateh guerillas based in Burj al-Barajina, as well as with the Druze and Lebanese Forces to the east of the capital.

As the Amal-Hizbullah confrontation in southern Beirut continued to simmer, Israeli forces launched yet another offensive into the area around Maydun. On 25 May units of the South Lebanese Army supported by IDF helicopters raided the villages north of the "security zone"; Amal forces succeeded in blocking the advance until an Israeli armoured column crossed the border heading for the village of al-Luwayza. At this point Amal's local commanders retreated to more secure entrenchments in the hills and requested reinforcements from the north. Caught in a pincer between Hizbullah and the IDF, the movement's leader, Nabih Birri, sent a delegation to Damascus to warn the Syrians "about the new plan being drawn up by the Revolutionary Guards and Fateh to gain control of the suburb" of al-Ghubayra and to ask for greater Syrian support.[39] Amal's deteriorating position in the suburbs of Beirut finally led the Syrian government to deploy its own troops throughout the area on 27-28 May.

Syrian intervention in south Beirut dampened the fighting between Amal and Hizbullah, but encouraged dissident Palestinians loyal to Abu Musa to step up their attacks on Shatila and Burj al-Barajina where guerrillas loyal to 'Arafat had reasserted control at the end of April. By the end of June, the dissidents had forced the defenders of Shatila to surrender and were redeploying around the much larger garrison at Burj al-Barajina. Fateh, whose leadership was attempting at the same time to cope with rising discontent from more radical factions within the PLO over the future direction of the *intifada*,[40] responded to the fall of Shatila by accusing Damascus of "colluding with the United States to disarm the Palestinians and expel them from Lebanon." In a statement issued from PLO headquarters in Tunis on 28 June, Abu Iyad called the forced evacuation of Shatila one component of an overarching agreement between the Syrians and the Americans designed to "uproot the Palestinian presence in Lebanon" and set the stage for the election of an anti-Palestinian candidate to replace Amin Jumayyil as president of Lebanon later that fall.[41] The Unified National Leadership of the Uprising echoed these sentiments in a statement broadcast from Baghdad three days later, calling Syria's role in the fall of Shatila "a new link in the chain of the ugly conspiracy against the Palestinian people and the PLO."[42]

By mid-July the Syrian regime and the mainstream PLO had fallen out completely. On the 14th, 'Arafat referred to al-Asad and his colleagues as "Zionists who speak Arabic" at a rally in Baghdad and accused them of "trying to finish the job of annihilating the Palestinian camps and killing women, children, and the elderly—a job left unfinished by Sharon."[43] Damascus riposted that 'Arafat had adopted a "capitulatory" strategy and was willing "to preside over a regime of self-rule in the West Bank and Gaza Strip with the occupation and settlements still in place." By abandoning "the revolution of the Palestinian people," 'Arafat and his lieutenants, like Saddam Husayn of Iraq, "have changed from revolutionaries to political merchants, and from men of principle to brokers of the land, rights, and dignity."[44] Syrian spokespersons subsequently distinguished between "our people's brave uprising in the occupied Arab territory" and the Fateh leadership's efforts "to bypass the uprising, deprive it of its liberation struggle content, and peddle the capitulatory and liquidatory deals" favored by Washington.[45]

Jordan's unexpected renunciation of responsibility for the West Bank reinforced the split between Damascus and the mainstream PLO in at least two complementary ways. In the first place, Amman's disengagement provided a potential geographical basis for a truly autonomous Palestinian nationalism, independent of the interests of the existing Arab states. Prior to August 1988, as Laurie Brand has observed, "the Palestinians' dispersal and lack of recognition internationally" made it highly "unlikely that the PLO or any other diaspora-wide Palestinian political entity could have been established and recognized without the support of the front-line Arab states, none of whom... sought to create the framework for independent Palestinian military initiatives."[46] This situation was transformed by King Husayn's announced willingness to "dismantle" his kingdom's connections with the occupied territories; Fateh activists immediately began discussing the form an independent Palestinian state located on the West Bank might take.[47] Damascus refrained from criticizing the King but responded vitriolically to the (perhaps premature) publication of the UNLI's draft declaration of independence naming 'Arafat president of the new state.

Secondly, Jordan's withdrawal from the West Bank firmly reinforced the ties between the mainstream PLO leadership "outside the occupied territories" and the organization's grassroots activists "inside the territories." As Lamis Andoni has argued, the altered circumstances of August 1988 virtually eliminated the most salient tactical differences dividing these two sets of actors: "the PLO leaders want to strengthen the leadership of the *intifada* and the popular committees as the national authority in the territories" by setting up a provisional government made up of the Palestine National Council, while the Unified National Leadership "has to ensure the continuation of the *intifada* in order to give substance to the suggested provisional government."[48] This growing congruence of interests made Syria's insistence on differentiating between a "capitulationist" outside leadership and a "revolutionary" internal cadre less and less convincing. By the time 'Arafat addressed the European Parliament in Strasbourg on 12 September, Palestinian activists across the political spectrum on the West Bank expressed their approval of the chairman's message; only the increasingly marginal PFLP-GC and Palestine National Salvation Front continued to reject what they referred to as "the two-state solution."[49]

Damascus' alienation from the leadership of the *intifada* and the mainstream of the PLO was underscored by the impromptu summit meeting of Egypt's Husni Mubarak, King Husayn and 'Arafat that took place in 'Aqaba the third week of October. Faced with growing instability in Lebanon,[50] the Syrian regime largely ignored the primary agreements reached at this meeting—that Jordan and the PLO would send separate but equal delegations to any international peace conference and that any Palestinian state would be independent of Amman, joined at most in a "confederal" arrangement with the kingdom—and held its silence throughout the extraordinary convention of the Palestine National Council held in Algiers in early November. The formal declaration of independence announced at the convention went unreported in the Syrian state media; Syrian policy towards the Palestinian national movement had clearly reached a dead end. As one observer remarked, "legitimacy in the Palestinian arena nowadays manifestly comes, not from control of this or that refugee camp in Lebanon, but from the uprising in the territories, where Syria's influence is negligible and the PLO enjoys total support."[51]

This observation captures some but not all of the strategic paradox confronting Damascus in the last quarter of 1988. The al-Asad regime faced a rapidly disintegrating political situation in Lebanon as Amin Jumayyil's term as president of the republic came to an end in late September; as a last chance at maintaining Syrian influence within the Maronite camp, Damascus opted to back Mikhail Dahir as Jumayyil's successor, but this selection was immediately vetoed by the Lebanese Forces on the grounds that Dahir "could not say no to the Syrians. He would be a toy, a puppet for them."[52]

Until some semblance of stability were restored in Lebanon, Syria could not risk encouraging violent resistance to foreign occupation in the West Bank and Gaza Strip for fear of its spreading northward. But at the same time, the possibility that 'Arafat might succeed in initiating serious negotiations with the Israelis over the independence of the West Bank and Gaza, excluding the occupied Golan Heights from consideration, made it incumbent upon Damascus to continue to challenge the predominant position of Fateh within the Palestinian national movement. Cross-pressured by these competing demands, the Syrian leadership retreated into a studied silence concerning the *intifada*, leaving the initiative—as well as the responsibility—for subsequent developments in the hands of the mainstream PLO.

Conclusion

Syrian policy toward the uprising in the West Bank and Gaza Strip during its first year remained clearly subordinate to the dictates of the regime's objectives in Lebanon and its persistent hostility to the mainstream of the PLO led by Yasir 'Arafat. Damascus ignored or de-emphasized the internal sources of the *intifada* whenever its own position in Lebanese affairs faced serious challenge; and it reconciled itself to Fateh only when it became evident that the overwhelming majority of the inhabitants of the occupied territories firmly supported the leadership of this organization. By the first anniversary of the rebellion, the conflicting demands of promoting stability in Lebanon and undermining 'Arafat's position within the Palestinian national movement reduced Damascus to virtual silence with regard to the course of the *intifada*. Most observers interpreted this passivity as moderation; but it can more plausibly be seen as the result of Syria's incompatible policies toward Lebanese and Palestinian issues.

As the uprising ground through a second and third year, Damascus' preoccupation with developments in Lebanon grew more and more pronounced. In the spring of 1989, the dominant Maronite political figure, General Michel 'Awn, initiated a campaign to drive Syrian forces out of the country by cutting off their allies' access to the Mediterranean and bombarding Syrian-held positions around Beirut. This offensive led to some of the heaviest fighting of the entire civil war, prompting Arab League mediation.

When Arab League mediators proved themselves incapable of stopping the shelling, the League's council of foreign ministers called an emergency meeting in Tunis at the end of April to discuss the situation. This virtually coincided with Yasir 'Arafat's official visit to Paris the first of May, in which 'Arafat (in his new capacity as president of the proposed State of Palestine) announced the "lapsing" of the Palestine National Charter and its supersedure by the declaration of independence adopted the preceding November. Syrian-backed Palestinian organizations immediately denounced

'Arafat's apparent abrogation of the Charter: PFLP-GC leaders called for the chairman to be replaced by "the rule of the people" on the grounds that he had become "a traitor" to the Palestinian cause.[53]

It was under these circumstances that Hafiz al-Asad traveled to Casablanca the last week of May to attend an emergency Arab League summit devoted to the twin issues of the *intifada* and the deteriorating situation in Lebanon. Syrian officials signaled just prior to the meeting that they would not block the reintegration of Egypt as a full participant in the organization; but they also made it clear that they would brook no further interference by the League's heads of state in Lebanese affairs. As the delegations assembled in Casablanca, Damascus allowed Iranian-sponsored Revolutionary Guards to reinforce their formations around Ba'lbak, where a sizable rally had been staged by Hizbullahis and the militias of the PFLP-GC and Palestine National Salvation Front earlier in the month.[54] Syria's position effectively sabotaged calls by Baghdad, Cairo and Amman for a Syrian withdrawal from Lebanon. Moreover, the time and effort devoted to the political crisis in Beirut "overshadowed what had been expected to be a major issue at the conference: the Palestinian uprising in the Israeli-occupied territories and the recent moves by the Palestine Liberation Organization to satisfy American conditions for a dialogue."[55]

After three months of stalemate, September 1989 saw the announcement of new initiatives designed to reduce the level of conflict in both the occupied territories and Lebanon. Egyptian President Husni Mubarak offered a straightforward plan to facilitate elections in the West Bank and Gaza and raised hopes among some Palestinian leaders that avowed PLO sympathizers might be permitted to take part in any elections held to choose delegates to negotiate with the Israeli authorities, although this optimism was not shared by the more militant wing of the Unified National Leadership in the occupied territories.[56] At the same time, the tripartite Arab League mediation commission proposed convening an extraordinary session of the Lebanese parliament to forge a revised National Pact and elect a legitimate president of the Republic. This proposal led to the gathering of 62 members of parliament in the Saudi Arabian resort city of Ta'if at the end of the month. Damascus' support for the meeting exacerbated a growing rift between Syria and Iran, as well as between their respective allies, Amal and Hizbullah. The last of these expressed particularly vituperative criticisms of the reforms adopted by the Ta'if conference, which improved the position of Lebanon's Sunnis but did little to enhance the power of the Shi'a.

Syria's position in Lebanon deteriorated markedly through October and November: General 'Awn immediately voiced his rejection of both the Ta'if agreement and any president elected according to its terms; Amal and the Progressive Socialist Party gradually distanced themselves from the accord, dissatisfied with its handling of Shi'i issues as well as with its provisions mandating the dissolution of all militias within six months; Lebanese Forces commander Samir Ja'ja' refused to sever his tenuous relations with General 'Awn; and high-ranking Iranian officials traveled to southern Lebanon to rally opposition to the new Lebanese government.[57] Furthermore, 'Awn's forces had begun to receive considerable levels of financial and material assistance from Iraq, the flow of which Damascus attempted to interrupt by stepping up its blockade of ports surrounding East Beirut. The Israeli air force added fuel to this already combustible situation at the end of November by launching a series of strikes against Palestinian strongholds in the southeastern Biqa', prompting Syrian overflights of Beirut in a calculated contravention of the 1976 Red Line agreement between the two sides.[58] Damascus moved armored and commando units into West Beirut in an effort to salvage its withering hold over Lebanese affairs, but this operation merely precipitated a flurry of diplomatic warnings against any attempt to impose the Ta'if agreement by force, along with armed clashes between Hizbullah fighters forced to retreat from the capital by the arrival of Syrian troops and Amal units protecting the Syrians' flanks.

To mark the second anniversary of the outbreak of the *intifada*, Dr. Tawfiq Saliha of the Ba'th Regional (Syrian) Command told a somewhat puzzled rally of Palestinians at al-Yarmuk University outside Damascus on 7 December 1989 that "Syria will continue to support the nationalist Lebanese stance, Lebanese legitimacy, the valiant nationalist Lebanese resistance in southern Lebanon, and unity of Lebanese territory, people and institutions." He went on to denounce General 'Awn and his presumed Iraqi and Israeli backers, as well as a group of French Deputies who had traveled to East Beirut to confer with the general earlier that year. Only then did Saliha praise "our kinsfolk's *intifada* in the occupied Arab territories and the Golan Heights." The uprising represented "an assertion of continued struggle and firm insistence on armed struggle until the land is liberated." Damascus had assisted in this struggle by "devot[ing] all [its] potential to achieving strategic parity with the Zionist enemy to liberate the land and restore the Palestinian people's usurped rights." It remained for other Arab states to learn the lesson of the *intifada*: that the policies of "deviants, capitulationists, defeatists, and agents" were certain to collapse in the face of renewed "Arab solidarity... in the common Arab battle against the Zionist enemy, its defenders, and those who deal with it."[59]

Dr. Saliha's address provided a considerably more cogent recapitulation of Damascus' policy regarding the uprising than did that of his colleague in the Ba'th Regional Command, Sulayman Qaddah, before an assembly of the governing Progressive National Front's Central Command two days later. The second speech, which focused more narrowly on Palestinian affairs, seemed platitudinous in the context of developments in Lebanon, the Gulf region and the occupied territories that posed serious threats to Syrian security and prestige across the board. But confronted with these threats—particularly the smoldering stand-off between 'Awn and newly-elected President Ilyas Hrawi around Beirut and the escalating fighting between Amal and Hizbullah east of Sidon[60]—only the most vacuous statements of support for the uprising seemed prudent. Deciding whether or not it can continue to play its Lebanese policy off against its Palestinian policy is the most salient item on the agenda created for the al-Asad regime by the stone-throwers of the *intifada*.

Notes

1. *al-Sharq al-Awsat* (London), 17 February 1988, in *Foreign Broadcast Information Service: Near East and South Asia* (hereafter, *FBIS*).
2. Fida Nasrallah, "Syria pays the price of isolation," *Middle East International*, 31 March 1989, p. 17.
3. *Damascus Domestic Service*, 16 December 1987 (*FBIS*).
4. *Damascus Domestic Service*, 22 December 1987 (*FBIS*).
5. *Damascus Domestic Service*, 13 January 1988 (*FBIS*).
6. *al-Safir* (Beirut), 8 February 1988 (*FBIS*).
7. *al-Sharq al-Awsat*, 17 February 1988 (*FBIS*).
8. *Damascus Domestic Service*, 14 April 1988 (*FBIS*).
9. *Damascus Domestic Service*, 9 July 1988 (*FBIS*).
10. *Damascus Domestic Service*, 14 July 1988 (*FBIS*).
11. *al-Thawra* (Damascus), 11 August 1988 (*FBIS*).
12. Jim Muir, "The divide with Syria widens," *Middle East International*, 18 November 1988, pp. 4-5.
13. Jim Muir, "The Arab states in solid support of the PLO," *Middle East International*, 2 December 1988, p. 5.
14. Nasrallah, "Syria pays the price of isolation," pp. 17-18.
15. *Agence France Presse* (Paris), 17 November 1987 (*FBIS*).
16. *Radio Free Lebanon*, 13 December 1987; *Voice of Lebanon*, 12, 13 December 1987; *Radio Free Lebanon*, 18 December 1987 (*FBIS*).
17. *Radio Free Lebanon*, 19, 20 December 1987 (*FBIS*).
18. *Voice of Lebanon*, 21 December 1987 (*FBIS*).
19. *Radio Free Lebanon*, 25 December 1987 (*FBIS*).
20. *Radio Free Lebanon*, 28, 30 December 1987; 5, 6, 17 January 1988; 13, 16 February 1988 (*FBIS*).
21. *Beirut Domestic Service*, 26, 27, 28, 30 November 1987 (*FBIS*).
22. *Beirut Domestic Service*, 12, 28, 29 December 1987; *Voice of Lebanon*, 14 December 1987; *Radio Free Lebanon*, 14 December 1987 (*FBIS*).
23. *Voice of National Resistance*, 1 January 1988; *Voice of Lebanon*, 1, 3 January 1988; *Beirut Domestic Service*, 3 January 1988; *Radio Free Lebanon*, 2, 4 January 1988; *Agence France Presse*, 2 January 1988 (*FBIS*).
24. *Jerusalem Domestic Service*, 3 January 1988 (*FBIS*).
25. Jim Muir, "The end of the 'camps war'?" *Middle East International*, 23 January 1988, pp. 10-11.
26. Safa Haeri, "Montazeri's plans for Lebanon," *Middle East International*, 5 March 1988, pp. 13-14.
27. Rashid Hassan, "The PLO's return to the Lebanese equation," *Middle East International*, 6 February 1987, p. 18.
28. Lamis Andoni, "The 18th PNC: no to US, yes to the USSR," *Middle East International*, 1 May 1987, pp. 3-4.

29. *Radio Monte Carlo*, 14, 16 November 1987 (*FBIS*).

30. *Voice of Lebanon*, 3 December 1987 (*FBIS*).

31. *WAKH* (Manama), 29 December 1987 (*FBIS*).

32. *SANA* (Damascus), 24 April 1988; *Damascus Domestic Service*, 25 April 1988 (*FBIS*).

33. *Jordan Times* (Amman), 24 April 1988 (*FBIS*).

34. *Radio Monte Carlo*, 27 April 1988 (*FBIS*).

35. *WAKH* (Manama), 1 May 1988 (*FBIS*).

36. Lamis Andoni, "PLO and Syria alter the political map," *Middle East International*, 30 April 1988, p. 3.

37. *Radio Monte Carlo*, 2 May 1988; *Voice of Lebanon*, 3, 4 May 1988; *Beirut Domestic Service* 3, 4 May 1988; *Voice of the Mountain*, 3, 4 May 1988; *Agence France Presse*, 4 May 1988 (*FBIS*).

38. *Radio Free Lebanon*, 5 May 1988 (*FBIS*).

39. *Voice of Lebanon*, 25 May 1988; *Beirut Domestic Service*, 25 May 1988 (*FBIS*).

40. Daoud Kuttab, "Next phase, civil disobedience," *Middle East International*, 11 June 1988, pp. 6-8.

41. *Radio Monte Carlo*, 28 June 1988 (*FBIS*).

42. *INA* (Baghdad), 1 July 1988 (*FBIS*).

43. *INA* (Baghdad), 14 July 1988 (*FBIS*).

44. *Damascus Domestic Service*, 17, 18 July 1988 (*FBIS*).

45. *Damascus Domestic Service*, 17 August 1988 (*FBIS*).

46. Laurie A. Brand, *Palestinians in the Arab World: Institution Building and the Search for State* (New York: Columbia University Press, 1988), p. 28.

47. Daoud Kuttab, "Plans for an independent Palestine," *Middle East International*, 26 August 1988, p. 3.

48. Lamis Andoni, "The PLO's thinking," *Middle East International*, 26 August 1988, p. 4.

49. Lamis Andoni, "Arafat turns to Europe as the PLO debate continues," *Middle East International*, 23 September 1988, pp. 5-6.

50. Godfrey Jensen, "Lebanon: Hanging together--just," *Middle East International*, 4 November 1988, pp. 6-7.

51. Jim Muir, "The divide with Syria widens," *Middle East International*, 18 November 1988, p. 4.

52. Jim Muir, "Lebanon set to plunge over the brink," *Middle East International*, 23 September 1988, p. 4.

53. Lamis Andoni, "Criticism of the boss," *Middle East International*, 12 May 1989, p. 5.

54. Jim Muir, "The fuse burns short," *Middle East International*, 26 May 1989, p. 12.

55. Youssef M. Ibrahim, "Arab Conference is Split by Syria," *New York Times*, 26 May 1989, p. 1.

56. Daoud Kuttab, "Glimmer of hope amid the gloom," *Middle East International*, 22 September 1989, pp. 7-9.

57. Jim Muir, "The imperative of removing Aoun," and Godfrey Jensen, "Syria and Iran: The glue is thinning," *Middle East International*, 17 Novemer 1989, pp. 4-6.

58. Jim Muir, "Can Hrawi and Syria get rid of Aoun?" *Middle East International*, 1 December 1989, pp. 3-5; Jim Muir, "Lebanon: Tantalising stand-off," *Middle East International*, 15 December 1989, pp. 7-8.

59. *SANA*, 7 December 1989 (*FBIS*).

60. *New York Times*, 24 December 1989; Muir, "Can Hrawi and Syria get rid of Aoun?"

PART THREE

The Superpowers

Within the broader international community, the Palestinian *intifada* has had two substantial effects. At one level, the uprising has had a significant impact on public perceptions of the Palestinian issue, especially in the West.[1] At another level, the uprising has also demonstrated the instability and cost of the status quo of occupation, in both human and political terms.

The diplomatic results have been significant. The European Community, for example, welcomed the resolutions adopted by the 19th session of the Palestine National Council in November 1988. During their July 1989 summit in Madrid, leaders of the twelve EC members appealed to Israel to "put an end to repressive measures." They also called for a negotiated political settlement, with PLO participation, which would respect both Israel's right to live within secure borders and the Palestinians' "right to self-determination, with all that this implies."[2] Nordic foreign ministers have expressed concern over "the repressive measures of the Israeli authorities" and called for "direct contacts between Israel and the PLO."[3] Several European countries joined the many Arab, Africa, Asian and Latin American states that formally recognized the state of Palestine declared by the 19th PNC.[4] Canada—once one of Israel's strongest supporters, as evidenced by its past United Nations voting record—has upgraded its contacts with the PLO, condemned Israeli human rights abuses, and expressed support (for the first time) for the principle of Palestinian self-determination.[5] Even the democratizing countries of Eastern Europe, although reducing political and material support for the PLO and strengthening diplomatic relations with Israel (severed in 1967), have shown no indication that they intend to reverse their previous positions in support of Palestinian statehood. In the General Assembly of the United Nations, resolutions critical of Israeli actions in the West Bank and Gaza have passed with overwhelming majorities.[6]

All this suggests that the global impact of the *intifada*, like its regional repercussions, has been substantial. International sympathy has encouraged Palestinians in their quest for self-determination, while growing political isolation has been another cost Israel faces as a consequence of the *intifada*. Still, one should be careful not to exaggerate the significance of international reaction. The attitudes of Western and Eastern Europe, of Canada, or of much of the third world, have only a limited impact in shaping the dynamics of the contemporary Palestinian-Israeli or Arab-Israeli conflict. It is, more than any other external actors, the superpowers—the Soviet Union and especially the United States—that can affect patterns of regional interaction, influencing processes of both conflict and negotiation.

Global Dimensions of the Palestinian-Israeli Conflict

The current and potential role of the superpowers is a reflection of the long internationalization of the Palestinian-Israeli conflict. In fact, the conflict has been internationalized virtually from its outset. With the Balfour Declaration of November 1917 and during the subsequent Mandate period, Britain helped shape the initial Palestinian-Zionist confrontation. In 1947 the United Nations proposed a partition plan, with the US and USSR acting as midwives at Israel's birth.

As the old European colonial order collapsed in the 1950s and 1960s (its passing marked by France and Britain's abortive Suez adventure in 1956), the United States stepped into the breach to bolster Western hegemony and safeguard access to Middle Eastern oil supplies. The Soviet Union too extended its influence in the region. The Middle East thus became another important geostrategic arena for global superpower competition, with each backing its own local clients. The US backed Israel and conservative Arab states, while the Soviet Union (from the time of the 1955 Czech-Egyptian arms deal) supported Nasir's Egypt, and Ba'thist Syria and Iraq. With the "oil shocks" of 1973-74 and 1979 (and again with the Gulf crisis of 1990) the Middle East gained even greater strategic significance, as "energy security" entered the lexicon of governments around the world. This global dimension has also been reinforced by the escalatory potential of regional inter-state conflict, a danger evidenced by the US nuclear alert at the time of the October 1973 Arab-Israeli war; by Israel's possession of a sizable arsenal of nuclear weapons; and by the more recent regional proliferation of chemical weapons, ballistic missiles, and other strategic delivery systems.

It is important to note, however, that the internationalization of the conflict has been driven not only by external intervention, but also by the actions of the principal local adversaries. Each has regularly sought outside political and material assistance. Before 1948, the Zionist movement sought the backing of Western powers; since its birth, Israel has looked to the United States for moral, economic and military support. As Fred Khouri observes, Israeli decision-makers have also made a deliberate effort to cement this relationship through a complex web of ties. In the early 1970s, Israel sought to integrate itself into US post-Vietnam strategy (then emerging as the Nixon doctrine) as a major regional ally—a status it successfully achieved thanks largely to its threats of intervention against Syria in the 1970 Jordanian civil war. In the 1980s under the Reagan administration, cooperation was entrenched still further with a formal strategic cooperation agreement and a vast network of bilateral ties at all levels of government.

For conservative Arab states like Jordan and Saudi Arabia, Israel's relationship with Washington has long presented complications for their own relations with the US. Others—Egypt under Nasir, and Syria in its continuing drive to achieve "strategic parity" with Israel—have sought to offset Israel's close ties to the West (and to the US in particular) by looking to the Soviet Union for counter-balancing support.

The scope of such superpower support for regional actors has been massive by any measure. US aid to Israel, for example, now totals some $3 billion per year. Egypt, once the recipient of significant quantities of Soviet aid, is now (in the context of its continuing problems of foreign debt) heavily dependent on the roughly $1.3 billion in economic aid it receives annually from Washington. The United States and other Western countries have been the major arms suppliers to Saudi Arabia, Jordan, and the Gulf countries. The Soviet Union, on the other hand, has been the major source of Syrian and Iraqi arms purchases and has provided significant numbers of military advisors for both armed forces.

The extent of external support, however, may overstate the influence that the superpowers might realistically exert on these or other states in the region. The United States, for example, has generally not exerted the degree of sustained influence over Israel one might expect— despite the even larger amounts of aid it supplies. The primary reason for this has been the political weight of Washington's pro-Israel lobby and the consequent constraints of US domestic politics, which have often aborted any American attempt to exert real pressure on the Jewish state. Soviet power has, if anything, been even less resilient. In Egypt, Moscow's influence proved negligible in the face of Sadat's realignment of Egyptian foreign policy in the mid-1970s. In the case of Syria, Soviet displeasure had no effect on Syrian intervention in Lebanon in 1976, nor on its conflict with the mainstream PLO after 1983. Equally, the USSR was unable to prevent either Baghdad's 1980 attack on Iran or its invasion of Kuwait a decade later.

It would be a mistake, therefore, to assume that external actors can provide externally-imposed solutions to the Palestinian-Israeli and Arab-Israeli conflicts. Quite apart from the objective limits to their ability to do so, initiatives that do not enjoy the participation and support of the parties most directly concerned are unlikely to prove enduring. Where the intervention of external actors (or more specifically, the United States) has proven critical, however, is in shaping the process of conflict resolution by providing an appropriate forum for the necessary negotiations while sustaining a political environment conducive to a settlement.

The Intifada, *the Superpowers and Conflict Resolution*

Of the two superpowers, it is of course the United States that has so far played the major role in Arab-Israeli negotiations. In recent decades alone, the US has launched the Rogers plan, bringing the War of Attrition to an end; dominated both the ill-fated Geneva peace conference and the Arab-Israeli disengagement agreements that followed the October 1973 war; mediated the Camp David accords and the Egyptian-Israeli peace treaty; and suggested other Arab-Israeli negotiating initiatives. In past Arab-Israeli diplomacy the modalities, framework and even outcome of negotiations has been heavily influenced by the US. And, as the evolution of the Shamir/Mubarak/Baker plan through 1989-90 clearly demonstrated, this continues to remain true in the era of the *intifada*.

Fred Khouri suggests, however, that US efforts at a resolution of the Palestine question have been marred by serious weaknesses. Successive US administrations, he asserts, have failed to pursue the objective of Middle East peace with foresight and determination. The US has been unwilling to place sufficient pressures on Israel to budge it from hardline positions; on the contrary, unconditional support has tended to inhibit Israeli concessions. Washington has been equally unwilling to prepare the ground at home in such a way as to weaken the domestic political constraints that deter the US from exerting such pressure. Finally, the US has tended to overlook the legitimate interests and concerns of the Palestinians, of other Arab states, and of the Soviet Union.

The net result, he concludes, has been detrimental to both US interests and regional conflict resolution. Moreover, it is a pattern which has generally continued despite the *intifada*. The uprising did generate somewhat greater sympathy for the Palestinian within US public opinion. Washington opened (but later suspended) a direct dialogue with the PLO. Both President Bush and Secretary of State Baker have been more outspoken than many of their predecessors on aspects of the Palestinian-Israeli conflict. Nonetheless, Khouri argues, they have generally failed to pursue energetically the political opportunities created by the uprising. Domestic factors—specifically, the influence of the pro-Israeli lobby on Capitol Hill—have again played a major role in this.

One aspect of American policy that Khouri criticizes is Washington's continued reluctance to endorse an international peace conference. In the past (notably at Camp David) the US has sought to exclude the USSR and its regional allies from Middle East conflict resolution. It remains wary of any arrangement that might dilute its centrality in the peace process.

Such efforts have done little, of course, to encourage Soviet support for past US-dominated peace efforts. This is not to say that the USSR has favored continuation of the conflict; on the contrary, Moscow long ago declared its acceptance of pre-1967 Israel, and has frequently acted to restrain local clients (a constant complaint of Sadat through the 1970s) or to put gentle pressure on the PLO. But, at the same time, viewed through the prism of East-West tensions, Moscow has also had every incentive to bolster local opponents of a potential Middle East *pax Americana*.

Still, as Tamar Weinstein observes, Soviet attitudes to Middle East conflict resolution have changed significantly in recent years. She further suggests that "new thinking" in Soviet foreign policy has played the major role in bringing such changes to the Soviet position towards the Palestinian-Israeli and Arab-Israeli conflicts. In other words, this shift has been primarily the consequence of internal developments: Mikhail Gorbachev's domestic program of *glasnost* and *perestroika*, and Moscow's consequent desire to reduce the economic costs associated with East-West tension and regional conflict. As a consequence of this, the USSR has cautiously reestablished some of the diplomatic links with Israel frozen after 1967—although reestablishment of full relations appears to have been made contingent on Israeli willingness to negotiate with the Palestinians and its Arab neighbors, and on Soviet involvement in the peace process. The USSR now seems to envisage a Middle East settlement as part of a broader process of ameliorating regional tensions through international cooperation. Overall, however, Soviet engagement in the region appears to be on the wane, reflecting the broader decline of its post-Cold War global influence. This in turn has raised considerable concern among Moscow's erstwhile Arab allies about the continued reliability of Soviet support and the apparent consolidation of Western hegemony in the region.

In some respects, the contributors to this section suggest some parallels in the respective reactions of the US and USSR to the *intifada*. In both cases, factors of domestic politics, rather than the Palestinian uprising *per se*, have played the major role in shaping or constraining policy. At the same time, the uprising has underscored in both Washington and Moscow that the unresolved Palestinian-Israeli conflict threatens current and future regional stability. The costs of conflict in this region—a region brimming with growing quantities of sophisticated arms (including chemical and nuclear weapons) and petroleum reserves of vital global economic importance—was further emphasized by the eruption of the Gulf crisis in August 1990.[7]

The magnitude of this latter danger to the global powers would seem to point to the potential importance of East-West cooperation in regional conflict resolution, whether in the form of bilateral US-Soviet coordination or multilateral action through the forum of the United Nations. Already, the late 1980s and early 1990s have seen significant progress toward resolution of a number of protracted regional conflicts, in Asia (Afghanistan, Cambodia), southern Africa (Angola, Namibia) and Central America, not to mention the rapid and generally peaceful transformation of the face of Eastern Europe.

During this period of remarkable thaw in East-West relations, the Palestinian-Israeli and Arab-Israeli conflicts have been largely absent from superpower agendas, a consequence of declining Soviet regional involvement and a residual US desire to exclude the USSR from a major role in any negotiating process. At their historic summit in Helsinki in September 1990, however, Presidents Bush and Gorbachev signaled the possible dawn of a new era of cooperation in the resolution of regional conflict in the Middle East. Certainly the contribution of both superpowers to any Palestinian-Israeli and Arab-Israeli peace process would be critical. While direct attention to Palestinian-Israeli issues through Palestinian-Israeli negotiation is a *sine qua non* of effective Middle East peace-making, it is also essential that other regional concerns be addressed and that any settlement enjoy international guarantees. Indeed, it is difficult to see how a stable solution can be attained and sustained among the principal actors without mediation and effective multilateral endorsement by the superpowers and the rest of the global community.

Notes

1. After August 1990, Western perceptions of Palestinian support for Iraq and its invasion of Kuwait threatened to undo some of the Palestinians' gains in public opinion —particularly in the US. Nonetheless, it is unlikely that the "humanization" of the Palestinian people brought about by the uprising, or the tarnishing of Israel's image caused by its response to the protests, could be completely reversed.

2. EC declaration on the Middle East, 27 June 1989, in *Journal of Palestine Studies* 19, 1 (Autumn 1989): 121-122. In 1988, the European Parliament delayed ratification of several trade treaties with Israel, and in January 1990 it passed a resolution condemning Israel's "increasing repression" and calling for an international peace conference with PLO participation. The following month, the European Commission suspended all scientific cooperation projects with Israel, citing the continued closure of Palestinian universities as a major reason. European Parliament Resolution on Repression in the Israeli-Occupied Territories, 18 January 1990, in *Journal of Palestine Studies* 19, 4 (Summer 1990): 134-136. See also Peretz, *Intifada*, pp. 165-166.

3. Nordic Foreign Ministers' Conference Statement on the Middle East, 7 March 1990, in *Journal of Palestine Studies* 19, 4 (Summer 1990): 150-151.

4. For a list of countries recognizing the state of Palestine, see *WAFA* (Palestine News Agency) 2 February 1989, in *Journal of Palestine Studies* 18, 3 (Spring 1989): 175-176. Other countries (notably France and Italy) have upgraded the diplomatic status of PLO representation but stopped short of full recognition of statehood.

5. On the changes in Canadian policy brought about by the uprising, see: Abdullah Abdullah, "The Policy of Ripples," *The Return* 2, 6 (February 1990): 11-13, 44.

6. Typical of these was UN General Assembly Resolution 44/2 of October 1989 on the "Uprising (*Intifada*) of the Palestinian People," which condemned Israeli practices in the occupied territories. The resolution received 140 votes, with six abstentions (Zaire, Uruguay, El Salvador, St. Vincent and the Grenadines, Antigua and Barbuda, and Grenada) and only two negative votes (the US and Israel). Text in *Journal of Palestine Studies* 19, 2 (Winter 1990): 140-141.

7. It is, of course, too early to predict the full impact of the Gulf conflict on either the superpowers or the Arab-Israeli conflict. The first months of the crisis made it clear, nonetheless, that the conflict is likely to strengthen the US role in regional security, and the intensify US cooperation with its key Arab allies (notably Egypt and Saudi Arabia).

9

Soviet Union

Tamar Weinstein

When the Gaza Strip exploded in demonstrations against Israeli occupation in December 1987, it took the Soviet Union some time to realize that an event of historic significance had occurred. In this respect, of course, the Soviet response was no different from that of the US, Israel—or indeed the Palestinians themselves. A *Tass* dispatch of December 11, two days after the beginning of what would become known as the *intifada*, reported that "some people were killed and dozens wounded" when Israeli troops fired upon "peaceful demonstrations". The press agency condemned such "new reprisals against protesters in the Gaza Strip" as "arbitrary actions by the Israeli aggressors," and proceeded to issue a standard denunciation of "the ruling Zionist clique of Israel":

> The policy of reckless military ventures and territorial expansion against Arab neighbors which is being pursued by Israel, is a challenge to the international public at large, defiance of the basic standards of international law and human rights and open violation of the UN Charter.[1]

On December 20, an *Izvestia* radio report cited the conclusion of "certain West European newspapers" that the occupied territories were "living through the bloodiest days in their history." By December 23, two weeks into the *intifada*, "the uprising of Palestinian Arabs" had been acknowledged, and *Tass* noted a "new element" in the Palestinian "demonstrations," namely, "their size and scope." The following day *Tass* commentator Sergey Medvedko said that "political observers in many countries are unanimous in their assessment of the current developments—never since the June 1967 aggression has terror reached such proportions and intensity on these lands."[2]

As these samples of early coverage suggest, the "story" for Soviet commentators often seemed to be not just the uprising itself, but the fact that *others* felt the demonstrations marked a new and qualitatively different stage

---

This chapter was coauthored with Adam Jones, a graduate research assistant in the Department of Political Science, McGill University.

in the Palestinian struggle, with uncertain but undoubtedly important implications for the Middle East peace process. Such early unwillingness of the Soviet authorities and media to issue decisive statements of their own also seems to have reflected a deeper uncertainty and ambivalence in the Soviet response to the *intifada*.[3]

Such Soviet ambivalence—for which further evidence will be offered later in this chapter—can be traced to the fact that the uprising began at a sensitive and in many ways inconvenient time for Soviet Middle East policy. Two-and-a-half years into the Gorbachev administration, the stage was set for the profound re-evaluation of Soviet foreign policy that would culminate in a new era of superpower cooperation. As one of the most volatile areas of tension in the world, and the one most likely to spark a military confrontation between the superpowers, the Middle East would clearly play a central role in the emerging Soviet policy.

At the time the *intifada* began, the Soviet Union's policy in the Middle East was focussed on three key areas: a resolution of outstanding problems with key countries of the Arab world (particularly Egypt); the Iran-Iraq conflict and possibilities for Soviet mediation; and finally a gradual and partial normalization of relations with Israel that would increase the role of the USSR in the Middle East peace process. As a result—as the British journalist Martin Walker has pointed out—the USSR was "in the ungainly position of a juggler who already has three balls in the air at once, when suddenly one more is thrown at him"—that is, the *intifada*. Walker quotes the statement of a veteran Arab diplomat, early in 1988:

> Moscow has simply not yet got its act together. Everybody was surprised by the Palestinian uprising but the USSR is taking longer to adapt than most countries. It is the traditional Soviet problem. Once they have a plan, they find it very hard to modify it when circumstances change.[4]

It is not immediately obvious why this should be the case. After all, the USSR had long presented itself as an energetic and devoted great-power supporter of Palestinian nationalism, and a strong critic of Israeli "oppression" and "expansionism." The *intifada* thrust the Palestinian question to the forefront of debate on the Middle East. In the pre-Gorbachev era, it might well have presented the Soviet regime with an historic opportunity to increase its influence in the region, as its Palestinian allies scored victories of considerable symbolic significance. Why was this not the case under Mikhail Gorbachev?

An understanding of the new Soviet policy in the Middle East, particularly since December 1987, must begin with the recognition that, now more than ever, Soviet foreign policy reflects and is subordinated to shifting configurations of domestic political power. Middle East policy emerges, of course, in the light of various opportunities and constraints presented by developments in the region itself. But while it can be difficult in any given case to gauge how much weight should be accorded either variable, there can be no doubt that Soviet *regional* policy arises primarily from the requirements of Gorbachev's *domestic* agenda—that is, the policies of *glasnost* and *perestroika*, with their focus on economic and political reform within the USSR itself.

The Soviet response to the *intifada* must also be seen in the broader context of Soviet regional policy, and the "New Thinking" that has reshaped it. The more ambivalent aspects of the response can be explained in terms of the USSR's desire to dissociate itself from excessively partisan positions in order to both expand its regional role and enlarge the area of common interests between itself and the wider international community, particularly the United States. In turn, such objectives are intimately tied to the need to foster international conditions which maximize *perestroika*'s chances for domestic success.

It is thus Soviet "New Thinking," more so than than regional developments in the Middle East, that has served to reshape Soviet Middle East policy. To understand the extent and direction the changes it has wrought, it is necessary to first consider the course of Soviet Middle East policy prior to Mikhail Gorbachev's ascent.

Old Directions in Soviet Policy

On June 10, 1967, hours before the war between Israel and the neighboring Arab states ended, the Soviet government severed diplomatic relations with Israel.

The Soviet move was unprecedented.[5] Never before had Moscow severed ties with states whose policies it condemned. This diplomatic impasse, however, did not lead to a withdrawal of Soviet recognition of the legitimate right of Israel to exist—a right the Soviet Union had supported ever since the 1947 United Nations decision to establish a Jewish state. It did, though, place the Soviet Union at a disadvantage in terms of its mediating role in the Arab-Israeli conflict, especially vis-à-vis the United States. The breaking of ties with Israel signaled the beginning of a steady decline of Soviet influence in the Middle East.

The Soviet disadvantage as conflict mediator in the Middle East was suggested most vividly by its inability to secure Israeli support—and on occasion even Arab support—for its peace plans. The Soviet plans of the late 1960s and 1970s were based on the USSR's interpretation of United Nations Security Council resolutions 242 and 338, which emphasized "respect for and acknowledgement of the sovereignty, territorial integrity and political independence of every state in the area and their right to live in peace with recognized boundaries free from threats or acts of force," Israeli withdrawal "from territories occupied in recent conflicts" and direct negotiations "under appropriate auspices." Soviet peace proposals called on

Israel to withdraw from all territories occupied during the 1967, and urged UN mediation of the conflict, either through special representatives or under the auspices of the permanent members of the Security Council.

The USSR, of course, was one of the permanent members of the Council, and this partly accounts for the emphasis which Soviet policymakers placed on the UN role during these years. But the Soviet strategy was also consistent with Arab opposition to direct negotiations with Israel. Israel, meanwhile, sought direct talks with the Arab states, and thus objected to all Soviet peace initiatives. The Israeli position was supported by the United States, which viewed Soviet strategy as a transparent attempt to compensate for their disadvantage as mediators by manipulating the forum of the United Nations.

The Soviet disadvantage was also made painfully clear by the USSR's inability to match the more practical political steps which the US took to decrease tensions in the Middle East. The most famous example of this came in 1973, while the Soviet Union was working to organize the Geneva conference—the first Arab-Israeli peace conference aimed at reaching a comprehensive solution to the conflict. While the USSR pulled strings in Geneva, the United States took on the flamboyant role of regional broker, with Secretary of State Henry Kissinger engaging in highly visible "shuttle diplomacy" between Egypt, Syria and Israel. Following Kissinger's mediation, the conflicting parties came to an agreement on the disengagement of military forces. While the Americans claimed their efforts respected the Geneva framework, it seemed the US brand of go-it-alone, incremental diplomacy was upstaging Soviet attempts to construct a more comprehensive framework for negotiations.[6] The Soviet approach was further undermined when Anwar Sadat seized the initiative with his visit to Jerusalem in November 1977. Given that the Sadat initiative bolstered the step-by-step approach to peace which had come to dominate Israeli-Egyptian negotiations, it was hardly surprising that the American government was once again invited to play broker in the process which led to the Camp David Accords of September 1978.

An evaluation by Soviet policymakers of the USSR's failure in the Middle East paved the way for many key elements of the policy which emerged under Mikhail Gorbachev. There is no doubt that the lack of diplomatic relations with a central Middle East actor—Israel—was seen as a major drawback. Even more important was the declining political influence of the Soviets vis-à-vis particular states in the region.

As noted earlier, Egypt had long been a key Soviet ally in the region. During the period between 1955 and the end of 1973 the Soviet Union invested three billion dollars in military aid to Egypt.[7] Most of this aid was given as long-term loans at low interest-rates. However, this military aid did not help Egypt win the 1967 or 1973 wars against Israel. Consequently, President Anwar Sadat of Egypt had begun looking for alternative ways of regaining lost Egyptian territories from Israel. The Americans stepped in, and from late 1973, Soviet-Egyptian relations followed a steep downward trajectory.

Syria also received arms from the Soviet Union and, following the Soviet-Egyptian rift, became the USSR's closest ally in the Middle East. But by 1976, strains in this relationship also became evident as the Soviets came to grips with the fact that they had virtually no control over the actions of their client.[8] In 1976, Moscow was unable to dissuade Syria from its military intervention against the PLO and Lebanese National Movement in Lebanon. Later, Soviet imprecations did not succeed in swaying Syrian President Hafiz al-Asad from his hostile stance toward PLO Chairman Yasir 'Arafat. Syria offered important diplomatic and military support for Iran's Ayatollah Khomeini in the Iran-Iraq war, despite growing Soviet unease and attempts to mediate an end to the conflict. And because of its alliances with states like Syria (or Libya)—in turn allied with extremist Palestinian factions—the USSR found itself increasingly depicted as a supporter of radical rejectionist elements in the Middle East conflict.

The USSR and the Palestinians

Until 1967, the Soviets had viewed the Palestinian problem primarily as a refugee problem. After the 1967 war and the occupation of Palestinian lands in the West Bank and Gaza, the issue became territorial. At this early stage, the Soviet Union supported Palestinian armed struggle in the occupied territories, but it also stressed accommodation with Israel. Because the USSR had never rescinded its recognition of Israel's right to exist, Moscow criticized the preference of most organizations within the PLO for a joint Jewish-Arab Palestine. In the Soviet view, this could only be achieved by liquidating Israel.

By the mid-1970s steps had been taken by the Palestinian National Council (PNC) to modify Palestinian demands. From 1974 onward a two-state solution slowly became the foundation of PLO policy. Welcoming this new moderation, and perhaps sensing a chance to seize some of the outside-mediator's spotlight from the United States, the USSR moved closer to the Palestinians and stepped up its international campaign for Palestinian national rights.[9] For their part, the Palestinians felt excluded from the mediating process negotiated between Israel, Egypt, and Syria; they were glad to have a partisan USSR as an ally and guarantor of their interests as attempts at conflict resolution proceeded.

It is not surprising, then, that when the Soviets determined in 1975 to reconvene the Geneva conference, they stressed the importance of the Palestinians to the regional peace process. Ever since—and continuing through to the period of the *intifada*—the indispensability of Palestinian representation has been a constant theme in Soviet proposals. It is worth noting, however, that the Soviet position (then, as now) could give rise to revealing ambiguities on specific issues of Palestinian participation. In January 1976, for example, the Soviets stressed that the PLO must participate in the Geneva conference from the beginning of the sessions and enjoy an equal footing with other delegations. One month later, the Soviets had altered their stance: the PLO might participate in the second, substantial stage of the conference but be excluded for the duration of the first, organizational stage. It further transpired that the Soviets were willing to accept PLO participation in the form of a joint Arab delegation.

These ambiguities reflected deeper inconsistencies in Soviet perceptions of a solution to the Palestinian problem. In general, Soviet peace proposals from the mid-1970s called for the satisfaction of the "legitimate rights" of the Palestinians, including the right to a separate state in the territories specified by UN resolutions 242 and 338 (i.e., the West Bank and Gaza Strip). But whenever the possibility of an international conference seemed closer to being realized, the Soviets proved more than willing to modify these demands. In September 1976, for example, Soviet Foreign Minister Andrei Gromyko was quoted as saying to President Carter: "If we can just establish a miniature state for the Palestinians as big as a pencil eraser, this will lead to a resolution of the PLO problem."[10] During the same period, high ranking Soviet officials such as Anatoli Dobrynin, the Soviet Ambassador to the United States, even expressed their willingness to drop the Soviet demand for a Palestinian state altogether. In October 1977, the US and USSR issued a joint communique calling only for "insuring the legitimate rights of the Palestinian people." Meanwhile, Soviet commentators suggested that a Palestinian-Jordanian confederation be considered as a viable solution to the Palestinian problem.[11]

Officially, however, the Soviets remained committed to Palestinian nationalism. Soviet criticism of the Camp David accords centered on the Accords' failure to provide a comprehensive solution which would allow for the establishment of a Palestinian state. (They also opposed the accord because it excluded the USSR from the Middle East negotiating process.) In February 1981, at the Twenty-sixth Congress of the Communist Party, Leonid Brezhnev once again called for an international conference to resolve the Arab-Israeli conflict. At the same time, however, the Soviets were unsuccessful in getting the PLO chairman to endorse their Geneva formula and their own position on a settlement of the Arab-Israeli conflict. Most important, Yasir 'Arafat refused to recognize the right of the Israeli state to exist without Israeli and American recognition of the Palestinian right of self-determination.[12]

The Lebanon war of 1982 cast the deficiencies of Soviet Middle East policy into sharp relief. In this war as in the 1967 and 1973 conflicts, Soviet weaponry and training proved ineffective. And when it came to negotiating an end to the fighting, Soviet leverage seemed more limited than ever. In

July-August 1982, the Soviets could only stand by while American negotiator Philip Habib arranged for the departure from Beirut of the PLO leadership and personnel. In September, Soviet leader Leonid Brezhnev announced a new Soviet Middle East peace plan, only to see it overshadowed by two other Arab-Israeli initiatives announced earlier that month by the US and the Arab League.

New Directions in Soviet Policy

After coming to power in March 1985, Mikhail Gorbachev spurred major revisions of the Soviet approach to foreign affairs. This critical assessment of foreign policy was stimulated, in part, by a perception that past Soviet policies (especially those of the late Brezhnev years) had proved weak and ineffective in advancing Soviet interests. In particular, there had been a disproportionate emphasis on military solutions to political problems, and the excessive rigidity of Soviet diplomacy had led to the marginalization of the USSR within the international arena.

In practical terms, Gorbachev's "New Thinking" has meant that Soviet policy makers have become more flexible, more ready to compromise and more inclined to cooperate with the international community. Recent years have seen declining tensions in many areas of global and regional conflict, in part because of Soviet initiatives and interest. Among these have been the abolition of intermediate-range nuclear forces under the INF treaty; the delineation of the Sino-Soviet border on the Amur river and an impending agreement on Sino-Soviet troop reductions along the common boundary; the Iran-Iraq ceasefire; and the Soviet withdrawal from Afghanistan.

The Soviet role in the Middle East peace process has not been untouched by these developments. "Much has changed," stated B.N. Chaplin, USSR Deputy Minister of Foreign Affairs, in December 1988:

> We have changed, and the attitude toward us abroad has changed. The new thinking that the Soviet leadership has proclaimed in international affairs is bearing real fruit. In the world today… the norms of civilized intercourse among states must gain an increasingly firm foothold.[13]

Chaplin spoke in the aftermath of the hijacking of a Soviet jet to Israel. In a striking symbol of the growing rapprochement between the USSR and the Jewish state, Israeli authorities had arrested the hijackers and returned them to the USSR to stand trial.

The moves toward normalization of relations with Israel represent only one Soviet regional initiative among many. The Soviets have also become increasingly flexible in their relations with moderate Arab states like Jordan. And there is now a greater Soviet willingness to air differences with allies such as Syria over sensitive issues like terrorism, political ties with Israel, and military and political strategy.

The Soviet Union and Israel

Mikhail Gorbachev's first Middle East initiative, after taking power in March 1985, was to approve a series of informal meetings in Paris and Washington between the Israeli and Soviet ambassadors. A year later, Israel's Prime Minister Shimon Peres and Soviet Foreign Minister Eduard Shevardnadze met at the United Nations. Further contacts followed. Perhaps the most significant meeting took place in Cairo in February 1989 between Shevardnadze and the Israeli Foreign Minister, Moshe Arens. The two agreed that the Arab-Israeli conflict had negative implications for international peace and that dialogue on the Middle East should continue at various levels. For example, they agreed that groups of Middle East experts should meet to exchange information and assess the prospects for a peaceful solution of the conflict in the near future.[14]

As is sometimes the case in diplomacy, what was said in these meetings was less important than the mere fact of conversation and communication. But improvements in Soviet-Israeli relations have not stalled at the rhetorical level. The Soviets and East Europeans have eased restrictions for Israeli tourists. The USSR has lifted its cultural boycott of Israel. Performing art troupes have toured Israel; at the same time, Soviet journalists have visited Israel, and Israeli journalists have been given permission to travel to and report from the Soviet Union. These events have been accompanied by the release of almost all Soviet Jews imprisoned for Jewish activism, most notably Anatoly (Nathan) Sharansky, and by an increase in the number of Jews permitted to leave the country. Two of the most important symbols of the new rapprochement were the Israeli response to the hijacking of a Soviet jet to Israel, mentioned earlier, and the Israeli contribution of a medical team in the aftermath of the horrific Armenian earthquake in early 1989.

The treatment of Israel and the Middle East peace process in the Soviet party press has also undergone a major transformation, one which speaks volumes about the impact of "New Thinking" on Soviet perceptions of regional issues and commitments. In early 1987, for example, *Pravda* reported a visit by Yitzhak Shamir to Washington. It referred to the "streams of unctuous encomium" which issued from the visit, and added sarcastically that "the two sides excelled in mutual praise, never tiring of extolling their 'close, special relations'." Another *Pravda* report from early 1987 discussed a "flare-up of anti-Syrian hysteria" as part of a "campaign of blackmail and threats that the forces of imperialism and Zionism have been conducting." This "very insidious conspiracy" was "aimed above all at destabilizing the political situation in the country and at undermining the progressive regime ruling there."[15]

Compare this tone with a *Tass* dispatch two years later assessing the international costs of Israeli policy in the Middle East. "One has to think," wrote *Tass*, that a perception of these costs "will prompt Israel to think about whether it should not make certain adjustments in some aspects of its approach."[16] Among other developments, a much more nuanced analysis of divisions within Israeli society became possible (mirroring the more complex picture of Soviet society which *glasnost* has also spawned). It is even possible to recognize that the previous picture of Israel and its "Zionist clique" was partly the product of Soviet ignorance. "I don't want to pass judgment or prescribe some remedy," an *Izvestia* reporter quoted a Palestinian journalist as saying in April 1988,

> But it seems to me that your country is showing the effects of a dearth of objective information, for your press provides very scant coverage of Israel and the everyday problems facing its citizens. For example, I can't understand why there isn't a single Soviet journalist working in Israel.[17]

Most recently, Soviet-Israeli negotiations have centered on the issue of emigration of Soviet Jews to Israel. Four thousand emigrés arrived in Israel from the USSR in the last two weeks of December 1989 alone. At one point, it was estimated that 230,000 Soviet Jews would settle in Israel in 1990.[18] Arrangements for an "air bridge," however, were disrupted by the furor which arose in the Arab world over settlement of the emigres in the West Bank. Arab protests increased in intensity after Yitzhak Shamir's statement that "for a big immigration, we need a big and strong state," widely interpreted as a call for continued Israeli control over the occupied territories.[19]

Other movement toward normalization of relations has also been evident. In July 1987, a Soviet consular delegation visited Israel—the first since the 1967 war—although the Soviets downplayed its significance to avoid arousing Arab ire. In mid-1988, an Israeli delegation visited the Soviet Union, ostensibly to inspect the Israeli interests section at the Dutch embassy. Soviet approval of the Israeli visit is significant, given that approval was granted as the Palestinian *intifada* was completing its first month, with harsh criticism of Israeli actions the norm among Soviet officials and commentators. This apparent anomaly was widely noted and commented upon in the Arab world.[20] Thereafter, a number of other, higher-ranking, Israeli delegations visited the USSR.

On the issue of normalization, however, the Soviets under Gorbachev are seeking clearly seeking a *quid pro quo* from Israel for the considerable benefits that would accrue to the Jewish state from a resumption of ties. Furthermore, despite the newly knotty relationship between the USSR and more radical actors in the Arab world, a resumption of relations that took place on Israeli terms—with the *intifada* still raging, and with Israel's commitment to control over the occupied territories intact—would be very difficult to justify to traditional Soviet allies. Thus, while the USSR has never succeeded in matching US policy successes in the region, it is not about to risk ties to the Arab world merely to satisfy Israeli demands for full normalization or to curry favor with the United States.

Instead, Moscow has emphasized linkage between normalization and an international peace conference on the Middle East. As Gorbachev put it in a speech during Hafiz al-Asad's April 1987 state visit to Moscow, although "the absence of [Soviet-Israeli] relations cannot be considered normal," any changes in Soviet-Israeli relations "are conceivable only in the mainstream of the process of settlement in the Middle East."[21] In a press conference in June 1988, Gorbachev re-emphasized the Soviet commitment to an international conference:

> We are in favor of having everything decided on the basis of a political settlement, taking into account the interests of all the parties concerned, and, of course, taking into account the fundamental provisions of the relevant UN resolutions.... I will let you in on something else: We said [to the US] that when the conference begins—a normal, effective conference, not just an umbrella for separate talks, but a forum that would be tied in with bilateral, trilateral and other forms of work—we will be ready to take up the question of regularizing diplomatic relations with Israel.[22]

Commenting on Hungary's resumption of diplomatic ties with Israel in September 1989, Soviet Foreign Ministry spokesman Gennady Gerasimov noted that while "the Soviet Union will not object to additional Warsaw Pact countries following in Hungary's footsteps," the USSR itself "continues to link restoration of diplomatic relations with Israel to substantial progress toward peace in the region." Three months later Soviet First Deputy Foreign Minister Yuri Vorontsov echoed the point, asking "as long as Israel refuses to move forward for a real settlement and convening an international conference, what would the meaning of relations be?" Yuri Stern, a spokesman for the Soviet Jewry Information Center, summarizes other important elements of the equation this way: "The Soviets are dragging things out for their own reasons, to minimize the risk in Arab lands, to test the influence on Soviet Jewish nationalism and because it is a problem ideologically after so many years of anti-Israel propaganda."[23]

The USSR has, however, followed with interest the resumption of ties between the newly-independent Warsaw Pact countries and Israel. The emphasis in Soviet statements and media coverage has been on the normalcy of such links, and this doubtless represents an effort to prepare domestic and international opinion for an eventual normalization of relations between the USSR and Israel.

The USSR and the Arab World

Significant changes are also evident in Soviet-Arab relations. Gorbachev's policy toward the Arab states involved directly or indirectly in the conflict with Israel, such as Egypt and Jordan, reflects his desire to increase perceptions of the USSR as a moderate actor capable of playing an objective and constructive role in a regional peace process.

Ever since the mid-1970s, when Soviet-Egyptian relations began to deteriorate, the USSR has worked to repair these ties.[24] The return of a Soviet ambassador to Cairo in 1985 was one of the first foreign policy successes for the Gorbachev regime, and signaled Egyptian receptiveness to the new leadership in the Soviet Union. The years since then have witnessed a series of official exchanges and declarations of goodwill. The most important exchange to date was the visit to Egypt of Soviet Foreign Minister Shevardnadze in February 1989. During his stay in Cairo, the Soviet foreign minister met with the Egyptian President Husni Mubarak, the Deputy Prime Minister Ismat 'Abd al-Meguid and with other high ranking officials. The Egyptian president and Soviet foreign minister agreed on the urgent need to settle the Arab-Israeli conflict, and stated that this could only be accomplished by taking into account the interests of all sides involved.[25] Furthermore, they proposed using the United Nations' peacekeeping apparatus to consult with all concerned parties—all this to prepare the groundwork for an international conference in which the parties would negotiate a peaceful resolution to the Arab-Israeli conflict. The agreement, when combined with the renewed political relations between the two countries, strengthened the potential Soviet position as regional mediator.

The breakthrough in Soviet-Egyptian relations was possible in part because the Soviets agreed to reschedule Egyptian military debts, which now total some three billion dollars. Among other provisions, Moscow granted a six-year grace period and generous terms for subsequent repayment stretched over 19 years.[26] The debt agreement enabled the two countries to sign new economic agreements and hold discussions on a possible resumption of Soviet military supplies to Egypt. Any such supplies, however, would be limited mostly to spare parts for matériel provided during the previous era of close military cooperation. There is no reason to believe Egypt is considering a reorientation away from its current close alliance with the United States.[27]

Soviet relations with Jordan have also improved. In December 1987 King Husayn visited Moscow. The visit took place despite strains that had surfaced in the relationship the year before, when leading Jordanian communists were arrested by Husayn's regime. The Jordanian king had also previously made efforts to arrange talks between the United States and the PLO (an act that clearly could have threatened Soviet involvement in any negotiating process), and then had turned his back on the PLO (a Soviet ally). In Jordan as elsewhere, then, it seems the Gorbachev government is willing to overlook policies it disapproves of in order to ensure smooth relations and increased regional prestige.

The Soviets, however, have a rather more limited interest in Jordan than in Israel or Egypt. Soviet-Jordanian ties have not been significantly diversified since 1985. Still, the warming trend in relations with Jordan has resulted in one important gain for the USSR: Husayn has insisted on the convening of an international conference with Soviet participation. Husayn is apparently seeking to counterbalance the strongly pro-Israel tilt of the United States by strengthening ties with the Soviet Union. This is a tactic which promises to be much less risky for "moderate" Arab leaders like Husayn, now that a suitably flexible and pragmatic leadership has emerged in the USSR.

The Jordanian call for Soviet participation represented an important achievement for Gorbachev's Middle East policy. It is a desire to preserve these gains which largely accounts for the initial ambiguity of Soviet policy statements concerning PLO representation at an international conference. In 1987, the Soviets suggested that Palestinian representation could come in the form of a joint Palestinian-Jordanian delegation or as part of a wider united delegation. Once again, the Soviets were attempting to convey their new flexibility on important matters of procedure and logistics in the peace process, and to dissociate themselves from past positions which were now seen as overly rigid and unconstructive.[28]

Meanwhile, however, the Soviets were working behind the scenes to mediate the reunification of the major groups of the PLO. From their point of view, a united PLO would be in a better position to negotiate for the Palestinian people. It would also be a positive step toward repairing the schisms among the Arabs in the wider sense, schisms which had caused no end of distress for Soviet policymakers attempting to construct (and oversee) a unified front to compete with the United States' system of alliances in the region. "We are distressed," Gorbachev announced in the presence of Syria's Hafiz al-Asad, "by the disunity, friction and conflicts in the Arab world, which are actively being taken advantage of by the imperialists and their accomplices. Naturally, we have seen the efforts currently being made to restore the unity of the Palestine Liberation Organization as a good sign." But when the Soviets put pressure on the Syrians to approve the inclusion of Syrian-backed factions of the PLO, they failed. At this stage, the importance of the Syrian-Soviet alliance was such that the USSR pressed no further.[29]

The new Soviet emphasis on moderation and accommodation was also evident during and after a meeting held between Gorbachev and PLO chief Yasir 'Arafat in April 1988. During 'Arafat's visit, Gorbachev urged the PLO to endorse publicly United Nations resolutions 242 and 338, and emphasized the need to take into account Israel's security needs. This pressure may have been a factor, though surely not a decisive one, in the PLO's subsequent decision to recognize Israel's right to exist, and in 'Arafat's call for Palestinian-Israeli talks within the framework of an international conference. Whatever the importance of Soviet pressure, the USSR welcomed the declarations made by the PLO in Algiers and Geneva. The Soviet Foreign Ministry referred to the various resolutions as "permeated with [a] keen sense of realism and responsibility" and "a major contribution to the process of fair political settlement in the Middle East."[30] Soviet Foreign Minister Shevardnadze elaborated:

> It is clear that the situation in the Middle East has changed recently. Preparations are underway to begin settling this conflict which is apparently the oldest and most difficult regional conflict. The credit for these [preparations] goes mainly to the peaceful Palestinian uprising and the realistic and constructive attitude of the Palestine Liberation Organization. By recognizing Security Council Resolution 242, affirming its readiness to open a dialogue with with Israel and its denunciation of terrorism in all its forms, the PLO has proved that it is a serious party to the peace talks. Now Israel or any other faction no longer has any pretext to reject the participation of [the PLO], which represents the Palestinian people, in preparing the convening of an international conference on the Middle East.[31]

The Soviet Union, of course, also recognized the declaration of Palestinian statehood made by the Palestine National Council at its Algiers meeting. Two months later, the USSR announced the upgrading of the PLO's office in Moscow to a full Embassy of Palestine.[32]

The Soviet Union has also worked hard to influence its traditional ally in the region, Syria. The relationship has become increasingly strained: the new Soviet policy in the region has disturbed and displeased the Syrians, while the USSR objects to many of Syria's policies, not only with regard to Israel but also in Lebanon and towards the PLO. The Soviets are unwilling to yield to Syrian demands for strategic parity with Israel, supplying them with a steady stream of military hardware but not with the quantity and quality demanded. And there is little doubt that Gorbachev views the fundamental hostility of Syria toward Israel as an impediment and an anachronism, given the warming trend in regional and global relations. Gorbachev's remark to al-Asad in April 1987 that "reliance on military force has completely lost its credibility as a way of solving the Middle East conflict," and comments made by the Soviet ambassador to Syria in 1989 that were critical of Syria's drive for "strategic parity," suggest the USSR's strong concern with Syria's emphasis on a possible military option against Israel. For his part, al-Asad has reiterated Syria's opposition to "defeatist" approaches and "surrenderist solutions" such as those put forward by the PLO at Algiers and Geneva (and welcomed by the USSR).[33]

These points of disagreement suggest that the Syrians, to some extent, have become a liability for Soviet interests in the Middle East. On the other hand, the Soviets are hardly about to abandon their Syrian allies. Rather, they will work to guide Asad's regime toward more moderate positions, partly because any international conference on Middle East peace would be virtually pointless without Syrian participation. It is possible that al-Asad's statement to Jimmy Carter in March 1990 (asserting that Syria might be willing to come to terms with Israel on the basis of a return of the Golan Heights) reflects such Soviet pressure.

In general, the Soviet relationship with Arab players in the Middle East conflict has undergone much the same nuanced re-evaluation as the relationship with Israel. On the whole, the more radical Arab forces have come off exceedingly poorly as a result.

Once again, the re-evaluation process can be discerned in the increasingly complex analysis of the Arab world offered in the Soviet official press. The newly-expanded range of permissible political opinion on Middle East issues is best typified by *Izvestia* correspondent A. Bovin's commentary, "The *Intifada*: What Next?" (August 1989). Bovin argues that the *intifada* showed the situation was stalemated, and calls for "the restoration of diplomatic relations between the USSR and Israel" as one way of helping end the impasse. He also articulates a perception of Arab actions which is markedly less sympathetic than was possible in pre-*glasnost* commentary. He refers to "the ambiguity and equivocation of many [PLO] documents and statements" which lent substance to Israeli charges of Palestinian "insincerity." He criticizes "extremists"—specifically citing a joint Syrian-Iranian statement calling for continued armed struggle—and praises those in the Arab world who "are gradually learning the lessons of history and shifting to more moderate positions."[34]

In December 1988, *Izvestia* political commentator K. Geivandov denounced those Arabs favoring "holy war" against the Israeli state, comparing this approach to the carnage of the Gulf war, which brought "only countless calamities, grief, death, and economic ruin...." An earlier *Izvestia* commentary had noted that the establishment of a Palestinian state, as specified by the UN in 1947, had "yet to be fulfilled, and it must be acknowledged that the leaders of certain Arab states are by no means the least to blame for this." The *Novosti* press agency similarly lamented the fact that "the new thinking which has taken hold in [the] Soviet Union does not unfortunately receive sufficient attention in the Arab world."[35] This tilt in Soviet policy statements and press commentary has been widely noted in the Arab world.[36]

The events in Eastern Europe during 1989 and 1990 have spawned a mixture of distress and resignation among the Soviet Union's traditional allies in the Middle East. The astonishing ease with which the USSR allowed its Eastern European allies to go their own way—together with the very mild Soviet response to the electoral defeat of the Sandinistas in Nicaragua—does not bode well for states and organizations dependent on the USSR for material and diplomatic support. The PLO, for one, has managed to find elements of the new Soviet policy which it believes may work in its favor. Faruq Qaddumi, head of the PLO's Political Department, has argued that "the axis of the two superpowers has come to an end," and that as a result, "Israel has lost much of its strategic importance for the West." Bassam Abu Sharif, a close 'Arafat adviser, has compared the upsurge of popular opposition which deposed the old-style communist regimes of Eastern Europe to the Palestinians' own uprising. "Change is coming because history is moving forward. This is a world where there's no place for colonialism and despotism. Those who broke down the Berlin Wall will break down the [Israeli] occupation."[37] But much of this commentary appears to be a matter of putting the best face on developments which Soviet allies in the Middle East find disturbing and disorienting.

There is a growing recognition that the new trend in Soviet foreign policy is likely to be a lasting one, with the local interests of traditional Soviet allies subordinated to a Soviet policy that is much less reflexive in its support for states and forces which threaten to upset the fruitful equilibrium in superpower relations. It is likely, for example, that key Soviet initiatives such as the move toward normalization of relations with Israel are in large part designed to ease relations with the United States. An end to the economically ruinous Cold War is viewed as absolutely indispensable to the success of economic "restructuring" within the USSR itself. Superpower relations therefore takes precedence over everything else on the Soviet foreign-policy agenda.

This is especially true when movement on a particular issue—the emigration of Soviet Jews—is explicitly tied by the US Congress to the easing of restrictions on American trade with the USSR. No development in Soviet Middle East policy has caused as much outcry in the Arab world as Soviet arrangements for Jewish emigration to Israel. For the Palestinians and the Arab states, the influx of Soviet Jews does not merely present the Israeli government with a new rationale for holding on to the territories. In a wider sense, it threatens to reverse the demographic trend as a result of which the Palestinians, early in the next century, were projected to overtake Jews as a majority of the population in Israel, the West Bank, and Gaza combined.

Thus, a memorandum dispatched to western consuls-general in Jerusalem by Palestinian leaders in the territories protested the settlement of Soviet Jews in the region, calling the policy "a rationalization for Israeli entrenchment, territorial expansion and intransigence [which] will inevitably have disastrous effects on peace in the region." The PLO warned that resettlement of immigrants in the territories was "very dangerous" and could lead the Palestinians to return to a policy of armed struggle. Chadli Klibi, the Arab League's secretary-general, stated in February 1990 that the influx of Soviet Jews could lead to a disaster for the Arab world equal to the founding of Israel itself and the defeat of the Arab states in 1967.[38]

The opposition was so passionate that the USSR chose to back away from establishing a direct air link between Moscow and Tel Aviv. But Arab influence on Soviet foreign policy is likely to be limited, in future, to this kind of holding action. This is even more likely to be the case when one considers that the Arab world has, in Moscow, nothing remotely similar to the efficient and well-established "Israel lobby" in Washington.

In the wider sense, given the revulsion with which the Brezhnev era is now viewed in Gorbachev's USSR, it can hardly help that two of the most egregious foreign policy setbacks of the Brezhnev years—the expulsion of Soviet advisers from Egypt and the military quagmire in Afghanistan—both occurred in the Muslim world. There seems to be a stereotypical perception among many Soviet policymakers, similar to that of their counterparts in the West, that Muslims/Arabs are prone to fratricidal violence and are generally "emotional and unpredictable," in the words of one Soviet specialist.[39] Soviet "New Thinking," of course, places great emphasis on orderliness and predictability, and holds out little hope for old-style rhetorical excess.

Soviet Policy and Regional Conflict Resolution

Changes in Soviet Middle East policy cannot be divorced from the USSR's changing approach to regional conflict resolution. According to Alex Pravda, one significant new trend in Soviet global as well as regional thinking is the emphasis on "the use of political rather than military means to try and resolve conflicts."[40] This trend, he adds, reflects Soviet awareness of the sheer complexity of international problems and, particularly, regional conflicts. A second characteristic that Pravda points to is the apparent desire of the Gorbachev government to collaborate, rather than compete, with the regional and international actors involved in specific conflicts. As he puts it: "The more co-operative attitude displayed towards the United Nations over... the Middle East suggests that Gorbachev may take practical steps to implement his rhetorical commitment to increasing the UN role in the management of international conflicts."

Pravda's view of Soviet New Thinking toward regional problems and, more specifically, the Arab-Israeli conflict is reinforced and elaborated upon by Soviet scholars and commentators. For example, Andrey U. Shoumikhin (head of the US Middle East policy sector of the USSR Academy of Sciences in Moscow) maintains that the Middle East conflict be resolved exclusively through political means by using "international methods and machinery of conflict resolution," recognizing that "no one's security may be attained at the expense of diminished security for others."[41] Due weight should be given to the legitimate interests of the various sides to the conflict and to their choice of "ways and patterns of ... development." If the problems in the Middle East are solved, Shoumikhin contends, the "zero-sum" approach which has dominated international politics and superpower relations since the end of World War Two will be replaced by a more moderate, less competitive environment. In other words, peace in the Middle East could lead to long lasting changes in East-West relations.

In fact, Gorbachev's attempts to improve Soviet political standing vis-à-vis particular states in the Middle East, and his desire to regain a position as mediator in the Arab-Israeli conflict, have been matched by a renewed emphasis on the United Nations as a regulator of political disputes. This became clear in 1987 when the Soviet Union agreed to pay dues owed for United Nations peacekeeping missions—including those in Lebanon and the Golan Heights. The same year, Gorbachev made an eleven-point proposal for reinforcing the status and scope of the United Nations. The specific proposals included the creation of a multilateral body, incorporating the five permanent members of the Security Council, to manage military and political conflicts.

Gorbachev and his advisers have consistently stressed the continuity of basic Soviet policy in the region, in particular the need to convene an international conference. Unlike his predecessors, however, Gorbachev has recognized the need for flexibility on the issue of international (and thus Soviet) involvement in the peace process. Realizing that Israel and the United States had rejected United Nations supervision in the past, the Soviet leader recommended a preparatory meeting to deal with contentious issues, including the question of Palestinian representation. And when this recommendation was not endorsed by the Americans and Israelis, Shevardnadze backed away, stating in Cairo:

> We do not insist on the preparatory committee. It is yet difficult to determine the form of the preparatory process, it will be indicated by the consultations among the sides. The entire process of preparation for an international conference on the Middle East is multiform, but we do not impose anything on anyone.[42]

The Soviets under Gorbachev, then, have consistently demonstrated a desire for a negotiated political solution to the Arab-Israeli conflict. These efforts are the result of the USSR's attempt to increase its political standing in the Middle East, and of Moscow's interest in internationalizing conflicts in order to strengthen its own role in situations from which it has been excluded. A more cynical perspective would suggest that the USSR, in the Middle East as in Central America, Eastern Europe, and Afghanistan, is also looking for solutions that enable it to retreat from tangled and expensive proxy relationships in a way that does not damage its credibility in the Third World (or that brings with it increased prestige in the First World to offset any such damage). Certainly the fear of this possibility is a consuming one for many of the USSR's traditional allies in the region, as we have seen.

While the changes in Soviet Middle East policy under Gorbachev have been considerable and even momentous, there remain significant constraints which so far have prevented the smooth evolution of this policy toward regional consensus, compromise, and conciliation. For one thing, the Middle East itself continues to harbor many uncompromising forces. Syria's government, while dependent on the Soviet Union for arms, pursues policies which often are at loggerheads with Soviet interests and initiatives. In Israel, political fragmentation and confusion are the rule of the day, which favors the status quo forged by Israel's former national unity government. Indeed this, coupled with the formation of a right-wing Likud government under under the hard-line leadership of Prime Minister Yitzhak Shamir in the spring of 1990, strongly mitigates against the convening of the international peace conference favored by the USSR. As well, the Arab world as a whole is badly divided on how (or whether) to bring an end to the ongoing conflict with Israel. This disunity creates difficulties for the Soviets, since their primary interest is to maintain good relations with all Arab states. Despite positive signs from the Soviet Union, then, the future prospects for the region remain unclear.

It will be obvious from this discussion that the new Soviet policy in the Middle East is not an opportunistic response to regional events. Rather, Soviet policy is inextricably tied to the "New Thinking" that has arisen in the Soviet Union—with its primary emphasis on domestic reforms, but a strong international and global component. To predict the future course of Soviet policy, then, it is not enough to outline possible developments in the Middle East region itself: the Soviet stance is not primarily a reactive one, but rather seeks to implement a complex agenda of regional initiatives designed to improve the international climate and permit a greater concentration of material and political resources on domestic problems.

Thus, any attempt to predict the future of Soviet policy must focus on the course of domestic reform under Gorbachev. Here too the future is full of uncertainty. Within the USSR itself, however, the Gorbachev regime has shown a notable willingness to institutionalize its reformist agenda, to an extent that would render much more difficult and complicated any future attempt to dismantle the reform apparatus. Something similar seems to have occurred in the realm of Soviet foreign policy. In an atmosphere now widely touted as "post-Cold War," such basic aspects of the new Soviet foreign policy as the emphasis on negotiations and flexibility of relations with regional powers may well prove to be stable and enduring features. As far as the Middle East is concerned, of course, it remains to be seen how the various other important elements coalesce in the light of regional and global developments. Among these elements is Palestinian nationalism as exemplified by the uprising in the occupied territories. It is this factor, and its relationship to Soviet policy, that we will return to in conclusion.

The Soviet Union and the *Intifada*

Today, the USSR and the Palestinians find themselves in a complex and dynamic relationship, in which the role of each is partly predicated on unusual, far-reaching, and unpredictable transformations in the other. Thus, in seeking to make use of the USSR's longstanding support for their cause, the PLO now must reckon with a Soviet regime which pursues a much less partisan policy in the Middle East than previously—and which is less likely to offer reflexive material and political support for Palestinian initiatives.

For its part, the Soviet Foreign Ministry is confronted with a Palestinian national movement that has finally succeeded in establishing itself as a legitimate actor on the world stage. Through a combination of diplomatic action and unceasing, highly visible resistance in the occupied territories, Palestinian nationalism is now far more than a bargaining chip in the negotiating process; in fact, some form of Palestinian statehood is increasingly perceived as a *sine qua non* for a Middle East settlement.

The irony is that this new Palestinian assertiveness has arisen at a time when the USSR appears more prepared than ever to subordinate its regional involvements and alliance—in the Middle East, Central America, or Eastern Europe—to the wider issue of superpower relations and the emerging Soviet role in a post-Cold War world. The emphasis today, and increasingly, is on a technocratic "global management" that stresses cool thinking, flexibility, and a minimum of inflammatory rhetoric.

Perhaps in an attempt to downplay the uprising's significance, the USSR has, from the start, emphasized the ways in which the *intifada* bolsters key elements of longstanding Soviet policy in the region. Along with other changes in the international environment which have lent new relevance to multilateral negotiations and international institutions, the *intifada* is portrayed as having vindicated the Soviet emphasis on negotiations under UN auspices involving key regional actors and the five permanent members of the UN Security Council.

Among the regional actors who must be represented in negotiations are, of course, the Palestinians. The *intifada* has lent further credence to the USSR's emphasis on Palestinian representation. In the aftermath of the declaration of the Palestinian state at Algiers in November 1988, the Soviet Foreign Ministry commented:

> An essentially new situation is taking shape, one that clears the way for a real breakthrough in achieving a settlement and creates the possibility of convening an international conference on the Middle East for this purpose. The PLO and Arab countries that have been drawn into the conflict are ready for this. Virtually the entire international community, including the UN Security Council's elective and permanent member-states, favors convening the conference. It is common knowledge that the Soviet Union has always championed this idea actively.
>
> The new situation also offers Israel the chance to rethink its position and, by renouncing its former stereotypes, to embark on the path of a joint search for constructive solutions.[43]

This renunciation of "former stereotypes" is a rule of thumb for the current Soviet reformism, both domestically and in the realm of foreign affairs. The *intifada* lends new urgency to the application of this rule in the Middle East. "It is important to grasp without delay the novelty of the situation coming about in the world," stated Soviet Deputy Foreign Minister Vladimir Petrovskiy in the UN debate at Geneva following the PNC declaration at Algiers. Petrovskiy urged other actors to "use [the new situation] to the fullest to overcome the former stereotypes, to progress from rhetoric to calm, businesslike, and well-considered work on building a lasting and just peace in the ancient land of the Near East."[44]

On closer inspection, Petrovskiy's statement offers some interesting insights into the Soviets' ambivalent response to the *intifada*. On the one hand, the uprising has been highly useful in clearing away old preconceptions and stale political formations. It has forced on Israeli society a growing belief that the occupation of the West Bank and Gaza is untenable in the long term. It has also given Palestinian nationalism an unprecedented degree of international credibility. The PLO has been able to undertake initiatives from a position of relative strength, and this has enabled the more moderate factions of the organization to downplay hostile rhetoric and to control the use of terrorism—both of these being weapons of the weak and marginalized. The PLO has thus been able to take explicit steps in the direction of a negotiated peace, one which would likely involve the Soviet Union as mediator and therefore realize one of the key aspirations of Soviet policy in the Middle East.

On the other hand, the *intifada* is anything but "calm and businesslike." It is a convulsion, filled with the kind of tension and confrontation that Soviet policymakers have long associated with the Middle East, and which they increasingly find cause for concern. "Let us be frank," said Soviet Foreign Minister Shevardnadze in Cairo (February 1989):

> There are people who believe that the great powers are not all that annoyed with the unsettled situation in the Middle East.... I would like to say, on behalf of my country, that this is not the case. Convulsions in the Middle East always affect us very strongly. The Soviet people are especially sensitive to everything that happens here, because tension in this region costs us dearly in all respects, including materially.[45]

Despite Shevardnadze's assertion that "It is more likely that the Pyramids will disappear than that the Palestinians will lose their longing for their homeland," it is possible that the USSR would be willing to accept a solution to the Palestinian question which falls short of full independent statehood. This chapter has noted the long history of ambiguous and contradictory Soviet statements on this count. It is a tradition which has continued into the Gorbachev era. A senior Israeli Foreign Ministry official, reporting on meetings with Soviet representatives in May 1988, stated that the Soviet officials "told us an independent Palestinian state is no longer their preferred option. They speak of federation [with Jordan].... They have not written off a Palestinian state but they are not advocating it as the exclusive solution as in the past."[46] This statement may be dismissed as inaccurate or self-serving. But is it realistic to expect that in the new atmosphere of compromise and flexibility, the Soviets would be willing to stake their entire Middle East policy on the attainment of Palestinian statehood? Certainly, if the present Soviet regime is prepared to sit idly by while Eastern Europe is transformed, then most time-honored tenets of Soviet policy must be seen as negotiable, even dispensable.

Given all this, one could be forgiven for wondering how strong is the Soviet commitment to the basic goals of the *intifada*—an end to the Israeli occupation and the realization of Palestinian national aspirations. The official (and usual) view of the *intifada* as an important catalyst for the regional peace process is not, in the era of *glasnost*, necessarily a consensus position among Soviet commentators. This may well reflect the ambivalence in Soviet policy-making circles.

As one indication, consider the broadcast on Moscow Radio Peace and Progress commemorating the second anniversary of the uprising in December 1989. On the matter of the *intifada*, the Soviet commentary revealingly slipped into the past tense: "In our view, the intifada *did fulfill* a certain role.... Both sides must now seek acceptable compromises." It noted further that "In the USSR... there is at present a controversy over the meaning of the *intifada* and its repercussions," with some analysts arguing "that the *intifada* does not advance the peace process and endangers the negotiations for a political settlement." Equally interesting was the fact that the broadcast was in Hebrew, and therefore intended for Israeli public consumption.[47]

Conclusion

This chapter has argued that the "New Thinking" in Soviet foreign policy under Mikhail Gorbachev is primarily a reflection of domestic programs and priorities, in particular the reformist agenda centered around political and economic "restructuring." The most pressing priority for the Soviet Union in the international sphere is an end to the Cold War tensions which had placed immense strain on the national economy. In pursuit of a more stable and cooperative relationship with the United States, the USSR has demonstrated its willingness to radically reorient the structure of its foreign policy. Among other things, it has permitted the transformation of its position in Eastern Europe, and is working toward peaceful resolution of conflicts in which Soviet clients are involved.

In the Middle East, the renewed prospect of international negotiations (in which the USSR would play a key role) has led to a much more moderate policy line which seeks to distance itself from radical actors like Syria and to establish ties with all powers in the region, particularly Israel. Given the global dimensions of the Soviet foreign-policy project, it would be unrealistic to expect that a regional upheaval such as the *intifada* could play a determining role. Rather, the Soviet response to the *intifada* has been to stress the elements of the new situation which appear to bode well for

Soviet policy in general. Officially, Palestinian nationalism is perceived as a *sine qua non* for a regional settlement in the Middle East. But the long-term commitment of the Soviet Union to the Palestinian nationalist agenda remains uncertain. This is especially true given the intimate relationship between the United States and Israel, and the deep and overriding desire of the USSR to preserve its foreign-policy achievements in the area of superpower relations.

Indeed, the Soviet Union's overriding concern with superpower relations seemed likely to only intensify in the wake of Iraq's August 1990 invasion of Kuwait. At a joint press conference with President Bush following a brief summit meeting in Helsinki, Gorbachev restated his views on the new approach to conflict resolution—an approach typified, for him, by the concerted great-power opposition to Iraqi aggression. "The way the world is changing," Gorbachev claimed, "...no single country, however powerful, will be able to provide the leadership which individual countries formerly tried to provide.... We can only succeed if we work together and solve our problems together." The Soviet President explicitly noted the connection between regional crisis and the supreme threat of global conflagration, and claimed that this threat was now considerably diminished:

> The fact that today we have taken a common approach to such difficult problems —[problems] which may well have tragic consequences for the whole world, not just for the peoples of that region—demonstrates that we are still moving forward in the right direction.... We shall find a solution which will be satisfactory and, above all, which will remove the danger of an explosion. And this is becoming a normal element of the new kind of cooperation...[48]

For their part, US officials pronounced themselves "exceptionally pleased with the Soviet role," without which "the whole color of the Gulf problem would be totally different." And, for the first time, the US suggested that it would consider accepting a Soviet role in any Middle East peace conference.[49] Given this apparent victory for Soviet diplomacy—given, too, that the Gulf crisis is widely perceived as having shunted the Palestinian question to the back-burner for some time—it is even more difficult to imagine the USSR investing heavily in the cause of Palestinian nationalism at the expense of their role as partner in an emerging system of great-power global management.

Notes

1. *Tass* (Moscow), 11 December 1987, in *Foreign Broadcast Information Service: Soviet Union* (hereafter, *FBIS*).

2. *Izvestia* (Moscow), 20 December 1987; *Tass*, 23 December 1987; *Tass*, 24 December 1987 (*FBIS*).

3. As late as 13 January 1988, for example, *Tass* seemed to down-play events,

referring only to "the Palestinian actions" and "the rioting in the Israeli-occupied territory." *Tass*, 13 January 1988 (*FBIS*).

4. Martin Walker, "Moscow gets its act together," *Middle East International*, 6 February 1988, p. 6.

5. Most observers of Soviet involvement in the Middle East agree that the Brezhnev government made this decision following Arab criticism of the USSR's passive role during the war. It may be that the formal Soviet break of ties with Israel was meant to appease Syria and Egypt, the two main Soviet allies in the area, who blamed the Soviet Union for refusing to supply aid for the war effort fast enough and also for supplying arms which performed poorly in the war. Galia Golan, "Gorbachev's Middle East Strategy," *Foreign Affairs* 66, 1 (1987): 44. Other analysts contend that the severing of ties was designed to bolster Soviet credibility, which had been badly damaged by Israel's "lightning success." Melvin A. Goodman and Carolyn McGiffert Ekedahl, "Gorbachev's 'New Directions' in the Middle East," *Middle East Journal* 42, 4 (Autumn 1988): 575.

6. Arthur Day Klinghoffer, *Israel and the Soviet Union: Alienation or Reconciliation?* (Boulder: Westview Press, 1985), p. 133.

7. Amnon Sela, *Soviet Political and Military Conduct in the Middle East* (London: MacMillan Press, 1981), p. 105.

8. Klinghoffer, *Israel and the Soviet Union*, p. 158.

9. Klinghoffer, *Israel and the Soviet Union*, p. 150; see also Galia Golan, *The Soviet Union and the Palestine Liberation Organization* (New York: Praeger, 1980).

10. Cited by Klinghoffer, *Israel and the Soviet Union*, p. 164.

11. Text of Joint Communiqué by the US and USSR, 1 October 1977, in *International Documents on Palestine 1977* (Beirut: Institute for Palestine Studies, annual), pp. 255-256; O. Alov, "For a Settlement in the Middle East," *International Affairs* 9 (1977): 67.

12. See, for example, the transcript of the 1979 discussions between 'Arafat and then-Soviet Foreign Minister Andrei Gromyko in Raphael Israeli, ed., *The PLO in Lebanon: Selected Documents* (London: Weidenfeld and Nicolson, 1983), pp. 34-73.

13. *Pravda* (Moscow), 4 December 1988, in *Current Digest of the Soviet Press* (hereafter, *CDSP*).

14. *Pravda*, 23 February 1989 (*CDSP*).

15. *Pravda*, 21 February 1987, 7 December 1987 (*CDSP*).

16. *Tass*, 23 February 1989 (*CDSP*).

17. *Izvestia*, 9 April 1988 (*CDSP*).

18. *Middle East International*, 2 February 1990, p. 4; *Jerusalem Post* (international edition), 10 March 1990, p. 1. These estimates, however, were contingent on establishment of direct flights between Moscow and Tel Aviv which would limit the flow of Soviet Jews to third countries.

19. *New York Times*, 5 February 1990, p. A12.

20. *Middle East Reporter*, 13 February 1988, p. 8.

21. *Pravda*, 25 April 1987 (*CDSP*).

22. Transcript of Gorbachev press conference, Moscow, 1 June 1988 (*CDSP*).

23. *Davar* (Tel Aviv), 22 September 1989; *New York Times*, 12 December 1989; *Middle East Reporter*, 30 July 1988, p. 10.

24. Golan, "Gorbachev's Middle East Strategy," p. 49.

25. *Pravda*, 21 February 1989.

26. Goodman and McGiffert Ekedahl, "Gorbachev's 'New Directions'," p. 577.

27. Golan, "Gorbachev's Middle East Strategy," p. 49.

28. Goodman and McGiffert Ekedahl, "Gorbachev's 'New Directions'," p. 578.

29. *Pravda*, 25 April 1987 (*CDSP*)

30. *Tass*, 18 November 1988 (*FBIS*).

31. *Novosti Press Agency*, 4 March 1989, in *Middle East Reporter*, 6 May 1989, p. 16.

32. The announcement was made at the precise time an Israeli cabinet minister was visiting the USSR—a clear attempt both to reduce PLO dissatisfaction with the visit and to pressure Israel. *Middle East Reporter*, 13 January 1990, p. 4.

33. *Pravda*, 25 April 1987, (*FBIS*); *Middle East Reporter*, 12 November 1988, p. 1.

34. *Izvestia*, 26 August 1989 (*CDSP*).

35. *Izvestia*, 18 September, 30 December 1988 (*CDSP*); *Novosti Press Agency*, in *Middle East Reporter*, 30 July 1988, p. 8.

36. *New York Times*, 6 March 1990, p. A1.

37. *Middle East Reporter*, 31 March 1990, p.12-13.

38. *Middle East Reporter*, 27 January, 10 March 1990; *Middle East International*, 6 February 1990, p. 9.

39. *Middle East International*, 4 November 1988, p. 17.

40. Alex Pravda, "Is There a Gorbachev Foreign Policy?" *The Journal of Communist Studies* 4, 4 (1988), p. 114.

41. Andrey Shoumikhin, "Soviet Perceptions of US Middle East Policy," *Middle East Journal* 43, 1 (Winter 1989): 18-19. See also Evgeni M. Primacov, "Soviet Policy Toward the Arab-Israeli Conflict," in William B. Quandt, ed., *The Middle East: Ten Years After Camp David* (Washington, D.C.: Brookings Institution, 1988), pp. 387-409.

42. Press Office of the USSR Embassy in Canada, "Shevardnadze—Cairo Speech," 24 February 1989.

43. *Pravda*, 18 December 1988 (*CDSP*).

44. *Tass*, 14 December 1988 (*FBIS*).

45. *Izvestia*, 23 February 1989 (*CDSP*).

46. *Middle East Reporter*, 28 May 1988, p. 4.

47. *Moscow Radio Peace and Progress*, 8 December 1989 (*FBIS*); emphasis added.

48. *New York Times*, 10 September 1990.

49. *New York Times*, 11, 20 September 1990.

10

United States

Fred Khouri

The *intifada* has had important effects on American public opinion and on US policy toward the Arab-Palestinian-Israeli conflict. In particular, it has promoted a better recognition of the dangers of perpetuating the status quo in the Middle East, and of the centrality of the Palestinian issue (and of the PLO) in the conflict. At the same time, however, American reaction to the *intifada* has also reflected many of the misperceptions and contradictions that have plagued US policy in the past.

This chapter will examine the changes which have taken place in American views and policies as a result of the *intifada*, and identify those changes which have yet to be made if the US is to play a truly constructive role in bringing lasting peace to the Middle East. Before it can do so, however, it is important to review the nature and sources of past US policy toward the Arab-Israeli conflict.

US Policy Before and After the 1967 Arab-Israeli War

After World War II America's declared interests in the Middle East were fourfold: to prevent the expansion of Soviet and communist influence; to promote peace and stability; to maintain friendly relations with key moderate states, both because of their strategic location and to ensure continued Western access to vital Middle Eastern oil; and to ensure the security and well-being of Israel. From the beginning it was clear that only a farsighted and balanced policy could serve the range of all four interests. In practice, however American leaders—out of ignorance of the region, and because of domestic political considerations—tended to emphasize the last of these objectives to the detriment of the others. The costs of this became particularly evident in the wake of the 1967 Arab-Israeli war.

The scope of Israel's victory in 1967 encouraged its government to resist serious negotiations, stalling for time in the hope of convincing Egypt, Jordan and Syria that their only hope of regaining lost territory was to negotiate directly, separately, and on Israeli terms. As former Israeli Foreign Minister Abba Eban observed, until then "we were not interested in peace.... We felt that we held the trump cards in our hands... but as time went on, we grew fond of them, and we were not ready to play them."[1]

The formal US position in the wake of the war was based on UN Security Council Resolution 242 of 22 November 1967, which called for the withdrawal of Israeli armed forces "from territories of recent conflict" and respect for "the sovereignty, territorial integrity and political independence of every state in the area and their right to live in peace within secure and recognized boundaries." While differences developed as to whether Israel would need to withdraw from *all* territories, it was widely agreed that if territorial changes did take place they would, as Secretary of State William Rogers stated in his 1969 peace plan, "be confined to insubstantial alterations required for mutual security."[2] This view was significantly at odds with those of both the Labor-dominated Israeli government, which insisted on the right to acquire large parts of the occupied territories for security purposes in any peace settlement, and of Menahem Begin's Herut Party, which laid claim to all of "Eretz Israel," both east and west of the Jordan River.[3] Moreover, Washington's willingness to press such issues was seriously constrained by domestic political considerations. The 1967 war had intensified Jewish nationalism, and American Jews rallied to Israel's support as never before. As a consequence of their enthusiasm, organizational skills, resources and knowledge of US political culture (as well as shortsighted Arab and Palestinian policies) the pro-Israeli lobby grew more powerful than ever. American liberal supporters of Israel were increasingly joined by American conservatives, who as a consequence of Israel's military prowess and Soviet military aid to Egypt in 1970-71 came to consider Israel as an important strategic asset in containing Soviet influence in the Middle East. As a result, US-Israeli relations became the cornerstone of US Middle East policy, and Washington became committed to fully and unquestioningly supporting Israel's position, even when this served to undermine other US objectives in the region.

The Nixon-Ford-Kissinger Period

President Richard Nixon and National Security Council Advisor Henry Kissinger looked at the Middle East largely in the context of East-West relations. They began to provide Israel with greatly increased economic and military aid, claiming that it would help combat the spread of Soviet influence, promote regional stability, prevent any Arab state from starting a war which might lead to US military involvement, and hence enable Israel to feel secure enough to make concessions for peace.

On December 9, 1969, Secretary of State Rogers proposed a more "balanced" American position and outlined what the US considered to be essential elements in any overall peace settlement. These included exchange of land for peace; the right of all parties to live in peace within secure borders; "insubstantial" border changes; a just solution to the Arab refugee problem; and no unilateral action in dealing with the Jerusalem issue. While some Arabs saw some value in the Rogers plan, Israel so strongly objected to it that the US refrained from actively pressing it and subsequently confined itself to dealing with only peripheral matters.[4]

The early 1970s saw King Husayn's defeat of the PLO in Jordan in 1970-71 and the assumption of power in Egypt and Syria by the more pragmatic Anwar al-Sadat and Hafiz al-Asad respectively. All revealed a greater willingness to accept the reality of Israel and the imperative of a political settlement. Despite this, Israel's position did not soften. It felt it had more to gain than lose from maintaining the status quo. Well-known British Zionist Jon Kimche noted that large-scale American military and economic aid "had strengthened Israel's armed forces to a point where they were masters of the Middle East,"

> ...why then, asked Mrs. Meir and her assenting colleagues, should Israel risk this strong position by making concessions to Egypt or anyone else... "Why change" became the slogan of 1972 and... 1973. Israel had everything she could want—except peace. And Mrs. Meir... did not believe that peace was obtainable at the price Israel might be willing to pay. This last proviso was crucial... The Government therefore believed that the best thing they could do...was to go on making sympathetic noises for a peace settlement, to be generally accommodating without making any commitments, and to rely on the Arab leaders to reject any American initiative, and to go on quarreling among themselves... Crucial, however, in this Israeli calculation was the assumption of continuing American support, diplomatic, military and financial.[5]

The October 1973 war, the resulting Arab oil embargo, and the near US-Soviet military confrontation destroyed US complacency and shattered two major assumptions underlying American policy: namely, that a strong Israel would deter the Arabs from resorting to war, and that the status quo in the Middle East could be maintained indefinitely in Israel's favor without serious risks for the US. The war also promoted greater appreciation of the importance of the Arab world in terms of geopolitics and oil. After the war, Henry Kissinger (now Secretary of State) initiated a step-by-step diplomatic process in an effort to defuse the explosive situation and, at the same time, postpone dealing with the Palestinian problem. He also sought to forestall significant Soviet involvement, establish the US as the sole diplomatic broker, and provide time for Israel to strengthen its bargaining position before entering serious direct negotiations.

By means of shuttle diplomacy Kissinger succeeded in attaining Egyptian-Israeli and Syrian-Israeli disengagement agreements in 1974. However, by the spring of 1975 both Kissinger and President Gerald Ford had come to consider Israel's intransigence as the main obstacle to a second Egyptian-Israeli disengagement agreement. Ford ordered a reassessment of American policy and temporarily suspended action on new military aid to

Israel in the hope of pressing it to be more forthcoming. However, a letter signed by seventy-five senators was sent to Ford demanding continued strong economic, political, and military support for Israel—thereby undermining administration efforts to elicit greater Israeli flexibility. Ford was later to criticize Israel for "dragging her feet" in the belief that its influence in Congress was such that it could always put enough "domestic pressure" on the administration to avoid concessions. He further complained that although the US had helped Israel become much more powerful than the Arabs in the expectation that it would feel secure enough to be "more flexible and more willing to discuss a lasting peace," Israel's position had become even more intransigent and "peace was no closer than it had ever been."[6]

Some American officials opposed the continuation of the step-by-step process in the belief that progress in one area could make it even more difficult to deal with broader and more vital issues. Kissinger disregarded this view and in September 1975 negotiated a second Egyptian-Israeli agreement. This, although achieving a very limited Israeli withdrawal along the Egyptian-Israeli front, was to have harmful long-term consequences because it ignored the Golan and Palestinian issues and further increased Arab distrust of the US. It also required Washington to provide Israel with such vast, long-term and unconditional economic, political, and military commitments that its leverage over Israel to obtain future concessions on more vital territorial and political issues was seriously undermined. Thus, the second disengagement agreement ended up doing more to impair than improve the climate for an overall settlement.[7]

Another effect of the October War was to bring into the open major differences between the US and its European allies over the conflict. Concerned about possible superpower confrontation emanating from some future Arab-Israeli war, anxious to maintain access to vital Arab oil, and convinced that moderate Arabs and Palestinians were increasingly prepared to accept a fair political settlement with Israel, many Western allies urged the US to deal with the PLO, accept Palestinian right of self-determination, and press Israel to be more forthcoming on the territorial and Palestinian issues as required by pertinent UN resolutions. Both the US and Israel disregarded Western European views.

The Carter Period

The Carter Administration gave priority to dealing with the Middle East. It was to go much further than any previous administration in developing an understanding of (and more balanced position toward) the conflict, and in making major, sustained efforts to promote a comprehensive settlement. Administration leaders concluded that the step-by-step process had exhausted its potential, leaving major elements of the problem still unresolved. Unless these elements were soon addressed, rising tensions would generate further violence—even war. This would undermine American influence and interests, and might even lead to a US-Soviet military confrontation. Thus, since the Arabs and Israelis were unable to reach any meaningful settlement on their own, it was in US interests to take the initiative by seeking a comprehensive settlement at a reconvened Geneva Conference. Moreover, it was important to act quickly, since the president enjoyed more room to deal with critical foreign policy matters in his first year in office than in subsequent years.[8]

Consequently, in early 1977 US diplomats and officials became involved in high-level consultations with Arab and Israeli leaders in an attempt to get as much prior agreement as possible on a comprehensive framework of principles that would then serve as guidelines to subsequent negotiations at a Geneva peace conference to be convened in September 1977. President Jimmy Carter played an active and key role in diplomatic talks, committing his influence and prestige to the peace process. He also began to reveal the broad outline of what the US considered fair principles essential to any lasting peace (an Israeli withdrawal to its 1967 borders with only minor border modifications, in return for full peace and security guarantees; PLO acceptance of Resolution 242 and Israel's right to exist; and a Palestinian "homeland" federated with Jordan) in an attempt to secure American public support. He made considerable progress in this regard.[9]

While Carter found all key Arab leaders, including President al-Asad of Syria, receptive to active American mediation, Israeli leaders were unhappy with the American initiative. US officials found Prime Minister Yitzhak Rabin "rigid" and "difficult to deal with."[10] Rabin admitted in his memoirs that Israel did not want a reconvened Geneva Conference and tried to "lay the matter of Geneva to rest." He preferred direct negotiations with each Arab party separately in order to gain the maximum benefit from Israel's superior bargaining power, rather than a conference which might require concessions he was unwilling to make. Indeed, he preferred the status quo to making such concessions.[11]

When the Likud Party won the May 1977 elections in Israel, Carter found himself faced with an even more intransigent leader. While Labor was willing to give up heavily populated parts of the West Bank so as not to endanger Israel's democracy, Jewish character, and security from within, incoming Prime Minister Menahem Begin and Likud opposed giving up any part of the occupied territories for ideological reasons. Begin's hardline position led Carter to complain that Israel was "more stubborn than the Arabs and put obstacles in the path of peace;" and that "we are financing their conquests and they simply defy us in an intransigent fashion and generally make a mockery of our advice and preference." Yet, for domestic political reasons Carter continued to assure the Israelis that he would not seek to impose a settlement on them. Thus, the Israelis remained convinced that they could do what they wished despite US concerns because their powerful supporters in Congress and American Jewish groups would assure that full American support would be maintained.[12]

By September Carter, concluding that Begin's opposition made agreement on a framework for peace impossible before going to Geneva, began to concentrate on such procedural matters as how the Palestinians would be represented at a conference. While the PLO was anxious to be invited to Geneva and 'Arafat personally was prepared to make a public statement conditionally accepting Resolution 242 as the US had demanded, most other PLO leaders opposed giving up the PLO's main bargaining card unless assured of getting to Geneva. The US failed to provide such assurances.[13]

On 1 October 1977, the US and USSR issued a joint statement regarding reconvening of the Geneva Conference, which the Soviet Union co-chaired with the US. Among other things, the US referred for the first time to the "legitimate rights" (and not mere "interests") of the Palestinians in the statement. While moderate Arabs and Palestinians generally welcomed this, Israel and its American supporters so strongly opposed it that Carter hastily drafted a "working paper" with Foreign Minister Moshe Dayan that effectively repudiated the joint statement. As one top administration official complained, this again encouraged Israel to feel confident that it could always get its way by mobilizing political pressures within the US; convinced the Arabs that American leaders would continue to bow to these pressures; and made the PLO more reluctant than ever to unconditionally accept Resolution 242.[14]

President Sadat's subsequent decision to take the initiative by going to Jerusalem undermined Carter's plans and forced him to return to the step-by-step approach. American officials now concentrated their efforts at attaining an Egyptian-Israeli peace treaty in the hope it would lead ultimately to a comprehensive settlement. But they found it difficult to make progress on even this more limited goal because, as Carter complained, "Whenever we seem to be having success with the Arabs, Begin would proclaim the establishment of new settlements or make provocative statements."[15] Even Israeli cabinet minister Ezer Weizman complained: that Begin and many cabinet members were "afraid of peace" and that "Israel seemed to be finding every possible tactic to impede the peace process," preferring the status quo to the concessions needed for a peace settlement.[16]

In a final desperate effort to salvage the situation, Carter invited Begin and Sadat to Camp David in September 1977. Sadat agreed to go only after he received prior assurances that Begin was prepared to give up the Sinai; he hoped that with Carter's support, an Egyptian-Israeli treaty would become a model for other treaties involving Israeli withdrawals from all occupied lands. However, Begin justified accepting the vaguely worded Camp David accords and the Egyptian-Israeli treaty, in which Israel gave up the Sinai, by assuring his followers that detaching Egypt from the Arab military equation would make it easier for Israel to retain the rest of the occupied territories. He also contended that Israel's withdrawal from the Sinai fulfilled all withdrawal requirements of Resolution 242. In addition, he resisted all efforts to implement the Camp David provisions calling for various steps to resolve the Palestinian problem in all its aspects. According to Weizman, Begin considered the withdrawal from Sinai to be "the end of the story" and thus "gave up promoting the peace process."[17]

Convinced that Begin would not abide by either the Camp David accords as a whole or his private commitment to halt new settlements, some administration officials urged a suspension of some economic aid to compel Begin to soften his policies. But with presidential elections approaching and his potential opponents taking a strongly pro-Israel stand, Carter took no action and sought to avoid any further active involvement in the politically sensitive issue.[18] Thus, the Camp David accords and the Egyptian-Israeli treaty ended up as a separate peace—one that removed Egypt as a confrontation state (thereby further weakening Arab bargaining power), and encouraged Israel to retain an uncompromising stand on other territorial and political issues. Israel soon felt free to intensify attacks on Lebanon and to accelerate its settlement program. In short, the agreements made it more difficult than ever to bring about a lasting comprehensive peace settlement.

The Reagan-Shultz Period: Before the Intifada

The Reagan Administration was convinced that the Soviet Union and communism posed the main threats to American security interests in the Middle East and elsewhere. Increasingly concerned about the Soviet role in Afghanistan and Iran's efforts to spread militant Islamic fundamentalism in the Gulf area, it downgraded the importance of the Arab-Israeli conflict.

While Secretary of Defense Caspar Weinberger and the Pentagon reportedly opposed too close ties with Israel because this could undermine US strategic interests in the Arab world, Reagan proved to be a stronger supporter of Israel than any previous president. He and Secretary of State Alexander Haig were so convinced of Israel's role as a dependable ally against Soviet expansionism in the Middle East that they greatly increased US aid; vetoed UN Security Council resolutions which criticized Israel's excessive use of force in Lebanon and against the Palestinians in the occupied territories; and, in November 1981, negotiated a Memorandum of Understanding on Strategic Cooperation to set up working groups to strengthen US-Israeli strategic cooperation.[19]

As a result, Israel felt even freer than before to take major military and political actions without regard to American views because it believed that while the American government might express disapproval of some actions, it would not halt or decrease economic and military aid. In fact, Secretary Haig even gave Israel a "green light" to invade southern Lebanon in June

1982.[20] When Israeli forces continued on to Beirut and bombed the city causing heavy civilian casualties, administration officials, American public opinion, the media, and even some members of Congress began to publicly condemn Israel. But the administration made no attempt to decrease aid to Israel (barring a temporary token suspension of F-16 fighter shipments). On the contrary, Congress actually increased that aid.

The Israeli invasion did, however, compel the Reagan Administration to reassess its Middle East policy. It finally recognized that an unresolved Arab-Palestinian-Israeli conflict posed a serious threat to American interests and could no longer be left on the back-burner. Thus on September 1 President Reagan announced a peace plan which provided for an exchange of land for peace as called for by Resolution 242; American opposition to both a Palestinian state and to permanent Israeli rule over the West Bank and Gaza Strip (including the establishment of new settlements); "full autonomy" for the Palestinians in the territories during a transitional period, at the end of which a self-governing Palestinian entity would become associated with Jordan; and an undivided Jerusalem, the future status of which would be determined in a final peace settlement. No specific reference was made to either Syria or the PLO.[21]

While the Labor Party saw some merit in the Reagan Plan, Begin strongly rejected it. He reiterated his opposition to any further Israeli withdrawals and the establishment of any kind of Palestinian entity, and initiated a greatly expanded settlements program. The State Department criticized these views and actions as creating obstacles to peace.[22]

PLO leader Yasir 'Arafat and Jordan's King Husayn did not reject the plan outright, believing that despite serious flaws it also contained some positive elements. Later that same month Arab leaders met in a summit at Fez and drew up their own peace plan. This called for a complete withdrawal from all territories occupied in 1967; a Palestinian state under the leadership of the PLO; and UN Security Council guarantees for the peace and security of "all states" in the region. Delegations of high-level Arab officials were dispatched to explain to the US and Western Europe that the plan implicitly recognized Israel. On September 15, 1982, Soviet leader Leonid Brezhnev proposed his own plan, similar to the Fez Plan except that it referred to Israel by name.[23]

'Arafat accepted both the Fez and Brezhnev plans and said he would even accept the Reagan Plan if it included a reference to Palestinian national rights. He opened talks with King Husayn in the hope that this might convince the US that he was serious about a political solution. In April 1983, 'Arafat and Husayn came to a tentative agreement on a joint negotiating formula. This agreement, however, was never finalized.[24]

After the Reagan Plan failed to get off the ground, administration officials returned to the piecemeal approach. Secretary of State George Shultz (who had succeeded Haig in July 1982) initiated a shuttle diplomacy which resulted in the signing on May 17, 1983, of an Israeli-Lebanese withdrawal agreement which limited Lebanese sovereignty and contained security provisions most favorable to Israel. However, because of strong opposition to the treaty within Lebanon and from Syria, President Amin Jumayyil eventually refused to ratify it.

Although Shultz had originally expressed some sympathy for the Palestinians, by late 1983 he had become the most pro-Israeli figure in a pro-Israeli administration. This change apparently began after the Israeli-Lebanese withdrawal agreement had collapsed. Shultz took this failure personally and blamed the Arabs—especially the Syrians, Saudis, and Palestinians—for it. By late 1983 he began to push for closer US-Israeli relations and a tougher joint US-Israeli posture to force Syria out of Lebanon and weaken Soviet influence. Once again, Israel became the central element in US Middle East policy and strategy.[25]

Despite the opposition of Secretary Weinberger and some senior generals and State Department experts (who believed that the US already had close enough military ties with Israel—and that a formal military accord would unnecessarily antagonize even pro-Western Arabs and undercut any mediatory role the US could play)[26] Shultz convinced Reagan to make another attempt at a strategic cooperation agreement to replace the one made in November 1981 but which had been suspended as a result of Israel's annexation of the Golan Heights in December 1981. An agreement for military and political cooperation was concluded on 29 November 1983. This provided for a joint military group to examine ways to further enhance US-Israeli cooperation, especially to counter "the threat to our mutual interests" posed by increased Soviet involvement in the Middle East. There would be combined planning, joint exercises, and prepositioning of American equipment in Israel. The US pledged to increase military aid; to negotiate an accord on reciprocal duty-free trade; to help Israel develop the Lavi fighter plane; and to provide access to secret electronic technology. Israel gave no *quid pro quo* for this agreement, nor did it produce greater flexibility on issues of US concern, such as Israel's rejection of the Reagan Plan, its opposition to arms sales to pro-Western Arab states, and the establishment of new settlements in the occupied territories.[27]

In early September 1983 and again in December 1983, the UN General Assembly passed resolutions calling for the convening by the UN of an international peace conference based on the UN Charter and pertinent UN resolutions in which all concerned parties (including the PLO) would participate. The resolutions also called for a Palestinian state and the right of all states in the Middle East to live within secure and recognized borders. These were supported by large majorities (the December vote was 124 in favor, 15 abstentions, and only Australia, Canada, the US and Israel voting against). In December 1983, the UN General Assembly passed other resolutions reiterating its prior stands on territorial withdrawal, settlements,

East Jerusalem, the Golan Heights and Israeli practices in the occupied territories. These resolutions were again passed by large majorities (with only the US and Israel—and occasionally Canada—generally voting against), thus showing how politically isolated the US and Israel had become. Close US allies repeatedly urged Washington to provide more balanced and effective leadership in the search for peace.[28]

Reagan's overwhelming victory in the 1984 elections provided a potential opportunity to provide such leadership. But Reagan had never taken the time and energy, as Carter had done, to master the complexities and realities of the Arab-Palestinian-Israel problem. Moreover, he did not want to become actively involved for fear of antagonizing a pro-Israeli Congress, Israel, and its influential American supporters.

Nor was Shultz prepared to take any initiative. After the failure of his Israeli-Lebanese accord he was unwilling to risk his prestige again unless assured of success. He had also become still more pro-Israeli. In an April 1985 address before a meeting of the American-Israeli Public Affairs Committee (AIPAC), the most powerful pro-Israeli lobby, Shultz declared that "We must make it clear to the world—through our material and moral support for Israel, our votes in the UN and our efforts for peace—that we are a permanent, steadfast and unshakable ally..." He went on to claim that the Soviet Union and its "radical allies," not Israel, were blocking the path to peace.[29]

In an address before an April 1986 AIPAC conference, Thomas A. Dine, Executive Director of AIPAC, quoted Shultz as saying that the point of strategic cooperation "is to build institutional arrangements so that eight years from now, if there is a secretary of state who is not positive about Israel, he will not be able to overcome the bureaucratic relationship between Israel and the US that we have established." Dine went on to say:

> ...the new constituency of support for Israel is being built in precisely those areas where we are weakest—among government officials in the State Department, Defense, and Treasury Departments, in the CIA, in science, trade, agriculture, and other agencies. These are the people responsible for proposing policy and for implementing it. In a crisis, these anonymous officials will play a vital role... In other words, we are talking not only about a revolution in relationship between two states, but also in the attitudes of key people responsible for that relationship.... The component of the strategic level is complemented by coordination on the diplomatic level. The US now only moves on the peace process after the closest consultations with ... Israel... Moreover, in its public diplomacy, this administration has demonstrated unprecedented support for the sometimes controversial actions Israel is forced to take... At the UN, the US has now gone beyond defending Israel to actively opposing and undermining the anti-Israeli efforts of the Arabs.[30]

At a May 1987 AIPAC conference, Dine referred to Shultz as a "warm, deeply committed partisan... There is widespread agreement that Ronald

Reagan has been the best friend of Israel ever to sit in the Oval Office, and that George Shultz has been a friend beyond words as Secretary of State." He also stated that despite the Pollard spy case, Israeli involvement in the Iran-Contra affair, renewed speculation about Israel's nuclear weapons, and Israel's opposition to US arms to pro-Western Arab states—despite all of these US-Israeli differences, "we have [had] one of the best years on record" in strengthening Israeli-US relations.[31]

Despite repeated urgings by King Husayn, President Husni Mubarak of Egypt, and even Israeli Foreign Minister Shimon Peres that there would be no progress without active high level American involvement and leadership, administration officials took no serious peace initiative in 1985 and 1986. Instead they concentrated their efforts on trying to promote direct talks between Israel and Jordan, with or without the involvement of non-PLO Palestinians as part of a Jordanian delegation.

In February 1985 King Husayn and 'Arafat reached a tentative agreement calling for a joint Jordanian-Palestinian delegation, peace negotiations with Israel under the umbrella of an international conference, and ultimately the formation of a Jordanian-Palestinian confederation. While Peres was finally convinced that Husayn needed a limited type of international conference as a face-saving device to enable him to risk direct negotiations with Israel, Israeli Prime Minister Yitzhak Shamir strongly opposed any type of conference. Shamir also objected to direct negotiations with Jordan since this might require Israeli territorial concessions. The US also continued to oppose an international conference and to insist on direct negotiations so as to forestall Soviet involvement in the peace process, maintain the US as the primary (if not sole) mediator, and bypass Syria and the PLO. Only after Husayn and Peres drew up an agreement in London in April 1987 which provided for a limited conference to facilitate direct negotiations did Shultz finally agree to back such a conference.[32]

In October 1987, Shultz made a trip to Israel in an attempt to gain Shamir's acceptance of a limited conference. But knowing that Shultz had "neither the will nor the inclination for a showdown," Shamir rejected Shultz's appeal. Peres accused Shamir and Likud of not having a "single proposal on which any Arab partner—even one—would be ready to negotiate" thereby killing all chances for peace because "there will be no movement in the peace process" if there will be "no give on the territorial issue."[33] Some administration officials regarded Shamir's opposition to a conference as a mask for his opposition to any territorial compromise. Shamir confirmed this when, in an interview with the *Jerusalem Post*, he stated that he opposed an international conference not because of procedural considerations but because "the dispute over the international conference is about the conditions for peace," such as "relinquishing territories."[34]

At the end of his fruitless trip Shultz felt frustrated and believed that it was useless to continue seeking peace. However, he finally realized, as he told reporters: "Excessive consultation on modality problems is not the way to pursue things. We ought to be scratching our heads more on what the substance ought to be."[35]

The Impact of the *Intifada*

The Reagan-Shultz Period

Until the *intifada* the Reagan Administration lacked the objectivity and will to produce any meaningful peace initiative. In fact, even after the *intifada* broke out in December 1987, the Administration believed that it would not last long, and that there would thus be no need for active American involvement. Some officials were convinced that, in any case, they could do nothing to control Israel's behavior and that Congress "would not let us, anyway." They argued that whenever they tried to pressure Israel in the past, Congress refused to go along. The lesson that was learned was that "Israel would get its aid, whatever it might do." So why should the Administration antagonize congressional backers of Israel by taking any initiative until all parties were prepared to accept it? To show continued strong support for Israel, on February 1 the US vetoed a Security Council resolution criticizing Israel's harsh treatment of civilians in the occupied territories even though American officials themselves had criticized such actions.[36]

However, by early February 1988 continuing violence in the occupied territories and mounting concern in the US (and even Israel) finally led Shultz to become actively involved in a major peace initiative. He also continued to reveal a better understanding of the situation. For example, he stressed that the status quo was "no longer acceptable" and that it was necessary to start dealing with "substance rather than procedure" and to focus directly on the problem of the Israeli occupation and how to bring it to an end. He also said that the "Palestinians must achieve control over political and economic decisions that affect their own lives and must be active participants in the negotiations to determine their future." Jordan, Syria, Lebanon, and the Palestinians outside the territories also had concerns which needed to be resolved. Thus, he began to stress both the importance of the overall Palestinian element and the need for a comprehensive settlement involving all parties to the conflict.[37]

In late February Shultz went to the Middle East to seek, as Carter Administration officials had done in 1977, agreement on several principles to guide future negotiations. He presented some ideas of his own which were incorporated in a formal Shultz plan. This plan proposed that an international conference with limited authority be convened in April 1988, consisting of the five permanent members of the UN Security Council and all parties to the conflict who accepted Resolution 242 and renounced terrorism. On May 1 Israeli and joint Jordanian-Palestinian delegations would begin negotiations on an interim phase of self-determination for the Palestinians in the West Bank and Gaza Strip. In December they would begin talks on the final status of these territories. An interim phase of self-administration would not go into effect until these latter talks had begun. Bilateral direct talks would be held with all other parties to the conflict, leading to a comprehensive peace settlement based on Resolution 242.[38]

While President Mubarak and Foreign Minister Peres supported the plan, most Arabs and Palestinians felt that it ignored the PLO, failed to provide for an effective international conference, and did not ensure the Palestinian right of self-determination. Prime Minister Shamir, meanwhile, quickly rejected the plan and vowed "war" on it. In a radio interview he said: "It is clear that this expression of territory for peace is not accepted by me." He would not give up any more territory beyond the Sinai, even in return for peace.[39] He came to Washington in mid-March in order to press the administration to scrap the Shultz plan, prepared to go over the heads of administration leaders and appeal to Congress and pro-Israeli groups if this became necessary to ensure its demise.

In early April Shultz returned to the Middle East in an attempt to persuade Arab and Israeli leaders to accept his plan. In statements in late February and early March, however, both Reagan and Shultz repeatedly assured Shamir they would not apply any pressures to change his views. They refused to hold up delivery of seventy-five F-16 jet fighters. Despite opposition from the National Security Council advisor and State Department Middle East specialists—who saw no reason to reward Shamir after he had rejected the latest American plan—Shultz singlehandedly and successfully pressed Reagan to respond favorably to Shamir's request for another memorandum of agreement. This agreement, signed on 21 April 1988, codified all existing formal and informal working arrangements involving cooperation on a range of military, economic, political, and intelligence matters which had developed during Reagan's Administration. It also officially stated for the first time that Israel was a major non-NATO ally.[40]

Some Israeli officials, who disagreed with Shamir's intransigence, criticized Shultz for failing to pressure Shamir to change his uncompromising position. One "senior official" complained that "it almost looks like Shultz gave him a reward for not cooperating." Foreign Minister Peres was reported as "telling confidants... that Mr. Shultz let him down by not forcing Mr. Shamir to make a [favorable] decision on the American plan during his recent visit to Washington."[41]

On arriving in Israel in April, Shultz said, in reference to the PLO, that "there is no place at the negotiation table for those who cannot accept that resolution [242] as the basis for negotiations."[42] Ironically, as former Foreign Minister Abba Eban noted, Shultz, as well as Israeli leaders and American Jewish supporters, "overlooked the awkward fact that the Israeli government does not support [242] at all."[43] Shultz never made an issue of this; and neither he nor his successors have yet pressed Israel to provide the same clear and unconditional acceptance of 242 they have demanded from 'Arafat and the PLO.

In April Shultz assured Israel that a withdrawal to the pre-1967 borders was "not in the cards" and that the US still gave highest priority to Israel's security. The US also vetoed on April 15 a Security Council resolution which asked Israel to allow the return of some Palestinians deportees, condemned the shooting of civilians, and called for a peace settlement under UN auspices. However, in early June, Shultz did break some more new ground on the Palestinian issue when he said: "There can be no settlement without addressing legitimate Palestinian political rights," going beyond the term "legitimate rights" as used in the past.[44]

At this point, King Husayn announced on 31 July 1988 that he was severing all legal and administrative links to the West Bank and was leaving all future negotiations over that area to the PLO. While still insisting on the need for active Jordanian involvement in any peace process, many US officials realized that Husayn's move had largely eliminated the "Jordan option" on which much of past American diplomacy had been based—and that the PLO and the Palestinians had therefore to be given a greater role in future peace efforts. For months some key State Department officials had been arguing that Israel had to negotiate with the Palestinians, and that the PLO under 'Arafat had been moving in a more moderate direction. Husayn's move strengthened their arguments. Moreover, by late 1988, Shultz had become increasingly disenchanted with Israel's refusal to accept his peace plan and had concluded that the US had to reassess its position on the Middle East. While he was still convinced that the continuation of the status quo was dangerous, he still was not yet ready to deal with the PLO until it had met tough American conditions; namely, accept Resolutions 242 and 338 and Israel's right to exist and unequivocally renounce terrorism.[45]

But during 1988 other important developments had taken place. A cease-fire had been arranged between Iran and Iraq. The USSR had decided to withdraw from Afghanistan and to improve its relations with both the US and Israel. 'Arafat was already convinced that, since American support was essential to achieving an Israeli withdrawal from the occupied territories and acceptance of Palestinian political rights, the PLO had to make a more serious effort to accept American conditions for opening a dialogue. Pressures from the Soviet Union and Western Europe, from Husayn's disengagement from the West Bank, and from the local leaders of the *intifada* strengthened Arafat's hand within the PLO. He pressed for resolutions at a forthcoming Palestine National Council (PNC) meeting which would enable him to convince the US, as well as many Israelis, that the PLO was prepared to take a more realistic and forthcoming approach than ever before.

At the Algiers PNC conference in November 1988, the PNC issued a declaration of a Palestinian state and passed resolutions by overwhelming majorities which 'Arafat hoped would satisfy American conditions. The declaration of independence cited UN General Assembly Resolution 181 of November 1947 (which partitioned Palestine into Jewish and Arab states) as its legal basis. PNC resolutions called for a UN-sponsored international conference based on Resolution 242 with the PLO representing the Palestinians; Security Council guarantees for peace and security for all states in the area; the establishment of a future confederacy between a Palestinian state and Jordan; and the rejection of terrorism "in all its forms," although affirming the right of all peoples under UN resolutions to resist foreign occupation.[46]

While Western European leaders and many American Middle East experts and even Israelis felt that the PNC decisions represented a "clear trend towards moderation," both Prime Minister Shamir and Foreign Minister Peres dismissed them as "nothing new." Shultz claimed that the PNC had not been explicit enough on Israel's right to exist and on renouncing terrorism.[47]

Despite the advice of top officials in the State Department, National Security Council, and US Mission to the UN, but with the support of some major Jewish organizations and a joint letter signed by fifty-one senators, Shultz denied 'Arafat's request for a visa so he could address the UN General Assembly in New York and personally explain the PNC decisions. Not only did US allies strongly criticize this move, but the General Assembly deplored it by a vote of 151 with only the US and Israel opposed.[48] 'Arafat instead presented a statement (based on one prepared with the help of five American Jews in Stockholm and the Swedish Foreign Minister, who had been quietly seeking to influence both 'Arafat and Shultz) to a special session of the UN General Assembly in Geneva on December 13. Since Shultz found this unacceptable as well, Sweden's Foreign Minister obtained the exact wording the State Department wanted and convinced 'Arafat to present it in English. Thus, 'Arafat told a press conference that the PLO accepted "the right of all parties... to exist in peace and security... including the state of Palestine, Israel, and other neighbors, according to resolutions 242 and 338;" and that it "totally and absolutely renounce[d] all forms of terrorism, including individual, group and state terrorism." He went on to say: "let it be absolutely clear that neither 'Arafat, nor anyone else for that matter, can stop the *intifada*... The *intifada* will come to an end only when practical and tangible steps have been taken towards the achievement of our national aims and establishment of our independent Palestinian state." This press statement was endorsed by the PLO Executive Committee in a meeting in Baghdad later in December.[49]

On December 14 Shultz indicated that he was finally satisfied with Arafat's statement and that a dialogue would now begin in Tunis between

US Ambassador Richard H. Pelletreau (the only authorized US channel for talks) and representatives of the PLO. He stated that the US objective was a comprehensive peace through direct negotiations; the US did not recognize the declaration of a Palestinian state; and American "commitment to the security of Israel remains unflinching." He also said: if "you're going to get a peaceful settlement in the Middle East you have to include Palestinians in the process from the beginning to the end;" and Israel should "show more flexibility" and should "face up to the reality of the difficult decisions that have to be made" to achieve peace.[50]

But to show continued strong support for Israel, on 14 December 1988, the US vetoed a resolution deploring an Israeli military attack on Palestinian positions in Lebanon. On December 15, only the US and Israel voted against a UN General Assembly resolution (supported by 138 other states, including all of Western Europe) that called for a UN-sponsored international conference with PLO participation and for an Israeli withdrawal to the pre-1967 borders. President Reagan also warned that the US would break off the talks if the PLO committed terrorist attacks.

In Israel, both Shamir and Peres, as well as many Israeli newspapers, vehemently condemned the US decision to open talks with the PLO. Dovish elements in Israel, however, welcomed 'Arafat's more moderate position and the opening of PLO-US talks, and urged their own government to begin talks with the PLO. They complained that Shamir and Peres "have tended to view signs of moderation in the PLO as a threat, rather than an opportunity" and preferred an intransigent PLO so that they need not face the need for major territorial concessions.[51]

The Bush Administration and the Intifada

The Bush Administration took office with some major advantages in dealing with the Arab-Palestinian-Israeli conflict. Compared to Ronald Reagan, George Bush had far more experience in foreign affairs, and greater open-mindedness regarding the Middle East. The Reagan Administration had already taken the domestic political risk of opening a dialogue with the PLO. Gorbachev had been following a more moderate policy in both internal and external affairs and US-Soviet relations had greatly improved, thus vastly lessening any Soviet military threat and opening new opportunities for US-Soviet cooperation in dealing with regional disputes.

Moreover, according to numerous public opinion surveys, most Americans—including a growing number of American Jews—had become increasingly critical of Israel's actions in dealing with the *intifada* and supportive of talks with the PLO and the convening of an international conference. According to *Time* (8 February 1988), as early as January 1988 polls showed 57 percent of American Jews and 72 percent of non-Jews disapproved of Israel's policies. The *New York Times* reported on 18

January 1989, that a recent *New York Times*/CBS poll showed 64 percent of Americans supporting US-PLO talks. In April 1988, a *Los Angeles Times* poll showed 63 percent were for an international conference; and a mid-December 1988 poll showed 46 percent supported a Palestinian state, while only 22 percent opposed.[52] According to a study of the American Jewish community taken for the American Jewish Committee's Institute on American Jewish-Israeli Relations, 58 percent of American Jews said Israel should talk with the PLO if it accepted Resolution 242 and Israel's right to exist and renounced terrorism; 47 percent believed the Palestinians should have a "homeland" in the West Bank and Gaza provided that it did not threaten Israel; and 54 percent felt that Israel was acting "wrongly" in the occupied territories, with 35 percent stating they were "morally outraged" by some of Israel's actions. The study also reported that younger Jews were less strongly attached to Israel than their elders; and "the very top leadership of Jewish organizations increasingly favor a two-state solution to the Palestinian-Israeli conflict."[53]

Moreover, according to the *Philadelphia Inquirer*, while some American Jews began to question Israel's policies during the 1982 war in Lebanon, Jewish criticism had "heightened" during the Palestinian uprising and had "intensified recently with the 'Who's a Jew' controversy." American Jews had become "more willing than in the past to engage in a public debate over Middle Eastern affairs and to express views not completely in accord with the Israeli leadership." Six leaders of three major American Jewish organizations criticized Israel's main lobby, AIPAC, for advocating "policies that are at variance with the consensus of the organized Jewish community" on some key issues, and for making it appear that it alone accurately represented the views of all American Jews. Leaders of some mainstream Jewish organizations—such as the American Jewish Congress and the Union of American Hebrew Organizations—began to call for an end to Israel's occupation and a halt to repressive occupation policies because these were considered as obstacles to peace and contrary to Jewish values.[54]

There was also a potential weakening of support in Congress. Some members of Congress warned Israel that, while support in Congress remained solid, it had been eroding badly among Americans at large and this could sooner or later "undermine congressional support for aid to Israel."[55]

In addition, developments were taking place in Israel. According to various reports, more and more Israelis—including mainstream newspapers, members of the Knesset, and soldiers and officers stationed in the occupied territories—were opposed to the increasingly harsh tactics used to try to suppress the *intifada*.[56] Mainstream Israelis, including Labor Party members of the Knesset, began to hold talks with pro-PLO leaders in the occupied areas. Eleven Israeli journalists interviewed 'Arafat in Cairo and a film of the interview appeared on Israeli television. In March 1989 the respected Israeli newspaper *Ha'Aretz*, became the first major publication to call on Shamir to drop his opposition to talks with the PLO. Around the same time, a poll conducted for the *New York Times* showed that although a majority of Israelis opposed early talks with the PLO, 58 percent said talks were ultimately inevitable; 44 percent saw a Palestinian state in the West Bank and Gaza within the next ten years; and 47 percent said that, because the US supplied so much aid, it had the right to influence Israeli policy (48 percent disagreed). Another poll in early 1989 indicated that 65 percent would be willing to give up some territory for peace. According to David Landau, such polls showed increasing support for talks with the PLO and a growing sense among broad segments of the Israeli public ("cutting across political and ideological lines") that there must be a political solution.[57]

Two major Israeli studies released in March 1989 also had significant influence on the Israeli public and strengthened the hands of both Israeli and American (including Jewish American) peace groups. These studies (by the Jaffee Center for Strategic Studies at Tel Aviv University and by army intelligence) concluded that continuing the status quo was intolerable and harmful to Israel's interests; that the *intifada* could not be ended without a political solution; that elements in the PLO had "undergone a real change and genuinely want to reach a political settlement with Israel;" and that a future Palestinian state could not be ruled out.[58]

Peace Now, founded by officers in 1978, came out openly for talks with the PLO and a two-state solution with security arrangements. Hundreds of senior Israeli reserve officers formed the Council for Peace and Security, which urged an exchange of territory for peace with security arrangements as the best way of promoting Israel's security and democracy. An informal poll taken by *Yediot Aharonot* revealed that "80 percent of the current General Staff... believe that the risks of retaining control of the territories and their 1.5 million inhabitants far outweigh the dangers Israel faces in returning them."[59] Peace Now and other Israeli peace groups have been active in the US, as well as in Israel, in trying to influence public opinion.

These favorable developments in the US and Israel made it easier for the Bush Administration to continue talks with the PLO and (given the necessary will and determination) to press Israel more vigorously to soften its positions on Palestinian and territorial issues. Such a move would have had broad support in the US and substantial backing even within Israel.

While the Bush Administration had some favorable factors to work with, it also had unfavorable ones. Although President Bush enjoyed considerable experience in foreign relations, only a small part involved the Middle East. Moreover, he was not considered to be a profound thinker or long-term strategist. He was known for approaching problems in a cautious manner, responding to situations rather creating them. For his part, Secretary of State James Baker lacked foreign policy experience. He too was cautious in approach and appeared to depend for advice primarily on a small inner circle and not on experienced State Department specialists.

According to the Washington correspondent of the international edition of the *Jerusalem Post* (19 April 1989), while both Bush and Baker lacked the strong warm, emotional ties to Israel which Reagan and Shultz had, they still were "sensitive" to Israeli concerns and security requirements; Vice President Dan Quayle was Israel's chief supporter at the highest level of the administration; and "there is no shortage of warmth and deep friendship for Israel among the second tier of foreign policy officials in this new administration." In fact, "at this level, there has been a net gain for Israel compared to the previous administration."[60] Moreover, as indicated earlier, close institutional and bureaucratic ties between Israel and the US had already been forged during the Reagan Administration.

The Bush Administration also faced a strongly entrenched and still very influential pro-Israeli lobby, and a pro-Israeli Congress. According to the *Jerusalem Post* (international edition, 18 March 1989) despite the changes in American public opinion, Baker and Bush still felt that although a peace plan would require "leaning" on Shamir, Israel's "support in Congress and among Jewish groups, while rapidly declining, is still strong enough to withstand massive American pressures at this point." It might also be noted that Bush undoubtedly plans on running again in 1992, and that Baker may have political ambitions for 1996.

These developments and conditions made it more difficult for Bush and Baker to develop the policies essential to a successful peace process—and also convinced Shamir that he could maintain his intransigent position with impunity. In fact, although in early February the State Department presented its 1988 *Country Reports on Human Rights Practices* (the most critical report ever made by the US about Israel) stating that there had been a "substantial increase" in human rights violations, and although from time to time American officials publicly condemned some of these violations, on February 17 the US was the only state to vote against a UN Security Council resolution deploring Israeli violations of Palestinian human rights. On April 20, only the US and Israel voted against a UN General Assembly resolution condemning Israel's violent repression of the *intifada* and calling for a UN-sponsored international peace conference.

In the early spring of 1989, the Bush Administration began to refocus US attention on the Arab-Israeli conflict. This was partly because of pressures (from Western Europe, friendly Arab leaders, and from American Middle East experts from inside and outside the government) to take the initiative while opportunities opened up by the *intifada* and PLO concessions remained alive and available. It was also because of the perceived need to counter a major Soviet peace initiative mounted in late February by the Soviet Foreign Minister. In mid-March, the Administration finally made some proposals on the Middle East. These were influenced not only by key pro-Israeli advisers, but also by the belief that while the *intifada* was unpleasant and needed to be dealt with, it still did not pose any serious threat to the US. The Administration also believed that there was little domestic pressure for any immediate, high profile Middle East peace initiative (while the domestic political risks for such an initiative requiring pressures on Israel would be great), and that the parties were unprepared to make the concessions for peace. Therefore, as one high administration official put it: "We should take our time, till the ground carefully and only move when we think there's a reasonable chance for success."[61]

Thus Secretary Baker made proposals which held that the best way to break the deadlock was through a step-by-step process. This would, at first, involve specific confidence-building measures by Israel and the Palestinians At the same time the parties would present ideas on a final settlement which would resolve Israel's security concerns and Palestinian "quest for self-determination," and which would convince the Arabs that the US was not "simply trying to reduce tensions or buy off the Palestinian uprising as an end in itself." Baker held that the Palestinians could not be expected to forgo their uprising without at least some general commitments to the future. If the first steps were successful, then Israel and local Palestinian leaders would negotiate an interim settlement (such as Palestinian autonomy) that would lay the foundation for a final settlement based on Resolution 242 and provisions for Israeli security and Palestinian political rights. According to Baker, if no such local leaders could be found, the need to negotiate directly with the PLO could not be ruled out. While noting that the US had "some differences with our staunch ally Israel"—such as over the land for peace formula—to allay some Israeli concerns Baker made it clear that the US was "completely committed to the security of Israel," and the US would "coordinate" its policies and strategy in dealing with the peace process with Israel. Moreover, he and Bush met with leaders of major American Jewish organizations both to assure them that no pressure would be placed on Shamir and to win their support for the Baker proposals.[62]

Neither Shamir nor 'Arafat were happy with Baker's proposals. Shamir especially objected to references to the exchange of land for peace and of the possibility of negotiating with the PLO. The Palestinians opposed any move that could drive a wedge between the Palestinians inside and outside the occupied areas; that could force the Palestinians to give up their *intifada*—their main bargaining leverage—in return for vague promises about a final status situation; or that could lead to a solution short of ending Israeli occupation and providing for a Palestinian state. The PLO was also concerned that a long drawn-out process would be exploited by Shamir to establish more facts on the ground and to wait out the *intifada* without making any reciprocal concessions.[63] In any case, the Baker proposals were soon shunted aside in favor of proposals Shamir was to bring with him to Washington.

While American officials urged Shamir to bring some new, constructive ideas for improving the atmosphere in the occupied territories and for interim and final status arrangements, both Bush and Baker publicly assured Shamir that the US would not apply any pressures on such a "friend" and "strategic ally" as Israel, no matter how much he differed with American views and concerns.[64] Thus, Shamir felt free to maintain a hard line. He permitted the setting up of a new settlement near Ramallah despite strong American opposition to such a move; he warned that he would arrest 'Arafat if he came to Jerusalem to try to negotiate peace as Sadat had done; he vehemently rejected the reports of the Jaffee Institute for Strategic Studies and his own army intelligence. In what the *New York Times* (13 February 1989) called a "fiery speech" before a Likud Party meeting, he said "folly and nonsense" to the US backed formula of exchanging land for peace; and added that "the time has come for the world to know that... the land of Israel belongs... only to the people of Israel" and "there is no power that can... force us to act otherwise." Some Israelis argued that Shamir and Likud did not really want any serious peace process because it could lead to a settlement requiring territorial and political concessions which they did not want to make—even for peace.[65]

Shamir's proposals involved, among other things, the holding of elections in the West Bank and Gaza to produce a delegation "to negotiate an interim period of self-governing administration." After about three years of autonomy, negotiations could begin about the permanent status of the territories. He insisted that no elections could he held until violence ended and that "Israel had no intention of ever leaving the West Bank and Gaza Strip," even as part of a final settlement. Confident that the Bush Administration was anxious to avoid a confrontation with him and his American supporters no matter what position he took, he rejected the most basic elements of the Baker proposals—claiming that "the land for peace formula" was a "deception" and rejecting any relaxation of Israel's occupation policies. He also said: "I don't think we have to give any guarantees to the Arabs... [or] take any measures for confidence."[66] To further strengthen his hand before coming to the US, Shamir met with the Presidents of Major American Jewish Organizations in February and hosted a world-wide Jewish Solidarity Conference in Jerusalem in March. He succeeded in obtaining warm support for Israel and his policies from the great preponderance of American and world Jewish leaders.

In short, Shamir came to Washington with a peace plan that he hoped would forestall any proposals from Bush that might provoke an open confrontation with the US. According to one senior member of Shamir's own party, the Israeli leader accepted the election idea "only because he was sure the PLO would turn it down." He also sought to play for time in the hope, as Ze'ev Schiff, military editor of *Ha'Aretz* stated, that "either the PLO will go back to terrorism, or the Bush Administration will lose interest, or something else will happen to spare him from giving up an inch of land."[67]

Shamir returned to Israel with his objectives fulfilled. He ignored

American urgings to soften his policies. He forestalled peace plans not only from the US, but also from Shimon Peres. Peres' proposals had called for a withdrawal from some territories, opened the possibility of indirect talks with the PLO, and declared to the Palestinians that Israel did not want to rule over them—and that they could ultimately opt for a federation with Jordan or Israel or both.[68] He was prepared to formally submit these for consideration should Shamir's plan be rejected by the US. Since Washington decided to go along with Shamir, Peres had no choice but to set aside his initiative. Ironically, Peres' proposals were far more acceptable to the Arab states, Palestinians, and that half of the Israeli population recognizing the need to exchange land for peace—and far more consistent with American views.

Administration officials were not elated with Shamir's proposals and outspoken public statements. They gave the proposals little chance of success, believing that they had not gone far enough on major issues (including that of a permanent settlement). Nevertheless, the Bush Administration, anxious to avoid a confrontation with Shamir and the possible need to come up with its own detailed proposals for a comprehensive settlement, decided to use the Shamir election idea in the hope that it could begin a dialogue that would ultimately create its own momentum for broader interim and final status negotiations. US officials began to claim that the plan provided a "foundation we can build on" and, in any case, that it represented the "only plan" presently "on the table" —apparently ignoring other peace plans (Western European, UN, Soviet, Arab, PLO and even the recent Baker proposals and Peres' as yet unsubmitted plan) that had been on the table or were otherwise available. The US thus concentrated its diplomatic efforts on promoting and, if possible, improving the Shamir election proposal.[69]

In Israel, the election proposal generated considerable opposition among Israeli doves (who claimed it did not go far enough, and was designed to be rejected)—and, more importantly, among a substantial number of members of the Knesset from Likud and ultra-right parties (who claimed it went too far and would ultimately lead to a independent state). Shamir assured his right-wing critics that in Washington "I gave away not a single political demand, not a single security aspiration... We shall not give the Arabs one inch of our land... We hold the veto in our hands."[70] He and his advisers also began to set forth positions that rendered his proposals even more unpalatable to Palestinians. These included limits on freedom of expression (such as showing the Palestinian flag) if necessary to prevent violence; opposition to allowing formal international observers to observe the elections; and non-withdrawal of troops from population centers during the election campaign. They also insisted that they would not hold elections until the violence had ended; that Palestinians running in the election "must agree [beforehand] that the occupied lands will not become an independent state;" and that Palestinians in East Jerusalem not be allowed to vote. Moreover, while having repeatedly assured the US and others that "all options are open" for a final settlement, Shamir and other Israeli officials insisted that the option of a Palestinian state was not really open.[71]

While the PLO rejected Shamir's plan, it did accept the principle of elections if they were truly free, held under international supervision, allowed Palestinians in East Jerusalem to vote, and were part of a process leading to Israeli withdrawal from the occupied territories under Resolution 242 and to Palestinian self-determination. While Palestinian leaders believed that Shamir was procrastinating in the hopes that the *intifada* would run its course, they realized that it would harm their position (especially with the US) if they took a completely negative position.

On May 22, Secretary Baker gave an important speech before AIPAC's annual policy council in which he both laid out the parameters within which a realistic solution (as envisaged by the US) would have to take place, and sought to facilitate a start of talks by dislodging both Palestinians and Israelis from what Baker considered unrealistic positions. He said that the US based its views on peace on certain principles, and that "the object of the peace process is a comprehensive settlement" achieved through "direct negotiations" and based on Resolution 242. These negotiations "must involve territory for peace, security and recognition for Israel and all the states of the region, and Palestinian political rights." Since the issues involved are "complex," some "transitional period is needed, associated in time and sequence with negotiations on final status." He added that the US did not support Israeli "annexation or a permanent control of the West Bank and Gaza" nor "the creation of an independent Palestinian state." Israel must "lay aside... the unrealistic vision of a greater Israel... stop settlement activity" and be prepared for some "territorial withdrawal and the emergence of a new political reality." Palestinians must recognize Israel and convince it of their peaceful intentions. They must also accept some form of self-government short of an independent state.[72]

Although Baker's remarks were consistent with longstanding American policy, their blunt tone was nonetheless such a major departure from that of the Reagan Administration that they stunned and angered many in the strongly pro-Israeli audience. While some American Jews felt that the speech was "courageous and overdue," most ardently criticized it for being "cold" and "hostile" to Israel and for causing "unnecessary tensions" between Israel and the US. Some even condemned it for being "too evenhanded."[73] Moreover, according to the *New York Times* (June 9), a letter, "tacitly encouraged by Israeli officials and AIPAC" and signed by 92 senators, urged Baker to be "fully supportive both in fact and appearance" of Shamir's plan. "The letter was meant to send a signal to the Bush Administration that [despite] the Baker speech, support for Israel on Capitol Hill remains very high and that flexibility in pressing Israel for concessions has narrower limits than the Administration may believe."

The Baker speech brought shock waves in Israel. Shamir condemned it as "useless." Right-wingers increased their opposition to the Shamir proposal. Moreover, this increased opposition and the strong support shown by both the Senate and many American Jewish leaders encouraged Shamir to toughen rather than soften his conditions for elections. Thus, he supported a Likud Central Committee resolution passed in July which provided that no Jerusalem Arab could vote; that there would be no surrender of territory or establishment of a Palestinian state; no stopping of the settlements program; and no elections until the uprising ended. While Israel opposed talks on final status, even Baker contended that such talks were necessary "at least in general terms" because this was the only way Palestinians could be convinced to go along with the elections proposal.[74]

While the PLO and West Bank leaders found something "positive" in Baker's speech, they felt that most of it was standard US policy. It did not mention the PLO, rejected a Palestinian state, and still had to be followed by concrete steps if it was to be taken seriously.[75]

In July 1989, Egyptian President Husni Mubarak, in an attempt to give impetus to the Shamir plan, offered to play host to Palestinian-Israeli talks in Cairo and presented a ten-point proposal that provided concessions to both sides. Although the proposal made no mention of either the PLO or a Palestinian state, it did call for voting by East Jerusalem Arabs; a temporary halt to Israeli settlement activities; acceptance of the principle of land for peace, and of Palestinian political rights; and agreement to start final status negotiations by a fixed date. The US, some Palestinian leaders, and even Labor Party leaders supported the proposal. Shamir opposed it, and it was eventually rejected by the Israeli cabinet in a tie vote. Israeli Labor Party leader Shimon Peres once again accused Shamir of "stalling and trying to avoid negotiations." He also complained that the US "was showing insufficient zeal in promoting the peace process," and that in trying to placate Shamir it was actually undermining the efforts of those in Israel who were sincerely trying to achieve peace.[76]

In an attempt to keep the elections idea alive, Secretary Baker presented his own five-point plan in October. This called for the Egyptian and Israeli foreign ministers to meet with him in Washington in early 1990 to consult on the composition of a Palestinian delegation, which would then meet with an Israeli delegation in Cairo. Although discussions in Cairo would focus on the Shamir plan, the Palestinians could "seek clarifications and make suggestions" about the plan.

Israel, Egypt, and the PLO gave only qualified acceptance of the Baker proposals. Shamir asked for assurances that the PLO would not be involved in any way and that the Cairo talks would be strictly limited to discussing his elections initiative. He also reiterated his willingness to face a confrontation with the US over giving up any territory. While making some minor changes in wording to placate the Israeli prime minister, Baker refused to give all the assurances requested of him.[77]

PLO leaders were growing increasingly frustrated at the lack of meaningful progress in the US-PLO dialogue in Tunis. They were unhappy at the failure of the two superpower leaders to give serious consideration to their problem at the Malta summit meeting in December 1989, and continued to complain that the US was trying to exclude the PLO from the peace process.. Still, they did not want to be blamed for any collapse in peace efforts, and felt that they still had more to lose than gain by ending their dialogue with Washington. Indeed, Yasir 'Arafat sought to provide further evidence of the PLO's hope for peace. In a private message to President Bush, he reiterated his desire for peace, urged the US to be more even-handed, and warned that continued failure to make progress would undermine Palestinian moderates and strengthen extremists.[78]

In the middle of November, Shamir made an unofficial visit to the US to speak before Jewish audiences to strengthen their support for his views. He met with Bush and Baker and, despite his major differences with them, once again averted any clash—largely because the administration did not want to precipitate a confrontation with him and his American supporters. Administration officials and some members of congress did complain privately about Israel's harsh policies in the occupied territories, but largely confined their public criticisms to Israel's military ties with South Africa since this represented less of a domestic political risk. Indeed, although some American policy makers again began to question Israel's commitment to peace negotiations, Administration officials assured Shamir that his proposal remained the only plan on the table, that no pressures would be applied to him, and that US-Israeli relations were as firm as ever.[79]

Shamir returned to Israel proclaiming his visit a great success, even though major differences with the US and some American Jewish leaders remained. Many of the latter were now openly criticizing Shamir's hardline views, especially on the land-for-peace formula. Moreover, because of the lack of US support for their position vis-à-vis Shamir, Israeli moderates felt helpless to act and were "weak and almost demoralized."[80] As a consequence Shamir remained confident that he could ignore both US views and those of Israeli Labor Party leaders with impunity. He made it clear that his primary goal was to play for time until he could obtain a settlement on his own terms, declaring that "the [Palestinian] population will... eventually grow disappointed in the *intifada* and with the PLO and then conclude that they must negotiate with us on the basis of our initiative. I hope that this will not take too long."[81]

In late 1989, Secretary Baker pressed Egypt and Israel to send their foreign ministers to meet with him in early 1990 in Washington, where they would discuss the composition of a Palestinian delegation which in turn would take part in discussions with Israel in Cairo regarding the elections proposal. Yet, as former Israeli foreign minister Abba Eban noted, "elections, however important, are not the basic peace issues... None of these [basic] issues is even remotely addressed in the 'only game in town'... In preoccupying itself exclusively with elections, the US is sidetracking the considerable Israeli and Arab opinion that is ready to think about central issues... Nothing is gained by procrastination."[82] As indicated earlier, even Secretary Shultz had concluded by late 1987 that the US was making a serious mistake in concentrating so much of its attention on mere procedural rather than substantive matters. He also realized, as Carter did in 1977, that no peace process could succeed without first attaining prior agreement by the parties on certain basic principles and a general framework essential to any lasting peace settlement. In his "tough" speech in May 1989, Baker himself spelled out such a framework and principles—a "comprehensive settlement" based on the principles of "territory for peace, security, and recognition for Israel and all states, and Palestinian political rights." While Arab and PLO leaders had accepted these principles before the beginning of any negotiations—indeed, the US had refused even to talk to the PLO until it had done so—the US, despite Baker's "tough" talk, appeared unwilling to make a serious effort to secure Israel's essential prior acceptance as well. In fact, Shamir had not only refused to accept most of these principles, but had firmly and publicly rejected them. As had repeatedly happened with the Reagan, Shultz, and other American plans in the past, the Administration then appeared to back away from its own proposals in the face of opposition from Shamir and his American supporters, even though the US continued to insist that the principles it espoused were vital to achieving peace.

The Administration also failed to take advantage of the unique and relatively favorable conditions that existed in 1989 and early 1990 for a real peace initiative. It was the first year of a new presidency, a period when a president is less subject to domestic pressures. Moderate Arab and Palestinian leaders had made virtually all the concessions asked of them by the US. Soviet President Gorbachev had made it increasingly clear that he would cooperate with the US in resolving regional conflicts, including that in the Middle East. Growing numbers of Americans (including American Jews) and Israelis wanted greater US efforts to promote more flexibility on the part of Israel. Western Europe, perturbed by an apparent lack of American concern and urgency, continued to press the US to provide more determined and enlightened leadership. However, the US continued to follow policies that did not work and, thereby, lost yet another uniquely favorable opportunity to promote peace.

In fact, prospects for peace were soon to deteriorate again. In late May, an Israeli gunman killed eight Palestinians. Israeli troops killed many more in the ensuing demonstrations. The Palestinians were further angered by American refusal to grant 'Arafat a visa to appear before the UN Security

Council, and by the US veto of a Security Council resolution calling for UN observers to be sent to the occupied territories. In June, the US decided to suspend its dialogue with the PLO because 'Arafat, while reiterating his opposition to terrorism, refrained from explicitly condemning an unsuccessful raid mounted by a radical PLO splinter group—even though Secretary Baker admitted that such a US move would further weaken Palestinian moderates. That same month, Yitzhak Shamir fashioned a narrowly-based, Likud-led hardline coalition government in Israel. This not only undermined Palestinian hopes of achieving progress through diplomatic means, but even led Bush and Baker to publicly blame Shamir for obstructing the peace process.[83] Frustrated Palestinians began to seek some other way to provide their peace strategy with a stronger base, particularly in the Arab world, which could increase their bargaining power vis-à-vis Israel and the US.

Some saw such an ally in Iraq. While the great majority of PLO leaders disliked President Saddam Husayn's brutal rule, many were attracted to his message: greater Arab unity and strength; stronger opposition to Israel and the US; more determined backing for the Palestinian cause. Moreover, he appeared to be the only Arab leader with both the military power and will to provide the Palestinians with badly needed support. Thus, well before the Gulf crisis erupted on August 2 with Iraq's invasion of Kuwait, many Palestinians—deeply frustrated, with no viable peace process in sight and nowhere else to turn—had begun to look to Baghdad for backing.

After the invasion, perceived PLO support for Iraq served to weaken the Palestinian position in much of the international community and among Israeli doves. Recognizing that support for Iraqi occupation of Kuwait would undermine the PLO's own opposition to Israeli occupation of the West Bank and Gaza, 'Arafat offered peace proposals that, among other things, called for both Iraqi and Israeli withdrawals from occupied territories. At the same time, Palestinians were particularly angry at what was seen as America's double standard: mustering vast military power, international cooperation, and the force of the UN and international law against Iraq's illegal occupation—yet not making any similar effort to end Israel's occupation (and, indeed, supporting Israel to such an extent that it was able to perpetuate its occupation with impunity).

Israel hardliners welcomed Arab disunity, more time to deal with the *intifada* freely, and respite from US pressures to negotiate with the Palestinians. At the same time, they were concerned that determined enforcement of international law and UN resolutions against Iraq, coupled with close cooperation between Washington and key Arab states (Egypt, Saudi Arabia, and even Syria), would ultimately weaken unconditional American support for Israel and possibly create eventual pressure on the US to insist on an Israeli withdrawal from the occupied territories. Meanwhile, Israeli (and American Jewish) doves warned that whatever the outcome of the Gulf crisis, an unresolved Palestinian problem would remain a threat to Israel's democracy and security. Thus, in their eyes, an Israeli peace initiative was needed now more than ever. They also suggested that the failure to find a solution to the Arab-Palestinian-Israeli conflict had a considerable bearing on the outbreak of the Gulf crisis and Palestinian support for Iraq, and that continued occupation of the West Bank and Gaza was not only immoral and illegal, but also harmful to Israel's long-term interests.[84]

At a superpower summit held in Helsinki in early September 1990, Presidents Bush and Gorbachev agreed that it was essential for them to deal actively and cooperatively to resolve the Arab-Palestinian-Israeli conflict, as well as the Gulf crisis. Bush also agreed to consider the eventual convening of some kind of international conference to help resolve the former conflict, as long as it was not linked to the Gulf situation. Secretary Baker stated in testimony to a congressional committee that "international cooperation engendered by the [Iraqi] invasion could become a springboard for ending the Israeli-Palestinian conflict." Moreover, in a meeting with Israeli Foreign Minister David Levy in early August, both men agreed that the Gulf crisis increased the need to revive a "credible" peace process. Baker even stressed that "the Palestinians must have reason to want to join the process"—by, one assumes, offering them adequate incentives and assurances that have so far been lacking.[85] None of this, however, suggested the form such a process might take, nor when and how it would begin. With the Bush administration preoccupied with the Gulf crisis (and fall congressional elections) and, in any case, having yet to give any meaningful sign that it was prepared to apply the necessary pressures on Israel, it seemed unlikely that the US would come up with a more credible peace process than those offered in the past. Yet if the administration did return to a policy of drift and double standards, there was a great danger that leaders of the *intifada* (and Palestinians elsewhere) would be left with little choice but to resort to armed violence—generating further instability and strife, with negative consequences for all sides.

As of September 1990, the outcome of the Gulf crisis remains uncertain. However it develops it seemed likely to have a negative impact on the *intifada*, on Israel's relations with the Palestinians and other Arabs, and with US relations with the area. If it is resolved peacefully and in compliance with UN resolutions, then the peoples and military forces facing each other in the area would be spared much death and destruction. President Bush might also end up with such prestige and popularity that he could—with courageous and farsighted leadership—mobilize Americans and the world community to do whatever is necessary to promote not only a fair, lasting and comprehensive settlement of the Arab-Palestinian-Israeli conflict, but also that new post-cold war world order which he claims to support and which the world desperately needs. To achieve these, he must promote effective enforcement of international law and UN resolutions, and do so consistently, and not selectively. Furthermore, the US itself must insure that it abides by the rule of law. If, on the other hand, the Gulf crisis ends in general war—a conflict that would almost certainly involve both the Arabs and Israel—then result could be disastrous for both the peoples of the Middle East and the US position in the area.

US Policy: An Assessment

The *intifada* has had a major impact in many ways and on many parts of the world. It has forced the Arabs, the PLO, Israel, USSR, the US, and others to reassess—and in some cases to change—their traditional views and policies. It has been unfortunate that all American administrations (with the exception of Carter) have waited for major regional upheaval before realizing either the dangers emanating from an unresolved Arab-Palestinians-Israeli conflict, or the pressing need for the US to reassess and change policies that have, in many ways, done more to exacerbate than resolve this conflict. Unfortunately too, lack of informed, effective, and courageous administration leadership, and the influence of the pro-Israeli lobby on Congress and domestic politics, have plagued (and continue to plague) American peace efforts. Peace-making has also been plagued by many myths and misunderstandings about basic aspects of the conflict and about what needs to be done to resolve it.

The Need for a Comprehensive Settlement

One of these is that direct negotiations are the only path to peace, even though, as Abba Eban has noted, "there is nothing about direct bilateral talks that is *per se* superior to other negotiating formats." On the contrary, in the "history of the Arab-Israeli conflict, all agreements reached have emerged from non-direct, non-bilateral frameworks while all bilateral talks have ended up by accomplishing nothing."[86] Israel, with a strong bargaining position insists upon direct, bilateral talks so that it could use its superior military power and occupation of the territories to compel each Arab party to accept a settlement largely on Israeli terms. An Israeli-imposed peace, however, would likely leave the explosive Palestinian and Jerusalem issues unresolved, Syrian irredentism, and intense Arab bitterness and humiliation—not real peace and stability in the Middle East. Nearly the entire world community—including US Western allies and many Israeli doves—understands this, and that is why it prefers to seek a comprehensive solution based on those principles and guidelines established by UN resolutions and accepted by nearly all states as essential to a just a durable peace. In the final analysis, whether there will be lasting peace will depend not so much on the procedures used as the fairness and mutual acceptability of the final peace terms. Therefore, the US should concentrate on attaining broad agreement among the parties concerned on these principles and guidelines and then use whatever procedures are best suited to achieving this goal. Under existing circumstances direct, bilateral negotiations based on the balance of power concept would be an unrealistic and ineffective procedure.

Moreover, as indicated earlier, agreements achieved through a step-by-step procedure have ended up making it more difficult than ever to deal constructively with other major political and territorial problems, and to promote an overall settlement which alone can produce real, lasting peace. Even the Israeli-Egyptian treaty can ultimately unravel if such a settlement is not achieved.

Finally, any lasting peace will require strong security guarantees from the international community. Consequently, a negotiating process that includes the USSR, Western Europe and the United Nations is more likely to result in an enduring outcome. The dramatic changes taking place in the Soviet Union and Eastern Europe provide a unique opportunity for greater US-Soviet cooperation in promoting Middle East peace. In fact, at the September 1990 Helsinki summit Bush indicated that the Soviet Union could play a helpful role on resolving the Arab-Palestinian-Israeli conflict.

The Question of US Pressure

Although experience seems to indicate that only resolute, effective pressures with major incentives by the US can bring about changes in Israel's hardline policies, various American administrations have continued to rely on mere oral persuasion to try to soften Israel's position even though, as one exasperated Reagan White House official complained: "we've been trying the soft-soap approach for years, and have nothing to show for it."[87] Actually, repeated unconditional US assurances that no pressures would be applied—apparently no matter how harmful and illegal Israeli actions were—have ended up merely encouraging Israel to maintain its hardline stance and to continue disregarding US views and interests.

What Washington appears to ignore, however, is that (as Mark Tessler notes elsewhere in this volume) there is more than one position in Israel regarding the peace process. There are Israeli peace forces who are convinced that Israel's uncompromising position will ultimately undermine its democracy and security and that, because they lack the political clout to influence Israeli policy, only effective pressures applied by the US against intransigent officials and in support of moderate Israeli leaders and groups can make it possible "to save Israel from itself."[88] Polls have shown that large numbers of Americans are prepared for such pressures.[89] Americans who oppose pressures as being counterproductive also overlook the fact that when seriously applied (as by President Eisenhower during the 1956 war) pressures have worked—and that failure to apply enough pressure to soften Israel's tough stands could ultimately prove to be even more counter-productive to American (and Israeli) longterm interests. Moreover, even America's new Arab allies and the international community would find it difficult to understand why the US was so determined to enforce international law and UN resolutions against Iraqi occupation of Kuwait but not against Israeli occupation of the West Bank, Gaza Strip, and Golan Heights.

American Policy and an Independent Palestinian State

US policy has long opposed the establishment of an independent Palestinian state. Much of this opposition has been based on the view that the PLO could not be trusted, and that the security risks to Israel would be too great. Yet, as Israeli strategic analyst Mark Heller has argued:

> The pursuit of a settlement with the PLO leading to an independent Palestinian state, with appropriate risk-minimizing provisions [such as demilitarization, verification measures, and international guarantees] would best promote Israel's fundamental strategic objectives of neutralizing the Palestinian issue as a factor in Israeli-Arab relations and reducing the overall threat to Israeli security, while preserving the Jewish, democratic character and vitality of Israeli society. Such a settlement... would not provide absolute security or guarantee perpetual peace. But given Israel's historic and geographical circumstances, no conceivable posture is without considerable risks and costs. This one, however, is almost surely the "least of all evils." Therefore, a settlement on this basis would probably leave Israel in a better overall position than a continuing stalemate or any other potential outcome.[90]

Similarly, Abba Eban has written "talk of Israel's extermination [by a weak and divided Palestinian state] is nowhere taken seriously by those who know the power balance; it is interpreted as justification for immobilism or pre-emptive aggression."[91] Therefore it is shortsighted for the US to adamantly and permanently oppose a Palestinian state under any and all circumstances. Not only has the world community and many Israeli moderates and Western experts considered such a state essential to any real, lasting peace, but even (as indicated earlier) reports of the Jaffee Center for Strategic Studies and Israeli army intelligence concluded that a future Palestinian state could not be ruled out.

As for the question of trust, former president Carter noted: "I don't think there is anything in the peace treaty between Egypt and Israel that relies on trust. An agreement can be reached based not on trust but on *mutual advantage*" [emphasis added].[92] A harsh, one-sided treaty (like the 1919 Versailles Treaty) will not last long if it lacks mutual advantages, while a fair magnanimous peace treaty (such as those made after WWII) will be more likely to endure since, as indicated earlier, both sides will have good reason to abide by it. Moreover, even Israeli army intelligence concluded that "elements of the PLO have undergone a *real change* and *genuinely* want to reach a political settlement with Israel" [emphasis added]. They want this not because they want to please Israel, but because they realize that this provides their only hope of ever attaining their own (if smaller) state. And whatever the outcome of the Gulf crisis, if moderate PLO leaders were provided with truly meaningful incentives and assurances in time—before more militant leaders might try to replace them—then they would once again be free to seek a compromise peace settlement for this very reason.

Terrorism and Violence

Another issue commonly raised is that of terrorism. This, of course, is a tragic phenomenon. It is, however, an issue that has come to obsess US policy, without the US ever coming to grips with its basic causes.

Fundamentally, terrorism is a symptom rather than a root of the problem. When unable to achieve their goals by peaceful means, many nationalist movements—including Zionist and Palestinian ones—have concluded that they have been left with no alternative to the resort to force. Lacking conventional military capabilities, they have resorted to the weapons of the weak—guerrilla and other acts of violence. Israeli military analyst Ze'ev Schiff stressed that Palestinian terrorism has been due to "deepening frustration and radicalization" as a result of Israeli policies which have pushed them "further in a corner."

> Yet the extremists among us have nothing to offer them except the advice to get used to Israeli occupation or commit suicide as a nation, or get out. We shouldn't be surprised that the Palestinians take up arms or resort to violence. Any people in this situation would do the same, including Jews.[93]

Indeed it is ironic that leading Jewish terrorists of the past, such as Begin and Shamir, now condemn the Palestinians for having recourse to political violence.[94]

To allow terrorism to influence US policy would be to cede control over the Middle East peace process to those who seek to abort it. The US should not have terminated its dialogue with the PLO and its peace efforts because of an attempted guerrilla raid by Palestinian extremists in May 1990; by doing so, it only played into the hands of rejectionists on both sides. As long as the root cause of terrorism has not been eliminated, it will remain very much alive; the US must be prepared to address it realistically and not use it as a pretext for giving up on efforts to promote peace. The long-term solution to Palestinian terrorism—as it was for Jewish terrorism—must be based not on force but on providing a political solution based on the Palestinian right of self-determination. Moreover, an end to dialogue and the peace process would result in more, not less, terrorism.

Israel and US Strategic Interests in the Middle East

As indicated earlier, after the 1967 war American supporters of Israel and increasing numbers of officials and members of Congress found it politically popular to contend that a strong Israel was a major strategic asset in promoting US interests in the Middle East. Various American Administrations thus felt justified in providing large-scale and virtually unconditional economic, military and political aid to Israel; in overlooking many Israeli transgressions; and in supporting Israeli policies and objectives without trying to seriously evaluate how compatible these policies have been with US interests in the Middle East.

This view, however, has been challenged by many top American political and military officials whose expertise and concerns involved US strategic and military interests. One of these, Harry J. Shaw, has written that "the Pentagon, particularly the Joint Chiefs of Staff, has long regarded a close military relationship with Israel with misgiving... and the US military continues to have reservations about Israel's value as a [strategic] partner. Similarly, Secretary of Defense Caspar Weinberger and some senior generals and State Department experts, were said to be concerned about the larger strategic realities in the Middle East and convinced that maintaining good relations with the more economically and geopolitically important Arab world was vital to American strategic interests, warned against neglecting American ties with friendly Arab states and allowing the US to become "a hostage to Israeli policy".[95] In fact, the Gulf crisis and the resulting strategic dependency on key Arab states—not Israel—only seved to underline the accuracy of these views.

Even the most pro-American Arab leaders had regarded the Soviet threat to be far more remote and less dangerous than the threat posed by Israel and by those extreme nationalist and Islamic forces whose strength and influence have been abetted by Israel's hardline policies (directly or indirectly condoned by the US) and by the failure to resolve the Palestinian issue. Even conservative Arab governments had turned to the USSR for military and political support because they felt they had no alternative. Thus, as a consequence of its militant and uncompromising stand, Israel became more of a liability than an asset in preventing the spread of Soviet influence. Moreover, given the revolutionary political changes that have taken place within the USSR, Eastern Europe, and US-Soviet relations, the Soviet challenge has virtually disappeared—thereby furthering undermining the argument that that the US needs a strong Israel to help block Soviet expansionism.

As for the claim that a strong Israel is essential to promote stability and ensure the survival of moderate Arab regimes, Israel's tough actions have actually had the reverse effect. By helping to prevent the solution of the Arab-Israeli conflict and thereby promoting the growth of radical Islamic and nationalist forces, Israeli policy has frequently served to foster conflict and instability (the *intifada* being a good example of this) and weakened rather than strengthened pro-Western governments in the area.

Therefore, as long as Israel continues to maintain a hardline stance, to disregard US concerns, and to follow policies harmful to US interests, it cannot seriously be considered a strategic asset. Moreover, as Harry Shaw has warned, the "strategic partner myth" has hampered and will hamper "American efforts to protect its interests when Israel's actions threaten them" because it will continue to encourage the US to acquiesce in even those aggressive policies with which it disagrees "in the name of preserving presumably critical strategic benefits."[96]

The *Intifada* and the Future of US Policy

Since the *intifada* broke out in December 1987, important changes have taken place that in some ways have improved the climate for peace. The PLO and all key Arab governments have publicly and clearly accepted Resolution 242 and Israel's right to exist. American officials and public opinion—and even many Israelis—have recognized the critical roles the Palestinian issue and the PLO play in the Middle East conflict. The US belatedly opened a dialogue with the PLO. The Soviets have been playing a moderating role and have been anxious to resolve the Middle Eastern and other regional conflicts. There has never been such broad international consensus about the urgent need for a political solution, and the broad principles essential to any just and lasting peace. There is also broad agreement among many experts, Western European leaders, and some Israelis that while moderate Arabs and Palestinians have for years been prepared to accept these principles, Israel's continued refusal to do so "remains the very core of the Middle East stalemate." As a result, many believe that there can be no serious progress on the peace process without strong, evenhanded, enlightened leadership by the US.[97] Whatever the outcome of the Gulf crisis, the explosive Arab-Palestinian-Israeli conflict will continue to plague the area and, therefore, must be resolved.

Over the years American officials have allowed ignorance, domestic politics, and lack of political courage to prevent them from adopting those balanced and farsighted policies essential to peace. Therefore, no peace initiative can succeed until top American officials themselves first acquire more accurate and complete understanding about the basic roots of the Arab-Palestinian-Israeli problem; the real obstacles to resolving it; and the policies needed to overcome those obstacles and achieve a settlement which adequately takes into consideration the legitimate interests and needs of all parties directly involved. They should then, as Carter tried to do in 1977, try to promote a better understanding in Congress and among the American public of the realities of the situation: of the dangers to the US (as well as to Arabs and Israelis) in an unresolved Arab-Palestinian-Israeli conflict; of the need to take risks for peace (because the risks of the status quo are far greater); and of the actions the US must take to promote that real durable peace so vital to America and the world. For many years, the US has allowed Israel to follow with impunity even those policies which US officials considered harmful both to peace and to US interests. It is now time for the US to back the moderates in Israel and to make the hardliners there understand that the US will start giving highest priority to what it considers most important to its own vital interests (and a fair and just peace settlement is such a vital interest), and that the US will take whatever actions necessary (including applying pressure) to achieve such a settlement. Most Americans and many Israelis would support such a move. Sooner or later these difficult and politically hazardous decisions and actions will have to be taken because they provide the key to peace in the Middle East.

Notes

1. Interview in *Ha'r*, 23 September 1983, in *Israel Press Briefs* (International Center for Peace in the Middle East, Tel Aviv) October 1989, p.9 [henceforth *IPB*].

2. *State Department Bulletin*, 5 January 1970.

3. Amnon Kapeliuk, "To Whom Does the West Bank Belong?" *New Outlook*, December 1977/January 1988, p. 47; Simha Flapan (ed.), *When Enemies Dare to Talk: an Israeli-Palestinian Debate* (London: Croom Helm, 1979), p. 24; Simha Flapan, "Begin and the Diaspora," *New Outlook*, June/July 1977, p. 18.

4. State Department *Bulletin*, 5 January 1970; Michael Brecher, *Decisions in Israel's Foreign Policy* (New Haven: Yale University Press, 1975), pp. 483ff; Malcolm Kerr (ed.), *The Elusive Peace in the Middle East* (Albany: University of New York Press, 1975), pp. 140, 293.

5. Jon Kimche, *There Could Have Been Peace* (New York: Dial, 1973), p. 311.

6. Gerald R. Ford, *A Time to Heal: The Autobiography of Gerald R. Ford* (New York: Harper & Row, 1979), pp. 245, 287; Edward Sheehan, "How did Kissinger Do It? Step by Step in the Middle East," *Foreign Policy* 22 (Spring 1976): 199; Peretz Merhav, "Challenge Facing the Doves," *New Outlook*, April/May 1976, p. 10.

7. Fred J. Khouri, *Arab-Israeli Dilemma* 3rd ed. (Syracuse: Syracuse University Press, 1985), pp. 379ff; *Israel Digest*, 12 September 1975, 5 December 1975; *New York Times*, 3 October 1975; *New Outlook*, July/August 1974, p. 2, One senior Israeli official noted: "We have been maneuvering since 1967 to gain more time and to return as little as possible. The predominant government view has been that stalemates are to our advantage." Sheehan, "How Did Kissinger Do It?" p. 64.

8. Zbigniew Brzezinski, *Power and Principle: Memoirs of the National Security Adviser, 1977-1981* (New York: Farrar, Straus Girioux, 1973), pp. 83ff, 87; Cyrus Vance, *Hard Choices: Critical Years in America's Foreign Policy* (New York: Simon Schuster, 1983), pp. 163, 166.

9. Jimmy Carter, *Keeping the Faith: Memoirs of a President* (New York: Bantam Books, 1983), pp. 280-281, 288; Vance, *Hard Choices*, pp. 164ff; Brzezinski, *Power and Principle*, p. 87.

10. Carter, *Keeping the Faith*, p. 280; Vance, *Hard Choices*, pp. 166-167, 173ff; Brzezinski, *Power and Principle*, p. 90; *New York Times*, 21 August 1977. Author's discussions with top officials in Jordan, Syria and Egypt in October-November 1977.

11. Yitzhak Rabin, *The Rabin Memoirs* (Boston: Little Brown, 1979), pp. 263, 293-

97; *New York Times*, 14 March 1977.

12. Moshe Dayan, *Breakthrough: A Personal Account of the Egypt-Israel Peace Negotiations* (New York: Alfred A. Knopf, 1981), pp. 59, 69; Brzezinski, *Power and Principle*, pp. 105, 110, 121.

13. Helena Cobban, *The Palestine Liberation Organization: People, and Politics* (Cambridge: Cambridge University Press, 1984), p. 240; Mattityahu Peled, "Talking to the PLO," *New Outlook*, March/April 1983, pp. 28ff; Robert O. Friedman (ed.), *World Politics and the Arab-Israeli Conflict* (New York: Pergamon Press, 1979), p. 229. Author's discussions with PLO officials in Damascus and Beirut in November 1977.

14. Brzezinski, *Power and Principle*, pp. 109ff; Vance, *Hard Choices*, pp. 192-193; Cobban, *The Palestine Liberation Organization*, p.90; *New York Times*, 5, 6 October 1977, 2 May 1978.

15. Carter, *Keeping the Faith*, pp. 191, 304.

16. Ezer Weizman, *The Battle for Peace* (New York: Bantam Books, 1982), pp. 137-138.

17. Weizman, *The Battle for Peace*, pp. 151, 190, 334, 383-384; Vance, *Hard Choices*, p. 197; Brzezinski, *Power and Principle*, p. 255-256.

18. Brzezinski, *Power and Principle*, pp. 276ff, 438.

19. *New York Times*, 8, 18, 19 April, 16 November, 1 December 1981.

20. *New York Times*, 18 April, 31 December 1981, 25 January 1982; *Washington Post*, 5 May 1982; Ze'ev Schiff, "Green Light, Lebanon," *Foreign Policy* 50 (Spring 1983): 78-82.

21. Department of State, *Current Policy* 524 (October 1983); *New York Times*, 9, 12 Sepember 1982.

22. *Washington Post*, 3, 11 September, 5 November 1982; *New York Times*, 22 December 1982; Larry L. Fabian, "The Middle East War Dangers and Receding Peace Prospects," *Foreign Affairs: America and the World*, (1983): 642.

23. *New York Times*, 15, 16 September 1982; *Journal of Palestine Studies*, 12, 2 (Winter 1983): 202.

24. *New York Times*, 4 September, 13 October, 16 December 1982, 12 April 1983; Fabian, "The Middle East War..." p. 638; *Christian Science Monitor*, 24 February 1983.

25. *New York Times*, 1, 5, 7 November, 4, 5 December 1983, 20 July 1984; *Philadelphia Inquirer*, 27 November, 3 December 1983.

26. *New York Times*, 15 February 1982, 11 December 1983, 20 July 1984.

27. *New York Times*, 30 November 1983; *Philadelphia Inquirer*, 30 November 1983.

28. *UN Report of the International Conference on the Question of Palestine*, Geneva/Conf. 114/12, pp.68-75; *U.N. Chronicle*, February 1984, pp. 81-88; *New York Times*, 24 April, 14 June 1980, 12 February, 15 October, 6, 10, 12 November 1981, 15 April, 30 June 1982, 11 December 1983; *Christian Science Monitor*, 11 June 1982; *Philadelphia Inquirer*, 5 December 1983, *Newsweek*, 9 March 1981, p. 2.

29. *New York Times*, 22 May 1986. Text of statement in *Journal of Palestine Studies* 14, 4 (Summer 1985): 123.

30. Text of statement in *Journal of Palestine Studies* 15, 4 (Summer, 1986): 138.

31. Text of statement in *Journal of Palestine Studies* 16, 4 (Summer 1987): 95.

32. *New York Times*, 24 February 1985, 3 May 1987, 3, 17 May, 3 November 1988; *Journal of Palestine Studies*, 17, 1 (Autumn, 1987): 187; *American-Arab Affairs* 22 (Fall 1987): 120.

33. *Davar*, 31 December 1987, in *IPB*, February 1988, p.2; *Yediot Aharonot*, 19 February 1988, in *IPB*, April 1988, p.4; *New York Times*, 19 February 1988. See also *Ha'Aretz*,4 December 1989, in *IPB*, December 1987-January 1988, p.7.

34. *New York Times*, 17 May, 18 October 1987.

35. *New York Times*, 21 October 1987.

36. Administration official quoted in *Philadelphia Inquirer*, 24 January 1988; *New York Times*, 5 February 1988.

37. *New York Times*, 24 (including editorial), 25, 26, 27 January, 5, 7 February, 2 March, 8 May 1988; *Philadelphia Inquirer*, 16 December 1987, 21 February 1988. A poll quoted in *Time*, 18 February 1988, held that 50 percent of Americans stated that Israel was using too much force and the US had the right to criticize Israel for this, and 56 percent said that Israel was treating the Palestinians in the occupied areas "unfairly."

38. *New York Times*, 4 March 1988; text in *American-Arab Affairs* 24 (Spring 1988): 142.

39. *New York Times*, 26 February 1988.

40. *New York Times*, 17, 18, 25 March, 5 April 1988; *Philadelphia Inquirer*, 22 April 1988; *Jewish Exponent*, 12 February 1988.

41. *New York Times*, 5, 22 April 1988; Yoel Marcus, *Ha'Aretz*, 7 April 1988, in *Journal of Palestine Studies* 17, 4 (Summer 1988): 153-155.

42. *New York Times*, 4 April 1988.

43. *Jerusalem Post*, 25 November 1988, in *New Outlook* (Tel Aviv), January 1989, p. C.

44. *Philadelphia Inquirer*, 7 April 1988; *Washington Report on Middle Eastern Affairs*, January 1989, p. 10; *New York Times*, 22 August 1988.

45. *New York Times*, 17 September 1988, 13 January 1989.

46. *New York Times*, 17 November 1988; *Washington Report on Middle Eastern Affairs*, December 1988, p. 5.

47. *Philadelphia Inquirer*, 17 November, 4 December 1988; *New York Times*, 18, 20 November 1988.

48. *New York Times*, 9, 26, 28 November, 1 December 1988.

49. *New York Times*, 15 December 1988; *Philadelphia Inquirer*, 28 December 1988.

50. *New York Times*, 15, 16 December 1988.

51. *New York Times*, 16 December 1988; *Philadelphia Inquirer*, 18 December 1988, 3 March 1989; *Davar*, 18 December 1988, in *IPB*, January 1989, p. 10; *Jerusalem Post*, 19 December 1988 in *IPB*, January 1989, p. 12.

52. *The Washington Report on Middle Eastern Affairs*, January 1989, p. 13.

53. *Jewish Exponent* (Philadelphia), 17 March 1989.

54. *Jewish Exponent*, 31 February 1989; *New York Times*, 12, 18 October, 2 November, 27 December 1987, 19 February, 7 March 1988, 4 February 1989; *Philadelphia Inquirer*, 26 January, 16 December 1988. In April 1990 AIPAC, the Anti-Defamation League of the B'nai B'rith, and other Jewish organizations openly criticized the Israeli government for funding a Jewish settlement in the Christian sector of East Jerusalem; see *New York Times*, 25 April 1990.

55. *Philadelphia Inquirer* 21 February 1989; *New York Times*, 4, 13 February, 15 March 1989; *Jerusalem Post* (international edition), 11 March 1989. Senate Republican leader Robert Dole was one of the few members of Congress to publically criticize Israeli actions. Others were said to share his views—but were "too politically insecure" to voice them. *New York Times*, 30 April 1990.

56. *New York Times*, 18 January 1989; *Philadelphia Inquirer*, 20 January 1989; *Newsweek*, 30 March 1988, p. 41; *New Outlook*, January 1989, pp. 4, 9.

57. *Jewish Exponent*, 3 March 1989; *New York Times*, 22 March, 2 April 1989; *Middle East International*, 17 February 1989.

58. *New York Times*, 9, 21 March 1989; *Christian Science Monitor*, 15 March 1989; *Jewish Exponent*, 10 March 1989; *Jerusalem Post* (international edition), 18 March 1989.

59. *Peace Now: A Newsletter to our Friends in North America*, Summer 1988, pp. 1, 5.

60. *Philadelphia Inquirer*, 4 April 1989 reported that key positions in the State Department and White House were filled with those who were "very supportive of Israel and sympathetic to its needs." In fact, Deputy Secretary of State Lawrence Eagleburger, Undersecretary for Political Affairs Robert Kimmitt, Assistant Secretary for Policy Planning, Dennis Ross, top Middle East adviser on the National Security Council, Richard Haas, and others had close personal ties with top Israeli leaders and officials and became key advisers to Bush and Baker on the Middle East. Three of the most influential of these men had been associated with the Washington Institute for Near East Policy, a relatively pro-Israeli "think tank," and helped write its 1988 study *Building for Peace in the Middle East*. The study advocated a cautious step-by-step approach, concentrating on reducing violence and urging confidence building measures; election of local Palestinian leaders to negotiate with Israel a transitional arrangement providing for limited self rule before negotiating a final settlement; supported direct negotiations; opposed a Palestinian state; and urged the US to work closely with Israel and to maintain Israeli military superiority. Bush and Baker appeared to have been strongly influenced by this report.

61. *New York Times*, 12 March 1989.

62. *New York Times*, 14, 15, 16, 17, 22 March 1989; *Jewish Exponent*, 17 March 1989.

63. For critical comment on the Baker proposals, see the editorials in the *New York Times*, 15 March 1989, and *Philadelphia Inquirer*, 19 March 1989. See also *Christian Science Monitor*, 13 March 1989; *Nation*, 3 April 1989; *New York Times*, 16 February 1989; *Philadelphia Inquirer*, 17 March 1989.

64. *Jewish Exponent*, March 31, 1989.

65. Critics included Labor Party figures (such as Peres and Eban), newspaper editorials (as in *Jerusalem Post*, 11 March 1989), former Israeli officials and experts (as Yehosofat Harkabi, Meron Benvevisti, and Yehoshua Porath) and others, who accused Shamir and Likud of trying to "sabotage the peace process;" of making proposals "when you know they will not be accepted so that you can blame the Palestinians and Arabs of being rejectionists" and using them to provide "a cover for what he really wants: to leave things as they are;" and of accusing the PLO of being an "unregenerate terrorist organization" out to destroy Israel not because of security considerations, but because it provides "an excuse for pursuing his maximalist aims" of a Greater Israel. See: *Jerusalem Post* (international edition) 7 February 1987, 10 March 1988, 11 February 1989; *Yediot Aharonot*, 3 December 1987, in *IPB* January 1988, p.4; *Yediot Aharonot*, 27 September 1988 in *IPB* November 1988; *New Outlook*, January 1989, p. B; *New York Times*, 21 August, 25 December 1988, 9 April 1989; *Philadelphia Inquirer*, 18 December 1988.

66. *Philadelphia Inquirer*, 7 April 1989.

67. *New York Times*, 7, 9 April 1989; *Philadelphia Inquirer*, 4 May 1989; *Jerusalem Post* (international edition), 29 April 1989.

68. *Jewish Exponent*, 24 March 1989.

69. *New York Times*, 8 April, 9, 10, 18 May 1989.

70. *Jerusalem Post* (international edition), 27 May 1989.

71. *New York Times*, 24 April 1989; *The Other Israel*, April/May 1989, p. 1; *Philadelphia Inquirer*, 4 May 1989, *Middle East International*, 28 April, 1989, p.5.

72. *New York Times*, 23 May 1989; *Philadelphia Inquirer*, 23 May 1989.

73. *New York Times*, 23, 24, May 1989; *Philadelphia Inquirer*, 23 May 1989.

74. *New York Times*, 24 May 1989; *Philadelphia Inquirer*, 24 May 1989; *Christian Science Monitor*, 25 May 1989.

75. *New York Times*, 24 May 1989; *Philadelphia Inquirer*, 24 May 1989.

76. *Philadelphia Inquirer*, 7 October 1989; *Middle East International*, 20 October 1989, p. 9

77. *Jewish Exponent*, 22 December 1989; *New York Times*, 16 November 1989; *Middle East International*, 1 December 1989.

78. *Middle East International*, 20 October, 1 December 1989; *Jerusalem Post* (international edition), 18 November 1989.

79. Quotation from *Jewish Exponent*, 22 December 1989. See also *Jerusalem Post* (international edition), 25 November, 2 December 1989; *Jewish Exponent*, 17 November 1989; *Middle East International*, 1 December 1989.

80. *Middle East International*, 1 December 1989. The *Jerusalem Post* (international edition), 25 November 1989, spoke of Shamir's reception by many American Jews as "lukewarm," and of open letters to him from mainstream Jewish leaders in the US that were extremely critical of his inflexible position, especially on the land-for-peace formula. See also *Jerusalem Post* (international edition), 2, 15 November, 2 December 1989; *Time*, 11 December 1989, p. 60.

81. *Washington Report on Middle Eastern Affairs*, December 1989.

82. *New York Times*, 30 December 1989.

83. *Washington Post*, 12, 18 June 1990.

84. Peace Now letter to its memebers, dated 17 August 1990; advertisement by the the Israel Council for Israeli-Palestinian Peace in *Ha'Aretz*, 17 August 1990; letter sent out by the Jewish Committee on the Middle East in Washington, D.C., dated 1 September 1990.

85. *Middle East International*, 14 September 1990; *New York Times*, 6,7 August 1990.

86. *Yediot Aharonot*, 3 December 1987 in *IPB*, December 1977/January 1988, p.5; *Maariv*, 20 February 1989 in *IPB*, March/April 1987, p.8.

87. *Philadelphia Inquirer*, 22 April 1988; *New York Times*, 25 January, 15 February, 8 August 1982, 26 February 1989; *Philadelphia Inquirer*, 22 April 1988, 14 April 1989; *Time*, 5 December 1988, p.5; Edward Sheehan, "It Changes, It Changes Not," *Journal of Palestine Studies* 7, 1 (Autumn 1977): 188. According to the *Jewish Exponent*, 12 February 1988, American diplomats and experts have warned that the "key to success" of any American peace move "may be the amount of pressure" that the US exerts on Shamir.

88. According to *Yediot Aharonot*, 31 August 1982, many Israelis were "praying in their hearts that Washington would save Israel from herself" by applying pressures. See also *Davar*, 29 September 1982; *Ha'Aretz*, 29 March 1984; *Jerusalem Post*, 7 November 1982; *IPB*, September 1982, pp. 6, 8; April 1984, p. 12; April 1988, p. 3; *Jerusalem Post* (international edition), 16 March 1989; *New Outlook*, January 1984, p. 28; Yehoshofat Harkabi, *The Bar Kokhba Syndrome: Risk and Realism in International Politics* (Chappaqua, NY: Rossel Books, 1983), pp. 178, 180; *New York Times*, 15, 22 April 1988; *Journal of Palestine Studies* 17, 4 (Summer 1988): 153-155.

89. *San Antonio Express*, 14 March 1989; *New York Times*, 26 February 1989; see also Rabbi Arthur Hertzberg, *New York Times*, 17 May 1984. *Washington Report on Middle Eastern Affairs*, April 1989, p. 22. See the polls in *Time*, 8 February 1988, 2 January 1989, p. 40; *New York Times*, 18 March, 7 December, 1988; *Philadelphia Inquirer*, 27 November, 15 December 1988, 4 April 1989.

90. Mark Heller, *A Palestinian State: The Implications for Israel* (Cambridge, MA: Harvard University Press, 1983), pp. 146-147, 153-154. See also *Trialogue* (Trilateral Commission), Winter 1983, p. 41.

91. *New York Times*, 2 January 1989.

92. *New York Times*, 26 March 1989.

93. *Ha'Aretz*, 28 July, 5 September 1985, in *IPB* August 1985, p. 15 and October 1985, pp. 3-4.

94. See, for example, Shamir's justification of violence in a 1943 Stern Gang publication on "Terrorism," *Al Hamishmar*, 24 December 1987, in *IPB*, December

1987/January 1988, pp. 22-23.

95. Harry J. Shaw, "Strategic Dissensus," *Foreign Policy* 61 (Winter 1985/86): 136; *New York Times*, 15 February 1982; 11 December 1983; 24 July 1984.

96. Shaw, "Strategic Dissensus," pp. 125, 128, 136, 138, 141. See also George Ball, "What is an Ally?" *American-Arab Affairs* 6 (Fall 1983): 9, 12; John C. Campbell, "The Security Factor in US Middle East Policy," *American-Arab Affairs* 5 (Summer 1983): 2.

97. *Time*, 25 April 1983, p.32; statement by Jimmy Carter quoted by *Middle East Perspectives*, April 1984; *New York Times*, 16, 20 December 1988; Mordechai Bentov, "Israel and Palestine: Siamese Twins," *New Outlook*, March/April 1983; International Center for Peace in the Middle East, *Newsletter*, December 1984, p. 1; *Yediot Aharonot*, 1 August 1983, in *IPB* September 1983, p.5; Fred J. Khouri, "Major Obstacles to Peace: Ignorance, Myths and Misconceptions," *American-Arab Affairs* 16 (Spring 1986): 53-62.

About the Editor and Contributors

Rex Brynen is assistant professor of political science and chairperson of the Middle East Studies program at McGill University. He is author of *Sanctuary and Survival: the PLO in Lebanon* (Westview Press, 1990) and a coeditor of *The Many Faces of National Security: Dilemmas of Security and Development in the Arab World*. His articles have appeared in *Arab Studies Quarterly*, *International Perspectives*, the *Journal of Refugee Studies*, the *Journal of Palestine Studies*, and elsewhere.

Lamis Andoni is an Amman-based journalist. Her articles have appeared in the *Jordan Times, Middle East International, Middle East Report, Washington Post, Financial Times, Guardian,* and *Christian Science Monitor.*

Neil Caplan is an instructor in the Department of Humanities, Vanier College. He is author of *Futile Diplomacy*, a two volume study of Arab-Zionist negotiation during the Mandate period. His articles and reviews on the evolution of the Arab-Israeli conflict have appeared in the *Journal of Contemporary History*, *Jerusalem Quarterly*, the *Wiener Library Bulletin*, *International History Review*, *Middle East Focus*, the *Journal of Palestine Studies*, and the *Historical Journal*.

Fred Khouri is professor emeritus, Department of Political Science, Villanova University. He is author of *The Arab States and the UN* and *The Arab-Israeli Dilemma* (now in its third edition). He has contributed chapters to a number of books and published articles in *Arab-American Affairs*, the *Middle East Journal*, *New Outlook*, *Middle East Forum*, the *Journal of South Asian and Middle Eastern Studies*, the *Review of Politics*, and elsewhere.

Bahgat Korany is professor in the Department of Political Science and director of the Arab Studies Program at the Université de Montréal. He is author or coauthor of *The Foreign Policies of Arab States* (Westview Press, second edition forthcoming 1991), *How Foreign Policy Decisions Are Made in the Third World* (Westview Press, 1986) and three other books. He has also contributed chapters to more than ten other books and authored some thirty-five articles in such periodicals as *Revue Française de Science Politique*, *Études Internationales*, *International Social Science Journal*, *Journal of South Asian and Middle Eastern Studies*, *Third World Affairs Yearbook*, *World Politics*, and others.

Fred Lawson is associate professor in the Department of Government at Mills College. He is the author of *Bahrain: The Modernization of Autocracy* (Westview Press, 1989). His articles on Syria have appeared in *International Organization*, *Middle East Report*, the *Journal of South Asian and Middle Eastern Studies* and *Power and Stability in the Middle East.*

Paul Noble is associate professor of political science, McGill University. He is a coeditor of *The Many Faces of National Security: Dilemmas of Security and Development in the Arab World.* His articles on the Middle East have appeared in *The Foreign Policies of Arab States*, *Canada and the Arab World*, and *International Perspectives.*

Nadim Rouhana is assistant professor of psychology at Boston College and formerly lecturer in the Department of Psychology at Harvard University. He is the author of numerous articles on Arab-Jewish interaction and the social and political transformation of the Palestinians in Israel. An earlier, abbreviated version of his chapter previously appeared in the *Journal of Palestine Studies.*

Raja Shehadeh is cofounder of *al-Haq*/Law in the Service of Man, the West Bank affiliate of the International Commission of Jurists. He is also author of a number of articles and books, including *The Third Way: A Journal of Life in the West Bank* and *Occupier's Law: Israel and the West Bank.* An earlier, abbreviated version of his chapter previously appeared in the *Journal of Palestine Studies.*

Salim Tamari is professor of sociology at Birzeit University. His articles on the occupied territories have appeared in the *Journal of Palestine Studies*, MERIP *Middle East Report*, *Occupation: Israel Over Palestine*, *Intifada: The Palestinian Uprising Against Israeli Occupation*, and elsewhere.

Mark Tessler is professor of political science at the University of Wisconsin, Milwaukee and president of the Association for Israel Studies. Among his many publications is *Israel, Egypt and the Palestinians: From Camp David to Intifada* (coauthored with Ann Lesch). Under grants from the US government, Professor Tessler currently administers academic partnerships between UWM and both al-Najah National University (Nablus) and the Hebrew University of Jerusalem. An earlier version of his chapter will appear in the *Wisconsin International Law Journal.*

Tamar Weinstein is a television producer with the Canadian Broadcasting Corporation's current affairs program *The Journal.* She holds a Ph.D. in political science from the University of Toronto, specializing in Middle East and Soviet politics.

Index

Abbud, 35
Abdallah bin Husayn, King, 120
'Abd al-Meguid, Ismat, 203-204, 206-207, 209, 251
'Abu Sharif, Bassam, 144, 148, 254-255
Abu Zant, 'Abd al-Munim, 185, 194(n64)
Acre, 103(fig)
Afghanistan, 152, 239, 256-257, 271, 278
Algeria, 137, 150, 215, 218, 220
Aloni, Shulamit, 76-77
American-Israeli Public Affairs Committee (AIPAC), 274-275, 281, 287
Amin, Mustafa, 211(n2)
Amman, 179
Amman Accords (1985), 124, 135, 167, 187, 275
Amirav, Moshe, 79, 82
Angola, 239
Ansar III, 100
Arab Cooperation Council, 150, 172, 188
Arab-Israeli wars, 129(n5)
(1948), 6, 105, , 115(n124), 120-121, 197
(1956), 6, 121, 197, 294
(1967), 1, 6, 121, 122, 197-198, 243, 246, 265
(1973), 20, 122, 137, 210, 216, 219, 236, 246, 267-268
(1982), 20, 86, 124, 126, 133, 135, 160(n14), 196, 201-202, 210, 213 (n19), 216, 246-247, 271-272
Arab League, 119, 150,195-196, 198, 255
Algiers summit (1988), 119, 140-144, 150, 168, 170
Amman summit (1987), 2, 125, 136-137, 140, 142, 168, 190(n7, 23), 196, 225
Baghdad summit (1978), 17, 171; (1990), 119, 128
Cairo summit (1990), 158
Casablanca summit (1989), 119, 127-128, 150-151, 196, 231
Fez summit (1982), 150, 272
Khartoum summit (1967), 198
Rabat summit (1974), 122, 124, 166, 170
Arab nationalism, 121, 122, 126, 211 (n2), 220-221
Araba Valley, 170
'Arafat, Yasir, 124, 127, 134-135, 139-142, 147, 149-150, 154-155, 158, 166, 169, 181, 183, 190(n7), 193 (n62), 204, 209, 216, 218, 220-221, 224-225, 228-231, 245-246, 252, 272, 275, 281, 284, 289
Arens, Moshe, 49, 52, 89, 114(n6), 193 (n60), 248
Ariel, 35
Arrabe, 106
'Arqub, 226
Asad, Hafiz al-, 121, 134, 140-141, 215, 225-226, 228, 231, 252-253, 267, 269
Association for Civil Rights in Israel, 56, 92(n25)
'Atallah, 'Atallah ("Abu Za'im"), 167, 175, 189(n6), 191(n38)
Australia, 273
Avenieri, Shlomo, 85
Awad, Lewis, 211(n2)
'Awn, Michel, 149, 230, 231-232
'Ayn al-Hilwa refugee camp, 225

Badran, Mudar, 187
Baka al-Gharbiyya, 107
Ba'lbak, 231
Balata refugee camp, 41(n15)
Bali, Ibrahim, 35
Baker, James, 238, 282, 284-285, 287-289, 292, 302(n60).
Bayt Sahur, 17, 34
Baz, Usama al-, 203-204, 206-207
Begin, Menahem, 123, 199, 202, 266, 269-272
Beilin, Yossi, 78
Beirut, 141, 149, 226-227, 232-233, 272
Ben-Eliezar, Benyamin, 56
Benvenisti, Meron, 16, 25(n1), 32, 302 (n60)
Berri, Nabih, 227
Biqa' Valley, 222-223, 226, 233

Bovin, A., 254
Brand, Laurie, 228
Burj al-Barajina refugee camp, 225-227
Brezhnev, Leonid, 247, 256, 263(n5), 272
Britain, 120
Bush, George, 238, 240, 280, 282-284, 289, 292, 294, 302(n60)

Cambodia, 239
Camp David accords (1978), 2, 20, 62, 123, 133, 151, 155, 169, 195, 197, 199, 202, 218, 221, 238, 244, 246, 270-271
Canada, 235-236, 273-274
Carter, Jimmy, 199, 246, 253, 268-271, 274, 293, 295, 298
Central America, 239, 257, 259
China, 152
civil disobedience, 9: strikes, 9, 24, 38, 64, 216; tax boycotts, 9, 24, 38
Cohen, Elon, 109
Cohen, Geula, 51, 53
Cohen, Ran, 53
collaboration, 8, 12(n6), 18, 26(n15)
Council for Peace and Security, 82-84, 86, 95(n95)

Dahir, Mikhail, 229
Dajani, Raja'i, 176
Damur, 223
Darwish, Samir, 107
Davis, Rick, 174
Dayan, Moshe, 270
Dayan, Yael, 94(n67)
Dayr Hanna, 106
Democratic Front for the Liberation of Palestine (DFLP), 12(n7), 21, 24, 140, 179, 183
Dine, Thomas, 274
Dobrynin, 246
Druckman, Haim, 31

Eagleburger, Lawrence, 302(n60)
East-West relations, 2-3, 133-134, 149, 152, 239-240, 255-256, 259, 261-262, 267, 269-270, 278, 280, 290, 292-294, 297
Eban, Abba, 53, 81, 94(n77), 265-266, 277, 290, 293, 295, 302(n60)
Egypt, 3, 62, 68, 88, 120-123, 126, 137, 150, 154, 157-159, 172, 179, 188, 192(n48), 198, 215-217, 219, 229, 231, 244, 267
  mediation efforts, 119, 126, 128, 139, 145-146, 152-153, 208-210, 213(n39, 40), 288-289
  political groups/parties: Arab Socialist Union, 197; communists, 203; Muslim Brotherhood, 203; National Democratic Party, 203; National Progressive Unionist Party, 201, 203; Socialist Labor Party, 201, 203; Socialist Liberal Party, 201, 203; Wafd, 203
  press, 201-202, 203, 205: *al-Ahali*, 201-202; *al-Ahram*, 201; 197, 201, 205; *al-Ahrar*, 201; *al-Akhbar*, 201; *al–Gumhurriya*, 201, 205; *al-Sha'b*, 201
  public opinion, 200-201
  recognition of Palestinian statehood, 146, 206-208
  relations with Israel, 123, 126, 152, 159, 195-197, 199-203, 205-206, 208, 210, 213(n19), 265, 267-268. *See also* Camp David accords; Egyptian-Israeli peace treaty
  relations with PLO, 122, 126, 136, 138-139, 145-148, 152-153, 156, 158, 193(n62), 202, 204, 206, 208-210, 220
  role conflict in foreign policy, 196-197, 199-202, 205-206, 208, 210
  See also Soviet Union, United States
Egyptian-Israeli peace treaty (1979), 123, 126, 138, 195-197, 199-201, 205-206, 208. 210, 217, 238, 270-271, 295
Egyptian National Committee in Support of the Palestinian Uprising, 203
Eilat, 80
Eisenhower, Dwight, 294
Eitan, Rafael, 51, 86
Elon Moreh, 55
Europe, 145, 268: Eastern, 152, 157, 235-236, 254-255, 257, 259, 261, 294, 297; Western, 204, 235-236, 268, 272, 278-280, 283, 286, 290, 294
  See also Britain, European Community, France, Italy.
European Community (EC), 38, 145, 229, 235, 240(n2)

Fahmy, Ismail, 200

Fajr, al-, 15,
Fateh, 12(n7), 21, 24, 124, 127, 134, 141, 149, 161(n29), 167, 175, 183, 194(n64), 216, 221, 224-228
Fawzi, Husayn, 211(n2)
Faysal bin Husayn, Amir, 119
Filastin al-Thawra, 22
Ford, Gerald, 199, 267-268
foreign policy roles, 211(n3)
France, 119-120, 145, 149, 215, 230, 232, 240(n4)

Galilee, 17, 106, 113
Gaza Strip, 1-2, 9, 33, 36, 48, 61, 64, 121, 184, 219
  See also occupied territories
Gazit, Shlomo, 83
Geivandov, K., 254
Geneva Convention, 31, 40(n1)
Gerasimov, Gennady, 250
Ghali, Butrus Butrus, 203, 207
Ginot Shomron, 35
Golan Heights, 29, 109, 121, 126-127, 224, 230, 257, 268, 273-274, 295
  See also occupied territories
Goodman, Hirsh, 82
Gorbachev, Mikhail, 2, 239-240, 242-243, 247, 249-250, 252-253, 256, 258, 261-262, 280, 290, 292
Gromyko, Andrei, 246
Grossman, Chaike, 53
Gulf crisis (1990), 126, 128, 129(n5), 131, 157-158, 188, 194(n71), 209, 236-237, 239, 240(n1, 7), 262, 291-293, 295-298
Gulf states, 128, 147, 149, 157-158, 160(n14), 177, 188, 271

Haas, Richard, 302(n60)
Habib, Philip, 247
Habibi, Emile, 113(n5)
Haifa, 66, 80, 102(fig)
Haig, Alexander, 271-272
Hakim, Tawfik al-, 211(n2)
Halamesh, 35
Halhul, 41(n15), 53
Hamas, 12(n7), 184-185, 189
Harish, Yosef, 54
Harkabi, 71-72, 85, 302(n60)
Hart, Aaron, 73
Hasan bin Talal, Prince, 178, 192(n47)
Haykal, Muhammad, 197
Hebron, 17, 35, 66
Heller, Mark, 295
Herzog, Chaim, 84
Hilal, Jamil, 22-23
Hilterman, Joost, 20-21
Histadrut, 104
human rights, 1-2, 9, 33-36, 54, 56, 68
  beatings, 33-34, 46, 53, 56
  censorship, 45, 47
  curfews, 34, 45, 47, 91(n10)
  demolition of houses, 34, 45, 47, 91(n10)
  deportations, 33, 45, 47, 52
  detentions, 33, 45, 47, 50
  shootings, 33, 45-46, 106-107; rubber and plastic bullets, 46, 50, 55-56
  tear-gas, 46, 55, 91(n6)
Hungary, 250
Husayn, Ibrahim Nimr, 107
Husayn, Saddam, 89, 129(n5), 157, 291
Husayn bin Talal, King, 121, 124, 135-136, 140, 142-143, 147, 156, 165-166, 168-172, 174, 178-179, 181, 183-184, 186-189, 228-229, 251, 267, 272, 275, 278

international law, 30-31, 199, 293
International Monetary Fund, 165, 177
intifada (1987-)
  casualties, 5, 12(n1), 33, 41(n18), 46-47, 50, 90(n4), 91(n7, 20)
  economic impact, 9, 12(n9), 38-39, 50
  eruption, 2, 22-23, 125, 131, 137, 165, 215, 241
  media coverage, 5, 31, 54, 68, 99-100, 119, 129(n1), 205, 241-242, 254
  social repercussions, 7-8
  See also human rights; Egypt; Israel; Jordan; occupied territories; PLO; Soviet Union; Syria; United States
Iran, 149, 155, 222-224, 227, 231, 245, 271
Iran-Iraq war, 2, 127, 136, 142, 149, 152, 155, 192(n48), 225, 242, 245, 271, 278
Iraq, 89, 120, 148-150, 157, 172, 179, 188, 192(n48), 236-237, 291
  invasion of Kuwait (1990). *See* Gulf crisis
  relations with PLO, 128, 137, 154-156, 158, 193(n62)
Irbid, 179

Islam, 120-121
Islamic Conference Organization, 195
Israel, 3, 6, 9, 59, 121, 123, 132, 135-136, 144-145, 147-148, 152, 154-156, 166, 170-171, 183, 185, 217-219, 221, 230, 232, 241, 244, 257, 259, 277
 Arab citizens, 10, 97-108, 110-113: Druze, 99, 114(n8); Bedouin, 99, 114(n8); protests by, 102-103(fig), 109, 117(n40); Follow-up Committee on the Concerns of Arab Citizens, 101-103(fig), 106-107; Jewish perceptions of, 97, 108-110
 "demographic dilemma," 7, 18, 42(n39), 59-60, 70-72, 255
 elections: (1977), 269; (1984), 65, 76, 114(n6); (1988), 52, 66, 69, 76, 79, 113(n2), 147
 national unity government (1984-90), 10, 44, 59, 85, 87, 89, 133, 151, 168, 209, 257-258
 political debates, 10, 43-44, 66, 86-90: concept of "tranfer," 42(n38), 68-70, 88; territorial compromise, 58-61, 71-79, 87-88; territorial maximalism, 58-62, 66-70, 79, 87-90
 political parties: Arab Democratic Party, 98, 113(n2, 3); Citizens' Rights Movement, 53-56, 76-77; Democratic Front for Peace and Equality, 98, 102-103(fig), 113(n2, 3, 5), 115(n16), 116(n34); Herut, 166; Kach, 70; Labor, 1, 10, 45, 47, 49, 52-53, 56, 61, 65, 67, 73-74, 77, 79, 101, 133, 139, 169, 172, 209, 266, 272, 281, 288-289, 302(n60); Likud, 1, 10, 29, 45, 47, 49, 51-53, 61, 64-65, 67, 69, 76, 79, 86, 101, 123, 126, 136, 152, 168, 188, 209, 258, 269, 275, 285-286, 288, 291; Mapam, 53, 77; Moledet, 69; National Religious Party, 31; Progressive List for Peace, 98, 102, 113(n2, 3), 114(n6); Rakah, 98, 102(fig), 114(n9), 116(n34); Tahiya, 51, 69; Tsomet, 51; Yahad, 56
 public opinion, 42(n38), 57-58, 66, 69-70, 72-73, 75-76, 78, 82, 90(n1), 117(n43), 282
 resurrection of the "Green Line," 63-66, 73, 110-113
 security concerns, 29-30, 40(n10), 79-86, 96(n99), 124, 266, 269, 282, 284
 See also Egypt; occupied territories; Soviet Union; United States
Israeli Defense Forces (IDF), 14, 34, 45, 48, 49-51, 53-55, 83-86, 124, 223, 226-227
Italy, 240(n4)
Ittihad, al-, 99-100, 102, 113(n5), 114 (n9, 10)

Jabaliyya refugee camp, 91(n10)
Jaber, Hisham, 37
Jaffa, 66
Jaffee Center for Strategic Studies, 282, 285
Ja`ja`, Samir, 232
Jalazun refugee camp, 34
Jazzin, 227
Jericho, 63
Jerusalem, 5, 6, 29, 47, 64-65, 102(fig), 109, 122, 133, 195, 216, 244, 270, 272, 274, 287-288, 293. *See also* occupied territories
Jibril, Ahmad, 218
Jordan, 1, 3, 88, 120, 124, 128, 129(n4, 5), 133, 139, 150, 154-155, 157, 215, 218, 229, 237, 246, 250-252, 265, 269-270, 275-277
 and the West Bank: 19, 37, 62, 105, 121, 135, 153-154, 162(n36), 166-167, 187: disengagement (1988), 119, 124, 140, 143, 146-147, 156, 165-166, 168-174, 176, 178, 187-189, 228, 278
 April 1989 protests, 125, 148, 165, 177-181, 188-189
 economic conditions, 125, 147-148, 165, 171, 173, 177-178, 180-181, 188, 192(n45), 193(n56) 194(n72)
 elections (1989), 126, 148, 166, 181-189
 political groups: "Arab Jordanian Nationalist Democratic Bloc," 194(n67); Jordanian Communist Party, 183, 185-186, 193(n61); Jordanian People's Democratic Party, 186, 188; Muslim Brotherhood, 181, 183-185, 189, 194(n64, 65)
 press, 174-175: *al-Dustur*, 174; Jordan Press Association, 175; Jordan Press Foundation, 174; *Jordan Times*, 174;

al-Ra'i, 174-175
"national charter," 181, 187
relations with PLO, 2, 122, 124-126, 135-136, 139-140, 142-143, 147-148, 153--156, 158, 159(n10), 161(n23), 165-167, 169-171, 179-183, 187-189, 267
Jordan Valley, 61, 80
Judea. *See* West Bank
Jumayyil, Amin, 229, 273

Kafr Qasim, 115(n24)
Kafr Yasif, 107
Kahane, Meir, 70
Kamel, Muhammad Ibrahim, 200
Karak, 177
Kawar, Samira, 174
Kayid, Mahmud al-, 174
Kelly, John, 209
Khaddam, 'Abd al-Halim, 219, 225
Khalaf, Salah, 193(n62), 225
Khasawna, Hani, 174, 191(n38)
Khatib, 'Umar, 193(n62)
Khomeini, Ayatollah, 245
Kimche, Jon, 267
Kimmet, Robert, 302(n60)
Kissenger, Henry, 199, 216, 244, 266
Kiryat Arba, 35, 69
Klibi, Chadli, 255

Labor party. *See* Israel, political parties
Lahat, Shlomo, 76
Land Day, 102, 106, 115(n24)
Landau Commission (1987), 31, 40(n5)
Lapidot, Amos, 83
League of Nations, 6
Lebanon, 122-124, 127, 133-135, 140-141, 150, 154-155, 231, 237, 257, 271-273
political groups: Amal, 124, 134, 140, 225-227, 231, 233; Hizbullah, 222-223, 227, 231, 233; Lebanese Communist Party, 222; Lebanese Forces, 222, 227, 229, 233-234; "Liberation Battalions," 222-223; National Movement, 224, 245; "Ninth of February Organization," 222; Progressive Socialist Party, 222, 233; South Lebanese Army, 223, 227 Syrian Social Nationalist Party, 222
See also Arab-Israeli war (1982); Syria
Levinger, Moshe, 35
Levy, David, 292
Libya, 150, 196, 206
Likud party. *See* Israel, political parties
Litani, Yehuda, 64

Ma'an, 177
Mahfouz, Naguib, 211(n2)
Majali, Rakan al-, 175
Majd al-Krum, 102-103(fig)
Mansour, Anis, 211(n2)
Marji'yun, 223
Mashghara, 226-227
Masri, Ghassan al-, 23
Masri, Zafir al-, 62
Medvedko, Sergey, 241
Meir, Golda, 121, 267
Meridor, Dan, 32
Milhelm, Muhammad, 193(n62)
Mitterand, François, 145
Mitzna, Amram, 55
Moda'i, Yitzhak, 52
Montazeri, Husayn 'Ali, 223-224
Mubarak, Husni, 126, 138, 147, 194 (n69), 195, 201, 204, 206-210, 217, 229, 251, 275, 277, 288
Mubarak, Suzanne, 204
Muragha, Sa'id Musa ("Abu Musa"), 225, 227
Murkas, Nimr, 107
Murphy, Richard, 218

Nablus, 17, 54-55, 62-63, 66
Nachmias, Aharon, 56
Naji, Ka'an, 222
Namibia, 239
Namir, Ora, 77
Naor, Arye, 71
Nasir, Gamal 'Abd al-, 121, 192(n48), 197-198
Nasirism, 197-199, 203, 207
Natan, Eli, 56
Natanyahu, Benjamin, 79
National Guidence Committee (NGC), 7-8, 20, 23, 62, 123
Navon, Michael, 38
Nawaysa, Riyadh, 192(n44)
Nazareth, 63, 100, 102-103(fig)
Nazi persecution, 56-57
Nicaragua, 254
Nixon, Richard, 199, 266
Nabulsi, Sulayman, 184
Nusseibeh, Sari, 15-16, 26(n8)

occupied territories, 58-63, 100-101, 105, 107, 113, 123, 132, 141, 152, 183, 215-216, 218-221, 228, 230, 232, 235, 245, 266, 270, 272, 276-277, 285, 291, 295
Civil Administration, 19, 32-33, 37-38, 123
demography, 1, 3, 18, 44
economy: conditions, 1, 18-19, 36, 62, 67, 73, 158; relationship with Israel, 9, 15, 17-19, 36-38, 42(n29)
elections proposal (1989), 78, 151-153, 172, 194(n69), 196, 208, 285-290
"iron fist" policy, 45, 124
Jewish settlers/settlements, 1, 3, 29-30, 34-36, 39, 40(n10), 51, 55, 63, 66, 69, 123, 133, 157, 228, 249, 272-273
land expropriation, 1, 29-30, 123
mass organizations/popular committees, 8, 20-21, 23-25, 27(n, 28, 39), 28(n40, 42, 43)
military orders, 29-30, 33, 41(n21), 42(n34)
social forces, 7, 13, 17
"steadfastness" (*sumud*), 14, 16-20
traditional elites, 7-8, 13, 19
universities, 45, 47
See also Jordan; Gaza Strip; Golan Heights; West Bank
oil. *See* petroleum
Olmert, Ehud, 109
Order of the Day, 84
Orr, Uri, 83
Ottoman empire, 5

Pakistan, 207
Palestine
declaration of independence (1988), 3, 9, 146, 206-208, 220, 229, 235, 253, 259, 279. *See also* PLO, Palestine National Council (19th).
Mandate, 6, 120, 266
rebellion (1936-39), 6
See also Israel; occupied territories
Palestine Communist Party, 12(n7), 21, 24, 140, 193(n61)
Palestine Liberation Organization (PLO), 7, 20, 23, 25, 62, 68, 74--78, 81, 90, 98-99, 106, 111, 114(n7), 122-125, 127-128, 131-159, 165, 260, 272-273, 277-278, 280, 284, 286, 288, 291, 302(n60)
internal politics, 2, 8, 13, 21-22, 134, 137, 141, 149, 158, 161(n29), 189(n6), 216, 225, 227
Palestine National Council (PNC), 13, 206, 229, 245, 278: 18th (1987), 125, 136, 225; 19th (1988), 3, 9, 23, 74, 94(n70), 98, 113(n5), 128, 144, 145-149, 165, 196, 206, 229, 235, 253-254, 278
Palestine National Fund, 181
peace initiative, 144-154, 156, 165, 286, 291
popular support for, 8, 12(n8), 62-63, 124, 141, 167, 189(n4)
See also DFLP; Fateh; PCP; PNF; PFLP; NGC; UNLI
See also Egypt; Iraq; Jordan; Syria; Soviet Union; United States
Palestine National Front (PNF), 7, 8, 123
Palestine National Salvation Front, 225, 229, 23
Palestinians, 12
in Israel. *See* Israel, Arab citizens
refugees, 6, 120, 124, 176
Paris, 77
Peace Now, 53, 76-77, 82, 89, 282
Peled, Beni, 86
Pelletreau, Richard, 280
Peres, Shimon, 1, 31, 52, 133, 136, 209, 248, 275, 277, 279-280, 286, 288, 302 (n60)
petroleum, 122, 265, 267
Petrovskiy, Vladimir, 259-260
Poleg, Zvi, 48
Popular Front for the Liberation of Palestine (PFLP), 12(n7), 21, 24, 140, 179, 183, 186, 194(n66)
Popular Front for the Liberation of Palestine—General Command (PFLP-GC), 141, 218, 223, 229, 231
Porath, Yehoshua, 302(n60)
Pravda, Alex, 256

Qaddah, Sulayman, 232
Qaddumi, Faruq, 193(n62), 225-226, 254
Qalqilya, 54
Quayle, Dan, 283
Quds, al- (radio), 141

Rabin, Yitzhak, 34, 44-45, 49--54, 63-64, 74, 79, 89, 115(n15), 125, 217, 269

Rahat, 103(fig)
Ramallah, 17
Ramon, Haim, 94(n77)
Rashadiyya refugee camp, 223, 225
Reagan, Ronald, 2, 271-275, 280, 283, 294
Rifa'i, Zaid, 125, 168-169, 173, 177, 185, 187-188, 190(n7)
Rogers, William, 199, 268
Ross, Dennis, 302(n60)
Ruby, Walter, 107

Sadat, Anwar al-, 121-122, 194(n69), 195, 198, 200-201, 216, 220, 237-238, 244, 267, 270
Said, Edward, 17
Sakhnin, 103(fig), 106
Salah, Kayid, 35
Saliha, Tawfiq, 232
Salim, 55
Salt, 177
Samaria. *See* West Bank
Sarid, Yosef, 54, 56
Sasson, Moshe, 203
Saudi Arabia, 120, 148-149, 157-158, 179, 198, 231, 237, 273, 291
Sayah, Shaykh al-, 206
Sayigh, Yusif, 15
Schiff, Za`ev, 296
Segev, Tom, 57
settlements. *See* occupied territories
Shafa 'Amr, 102-103(fig), 108
Shahal, Moshe, 52
Shakshir, Tahani, 51
Shalev, Avraham, 35
Shamir, Yitzhak, 1, 10, 34, 45, 50-54, 61, 78, 157, 172, 193(n60), 194 (n69), 209, 248-249, 258, 275, 279-280, 283-288, 291
Shar', Faruq al-, 219, 226
Sharansky, Anatoly, 248
Sharif, Mahmud, 174
Sharon, Ariel, 51, 85, 124, 202, 217, 228
Shatila refugee camp, 226-228
Shaw, Harry, 297-298
Shawa'a, Hisham, 36
Shevardnadze, Eduard, 248, 253, 257, 260
Shin Bet, 31, 32, 40(n5)
Shomron, Dan, 35, 48, 51, 82
Shoumkin, Andrey, 256
Shubaylat, Layth al-, 191(n38), 192(n44)
Shultz, George, 139, 146, 224, 272-276, 283
Sidon, 149, 223, 233
Sinai, 45, 121, 195, 270-271
Sneh, Ephriam, 83
Sofer, Arnon, 116(n32)
South Africa, 60, 289
Soviet Union (USSR), 2, 152, 168, 171, 219, 236, 240, 241-262, 271-272, 274-275, 283, 286, 294, 297-298
  domestic factors in foreign policy, 239, 243, 255, 258, 261
  Jewish emigration to Israel, 39, 60, 157, 249, 255, 263(n5)
  "new thinking" in foreign policy, 243, 247-248, 256-258, 261
  relations with Egypt, 236, 242, 244-245, 250-251, 263(n5), 266
  relations with Israel, 238-239, 243-244, 247-250, 278
  relations with PLO, 157, 245-246, 252-253, 258-261
  relations with Syria, 68, 149, 215, 218, 236-237, 245, 253, 263(n5)
  See also East-West relations
Steadfastness and Confrontation Front, 216
Suez Canal, 199
Sweden, 146, 279
Syria, 3, 68, 119-122, 124, 126, 128, 135, 141, 150, 159, 179, 186, 192 (n48), 195, 206, 244, 265, 267, 269, 272-273, 291, 293
  Ba'th Party, 217, 224, 232
  position in Lebanon, 124, 127, 150, 154, 216, 221-224, 226-233
  relations with PLO, 2, 122, 124, 127, 134-135, 140-141, 148-149, 154-156, 158, 215-216, 218, 220-221, 224-230, 245
  See also Soviet Union

Tafilah, 177
Ta`if agreement, 231-232
Taraki, Lisa, 20-22
Tayiba, 103(fig)
Tel Aviv, 63, 76-77, 79, 80, 157
terrorism, 79-80, 157, 260, 279, 285, 291, 296, 302(n60)
Tiberias, 80
Transjordan. *See* Jordan
Triploi, 225
Tsaban, Yair, 53, 77

Turkey, 207
Tyre, 222-223

'Ubaydat, Ahmed, 179
Umm al-Fahm, 102-103(fig)
Unified National Leadership of the *Intifada* (UNLI), 8, 12(n7), 23, 24, 28(n40), 106, 161(n23), 167, 190 (n8), 224, 226, 228-229, 231
United Nations (UN), 31, 34, 47, 101, 122, 128, 144-146, 149, 156-157, 219, 235, 239-240(n6), 241, 244, 251, 256-257, 259, 268, 271-274, 276, 279, 283, 286, 290-295
  General Assembly Resolution 181 (1947), 6, 94(n70), 144, 206, 243, 279
  Security Council Resolution 242 (1967), 1, 45, 74, 121, 144-145, 166, 206, 216, 243, 246, 252-253, 266, 269-271-272, 276-279, 284, 298
  Security Council Resolution 338 (1973), 45, 74, 144-145, 166, 206, 243, 246, 252, 279
United Nations Relief and Works Agency (UNRWA), 37, 162(n36)
United States (US), 123, 127, 133, 135, 154-155, 171-173, 183, 190(n17), 194(n71), 215-218, 236, 240, 241, 246, 257, 266
  Baker initiative (1989), 157, 188, 194(n69), 209, 284-289, 291
  dialogue with PLO, 9, 126, 128, 145-146, 151, 156-157, 188, 208-210, 238, 279-280, 282, 289, 291, 296
  domestic factors in foreign policy, 237-238, 255, 266, 268-271, 276-277, 281, 283, 287, 289-290, 293
  Kissinger shuttle diplomacy, 122, 267-268
  public opinion, 280-281, 301(n37)
  relations with Egypt, 126, 152, 195-196, 199-200, 202, 208-210, 237, 270
  relations with Israel, 39, 50, 129(n5), 132, 151-152, 157, 202, 236-237, 266-268, 271-278, 280-281, 284-289
  Reagan Plan (1982), 2, 133, 272-273, 290
  Rogers plan (1970), 121, 238, 266-267
  Shultz initiative (1988), 139-140, 142, 169, 219, 276-278, 290
  See also East-West relations

Van Crefeld, Martin, 85
Vietnam, 215, 220
Village Leagues, 18, 62, 92(n43), 123, 189(n5)
Vorontsov, Yuri, 250

Washington Institute for Near East Policy, 302(n60)
Wazir, Khalil al- ("Abu Jihad"), 140, 167, 194(n64)
Weinberger, Caspar, 271, 273, 297
Weiss, Shevah, 52
Weizman, Ezer, 270-271
West Bank, 1, 7, 9, 18, 29, 38, 61-62, 64, 80, 83, 121, 177, 228-229, 249, 288
  See also Occupied territories
West Bank Data Base Project, 32, 37

Ya'acobi, Gad, 49, 71, 74
Yahya, 'Abd al-Razzak, 161(n23)
Yariv, Aharon, 82
Yemen, 120: North: 150, 172, 198; South: 137, 150

Zaid bin Shakir, Sharif, 174, 177, 180
Zarqa, 179
Zionism, 5-6, 58-60, 104, 112, 120
Zucker, Dedi, 55